S0-ABA-783

THE BOOK THAT TAKES YOUR B R E A D T H AWAY

Overweight is *dangerous*—to your health, to your looks, to your very life expectancy.

But dieting is . . . *dull.*

Now, in this monumental, carefully researched book, expert gourmet Leonard Louis Levinson presents the full facts you need to eat well—without dangerous caloric intake.

Indispensable to the reducer—invaluable to the housewife—important for people with special health problems, such as diabetics—here is the book that will show you how to become slimmer, look younger, and feel better than you have in years!

New and Revised Edition

THE COMPLETE BOOK OF
LOW CALORIE COOKING

Leonard Louis Levinson

PYRAMID BOOKS **NEW YORK**

*To the thin person, inside every fat person,
fighting to get out*

THE COMPLETE BOOK OF LOW CALORIE COOKING

A PYRAMID BOOK

Published by arrangement with Hawthorn Books, Inc. *Publishers*

Hawthorn Books edition published March, 1956

Pyramid edition published January, 1968

Copyright © 1964, 1956 by Leonard Louis Levinson.

Copyright under International and Pan-American Copyright Conventions.

All rights reserved, including the right to reproduce this book, or portions thereof, in any form except for the inclusion of brief quotations
in a review.

Library of Congress Catalogue Card Number: 64-19702

Printed in the United States of America

PYRAMID BOOKS are published by Pyramid Publications, Inc.
444 Madison Avenue, New York, New York 10022, U.S.A.

This book is full of practical help for dieters and weight watchers. And practical help for overweight people is not too easy to find. Most advice has consisted, in essence, of a mere caution to eat less. Specific details in many important areas have been sadly lacking.

Many books written on reducing have not taken into account the real difficulties of dieters. Physicians who treat overweight patients realize that these patients know which foods are fattening, the caloric values of practically all common foods, and many specific diets for weight reduction. Lack of this knowledge is not the real difficulty.

Therefore, some books have hopefully offered specific advice based on the limited experience of one patient, the author. Others have offered general advice based on no real knowledge of the characteristics of people who are overweight. In both situations this advice is often unrealistic and impossible for the dieter to carry out.

In the treatment of overweight people, doctors have observed that they have very special traits that differentiate them, in *personality,* from thin people. They are usually not rigid perfectionists but sensitive and easily discouraged by temporary setbacks. For this reason they cannot be expected to carry out very rigid schemes involving too specific calorie counting. It is therefore obvious that they are dependent on very detailed advice in every area—especially on how to prepare low-calorie food attractively.

A very common question asked by the dieter of the physician is how to prepare food that tastes good but is not fattening. Because of his basic personality, the overweight individual generally will not have the drive and initiative to find out by trial and error. Yet the physician cannot be expected to have the knowledge and experience of an expert chef. This book by Mr. Levinson is an authoritative and welcome answer to this important problem.

The psychology of the dieter is the important consideration for success in reaching normal weight and staying there. In dieting, the overweight individual is performing a most unpleasant duty. He is required to give up an immediate pleasure in order to reach a goal that is still distant. Consequently, the only real problem in dieting is one of morale. And this keeping up morale is the great task in weight reduction.

For this the dieter needs all kinds of support in the way of specific advice on many matters. If food can be prepared to taste and look attractive, and yet fit into the dieter's scheme of things, this is most valuable advice and support. It lessens the rigors of diet and helps keep up the dieter's morale.

Even after normal weight is reached, there still remains a most important task—and that is *staying* normal. In becoming thin, the overweight individual has not yet completely solved his problems, for his personality has not been altered during the process of dieting. He continues to have overwhelming drives to overeat, and especially to eat fattening foods. Of course weight watching *after reducing* is not so rigorous as dieting *to lose weight,* but reducers tend to regain weight if they relax completely. To any previously overweight person, what many of us think of as normal eating is always *more* food than the food needed to keep him at normal weight. For this reason the advice and information in this book will be just as valuable to the "ex-fatty" who wants to keep his present weight as it will be to the person who wants to reduce.

LEONID KOTKIN, M.D.

Not one of us is interested in losing weight for a week or a month and then slowly eating it all back. But that is exactly what a majority of reducers do.

Do not look on this book as an aid to "going on a diet." The advice and facts it gives are to help you and your doctor get your weight to where it no longer handicaps your health, appearance, or chance to live longer—and then keep it there.

Look on what you will learn and do as a new way of life. And remember that it is neither terribly complicated nor agonizing to achieve a trim figure and all its benefits. The rules are simple and the food can be delicious.

Then, after you have reached your ideal weight, when you are feeling better than you have in years and looking younger and slimmer, only one person can keep you that way—yourself.

Keep applying the same successful principles of good nutrition and self-control . . . and do one thing more. Remember that we are the only nation menaced with overeating; half the people in the world are seriously underfed. You can help those who don't have enough to eat through your local civic or religious charities, through CARE, U. S. Committee for the International Children's Emergency Fund, United Nations, N.Y., or the Food for Freedom Fund, 648 South Broadway, Los Angeles, Calif., which sends three-cent meals of Multi-Purpose Food, developed at Cal Tech, to hungry people throughout the world.

LEONARD LOUIS LEVINSON

The author wishes to express his thanks to the many people who helped him assemble this book.

First, to the late Alice Brown Kline, consultant to Abbott Laboratories, who was most generous with time and guidance drawn from her wide experience in preparing dishes without sugar.

Then to Miss Llewellyn Miller, author of *The Reducing Cookbook*, whose counsel and extensive library were always available.

And Mary Anderson Gregg, dietician of the University of California Medical Center at Los Angeles, as well as Netty Prosterman, staff dietician of Mt. Sinai Hospital in New York, who checked recipes and calorie counts.

Also to a number of physicians for their advice and answers to question, including Norman Jolliffe, M.D. of the Bureau of Nutrition, Dept. of Health, City of New York; Herbert Pollack, M.D.; Henry Dolger, M.D., S. I. Heller, M.D.; Gerald F. O'Brien, M.D.; Sidney J. Robbins, M.D., all of New York; William H. Grishaw, of the Beverly Hills Clinic; Raoul Esnard, M.D., of Los Angeles, California, as well as the New York Academy of Medicine Library.

To Marjorie Child Husted of Minneapolis, Sara Hervey Watts of Ithan, Pa., who succeeded Alice Kline, Deaconess Maude Behrman and J. Richard Connelly of the American Diabetes Assn., Inc.; Mabel Stegner of Waring Products, Inc.; Anna A. Noone of Electrical Merchandising; Lea Kates of the Tea Council of the U.S.A.; and Executive Chef Otto Bismark of the S.S. *United States*.

And to the directors of Home Economics of the following institutions and firms: Kathryn B. Niles, Poultry and Egg National Board; Monica Clark, formerly of the American Meat Institute; Reba Staggs, National Live Stock and

Meat Board; Gertrude Austin, Sunkist; Jean Griffin, National Cranberry Assn.; Deborah Personius, "Junket"; Helen C. Hamilton, Mazola; Eleanor Lynch, Reynolds Metals Co.; Helen J. Britt, The Nestle Co.; Mona Van Dyke Schafer, California Fresh Peach and Plum Advisory Boards; Mary B. Horton, Sealtest; Helen E. Goodrich, Western Growers Assn.; Janet E. Bonnell, John Oster Mfg. Co.; Patricia Collier, Dole Pineapple; Elspeth Bennett, Ralston Purina Co.; M. Dorothea Van Gundy, International Nutrition Foundation; Catherine Haigler, Pet Milk Co.; Helen Kirtland, Hotpoint Inst.; Ann Dawson, Aluminum Cooking Utensil Co.; Joan E. Thimm, Buitoni Foods Corp.; Marjorie Deen, Fay Burnett, and Rowena R. Garber of General Foods; Josephine F. Williams, Battle Creek Food Co.; Evelyn Miller, The Peerless Corp.; Kathleen Burke, Knapp-Monarch Co.; Dorothy Z. Bergman, National Presto Industries, Inc.; Laura Wilson, Mirro; and Rose Kerr of the Fish and Wildlife Service, U.S. Dept. of the Interior.

Cooperating with information regarding various foods and utensils were J. B. Maloney of the Sunbeam Corp.; J. E. Metzger, Jr., of Dannon Milk Products, Inc.; Dr. David A. Copson of Raytheon Mfg. Co.; Nancy Webb for the Fresh Fruit and Vegetable Council, Inc.; Martha Tupper for Knox Gelatine, Ac'cent, Florida Citrus Commission, Tabasco, etc.; Gertrude Michalove for Borden's Starlac; Edna Willmont, General Electric Co. For health information, statistics, and tables from the Metropolitan Life Insurance Co., June Bricker, director of Home Economics bureau and Herbert H. Marks and William Holland of the Insurance Medical Statistics department.

Especial thanks are due to W. S. Bussey and M. W. Jensen of the Office of Weights and Measures of the National Bureau of Standards for their suggestions and checking of the Tables of Weights and Measures in this book; to J. K. Kirk of the Food and Drug Administration; and to Samuel A. Simon of the Better Diet Shop in New York for information on new low calorie food products.

And lastly to Duncan Hines, the culinary Columbus; Mort Weisinger, who frequently writes about nutrition and health for the national magazines; and Dean Jennings, author of "The New Non-Fattening Sweet," which appeared in Reader's Digest.

CONTENTS

THE ABCs OF REDUCING AND NUTRITION

If each one of us who is overweight had to carry that excess baggage around in a bag chained to the arm, like a bank messenger, he would very quickly find ways of getting rid of it.

Yet that inconvenience is a trifle compared to the harm that our unneeded fat can do. All the statistics available tell us that we can live longer and have less illness, sometimes 50 per cent more successfully, if we are slightly on the lean side of our ideal or desirable weights.

SHOULD YOU REDUCE?

What are these desirable weights and how much in excess makes us too fat, overweight, or obese?

Consult the charts on the following pages. They give the ideal "bathroom scale" weights for men and women who have stopped growing, the amounts authorities in the field feel we should weigh, according to height and body frame, to be healthiest and longest lived.

If your own weight is more than 10 per cent above the desirable, you should do something about it. According to most recent surveys about 30 per cent of the people in this country are that much overweight. And the higher your percentage of overweight, the more serious is your need to do something about it.

DESIRABLE WEIGHTS FOR GOOD HEALTH

In pounds, for people twenty-five and over, as you stand on the bathroom scales, without clothes or shoes.

These tables are adapted for home use from ones prepared by the Metropolitan Life Insurance Co.

When dressed, add 1 inch for men's heels and 2 for women's. Men wearing ordinary street clothes add 6 pounds; women, 4 pounds.

FOR MEN

HEIGHT WEIGHT ACCORDING TO FRAME
(Without Shoes) *(Without Clothes)*

Feet	Inches	LIGHT *Frame*	MEDIUM *Frame*	HEAVY *Frame*
5	1	110—119	118—127	125—136
5	2	113—122	121—130	127—138
5	3	116—126	124—134	131—143
5	4	120—130	128—138	135—147
5	5	123—133	131—141	139—151
5	6	127—137	135—145	143—156
5	7	130—141	139—150	147—160
5	8	134—145	143—154	151—164
5	9	138—149	147—158	155—169
5	10	142—153	151—162	159—174
5	11	146—158	155—167	163—179
6	0	151—163	160—172	168—184
6	1	157—169	165—176	173—190
6	2	162—174	170—183	178—196

FOR WOMEN

HEIGHT WEIGHT ACCORDING TO FRAME
(Without Shoes) *(Without Clothes)*

Feet	Inches	LIGHT *Frame*	MEDIUM *Frame*	HEAVY *Frame*
4	9	100—107	106—114	114—124
4	10	101—109	108—116	115—125
4	11	103—111	110—118	119—127
5	0	106—114	113—121	120—131
5	1	109—117	116—122	123—134
5	2	112—121	120—128	127—138
5	3	115—124	123—131	129—141
5	4	119—128	126—136	134—146
5	5	122—132	130—140	138—150
5	6	125—135	133—143	141—154
5	7	129—139	137—147	145—158
5	8	132—143	141—151	151—165
5	9	135—146	144—154	151—165

For girls between eighteen and twenty-five, subtract 1 pound for each year under twenty-five.

WHAT THIS BOOK CAN DO

There is no magic potion or formula that can make you thin. Each time one is announced in the advertisements, just ask yourself what became of the last "reducing discovery" that recommended itself in the same glowing terms. Do the same with those quick-trick diets that guarantee to cut your weight in no time by abstaining from or accenting some particular food.

Successful reducing — which means permanent weight loss—is so personal a problem, depending on so many different facts, with so many different answers or solutions, that the only person qualified to tell you what to do is your physician.

He can tell you what to do, but he probably won't have the time to tell you how to cook less fattening dishes, which foods have the least calories, and the hundreds of other facts, figures, and details of weight-reducing.

That is why this book was written—to supplement the doctor's general instructions and to help you carry out his orders. Use it as you would any other prescription he gives you. This one has one advantage—you won't have to have it refilled.

Every endeavor has been made to give you a complete book of low calorie cooking, with charts and instructions for less-fattening dishes and cooking methods. Here, also, is the first complete cata-logue of low calorie commercial foods ever assembled; a description and list of kitchen appliances that aid low calorie cooking, and a Spice Dictionary, as well as special sections on spices in each recipe section. Other lists and collections of facts are scattered throughout the book.

FACTS ABOUT GETTING THIN

Millions of words have been written to explain why we get fat and what we should do about it. Out of this flood of heavy literature have come facts, backed by both scientific and practical experience, which the author has reduced to simple answers. They apply to 99 per cent of overweight cases.

Why do we get fat?

Because we eat too much food—or too much of the wrong food.

It is as simple as that. Science has swept away all the other theories and we are back to the original, basic reasoning:

If we feed our bodies more

fuel than we burn up in energy, we store it in the form of fat.

Why do we eat too much?

For any one or combination of the following reasons:

Because of set patterns. Eating is a nervous habit. Frequently it is part of family tradition. As children, many of us were stuffed with loving care.

For enjoyment. Eating is a pleasure. It is a substitute for boredom; an outlet for frustrations; something pleasant to do for the lonely, the unloved, the discontented.

For sociability. This is the opposite of the last reason. The ability to eat when, what, and where we please is a symbol of success. We frequently eat between meals only to be able to sit and talk and visit with others.

And we usually eat too much of the wrong food because we don't know better.

WHAT TO DO ABOUT IT

No one in the world knows you like you know yourself. Observe the what, how, where, when, and why of your eating habits and begin experimenting.

Investigate unfamiliar, less-fattening foods. Try different, less-caloried ways of fixing your favorite dishes.

Don't let eating be your only pleasure. As you change your feeding pattern, find new interests—studies, hobbies, friends. Become more active. It will give you less time to think of food.

Are you an "emotional eater," building a fortress of fat between you and the world? Simple psychotherapy, explaining the connection between these emotional disturbances and eating too much, may be your solution. More and more this is being done in weight-control groups, weekly or semiweekly meetings of six to twelve overweight people who talk out their problems and exchange experiences and advice. Inaugurated by the U.S. Public Health Service, they have proven quite successful for those who are regular in attendance.

Cut down on betweenmeal eating by breaking coffee-break, cocktail-hour, and midnight-munch habits or by substituting nutritious snacks for the usual rich ones. (See 50 Sensible Snacks)

And change from eating the wrong food by learning what the food we eat does to and for us.

PROPER NUTRITION

If digestion was not automatic—if it took just one tenth as much thinking to put our food through our digestive systems as it does to earn it, we would be far more careful of what we ate.

We wouldn't keep putting more cans of fat on our already overcrowded shelves. We wouldn't neglect the effective and wonderfully complex vitamins that nature provides in food and then attempt to make up deficiencies with the crude manufactured versions modern science has perfected.

We would eat sensibly, and we would know something about nutrition—the science of nourishing the body properly, providing it with the proteins, carbohydrates, fats, vitamins, minerals, and water needed for its proper growth, maintenance, and repair.

Since we will be discussing them from here on, let us describe the three types of food elements:

PROTEIN. Meat, fish, eggs, and cheese contain large amounts of protein. It is vital to our well-being because our own meat or muscle is largely protein and we need outside protein to keep ours from sagging or wasting away. Protein also provides some energy and does a large number of other odd but vital body jobs. We do not store up proteins. Any excess in the diet is rejected or dis-

carded. But if there is a deficit, the body will draw upon its own muscles to balance its requirements. That is why it is important to eat sufficient protein and guard against muscle loss.

CARBOHYDRATE. Sweets, cereals, bread, fruits, and potatoes are largely carbohydrate — sugars and starches that the body transforms into sugar. This sugar is poured into the blood where it supplies quick energy for muscular exertion. But since our blood can hold only a limited amount, most of the surplus is stored away as fat. We require *some* carbohydrate because fat will not be consumed by the body unless there is carbohydrate to make it burn properly. And to reduce weight is to burn the body's excess fat.

FAT. Butter, oil, bacon, lard, cream, egg yellow are the principal sources of fat. In our bodies the surplus calories we have taken in are stored as fat, at about 4,000 calories a pound, the same as lard. Some fat is needed in a normal diet, but if you are well overweight your doctor will probably take you off outside fats until your body has finished consuming its own.

Simply eliminating fats and other high-calorie dishes

is not the answer to losing weight if you want to go about it safely and for keeps. You can starve yourself skinny and be nervous and lifeless and ill. You can slim down to the most ideal of weights and then slide right back up into your old clothes if you switch back to your old eating habits.

The simple but not easy answer is to learn to eat what is best for your body and eat that way the rest of your life. To get the foods, vitamins, and minerals we require to function best we need a balanced diet that contains the basic seven foods.

THE BASIC SEVEN FOODS

While we are the richest nation, spending by far the most money on food, we are not always the best fed. To remedy this, the Food and Nutrition Board of the National Research Council set standards that apply for people of all ages and types. They have named the seven basic food groups necessary for proper nutrition. To feed our bodies scientifically and sensibly we should eat some food from each group every day. The list has been adapted slightly for low calorie diets.

1. Especially for vitamin A. *Leafy, Green,* and *Yellow Vegetables, Apricots, Peach-*

es: raw or cooked. 1 or more servings a day.

2. Especially for vitamin C and roughage. *Citrus Fruits, Tomatoes, Cabbage, Salad Greens, Cantaloupe, Pineapple, Strawberries, raw.* At least 1 serving a day.

3. For a wide variety of vitamins and minerals, roughage. *Artichokes, Beets, White Cabbage, Cauliflower, Celery, Cucumbers, Eggplant, Leeks, Mushrooms, Onions, Radishes, Sauerkraut, Summer Squash, Turnips, Zucchini; Apples, Apricots, Berries, Cherries, Cranberries, Grapes, Peaches, Pears, Plums, Rhubarb, Watermelon, Vegetables and Fruits* not mentioned elsewhere; raw or cooked—2 or more servings a day.

4. For vitamin A, protein, calcium, other minerals, and vitamins. *Skim Milk, Buttermilk, Yogurt, Cottage Cheese, Ice-Cream Products.* Children through the teen years need 3 to 4 cups of milk or equivalent a day; adults, 2 cups.

5. Especially for protein, iron, vitamins. Lean *Meat, Poultry, Fish*—1 to 2 servings daily, plus *Eggs,* at least 5 each week.

6. Calories for energy; vitamins, iron, roughage. *Bread,* other *Flour Products,*

Cereals—2 to 3 servings a day.

7. Calories for energy, vitamin A. *Butter, Margarine* (fortified), or *Fats, Oils*—1 to 3 tablespoons (100 to 350 calories) every day.

In addition most people need from 4 to 8 glasses of water a day.

WHAT IS A CALORIE?

Normal body temperature is 98.6° because food is burning or oxidizing in our bodies to replace the heat we are losing by physical exertion, bodily radiation, breathing, etc. Even while we are asleep we are burning food, at about 1,700 calories per day for a 160-pound body.

A calorie is a measure of heat, or energy, produced by food as it burns in the body (or in a vacuum in a laboratory, which is one of the ways caloric values are determined). One calorie is the amount of heat used to raise the temperature of a pint of water 4° Fahrenheit and 1 calorie will keep that sleeping body running for about 51 seconds.

One gram of protein or carbohydrate (less than ¼ teaspoon) will supply 4 calories of heat or energy. One gram of fat equals 9 calories. (Breaking down a food into these three types and determining the amounts of each

is another way caloric values are established.)

All foods have been measured and given caloric values and in the Composition of Foods section in the back of this book about 200 of the principal ones are listed, with figures for common household units; proteins, fats, and carbohydrates in grams; and a new calories-per-net pound listing that gives the caloric value of a completely edible pound of each food. Also, the calorie count of servings is given in all recipes, the figures having been calculated from this list, which is based on the standard authority, "Composition of Foods," U. S. Dept. of Agriculture Handbook No. 8.

But bear in mind that any calculations are "approximate." Food is perishable and the amount of calories for any given one depends on freshness, time of year, variety or type, maturity, where grown, amount of sun and water, soil conditions, and other variable factors. While it is impossible to be correct down to the single calorie, such accuracy is not necessary, since variations will average out and daily requirements run from 1,200 calories on up.

Recommended by the National Research Council are the following:

Individual Work	Calories per day
154-pound man	
Sedentary	2,400
Physically active	3,000
Heavy labor	4,500
123-pound woman	
Sedentary	2,000
Moderately active	2,400
Very active	3,000
1-to-3-year-old child	1,200
13-to-15-year-old boy	3,200
" " girl	2,600

HOW MANY CALORIES A DAY FOR ME?

So many different factors are involved in prescribing the caloric intake and the eating routine for a reducing dieter that it requires the knowledge and experience of your physician. Here are some of the facts and figures that must be taken into consideration:

Your sex
  age
  weight
  height
  frame size
    general health
    proportion of muscle to fat
    metabolism (rate at which you burn calories)
    physical activity
    previous eating habits

Your doctor will not only tell you how to begin, how many calories of what kind of food you should eat, the amount and type of exercise you should take and what your vitamin and mineral requirements are, but he is the man to check your progress as you go along, alter your diet, and, when you have reached your ideal weight, tell you how you can stay at that weight for a healthy and longer life.

DO's AND DON'Ts FOR DIETERS

DO . . .

it yourself. Nobody can do it for you. *Mort Weisinger.*

seek the assistance and encouragement of family and friends in changing your lifetime eating habits.

if you are a man, wear sus-

DON'T . . .

exercise. Buy a dog and it will exercise you. *Fred Allen*

bore everyone with continual news bulletins on your dieting. *George Frazier*

be discouraged if it takes time to lose those first few

DO . . .

penders or an elastic belt, so you won't be constantly pushing out your tummy to keep your pants up. *Toots Shor*

if you are a woman, buy a new dress—a dress more expensive than you can afford and one size too small. That'll make you reduce. *Arlene Francis*

weigh yourself on the same scale, under the same conditions, every week at the same time. *Leonid Kotkin, M.D.*

have a good breakfast, rich in protein food, every morning for a consistent sense of well-being. *United States Department of Agriculture report.*

eat as though your life depended on it, for frequently it does. *Raoul Esnard, M.D.*

take the edge off your appetite by starting lunch or dinner with your soup or salad. *Marjorie Child Husted*

cook yourself thinner if your kitchen fits too snug around the hips. *Poppy Cannon*

avoid fat meat and fish, fried foods, gravies, rich sauces, mayonnaise, oily salad dressings, nuts, whipped cream, candy, jelly, pastries, too much bread, cereal or potatoes.

get as satisfactory an amount of bulk as you can for the calories eaten. *W. H. Grishaw, M.D.*

have dinner an hour earlier

DON'T . . .

pounds. Water frequently displaces fat temporarily.

worry if your weight fluctuates up and down during the week. It's that once-a-week result that tells the story.

let your blood sugar get so low that you become irritable and snappish.

let up. Eternal vigilance is the price of a good figure. *Haynes H. Fellows, M.D.*

skip meals. You're bound to overload your digestive system later.

forget that, as we grow older, our lean tissue turns to fat. *Joseph Brozek, M.D.*

neglect green salads, lean meat and fish, cranberries, melons, cucumbers, skim milk, tomato juice, unsugared gelatines, and slim soups. *Donald G. Cooley*

play doctor by giving your diet to your friends. It may not fit them any better than your shoes. *Stephanie H. Robbins, M.D.*

take any drugs or medicine for reducing without your physician's advice. *Fredrick J. Stare, M.D.*

eat a heavy meal when overly tired or emotionally upset. Rest first. *Lucile H. Parker*

serve diet portions in large plates or cups. Cutting down the size of the dishes makes the eye help the mind adjust the stomach. *Frank Scully.*

DO . . .

and avoid the cocktail hour. *Alfred Hitchcock*

use a 1-cup Pyrex measure to drink from at meals if you want to check your liquid intake.

remember that you are what you eat. The more you eat, the more you are. *Fred Beck.*

consider, when you are tempted by a beautiful but fattening dessert, how it will look in a bathing suit. *Esther Williams*

remember there is no law that makes you finish everything on your plate. Stop when you're still a little hungry. *Rudy Vallee*

recall the ancient Roman proverb—"*Plures crapula quam gladius*," or "Gluttony kills more than the sword." *Dr. George Gamble*

keep in mind, when giving a party, those who are dieting, and have some non-fattening foods. *Emily Post*

remember, a full belly makes a dull brain. *Benjamin Franklin*

broaden your mental viewpoint while narrowing your physical foundation. *Spike Jones*

take it easy . . . shrink without wrinkling. *S. I. Heller, M.D.*

DON'T . . .

keep getting in the way of temptation. If those French fries are not on your plate, you can't eat them. *Betty Betz.*

load your system with "empty calories," the cooking oils and sugar devoid of protein, vitamin, or mineral values. *Norman Jolliffe, M.D.*

bolt it and beat it. Eat slowly and eat less for better digestion. *Duncan Hines*

forget that one of the finest reducing exercises is turning your head from side to side when offered a second portion and another is simply pushing yourself away from the dining-room table. *Louis L'Amour*

abandon your diet just because you go on one mad eating spree. *Sheilah Graham.*

start unless you've made up your mind to keep holding down your weight all of your days. *Walter C. Alvarez, M.D.*

sleep more than 8 hours a night during a reducing schedule unless your doctor advises otherwise. *Donald B. Armstrong, M.D.*

forget that Rome wasn't built in a day. Habits of years cannot be broken by magic overnight. *Walter Wilkins, M.D., PhD. and French Bold, B.S.*

. . . and there will be no pot at the end of your rainbow

—SAM LEVENSON

SUCARYL AND OTHER ARTIFICIAL SWEETENERS

Throughout this book you will find recipes with Sucaryl as the sweetening agent instead of sugar. That is because Sucaryl has the ability to sweeten without adding calories, to retain its sweetness when frozen or heated in any cooking process, and because, used in ordinary amounts, it is not known to give any bad physical reaction. Perhaps as important as anything else, it leaves less of a bitter aftertaste than any other artificial sweetener known.

Sucaryl (pronounced "Soo'-ka-ril") was discovered accidentally by Dr. Michael Sveda in 1937 when he was a graduate chemistry student at the University of Illinois. After a day of compounding new variations of sulfamic acid, he picked up his cigarette from the lab bench and noticed an unusual, sweet taste. A chemist is an extremely able detective. It didn't take him long to travel from the wet end of the cigarette, through a dozen different new chemicals he had created that day to some crystals that had spilled on the cigarette. Sveda jotted down the formula, named it Sodium Cyclohexylsulfamate, made a note of its properties, and filed it away for later action.

This did not come until several years later, after the chemist had gone to the Dupont Laboratories in Delaware. Dr. Ernest H. Volwiler, now president of Abbott Laboratories, was visiting Dupont when he heard of Sveda's unusual but neglected compound. Arrangements were made to take the formula back to the Abbott plant in North Chicago and the experimenting began. Sample batches were tried on animals and then, as no harmful symptoms developed, a dozen company volunteers began testing the effect of Sucaryl, as it was trade named, on all the internal organs. Radioactive

Sucaryl was traced through the bodies of other volunteers and physicians in many cities tried the new sweetener on their diabetic patients.

Clinical tests in which as many as 50 Abbott workers were involved at one time continued for nine years before most of the technical and manufacturing problems were solved. The U.S. Food and Drug Administration spent two years on its own investigation before it approved the sale of Sucaryl to the public.

It was introduced to the public in May 1950 at a banquet given by Abbott for science editors and newspapermen. After the guests had finished their dessert they learned for the first time that they had just eaten the first complete meal ever sweetened solely without sugar. The chef had cut the calorie count from 832 to 649, a saving of about 22 per cent, by using Sucaryl and eliminating 9.18 teaspoons of sugar.

Public acceptance of the product was prompt and its popularity has increased each year.

SACCHARIN

Where Sucaryl resulted from the discovery of a naturally sweet chemical, saccharin, first compounded in 1879 by Remsen and Fahlberg, was the result of tremendous research to produce an artificial sweetening agent. (Originally they were going to call it Anhydrourthosulphaminebenzoic Acid, but then they cut it to Benzoic Acid.) Therefore it is not strange that the manufactured sweet has two drawbacks not known in the naturally (or naturally chemically) sweet Sucaryl. These are saccharin's instability when exposed to heat and its fairly apparent bitter aftertaste. There have been a number of attempts to eliminate this off-taste by various refining processes and several refinements, notably Crystallose, Sweeta, and Saxin have succeeded in minimizing it. However, in tests of concentrated sweeteners people have been aware of the off-taste of saccharin long before they sense any "chemical" taste in Sucaryl. Saccharin's notable attribute is its 50-year history as the dominant sugar substitute, without harm to the human system.

Since chemists are detectives by profession, a group of them at Abbott decided to learn what would happen if Sucaryl and saccharin were combined. Experiments and taste panels were held for some time and the results exceeded any of the chemists' expectations.

IMPROVED SUCARYL

A combination of 10 parts Sucaryl (which has a sweetening power 30 times that of sugar) with 1 part saccharin (400 times as sweet as sugar) was found to be the best. But instead of being as sweet as the two combined, for some unknown-as-yet reason the combination is quite a bit sweeter than the arithmetic says it should be. This means that less of the new sweetener need be used to do the job.

In the important realm of taste, even finer results were discovered. A tremendously sweet concentration of the new compound had to be tasted (about 13 tablets in 1 cup of water) before anyone at all complained about aftertaste.

With these advantages checked and double checked, Abbott in the fall of 1955 announced "Improved Sucaryl." The new Sucaryl, in smaller tablets, has the same sweetening power as the old and in all of our recipes and directions listing Sucaryl either can be used.

Sucaryl is made in two formulas:

Sucaryl Sodium tablets and Sucaryl Sodium solution (liquid) are for general use.

Sucaryl Calcium tablets, Sucaryl Calcium solution, and Sucaryl Calcium Sweetening powder contain no sodium and are for people on low-salt diets.

The sweetener has also created virtually a new industry in dietetic foods, notably fruits, and diet soft drinks. (See Dietetic and Low Calorie Food Products.) First commercial user was the Colfax Mineral Springs Co., Colfax, Iowa, which began making soft drinks in June 1950.

Experimenting independently, Kirsch Beverages, Inc., of Brooklyn, N. Y., sought to furnish diabetics at Brooklyn Jewish Chronic Disease Hospital with sugar-free soft drinks. When the hospital personnel began diverting part of the samples to their own use, the Kirsches realized how successful a taste test this was. One result of their philanthropic gesture is the marketing on a national scale of their discovery as "No-Cal."

In the food-packing field Richmond-Chase of California was the first to begin experimenting with Sucaryl, but the first to reach the retail market was the National Cranberry Association with their Ocean Spray Dietetic cranberry sauce.

SUGAR

In 1953, according to United States Department

of Agriculture figures, each of us used 109 pounds of sugar and syrup. This was about double what it had been twenty-five years before and we seem to be becoming sweeter all the time. And stouter.

Another government survey estimates that the average person consumes 500 calories of sugar a day. It would seem to be so simple to lose weight by just cutting out all this sugar. However, sugar is hidden in many of our foods for reasons other than its sweetening power.

For example, it is in bakery products to add flavor, for its tenderizing effect on gluten, to raise coagulation temperature of eggs, to give desirable brownness (partly by reaction with protein, partly by carmelization), and to improve texture, since it incorporates air during creaming of sugar and fat.

In canning and preserving it is an effective preservative. It adds bulk to some foods, gives a syrupy consistency to others, helps jell some, and is a glaze or coat on ham, pineapple, hot-cross buns, and candied cherries.

Sugar is in so many things we eat and for such varied purposes that it is not easy to eliminate it even from the most stringent of diets, and the search for substitutes for its non-sweetening effects continues.

SUCARYL ALONE NOT THE ANSWER

Even if you could cut out every ounce, eliminating sugar from your diet won't make you thin.

Used in conjunction with a "way of life" worked out for you by your physician, a non-caloric sweetener such as Sucaryl will help in your campaign to reduce effectively and safely.

And you can hold those losses only by continuing that regime, modified by the doctor, after you have reached your desired weight.

This may seem harsh, but it is realistic. The "Miracle Diets," the "Wonder Cures," the "Amazing Methods" of today will fade away as soon as the gullible stop patronizing them, just as similar promotions in the past have disappeared. There is no more a way to get slim quick than to get rich quick.

OTHER SWEETENERS

Sorbitol and Mannitol are sugar alcohols that have been used in dietetic foods because, while they have the same number of calories as sugar, they are absorbed far slower into the bloodstream and therefore have been considered by some doctors more advantageous for diabetics. Used in large quantities, they can bring about strong cathartic action. According to medical authorities, "It seems doubtful that they possess any advantages over any other sugars in the diabetic diet." This applies possibly even more to the straight reducing dieter.

Lactose or milk sugar is sometimes suggested by patients as a replacement for table sugar, but your doctor will point out that it contains the same amount of calories but tastes only half as sweet.

Sodium and Calcium Cyclamate, the chemical names for Sucaryl, are now being produced by several other laboratories under agreement with Du Pont, the patent owner, and marketed, at much lower prices than Sucaryl, under a number of brand names.

Here are some of the ways saccharin and Sodium and Calcium Cyclamate are available. If you are unfamiliar with their taste, buy small quantities of several and try them. Shop around until you find the one that suits your palate best.

Adolph's Granulated Sugar Substitute
Soluble saccharin, Glycine, Gum Arabic. One-fourth teaspoon equals 1 tablespoon sugar. Adolph's Ltd., Burbank, Calif.

Cellu Saccharin
In ¼, ½, and 1 grain tablets.

Cellu Sugarless Sweetener
Powder, no food value.

Cellu Liquid Sweetening
Saccharin in liquid form.

Colfax Sugar Fré Concentrated Sweetener
4 drops sweetens a cup of coffee or tea. One teaspoon equals 20 teaspoons of sugar. One tablespoon sweetens like 1 cup of sugar. No calories. Contents: Water, Methylcellulose, 12½ per cent Sucaryl Calcium; 4 per cent Calcium Saccharin; also 1 per cent Benzoic Acid; .05 per cent Methyl Parabon preservatives. Formula United States patent #2691591.

Crystallose
Calorie-free crystals of saccharin sodium, 1 crystal equals 1 lump of sugar. Also in liquid form, 2 drops equal 1 teaspoon sugar. Jamieson Pharmacal Co., Inc., New York, N. Y. 10022.

Diamel Sugar Substitutes (no food value)
Powdered Sugarless Sweetener
Sweet'n-it liquid
Saccharin tablets (½ grain)
Saccharin crystals

Dietician Sugar Substitutes
Sugarless Sweetener powder

Sacrose Liquid Sweetener, a solution containing saccharin 3 per cent, Sodium Benzoate 0.1 per cent. Six drops equal about 1 teaspoon sugar in sweetness. One teaspoon Sacrose has sweetness of about 3 tablespoons sugar. In cooking, use Sacrose toward end when possible.

Fortissimo Life Sweetener

Powder, contains slow-absorption carbohydrates and Sucaryl, 4 calories per gram.

Hermesetas

Pure crystallized saccharin without Sodium Bicarbonate. One tablet equals 2 lumps of sugar. Hermes Ltd., Zurich, Switzerland.

Jelsweet Liquid Sweetner

Calcium Cyclamate, Calcium Saccharin, Benzoic Acid, Methylparabon. One-fourth teaspoon equals 1 tablespoon sugar. Also for use with M.C.P. "Low Sugar" Pectin for jams, jellies, etc. Mutual Citrus Products Co., Anaheim, Calif.

Tillie Lewis Tasti-Diet Sweetenin'

One teaspoon equals 16 teaspoons of sugar. No caloric value. Contains Calcium Saccharin, Pectin, Benzoic Acid, Vanillin.

Loeb's Sweeteners

Saccharin tablets, crystals, liquid, powder.

Loeb's Steda-sugar

Sucaryl (Cyclamate Calcium) liquid, powder.

Necta

Soluble saccharin in liquid base. Three drops equal 1 teaspoon of sugar. Norwich Pharmacal Co., Norwich, N. Y.

Norwich Saccharin

In ¼, ½, and 1 grain soluble tablets. Norwich Pharmacal Co., Norwich, N. Y.

Pharma Vita Sutabs

Tablets of Sodium Cyclamate and saccharin. Pharma Vita Co., New York, N. Y.

Saxin

Compressed tablets of ¼ grain saccharin. No food value. Burroughs Wellcome & Co., Inc., Tuckahoe, N. Y.

Slenderella Non-Caloric Sweetener

Liquid and granulated Sodium Cyclamate, Slenderella Inc., Long Island City, N. Y.

Sucaryl (Improved)

Tablets and liquid of Sodium Cyclamate and saccharin; tablets, powder, liquid of Calcium Cyclamate and saccharin. Powder contains 10 per cent Cyclamate Calcium and 1 per cent Saccharin Calcium with Acacia as diluent. Abbott Laboratories, North Chicago, Ill.

Sugarine

One teaspoon equals 16 teaspoons of sugar, 1 tablespoon equals 1 cup sugar. No food value. Propylene Glycol N.F. 25 per cent, trace of Vanillin U.S.P. Eugenol. Saccharin Sodium soluble 5 per cent, demineralized Aqua 70 per cent. The Sugarine Company, Mt. Vernon, Ill.

Superose Sweetener

Propylene Glycol U.S.P. 15 per cent, water 80 per cent, Cyclamate Calcium 1 per cent, Saccharin Sodium Soluble U.S.P. 4 per cent. Four drops approx. 1 teaspoon sugar in sweetness. C. G. Whitlock Process Co., Springfield, Ill.

Sweet Tabs

Tablets of Sodium Cyclamate and Sodium Saccharin. E. J. Korvette, New York, N. Y.

Sweeta

Two drops equal 1 level teaspoon sugar. Soluble saccharin. E. R. Squibb & Sons, New York.

Sweet'n Low (powder)

In packets equal to 2 teaspoons of sugar. Lactose, Calcium Saccharin, Calcium Cyclamate. Three calories each. Cumberland Packing Co., Brooklyn, N. Y.

Table Sweet

Liquid Calcium Cyclamate, Soluble Saccharin, Sorbitol, Benzoic Acid, Methylparabon; ½ teaspoon equals 2 teaspoons of sugar.

Names and addresses of firms not listed above can be found in Brands and Their Distribution section, following Dietetic and Low-calorie Food Products.

Cheating on the diet is the most serious problem that faces the reducing patient and the physician trying to help him. For one thing, the concentration on a lower caloric intake keeps the thought of food uppermost in the mind and any but the strongest willed are inclined to couple thought and action by nibbling between meals and after dinner.

If you find it too difficult to resit the midnight call of the icebox, the afternoon snack at coffee-break time, or the drink before dinner, make provision for it in your daily menu— keep your intake 100 to 150 calories lower than your allowance—and spend those units on between-meal snacks.

Now, 100 to 150 calories won't take you far on bread and butter. One slice and you're finished. But doled out wisely for the cheap-but-healthful substitute snacks, they can furnish from 3 to 17 different chewy-eating items a day without cheating on yourself, vexing your doctor, or disturbing your conscience.

As you experiment, add favorite substitutions of your own to the list below, which has 50 of the usual fattening snack and cocktail items and 50 substitutes that have practically the same bulk as their richer counterparts.

Included are low or non-caloric replacements for liquor in various forms. Alcohol is not only fattening but whets the appetite and breaks down will power at mealtime. You can drink calories a lot faster than you can eat them. Many a man has trimmed down to ideal weight by doing no more exercise than climbing on the water wagon.

BEVERAGE SUBTITUTIONS

(OF COURSE THEY ARE NOT THE SAME, BUT MAKE THIS A HABIT AND YOU WON'T BE THE SAME, EITHER.)

The Beverage	Grams	Serving	Calories	The Substitute	Grams	Serving	Calories	Calories Saved
Beer	180	6-oz. glass	86	Bouillon	191	1 portion	27	59
Daiquiri	56	1 cocktail	124	Low cal. lime soda	180	6 oz.	0	124
Gin rickey	240	1 glass	153	Suc.-sweet. lemonade	240	1 glass	8	145
Highball	240	1 glass	170	Iced tea	240	8 oz.	0	170
Manhattan	56	1 cocktail	167	Low cal. cherry soda	180	6 oz.	0	167
Martini	56	1 cocktail	143	Demitasse	56	1 cup	0	143
Mint julep	240	1 glass	217	Mint tea	240	1 glass	0	217
Old-fashioned	240	1 glass	183	Suc.-sw. grapefruit juice	100	3¼ oz.	36	147
Tom Collins	240	1 glass	182	Tomato juice	240	8 oz.	50	132
Rye	43	1½-oz. jigger	122	No cal. broth	190	1 bowl	0	122
Scotch	43	1½-oz. jigger	107	Black coffee	240	1 cup	0	107
Red wine	100	1 wineglass	73	Low cal. raspberry	180	6 oz.	7	64
White wine	100	1 wineglass	85	Low cal. ginger ale	180	6 oz.	0	85
Champagne	100	1 wineglass	85	Skim milk	123	½ cup	44	41
Port, Muscatel	100	1 wineglass	160	Tea	240	1 cup	0	160
French vermouth	100	1 wineglass	108	Low cal. root beer	180	6 oz.	0	108
Italian vermouth	100	1 wineglass	170	Low cal. cola	180	6 oz.	0	170

SNACKS VS. SENSIBLE SUBSTITUTES

(TEAR OUT AND PASTE ON REFRIGERATOR DOOR)

The Snack	Wt. in Grams	Size of Portion	Calories	The Substitute	Wt. in Grams	Size of Portion	Calories	Calories Saved
Apple pie	160	½ medium	377	Raw apple	150	1 medium	76	301
Avocado	114	½ peeled	279	Raw papaya	121	⅔ cup	44	235
Brownie	30	2 x 2 x ¾	141	Carrot	30	15 thin strips	12	129
Butter	14	1 tablespoon	100	Unsw. applesauce	15	2 tablespoons	6	94
Choc. cake	100	½2 of cake	356	Honeydew melon	100	2 x 5 wedge	33	323
" nut bar	58	10¢ almond	316	Gregg candy	28	4 fruit jels	72	244
" malted	365	regular	502	Buttermilk	366	12 oz.	129	373
" sundae	224	with nuts	543	Watermelon	225	½ pound	63	480
Cookies	48	2 icebox	232	Raw cucumber	50	4 slices	6	226
Cupcake, white, iced	55	regular	229	Apricot	50	1 medium	25	203
Dates	30	3 to 4 pitted	85	Radishes	30	3 small	6	79
Doughnuts	64	2 medium	272	Green pepper	64	1 medium	15	257
Eclair, cream puff cream filling	105	regular	296	Stewed rhubarb	112	Suc. sweet.	18	278
Eggnog	204	5 oz. glass	200	Consommé	191	1 serving	29	171
Fig, dried	21	1 large	57	Cauliflower	20	⅓ cup, raw	5	52
Frankfurter	100	2 av., cooked	248	Dill pickles	100	1 large	11	237

Food	g	Measure	Calories	g	Sensible substitute	Measure	Calories	Calories saved
French dress.	30	2 tablespoons	118	30	Vinegar	2 tablespoons	4	114
Gelatin Dessert	120	½ cup, plain	77	120	Low-cal. gelatin	½ cup, plain	12	65
Hamburger	82	large patty, cooked	300	80	Raw tomato	thick slice	8	292
Jelly, jam	40	heaping tablespoon	110	40	Low-cal. jam	heaping tablespoon	9	101
Lemon meringue pie	160	⅙ medium pie	281	145	Cantaloupe	1 cup, diced	30	251
Mayonnaise	26	2 tablespoons	184	26	Yogurt	2 tablespoons	20	164
Mince pie	160	⅙ medium pie	398	180	Grapefruit	½ medium	72	326
Muffin	45	1 corn meal	128	50	Celery	3 inner stalks	9	119
Pancake	45	1 average, 4"	74	50	Mushrooms	2 large broiled	8	66
Peanut Butter	20	1 tablespoon	100	20	Low-cal. orange marmalade	1 tablespoon	4	96
Potato chips	20	10 medium	108	20	Celery root	10 slices	7	101
Potato salad, mayonnaise	123	½ cup	200	100	Sauerkraut	⅔ cup	22	178
Raisins	170	1 cup, cooked	218	200	Cranberry sauce	7 oz. jar	20	198
Rice pudding	145	¾ cup	249	146	Diet peaches	⅔ cup	40	209
Roll, sweet, white flour	55	average	178	15	Whole-grain wafers	5	25	153
Waffle, plain	73	5½ inches	232	74	Raw strawberries	½ cup, capped	27	205
Whipped cream	32	2 heaping tablespoons	104	32	Skim-milk whipped topping	2 heaping tablespoons	38	66

Americans have always relied on butter, flour, sugar, and other rich ingredients to make their dishes taste good. In less fortunate countries various seasonings—home-grown herbs or easily available spices—are used to make foods more attractive and varied. These seasonings have, for dieters, the advantage of being practically free of calories; also in some instances valuable vitamins and minerals are present.

Now is the time to enlarge your knowledge of the wide world of seasonings, push back the frontiers of your palate, and have fun becoming an authority on how to give food unusual and delicious flavoring.

It isn't expensive to make a collection of seasonings, either by picking up one or two new ones each time you shop at your grocer's, or by going on a spice spree in a specialty shop, where you will find greater variety, fresher stock, and usually lower prices.

Learning the difference between such black peppers as Alleppey, Java, Johore, Lampong, Penang, Saigon, Singapore, Tellicherry, and Trang, or the attributes of Dalmation sage versus Cyprus, Rose, White, Pineapple, or Spanish can make you the neighborhood culinary authority.

And experimenting with new uses for old spices or new blendings and combinations is a hobby that pays off at dinnertime.

More and more, as America becomes herb conscious, people are growing their own in kitchen gardens and windowsill pots. The United States Department of Agriculture has published *Savory Herbs: Culture and Use*, which is a valuable handbook on the subject. (Send 15c to Supt. of Documents, United States Government Printing Office, Washington, D.C. 20025). And Cornell University offers "Culinary Herbs," Bulletin No. 841, which is free to residents of New York State. (Address W.H.C.U., Ithaca, N. Y.)

Here are a few rules for the purchase and use of seasonings:

1. Before buying, check them for freshness.

2. Purchase in small quantities; keep container tightly covered and away from heat; throw out old, weak flavorings.

3. Buy a small hand pepper mill to grind peppercorns fresh each time used; also one for fresh-ground cloves; and a little mortar and pestle to bruise, crack, and grind herb and spice seeds yourself.

4. Use fresh herbs in season, chopping or crushing them in mortar just before using, to bring out volatile oils and true flavors. They will keep for days in refrigerator, in tightly covered jars.

5. Dried or powdered herbs may be used in place of fresh, but in smaller portions: powdered, ⅛ as much; dried, ¼ as much.

6. Begin with about a teaspoon of fresh or ¼ teaspoon of dried herbs in a dish for 4. Add herbs to soups and stews in the last hour of cooking.

7. For sauces, dressings and lightly cooked dishes, first steep herbs in hot water 10 to 15 minutes. Or dried herbs are often placed in a strainer and given a hot-water bath for 10 seconds, followed by a similar cold-water bath.

8. If you put the herbs and spices in cheesecloth bags when cooking soups and stews, it saves the trouble of straining later.

9. You would no more use the same seasoning for every dish in a meal than you would dress in the same fabric and color from head to foot.

10. Extended cooking will kill the delicate aroma and flavor of many seasonings.

11. Don't just stick to the familiar, reliable flavors — keep trying new ones and new combinations.

12. Let your blending imagination soar, but begin cautiously as to quantities. Season with a light hand. Don't drown the food.

13. If you are dieting because of stomach or gastric disturbances, your doctor

will undoubtedly tell you to skip this section.

Here is a complete Dictionary of Seasonings, including all but the most obscure spices and herbs; listing their names, categories, form in which they can be obtained and are used, plant family, aroma, taste, etc.

Rather than list the various uses of Seasonings here, for the convenience of readers, separate seasoning recommendations have been compiled at the end of each recipe section.

DICTIONARY OF SEASONINGS

Barks, Beans, Berries, Blends, Buds, Bulbs, Combinations, Condiments, Flowers, Fruits, Herbs, Leaves, Plants, Powders, Sauces, Seeds and Spices.

ALLSPICE, spice; whole or ground berry of Allspice tree (Jamaica Pimento). Nature's own blend, combining cinnamon, nutmeg, and clove flavors.

ANGELICA, herb; fresh stems and leaf stalks; Parsley family. Sweet, aromatic, somewhat like licorice.

ANISE, herb; seed, and fresh and dried leaves; Parsley family. Sweet, spicy taste and odor, adds licorice taste to cookery.

BALM (or Lemon Balm), herb; fresh and dried leaves; Mint family. Sweet, lemon-mint scent and flavor.

BASIL (or Sweet Basil), herb; fresh and dried leaves and tender stems and essential oils; Mint family. Highly aromatic, spicy flavor, between clove and licorice. Can be cooked for long periods.

BAYLEAF, dried leaf of Sweet Bay or Laurel shrub or tree. Familiar strong, pungent smell; woodsy, almost bitter taste.

BEEF EXTRACT, in liquid, powder, cube form.

BERGAMOT (also Wild Bergamot), herb; dried leaves. Mild aroma; pleasant, peppery taste. Brewed as tea by protesting New England colonists after Boston Tea Party.

BORAGE, herb; fresh and dried leaves and flowers. The tender young leaves have a fresh, cool, cucumber flavor and can be cooked as spinach or greens.

BOUQUET GARNI, a blend of fresh or dried herb sprigs, tied with white thread, placed in soups and stews while cooking and removed before serving. See Seasoning Blending.

BURNET (or Salad Burnet), herb; fresh and dried leaves. Tender young leaves have distinct, delicate flavor, like cucumber.

CAPERS, flower buds of wild bushy herb; pickled, bottled, and used as condiment. Bitter, salty taste.

CARAWAY, herb; fresh leaves, roots and seedlike fruit; young leaves have flavor similar to seed, but more delicate. Root is very sweet, more delicate than parsnips, and does not resemble taste of seed. Seed has spicy, aromatic flavor.

CARDAMOM, whole or ground seed of herb, related to Ginger, although milder. Pleasant, pungent aroma and aromatic taste.

CASSIA, whole and ground bark and buds of a tree native to Burma and India that resembles Cinnamon in flavor, but of an entirely different botanical family. There are numerous geographical varieties, varying in warmth, sweetness, pungency, and color. Sold throughout United States as cinnamon.

CATSUP, condiment. "Catsup" is as near as the English language can come to a Chinese word meaning "brine of pickled fish." A sauce made with mushrooms, tomatoes, or walnuts.

CAYENNE. See Pepper.

CELERY, vegetable herb; fresh and dried leaves, fresh stalks and root, seed and salt. Every part is edible, useful, in all cookery except desserts.

CHERVIL, herb; fresh and dried leaves. Resembles parsley, but more subtle flavor, somewhat like tarragon and a little like licorice in taste. Very fragrant and useful.

CHILI. See Pepper.

CHIVES, herb; fresh leaves, bulbs, salt; Onion family. Young tender leaves have delicate onion flavor. Bulbs are pickled as tiny onions.

CHUTNEY, condiment; highly-seasoned, sweet, pickled combination of tropical fruits, herbs, spices, and nuts, with mango and raisins usually predominating.

CINNAMON (or True Cinnamon), spice; aromatic inner bark, stick, or ground, of Cinnamon tree. More delicate than Cassia. Practically all "cinnamon" sold in United States is Cassia.

CLOVES, spice; whole or ground dried unopened flower buds of Clove tree.

Spicy, aromatic, very warm taste. Pungent; use sparingly.

CORIANDER, whole or ground, dried seed of herb. Taste and smell reminiscent of orange, or, to some, mixture of lemon peel and sage. One seed, crushed in demitasse cup, gives a delightful aroma and taste to coffee.

COSTMARY, herb; fresh or dried leaves; Aster family. Very agreeable minty odor and bitterish flavor.

CRESS (or Land Cress), herb; fresh leaves; Mustard family. Young leaves and stems have spicy, piquant taste like mustard plant or nasturtium leaves. See watercress.

CUMIN, whole or ground dried seed of herb; Parsley family. Has aromatic flavor and warm, bitterish taste, somewhat like caraway seed, which it resembles in appearance.

CURRY POWDER, condiment; combination of spices in powder or paste. According to different manufacturers' formulae, taste varies from fairly mild to very hot, depending on proportions of Allspice, Black Pepper, Red Pepper, Cayenne, Ginger, Cinnamon, Cardamon Seed, Coriander Seed, Fenugreek, Caraway Seed, Curry Leaf, Mustard Seed, Nutmeg, Saffron, Turmeric, White Pepper, and/or other spices used. Has pungent, tempting aroma. Known as "the salt of the Orient."

DILL, herb; fresh leaves, fresh or dried flowers, seed; parsley family. Pungent flavor. Use sparingly. Do not overcook.

FENNEL (also called Sweet Anise, Finocchio, or Sweet Fennel), herb; fresh and dried leaves and stalks, seeds, essential oil; Parsley family. Pungent licorice taste. Use like Anise. Blanched stalks and bulbs can be eaten and cooked like celery.

FENUGREEK, seeds of herb, allied to Clover. Peculiar but pleasant aromatic odor, rather bitter taste. Use sparingly.

FILE, powdered Sassafras leaves, used in gumbos.

FINES HERBES (in French, "fin-erb"), combinations of three or more finely chopped herbs used to flavor many dishes. See Seasoning Blending.

GARLIC, bulb, dried, powder, salt, oil. "The most pungent and wholesome member of the large On-

ion family. Like all that is best, it must be used with care and discretion."
—André L. Simon.

GERANIUM, flower herb; fresh and dried leaves. There are many varieties, including Apple, Balm-Scented, Camphor-Rose, Lemon-Scented, Nutmeg, Orange, Peppermint, Rose (the most popular), and Spicy, each with the aroma and flavor of its name.

GHERKINS, small, prickly cucumbers after pickling.

GINGER, herb; dried whole and ground root and essence of semi-tropical plant. Aromatic and stimulating, sweet and spicy.

HERB, any fragrant plant with culinary or medicinal use.

HORSE RADISH, fresh root of herb of Mustard family. Noted for pungency. Use sparingly.

HYSSOP (or Blue Hyssop) herb; fresh and dried leaves and flowering spikes or tops; Mint family. Sweetly scented, minty taste and aroma.

JUNIPER BERRY, aromatic fruit of cedarlike shrub or tree. Tastes slightly bittersweet, with fragrant, spicy aroma. Useful in

many dishes aside from flavoring gin.

LEEK, herb; fresh bulbs or stalks; Onion family. Mild onion flavor, strong fragrance. Can be boiled, braised or baked as vegetable.

LEMON, fruit; rind, juice, essential oil. Indispensable flavoring in preparing food.

LICORICE, dried root of shrub. Sweet and slightly astringent.

LIME, fruit; rind, juice, oil. Aromatic, tart flavor. One sixth as much sugar as Lemon. Good in blending other flavors.

LOVAGE (Love Parsley), herb; fresh and dried leaves, dried roots, seed; Parsley family. Flavor and odor similar to celery, but stronger taste. Leaves and stalks can be cooked and eaten as a vegetable, like celery or spinach.

MACE, spice; flakes or ground dried fleshy layer between kernel and outer husk of Nutmeg. Same flavor as Nutmeg, except stronger, more pungent. Adds color and character to dishes.

MARIGOLD (Calendula, Pot Marigold), flower herb; fresh and dried whole and powdered flowers and petals. Fresh petals used as flavor and garnish, both fresh and dried add subtle, bitter taste. Also used to color dishes.

MARJORAM (Sweet Marjoram), herb; fresh and whole, crushed and powdered dried leaves; Mint family. Has fragrant, spicy odor and warm, aromatic flavor. A less pungent substitute for Sage. Use with discretion. For Wild Marjoram, see Orégano.

MINT, herb; any of a number of different-flavored perennials, including Curlyleaf, Apple, Apple Variegated Golden, Orange, Spearmint, Peppermint; fresh and dried leaves and flowering tops.

MUSHROOMS, edible fungi; alone or as a sauce add a distinctive flavor and negligible food value.

MUSTARD, herb spice; fresh leaves or greens, seed, powdered (flour), condiment. Tender young leaves are cooked like and with spinach. The lighter the seed, the milder the flavor. Dry mustard or mustard flour is pale yellow. When color is brighter, turmeric has been added. Prepared mustard or mustard sauce comes in a great variety of flavors and nationalities. More can be created by the addition of various spices. See Seasoning Blending.

MYRTLE, leaves and seeds of shrub; can be used as substitute for Bay Leaf in marinades and stews.

NASTURTIUM (Indian Cress), flower; the word means "Twist the nose." Leaves and flowers used like water cress; seed pods, pickled, are similar to capers.

NUTMEG, spice; whole and ground dried kernel of Nutmeg tree. Best and strongest when freshly grated. Aromatic with spicy, almost bitter taste. Good for blending. See Mace.

ONION ("The Kitchen Lily"), bulb; young and green called Green Onion or Scallion, has delicate flavor; matured bulbs are sundried, can be used raw or cooked for flavoring or cooked as vegetable. Also comes in dried flakes, powder, salt.

OREGANO (Wild Marjoram), herb; used same as Marjoram, more pungent. Gives Latin flavor to dishes.

PAPRIKA. See Pepper.

PARSLEY, herb; fresh, dried

leaves. Contains more iron than spinach. Also a great deal of vitamins A and C. It is unfortunate that Parsley is used predominately as a garnish when it can be better utilized in almost any dish as a seasoning.

PENNYROYAL (Wild Thyme), herb; dried leaves; Mint family. Aromatic flavor.

PEPPER, BLACK and WHITE, spice; dried berries of vine that grows in East Indies and India. Black Pepper is the whole ripe berry, cured; White Pepper is the mature berry after the outer hull is removed and is milder than the black. Best grades are sun-dried rather than over slow fire. Freshest, best flavor comes when black peppercorns are ground in mill as needed. White Pepper should be used where, in cooking, black specks are to be avoided.

PEPPER, RED CAYENNE, PAPRIKA, vegetable spices; dried whole, crushed and ground pods and seeds of ripe Chili or Red Pepper pods of the Capsicum family. Red Pepper is made from the long red Mexican chili and is extremely hot and therefore should be used with great restraint. The crushed pepper, consisting of pod and seeds, is hotter than the ground pods. Cayenne Pepper is the dried whole pods or ground powder of very small, very fiery chilis. A pinch or a dash is usually sufficient. Paprika is the ground dried pod and seeds of large sweet red peppers. It is rich in vitamins C and P, the latter a new one found in Paprika. Sweet and pungent, Paprika is also useful as a garnish because of its deep red color.

PICCALILLI, condiment; mixture of chopped green peppers, green tomatoes, onions, etc., highly seasoned and cooked slowly in vinegar.

PICKLES, condiment; cucumbers, small onions, cauliflowerets, and other vegetables and fruits pickled in salted vinegar bath; useful in sauces, salads, and dressings.

POPPY SEED, tiny, dried whole and ground seed of Poppy plant. There are more than 50,000 seeds to the ounce. Fragrant, nutty, oily flavor. Interesting with eggs.

ROSEMARY, herb; fresh and dried leaves; Mint family. Refreshing, spicy scent; piny flavor; combines well with Basil and Bay Leaf. Use with great discretion.

RUE, herb; fresh and dried leaves. Next to wormwood, the bitterest herb, but has strange, welcome flavor when used sparingly.

SAFFRON, spice; dried stigmas of a crocus of Iris family. Sweetish, aromatic odor, somewhat bitter taste. Expensive, but a small pinch goes a long way. Use for coloring as well as flavor.

SAGE, herb; fresh and whole and powdered dried leaves; Mint family. About 500 varieties exist. Most used include Common Garden, Cyprus, Dalmatian, Pineapple, Rose, White. Very pungent, mildly astringent taste, therefore use quite sparingly; do not cook long and do not use in foods to be frozen, as they will develop a bitter taste.

SALT, oldest, most indispensable seasoning and preservative. Brings out the natural flavor of almost every food. Herb Salts include commercial blends such as Lawry's, also Celery, Charcoal, Chive, Curry, Garlic, Hickory, Onion, and Smoked.

SAUCE ALONE, English pot herb, also known (explaining the name) as Garlic Mustard.

SAVORY, SUMMER and WINTER, herbs; fresh or dried leaves and flowering tops; Mint family. Summer Savory is a fragrant annual with flavor resembling Thyme and a slight resin smell. The Winter variety is a perennial with a stronger flavor. Both are good mixers with other herbs.

SESAME (or Bene), seed of a tropical herb; seeds and oil. Toasted, it has a flavor similar to roasted almonds.

SHALLOT (Eschalot), fresh or dried bulb or herb. A small brown brother of the Onion, with a stronger but mellower, more subtle flavor and a shape like Garlic.

SORREL (Garden Sorrel, Indian Sorrel, Sour Grass, Dock), herb; fresh leaves and stems. Cooked with other greens, it has a pleasant acid or sour flavoring. (JAMAICA SORREL, a bushy hibiscus, has seed pods, berries, blossoms, and stems that are all usable.

SOY SAUCE, Chinese catsup, fermented juice of soybeans. Very salty. Can be sweetened slightly with

Sucaryl solution for meat or fish.

SPICES, aromatic, often pungent plant substances used to season food and beverages.

SUGAR, the principal sweetening agent used everywhere except in low calorie cookery.

TABASCO SAUCE, fiery hot essence made from vinegar and small red peppers originally imported from the state of Tabasco, Mexico. Use very sparingly, a drop at a time.

TANSY, herb; fresh or dried leaves. Strong aroma and bitter flavor.

TARRAGON (means: "Little Dragon"), herb; fresh and dried leaves and flowering tops; Aster family. Distinctive flavor. Use with light hand. Can be cooked for long periods.

THYME (pronounced "time"), herb; fresh and dried whole and ground flowers and leaves; Mint family. Strong, pungent, agreeable, fragrance. There are varieties with Lemon, Orange and Caraway scent and flavor. Most versatile herb. Use sparingly.

TRUFFLES, black underground fungus tuber. Use as garnish or seasoning for distinctive fragrance and flavor.

TURMERIC (also Tumeric), spice; ground and whole rootstock of mild cousin of Ginger. Has aromatic, warm flavor and beautiful yellow color. One pinch will color a big dish. Used in mustards, chowchow pickles, etc.

VANILLA, spice; bean of climbing vine of Orchid family. Stick and extract of soluble part in alcohol are used.

VERBENA (or Lemon Verbena), herb; fresh or dried leaves. Fruit aroma and flavor like Lime or Lemon.

VINEGAR (French *vin*, wine, and *aigre*, sour), dilute acetic acid, condiment and preservative. There are many commercial varieties: Malt, Cider, Red and White Wine, Perry (pear), Corn, Distilled, Herb, and Spice. To make your own herb and spice vinegars see Seasoning Blending.

WATER CRESS, herb; fresh leaves and stems; Mustard family. Peppery, pungent, resembling nasturtium.

WINE, fermented juice of fresh, ripe grapes. There are many varieties: dry, sweet, semi-sweet, sour, in red, rosé and white. Wine is a cornerstone of European cuisines and adds much character to many dishes. The alcohol, and consequently most of the calories, evaporates in cooking, unless very sweet wines are used.

WORCESTERSHIRE SAUCE, condiment. Adds color and spice to all except sweet foods.

SEASONING BLENDING

In mixing together herbs and other flavors new and unusual combinations can be achieved according to your own taste and the skill which you acquire from experience. There is one rule to remember—pick one leading flavor as the foundation for your blend and surround it with from one to four other, more subtle seasonings. Never let two strong seasonings fight it out in a blend.

The "leading flavors" are the pungent, dominating herbs such as Rosemary, Sage, Winter Savory; then come Sweet Basil, Peppermint, Spearmint, Sweet Marjoram, Tarragon, Thyme, and, of course, Garlic.

Especially good in blends are Chervil, Chive, Curled Parsley, Summer Savory, Lovage, and Celery. Then there are all the others with which to experiment. If you are extrasensitive in your blending, you can flavor your dishes with such unusual and pleasing combinations that only an expert could name the components.

There are two types of blends in French cuisines that are traditional and point the way for you to start your blending experiences—*les fines herbes* (the fine herbs) and *bouquets garnis* (garnished bouquets).

LES FINES HERBS

These are different blends of fresh herbs finely chopped or dried ones crushed, powdered, and strained through a fine sieve.

There are several versions of what constitute the traditional *fines herbes*. One is Sweet Basil, Chervil, Sweet Marjoram, Thyme, Rosemary, and Tarragon. Another is fresh Chervil, Tarragon, Chives, Parsley, and sometimes Fennel, Truffles, and Mushrooms, too. Twice as much Parsley is used as the other herbs. This is a blend used for almost any herb seasoning.

Here are some other combinations for specific uses. For 2 eggs: ¼ teaspoon each powdered Parsley, Thyme, Sweet Basil, Onion powder, plus a dash of cracked Black Pepper.

For soups, stews, and sprinkled over beef and pork roasts and beef and veal steaks before cooking: 6 crushed Bay Leaves, 1 tablespoon each of powdered Sage, Parsley, Marjoram, Summer Savory, Thyme, grated Lemon rind, and Celery seed.

For pork dishes: equal quantities of Sage, Basil, and Savory. As a blend for vegetables: 3 tablespoons each dried Mint and Sage, 1 teaspoon each Celery seed and White Pepper. Reduce all ingredients to a fine powder. Use ¼ teaspoon or more of mixture to season boiled vegetables such as string beans, carrots, cauliflower, and peas.

BOUQUETS GARNIS

There are bunches of fresh herbs tied with white thread or dried herbs in cheesecloth sacks (like teabags) that are cooked with food or soup and removed when dish is ready to serve. Here are some combinations.

1 piece each Bay leaf, Parsley, and Thyme or Onion.

Marjoram, Savory, and Basil sprigs and Celery stalk with leaves.

For stews: 1 sprig each Basil and Parsley and 2 Scallions; 1 sprig each Parsley, Savory, Thyme; 1 sprig Sweet Marjoram, 1 stalk Celery, and leaves, 2 Scallions.

For lamb stew: Parsley, Thyme, Clove.

For soups: 2 stalks Celery with leaves, 5 Chive blades, 1 sprig each Chervil, Parsley, and Summer Savory, small sprig Basil.

Dried Herb Bag Mix for soups: 1 teaspoon each dried Parsley, Thyme, Marjoram; ½ teaspoon each Savory, Sage, Bay leaves; 2 teaspoons Celery leaves. Crush and blend well. Put in 6 small cheesecloth or muslin sacks and tie like tea bags. Use each sack to season 1 to 2 quarts of soup.

OTHER COMBINATIONS AND PROPORTIONS

(Freshen the dried herbs before blending by soaking in lemon juice a few minutes.)

- 2 dried Tarragon to 1 dried Marjoram.
- 2 dried Summer Savory to 1 chopped Chives.
- 4 minced Dill to 1 minced Garlic
- 2 dried Thyme to 2 dried Orégano or 1 dried Marjoram.
- 2 dried Basil to 1 chopped Chives. Add 1 dried Marjoram (optional).

1 dried Borage to 1 dried Burnet and 2 chopped Chives.

2 minced Parsley to 1 dried Burnet and either 2 dried Mint or 1 dried Thyme.

2 minced Parsley to 4 minced Celery and 1 dried Rosemary.

1 dried Parsley to 1 chopped Chives and 2 dried Chervil.

2 minced fresh Lovage to 1 minced fresh Parsley and pinch of Orégano.

2 minced fresh Marjoram to 2 minced fresh Parsley and 1 dried Rosemary.

2 chopped Chives to 1 dried Marjoram and 1 dried Summer Savory.

2 minced fresh Parsley to 2 dried Mint and 1 Burnet.

HERB BOUQUET
calories negligible

With an electric blender you can make a blended herb seasoning to add flavor to vegetable or tomato-juice cocktails, soups, and sauces. Simply place ½ ounce onion, ½ cup parsley leaves, 4 cups celery leaves, 2 teaspoons salt, and 2 cups water in glass container of Waring or other blender. Cover container and blend until smooth, at least 1 minute. This will flavor 6 quarts of beverage or soup. Small amounts of fresh herbs can be blended in as desired. Makes 3 cups.

HERBED AND SPICED VINEGARS

Cider, malt, red and white wine, distilled and other vinegars all have individual flavors. And almost all the herbs, spices, and seasonings will blend with them, giving them mellowness as well as flavor. So any dieter who cares to mix his own can certainly, with a little practice and discrimination, achieve wonderfully subtle and unusual results with seasoned vinegars.

Fresh leaves: Place 1 packed cup minced and gently bruised leaves, which have been washed and drained, and 1 pint vinegar, in jar with tight cover. Let stand 1 to 2 weeks in warm kitchen or sun, shaking once daily. Strain and bottle.

Dried leaves, crushed seed, or powder: 2 teaspoons to 1 pint hot vinegar, then proceed as with fresh leaves.

Seasonings for use in vinegars: Allspice, Basil, Bay leaves, Borage, Burnet, Capers, Caraway, Cardamom, Cayenne, Celery, Chilis, Chives, Cinnamon, Coriander, Black Cumin, Curry powder (1½ ounces to pint), Dill, Fennel, Garlic (1 ounce minced to pint), Geranium,

Horse radish (2 tablespoons fresh-ground to pint), Ginger, Juniper berries, Marjoram, Mint, Mustard, Onion, Paprika, Red Peppers, White Pepper, Black Peppercorns, Rosemary, Shallot (2 ounces minced to pint), Sorrel, Spearmint, Tarragon, Thyme.

Herb combination: Allspice, Basil, Bay leaves, crushed Cloves, Dill seed, Marjoram, Mint, Rosemary, Tarragon. Crush and blend in jar, add vinegar of choice, infuse for 2 to 3 weeks, filter, and bottle.

Mint, Spearmint, Wintergreen, or Rose Geranium can be used to make sweet vinegars by chopping and bruising 1 cup of fresh leaves and adding them to 1 pint cider vinegar and 1 tablespoon Sucaryl solution. Boil together for 5 minutes, then strain through fine strainer (or filter) into hot, sterilized bottles and cork tightly.

Tarragarlic vinegar: Place 2 cups tender Tarragon leaves, washed, dried, and crushed, in wide-mouthed jar, pour 1 pint distilled vinegar over, add 2 crushed cloves and 1 split clove garlic. Keep in warm room 1 day, remove garlic, keep in warm place 2 weeks, shaking daily. Strain and bottle.

Blending different seasonings for infusing vinegars: Begin cautiously, mixing only two flavors together at first. After all, the vinegar provides a third one. Be guided by the rules for Seasoning Blending. Don't use too much of a strong seasoning (Garlic, Chives, Tarragon, Basil) with a milder one, or only the strong will come through. Try blending the different vinegars together, also.

GENERAL KITCHEN RULES

The first kitchen rule is—clean up as you go along.

Ingredients in recipes are listed in the order in which they are used.

All temperatures given are Fahrenheit.

A set or nest of standard measuring cups and spoons is essential. A small food scale is very helpful in preparing diet foods. Every home should have at least one heavy iron or aluminum skillet with a tight cover. These are the all-purpose restaurant utensils and are used for roasting, braising, poaching, and preparing sauces, as well as for frying.

Oven-crisp crackers and other baked goods just before serving.

Duncan Hines says, "If you insist on long boiling of vegetables in a lot of water, then drink the water and throw away the vegetables. The water will be more nutritious."

In cutting recipes to half, a short-cut is to substitute "tablespoons" for "ounces" and "cup" for "pint" or "pound."

In cutting baking recipes remember to use a smaller pan and shorter baking time.

COOKING TERMS

AU GRATIN. To brown under the broiler.

BASTE. To moisten cooking or roasting food, using a long-handled spoon, ladle, or large "eyedropper" type vacuum tube and bulb.

BLANCH. To clean meat, place in water, bring to a boil, remove, and wash again. Also, to dip in boiling water to loosen fruit or tomato skins.

CUBE. To cut food into even squares.

DICE. To chop food into small pieces.

FOLD. To mix together very gently by hand ingredients that have air beaten in them. Never use mechanical mixer.

MARINADE. A pickling liquid, especially for barbecues.

MARINATE. To soak, pickle, or coat with a marinade or seasoned dressing.

MINCE. To cut or chop fine or grate medium or coarse.

OVER HOT WATER. In top of double boiler or similar utensil.

PUREE. To put foods through fine sieve or cut with electric blender so that they are smooth liquid or semi-liquid.

REDUCE. To evaporate part of the liquid by boiling or simmering until it is thicker.

SAUTE. To fry quickly with little grease, keeping food moving in pan to prevent burning. (*Sauter*, French, to jump.)

SCALD. To heat below boiling point. Milk scalds at 190° when a row of fine bubbles appears around the edge of the pan.

SEAR. To cook the surface of food quickly with intense heat to seal in juices.

SIMMER. To cook below boiling point. Water simmers at 180 to 185°, boils at 212°.

WHIP. To add air into food or mixture of food by beating with French whisk or rotary (egg) beater or electric mixer.

MEASURING FOOD

There are two ways of measuring food. One is by bulk or volume; the other by weight.

The volume measurements are either liquid (pints, quarts, gallons) or dry (pints, quarts, pecks, bushels). Dry measurement is disappearing in favor of weight (avoirdupois) measurement.

The liquid (or fluid) pints and quarts do not have the same volume as the dry, which are about 1/6 larger.

Another difference is between the liquid ounce and

the avoirdupois ounce. The first is a measure of size, 1/16th of a liquid pint; the second is of weight, 1/16th of a pound.

In this book most of the measurements are in liquid spoons, ounces, and cups. Avoirdupois ounces and pounds are given mainly for raw and canned foods. Since the average canned food weighs about 15 liquid ounces per pound, 1 full liquid ounce of can contents has approximately the same number of calories as an Avoirdupois ounce.

Remember in measuring that all spoons and cups must be *level* to be accurate.

TABLES OF WEIGHTS AND MEASURES
(all level)

LIQUID OR FLUID MEASURE

"A pinch," "dash," or "few grains" = less than ⅛ teaspoon
1 teaspoon = 60 drops = ⅓ tablespoon
1 dessert spoon = 2 teaspoons
1 tablespoon = 3 teaspoons = ½ liquid ounce
1 liquid ounce = 2 tablespoons = ⅛ cup
¼ cup = 4 tablespoons
⅓ cup = 5 tablespoons and 1 teaspoon
1 gill = ½ cup = 8 tablespoons
⅔ cup = 10 tablespoons and 2 teaspoons
¾ cup = 12 tablespoons
⅞ cup = 14 tablespoons
1 cup = 2 gills = ½ liquid
    pint = 8 liquid ounces = 16 tablespoons
1 pint = 2 cups = ½ quart = 4 gills = 16 liquid
    ounces = 32 tablespoons
1 quart = 2 pints = ¼ gallon = 4 cups = 32 liquid
    ounces = approx. 945 cubic centimeters = 57.75
    cubic inches
1 gallon = 4 quarts = 8 pints = 16 cups = 231 cubic inches

DRY MEASURES

1 dry quart = 2 dry pints = ⅛ peck = 67.2 cubic inches
1 peck = 8 dry quarts = 16 dry pints
1 bushel = 4 pecks = 32 dry quarts = 2150.42 cubic inches

AVOIRDUPOIS WEIGHT

1 avoirdupois ounce = 28.35 grams
1 pound = 16 avoirdupois ounces = 453.6 grams
1 kilogram = 1000 grams = 2.2 pounds

OVEN TEMPERATURES
(all Fahrenheit)

Very slow	250°
Slow	300°
Moderately slow	325°
Moderate	350°
Moderately hot	375°
Hot	400°
Very hot	450° to 500°
Broiling	500° and over

Water boils at 212° Fahrenheit and 100° Centigrade at sea level.

Water freezes at 32° Fahrenheit and 0° Centigrade.

ROASTING GUIDE

	Minutes to leave in oven	*Fahrenheit*
Beef roast, 3—4 pounds, rare	20 per pound	300
" " " well-done	30 " "	325
Chicken, 4—5 pounds	1½—2 hours	350
Custard, individual	30—40	350
Fish, whole, 4 pounds	30—35	350
Ham	30 per pound	300—325
Lamb or veal, 3—4 pounds	35 per pound	325
Turkey, 10—13 pounds	25 per pound	325

COMMON SIZES OF CANS

Size of Can	Approximate Net Weight*	Net Liquid Contents†	Approx. Cupfuls	Average No. Servings
6 oz.	6 oz.	6 fluid oz.	¾	2 small
8 oz.	8 oz.	7¾ fluid oz.	1	2
No. 1	10½ oz.	9½ fluid oz.	1¼	2—3
No. 300	15½ oz.	13½ fluid oz.	1¾	3—4
No. 303	1 lb.	15 fluid oz.	2	4
No. 2	1 lb. 4 oz.	1 pint 2 fluid oz.	2½	5
No. 2½	1 lb. 13 oz.	1 pint 10 fluid oz.	3½	7
46 oz. or No. 3 cyl.	3 lb. 3 oz.	1 quart 14 fluid oz.	5¾	11—12

* The net weights of various foods in the same size can vary with the density of the product. The weights cited are for foods of average density.

† The volume figures cited are average commercial fills.

It is possible to drink (alcoholic beverages, that is) and reduce, but then you don't need to diet. Just drink and don't eat.

Alcohol is not only fattening (figure 1 calorie per proof point per ounce*) but it furnishes those empty calories Dr. Norman Jolliffe tells us about, containing none of the needed proteins, vitamins, or minerals.

If your social life exposes you to the high-caloric hospitality of cocktail parties, or if you have been accustomed to taking a shot along with the sunset gun, try substitution and subterfuge. Quietly pour or ask for plain carbonated water or one of the non-caloric sodas—something which can pass for a gin and tonic or a vodka and whatever they are mixing with vodka in your set. Or if you have the mental strength of a saint, accept a glass of strong waters and hold it in your hand all evening without succumbing to the demon. This also cuts down the number of hands you have available to nibble at snacks.

If you usually have a drink before dinner, try cold bouillon or soup on the rocks, fruit or vegetable juice, clam juice, or one of the cocktails in the Anti-appetizer section.

TEA

Ever heard of Richard Blechynden? One of the world's great unsung heroes. He invented iced tea. According to tea-industry lore, young Mr. Blechynden came from Calcutta to represent the Indian and Ceylon tea planters at the St. Louis World's Fair and to popularize the use of tea in this country.

With a colorfully costumed group of young na-

* For instance, 1 ounce of 85-proof Bourbon is 85 calories; 1 wineglass (4 ounces) of California red wine (10½% per cent alcohol, or 21 proof) is 84 calories.

tives to do the serving, he opened his booth just as a stifling hot spell set in. For days perspiring crowds streamed right by the steaming teapots to the iced-drink stands, until out of desperation Blechynden did something that no other Englishman has even been able to forgive. He experimented with some blends, filled a few tall glasses with chunks of ice, and poured in his hot tea. Gad, the man knew his market! In England he would have been lynched. In St. Louis he was mobbed. Iced tea was on its way to becoming an institution.

Americans now drink well over 10 billion glasses during the hot season. Into this they squeeze 710 million lemons, and pour 170,836,-000 pounds of sugar. Here are a few ways to prepare tea without any sugar.

TIPS ON TEA

Use a teapot, preheated. That means first filled or rinsed with scalding water.

Use fresh, cold water, brought to a full rolling boil.

Use 1 teaspoon or 1 teabag per cup.

Brew by the clock 3 to 5 minutes. Longer gives the tea a bitter taste.

Don't judge the strength of tea by its color. Some weak teas produce a dark brew. Some strong ones brew light. The color may also be affected by differences in water. Go by the flavor.

If you prefer weaker tea, prepare as usual, then add hot water to dilute.

When you buy a package of teabags, remember that a box of 16 weighs about 1¼ ounces, a box of 48 is not quite ¼ pound, and it takes 200 to make a pound. Compare the cost with that of a pound of loose tea.

Tea stays best when kept in a tightly covered container away from spices and cooking odors.

Experts recommend milk, not cream, because it lets the true flavor of the tea come through.

ICED TEA

It is not necessary to refrigerate iced tea, as this may cause clouding, which is not harmful to flavor or quality. Restore to clear by adding a little boiling water.

FROSTY SPICED TEA
2 calories per cup

¾ cup cold water
1 tablespoon Sucaryl solution
   dash of salt
½ teaspoon whole cloves
6 2-inch cinnamon sticks
   dash of nutmeg
4 cups water
3 tablespoons tea
6 lemon wedges
   ice cubes

Make syrup by combining and simmering water, Sucaryl, salt, and spices over low heat for 10 minutes. Drain, and set aside. To make tea base, bring 4 cups of water to a full rolling boil. Remove from heat and immediately add 3 tablespoons tea. Cool 3 to 5 minutes. Stir and strain into spiced syrup. Pour over ice cubes in tall glasses. Serve with lemon wedge and a stick of cinnamon in each glass. Serves 6.

VARSITY TEA
28 calories per serving

- 2 cups water
- 1 tablespoon tea
- 2 tablespoons Sucaryl solution
- ¾ cup orange juice
- ⅓ cup lemon juice
- 1 pint club soda
- 12 slices orange

Bring water to full rolling boil. Remove from heat and immediately add tea. Brew 3 to 5 minutes. Stir and strain into container holding Sucaryl, and add fruit juices. Pour into small punch bowl over piece of ice. Just before serving, add the club soda and the orange slices. Serves 6.

TEA DELIGHT
25 calories per serving

- 1 cup boiling water
- ½ tablespoon tea
- ½ tablespoon Sucaryl solution
- 1 12-ounce can low calorie unsweetened apricot nectar
- ¼ cup fresh lemon juice
- ½ pint orange juice
- 1 quart non-caloric ginger ale
- lemon slices

Bring water to full rolling boil. Remove from heat and immediately add tea. Brew 5 minutes. Strain and pour into container with Sucaryl and add apricot nectar and fruit juices. Chill. Just before serving, pour over ice blocks in punch bowl. Stir in ginger ale and garnish with lemon slices. Serves about 12.

FRUIT TEA PUNCH
30 calories per serving

- 2 cups water
- 1 tablespoon tea
- 1 No. 303 can unsweetened grapefruit juice
- 1 No. 303 can unsweetened pineapple juice
- 1 tablespoon Sucaryl solution
- 1 quart non-caloric ginger ale
- 1 lemon, thinly sliced

Bring water to full rolling boil. Remove from heat and immediately add tea. Brew 4 minutes. Stir and strain into container holding fruit juices and Sucaryl. Chill. Just before serving, add ginger ale. Pour over ice cubes in tall glasses and garnish with lemon slices. Makes 14 6-ounce servings.

SPICED FRUIT PUNCH
19 calories per serving

2 cups boiling water
3 teabags
12 whole cloves
1 2-inch stick whole cinnamon
3½ cups fresh orange juice
1½ teaspoons grated lemon rind
½ cup fresh lemon juice
1 cup pineapple juice
½ teaspoon ground nutmeg
¼ teaspoon ground allspice
1 tablespoon Sucaryl solution, or to taste
1½ quarts non-caloric ginger ale

orange slices, grapes

Combine water, tea, and whole spices. Steep about 5 minutes. Remove teabags. Cool tea. Add rest of ingredients except ginger ale. Strain over cracked ice in punch bowl and add ginger ale. Garnish bowl with slices of fresh orange and clusters of grapes. Serve at once. Makes 28 4-ounce servings.

HERB TEAS

Teas can be brewed from many of the herbs, either individually or in combination with regular teas. And they can be served hot or iced, according to the season. Here are the principal herbs used for tea:

Angelica, Anise, Balm and Lemon Balm, Bergamot, Burnet, Borage, Camomile, Catnip (!), Costmary, dried Clover, Dill, Fennel, Horehound, Hyssop, Lovage, Marjoram, Mint, Marigold, Mullein leaves, Parsley, Pennyroyal, Peppermint, Lavender, Rose Geranium, Rose petals, Rosemary, Rye, crushed Saffron stigmas, Sage, Sarsaparilla, Sassafras, Strawberry leaves, Garden or Lemon Thyme, Tilia leaves, Verbena, Vervian, Wintergreen, Woodruff, Yerba Maté.

Don't use a metal pot for brewing herb teas. Use 1 teaspoon of the dried leaves per cup and one for the pot. Or 1 tablespoon of the fresh leaves, bruised gently, per cup.

Seed tea is made by crushing 1 tablespoon of the seed (in a mortar, if you have one) to bring out the oils. Add to water before it comes to a boil, then simmer gently 5 to 10 minutes, strain, and serve.

For iced herb tea, crush the herb in a pottery pitcher, pour boiling water over; steep 5 minutes; strain; cover pitcher and cool in refrigerator. Either fresh or dried leaves, as for hot tea, can be used in making iced tea. Some herbs especially suited for iced herb tea are:

Anise, Borage, Lavender, Lemon Balm, Lemon Verbena, Sweet Marjoram, Mint, Rose Geranium, Rosemary, Rose petals, Garden or Pineapple Sage.

Crushed seeds to be served hot are:

Anise, Caraway, Dill, Fennel, Fenugreek, Parsley.

Herbs to blend with the Mints in tea-making are:

Costmary, Lavender, Lemon Balm, Lemon Verbena, Sweet Marjoram, Rose petals, Rose Geranium, Sage.

Try blending Rosemary with Lavender flowers.

OTHER BEVERAGES

ICED COFFEE FIZZ
No calories

Combine 1 cup hot, strong coffee, 1 teaspoon Sucaryl solution, and 1 teaspoon vanilla. Pour equal amounts into each of 4 10-ounce glasses; add ice cubes. Fill glasses with sparkling water; stir gently to mix. Serves 4.

FROSTED SPICE COFFEE
No calories

Combine 3 cups of strong coffee, 2 tablespoons broken stick cinnamon, 8 whole

cloves, 8 allspice berries; simmer 15 minutes. Strain. Add 1 teaspoon vanilla and 1 teaspoon Sucaryl solution. Pour over ice in 4 tall glasses. Serves 4.

ICED COFFEE CARIBBEAN
No calories

In a tall glass combine ¼ teaspoon Sucaryl solution and ½ to 1 teaspoon imitation brandy or rum flavoring; add ice cubes. Fill glass with strong, hot coffee. Stir gently. Serves 1.

ICED COFFEE MANHATTAN
No calories

Combine 1½ teaspoons Sucaryl solution, 1 cup hot, strong coffee, and 1 teaspoon Angostura bitters. Pour equal amount into each of 4 10-ounce glasses. Add ice cubes and fill glasses with sparkling water. Stir gently to mix. Serve with twists of lemon peel. Serves 4.

MOCHA PEP-UP
26 calories per serving

4 ounces skim milk
½ teaspoon powdered coffee
few drops vanilla
Sucaryl, saccharin, Crystallose, Saxin, or Sweeta to taste

Mix thoroughly with an electric mixer, blender, or egg beater. Serve chilled or over ice cubes. Serves 1.

COCOA

76 calories per serving

¾ teaspoon Sucaryl
  solution
3 cups skim milk
3 tablespoons cocoa
  pinch of salt
½ cup water
⅛ teaspoon vanilla

*Combine Sucaryl with 2 ta-
blespoons of the milk. Combine cocoa, salt, water, and
Sucaryl mixture in top of
double boiler. Cook 2 minutes over direct heat, stirring constantly; add remaining milk and vanilla. Cinnamon may be used instead
of vanilla. Place over boiling water. Heat thorough-
ly. Makes 4 servings.*

If made with sugar, this
would be 117 calories per
serving.

HOT CHOCOLATE

118 calories per serving

1½ ounces bitter chocolate
1½ teaspoons Sucaryl
  solution
  pinch of salt
1 cup water, boiling
3 cups skim milk,
  scalded

*Melt chocolate in double
boiler. Add Sucaryl, salt,
and water slowly; stir until
smooth. Boil 1 minute. Add
to scalded milk. Makes 4
cups.*

If 3 more cups of boiling
water are used, instead of
skim milk, the calorie count
is 53 per serving.

Joseph Metzger, Jr., who
lives in a world of yogurt—
he makes a million jars of
Dannon Yogurt a month—
has earned the gratitude of
all dieters by making the
product less caloric. Dannon has cut its count per 8-
ounce jar from 160 to 120
and it is at the latter figure
that we calculate Mr. Metzger's favorite pick-me-up,
an extremely bland drink.

RED VELVET

85 calories per cup

½ cup Dannon yogurt
½ cup tomato juice
  dash of celery or other
  seasoned salt

*Mix first 2 items together
by hand, in mixer or, best
of all, in electric blender.
Add celery salt. Serves 1.*

VEGETABLE BUTTERMILK COCKTAIL

90 calories per serving

¼ cup finely grated cu-
  cumber and juice
½ teaspoon finely grated
  onion and juice
2 teaspoons finely grated
  celery and juice
1 tablespoon finely
  grated carrot
1 teaspoon lemon juice
2 cups Sealtest or other
  buttermilk
  salt

*Add cucumber, onion, cel-
ery, carrot, and lemon juice
to buttermilk. Mix well.
Season to taste with salt.
Chill thoroughly in refrig-*

erator. *Strain and serve. Makes 2 generous servings.*

BUTTERMILK LEMONADE
49 calories per serving
3 tablespoons lemon
juice, chilled
1½ teaspoons Sucaryl so-
lution or to taste
1 cup buttermilk, chilled

Blend juice and sweetener, add buttermilk, and mix well. Serve cold. Serves 2.

BLACK CHERRY FIZZ
43 calories per serving
Fill 8-ounce glass half full of cold Sealtest or other buttermilk. Slowly fill to top with cold non-caloric black cherry soda. Stir gently and serve immediately. Serves 1.

SLIM GINGER
44 calories per serving
Fill glass half full of cold Sealtest or other buttermilk. Slowly fill to top with cold, low calorie ginger ale. Stir gently. Serve immediately. Serves 1.

FRUIT DRINKS
APRICOLA SLING
22 calories per serving
Mix ¼ cup grapefruit juice, ¼ cup pineapple juice, and 1 cup apricot nectar with ½ teaspoon Sucaryl solution. Add 24 ounces Hoffman's Streamliner Cola or other non-fattening carbonated cola. Serves 4.

CRANBERRY COCKTAIL
29 calories per serving
1 quart cranberries
1 quart water
2 tablespoons Sucaryl
solution
¼ cup lemon juice
¼ cup orange juice
pinch of salt

Boil cranberries in water until soft. Strain, and add Sucaryl, lemon juice, orange juice, and salt. Bring to boil. Chill and serve. Serves 10.

CRANBERRY PUNCH
15 calories per serving
Proceed as above, except serve from punch bowl containing block of ice and add 2 quarts soda water. Makes 3½ to 4 quarts. Serves 20.

This is an egg drink with an unusual name. It is best made with the Ocean Spray diet cranberry juice that is put up without sugar. Since only the ripest berries are picked, the supply is small and it may be difficult to obtain. In that case, make your own with fresh cranberries boiled until soft, strained, and sweetened with Sucaryl.

SPIZZERINKTUM
59 calories per cup
2 eggs
⅛ teaspoon salt
1 tablespoon Sucaryl
solution
juice of 1 lemon
juice of 3 oranges
2 cups diet cranberry
juice

Beat eggs and salt until lemon colored. Add Sucaryl and fruit juices and blend. Pour over cracked ice in glasses or punch cups. Makes 5 8-ounce glasses.

OCEAN SPRAY COCKTAIL
62 calories per serving

1 pint Ocean Spray unsweetened cranberry juice
1 tablespoon lemon juice
1 egg white
nutmeg

Blend cranberry and lemon juice, chill. Beat egg white stiff. Add juice and beat until frothy. Pour into glasses and sprinkle with nutmeg. Serves 4.

LEMONADE
8 calories per glass

Put scant ½ teaspoon Sucaryl solution, or 3 tablets, in 2 tablespoons of fresh strained lemon juice. Add enough water to make 8 ounces. Add ice as desired; garnish with a slice of lemon or mint leaves. Serves 1.

Lime juice as well as carbonated water may be substituted.

APPLE LEMONADE
47 calories per serving

1 quart apple juice
1 cup lemon juice
1½ tablespoons Sucaryl solution (or to taste)

Combine ingredients and serve with ice and mint sprigs. Serves 12.

TEA LEMONADE
4 calories per serving

4 cups water
6 tablespoons tea
3 cups cold water
¾ cup cold water
1½ tablespoons Sucaryl solution
¾ cup fresh lemon juice

Bring 4 cups of water to full rolling boil. Remove from heat. Immediately add tea and brew 3 to 5 minutes. Stir and strain into pitcher holding 3 cups cold water. To make syrup, mix ¾ cup cold water with the Sucaryl. Add to the tea, then add lemon juice. To serve, pour over ice cubes in tall glasses. Makes 10 8-ounce servings.

MINT COOLER
23 calories per serving

1 cup water
3 tablespoons Sucaryl solution
2 dozen sprigs mint, chopped, or 5 to 6 dashes Mintit
1 cup fresh lime juice
2½ cups canned or fresh grapefruit juice
½ teaspoon salt
1 quart carbonated water

Simmer Sucaryl and water. Pour over chopped mint or combine with Mintit. Cool. Combine fruit juices and mint mixture. Add salt and pour over ice in 8 tall glasses. Fill with carbonated water. Serves 8.

MINTIT FRUIT JUICE
57 calories per serving

1 cup orange juice
1 cup pineapple juice
few drops of Mintit

Combine juices and chill. Add Mintit (or mint extract) just before serving. Serves 4.

PEACH CREAM
56 calories per cup

2 halves Monarch or
  other Sucaryl sweetened peaches
4 tablespoons peach juice
  from above
3 medium ice cubes,
  crushed

Put all ingredients into glass container of Waring or other blender and mix at high speed for 1½ minutes. Serve at once. Makes 1 cup.

Frappéed watermelon was one of the many pleasant drinks this writer encountered years ago at the Café Florida on the Prado in Havana. The Waring Blendor people suggest this way to make it.

WATERMELON FRAPPE
48 calories per serving

Remove seeds and cut red watermelon flesh into small chunks. Put 4 cups into blender and run 15 to 20 seconds, until watermelon is puréed. Makes 2 cups of purée. Serves 4.

Can be chilled to mush in freezer tray of refrigerator and served as a first course.

MIXED SODAS

Just because there are few or no calories in the new sugarless carbonated drinks don't step up your intake of them. Since in large quantities they supply water, bulk, and distend the stomach, keep your consumption of them to normal.

Here are a few ways to vary the flavors.

CREOLE COOLER
Calories negligible

2 bottles No-Cal black
  cherry
1 bottle No-Cal cola
8 ounces No-Cal ginger

Any other available non-caloric brand will do. Chill bottles thoroughly and pour sodas slowly into pitcher. Serve at once without stirring. Serves 6.

NO-CAL REFRESHER
32 calories per glass

1 ounce Ocean Spray
  dietetic cranberry
  juice
1 ounce fresh orange
  juice
1 ounce fresh lemon
  juice
  No-Cal ginger to fill
  glass

Mix juices. Pour into 12-ounce highball glass filled with ice cubes. Fill up with No-Cal ginger. Serves 1.

MINT COLA
Calories negligible
- 2 teaspoons lemon juice
- ¼ teaspoon Mintit or mint flavoring
- 12 ounces non-caloric cola drink
- 2 Maraschino cherries
- 2 lemon slices

Pour lemon juice and mint into 2 10-ounce glasses. Add ice cubes. Pour cola into glasses and stir. Add cherries and lemon slices. Serve with sprigs of mint. Serves 2.

TEA PUNCH
Calories negligible
- 3 ounces cold strong tea
- 2 dashes Angostura bitters
- No-Cal ginger to fill
- grated lemon rind

Put tea and bitters into tall glass filled with cracked or cubes of ice. Fill glass with No-Cal ginger and serve with lemon rind. Serves 1.

COLA JACK
31 calories per serving

Mix ½ cup apple juice, ⅛ teaspoon Sucaryl solution, and 12 ounces non-fattening carbonated cola. Pour into glasses containing slices of lime and ice cubes. Serves 2.

YOUNG-FASHIONED
5 calories

Put a slice each of lemon, orange, and pineapple, a Maraschino cherry, and a few drops of Sucaryl liquid solution in an old-fashioned glass. Add 4 ounces Streamliner cola or other low-calorie cola. Ice and serve.

CARBONATED ICE CUBES

Freeze any of the non-caloric carbonated beverages and use the ice cubes with the same or contrasting flavors. Lemon poured over black cherry or cola cubes and cream soda poured over lemon cubes give a lot of interest to drinks. Also, serve iced tea with frozen lemon soda cubes instead of slices or juice of lemon and sweetener.

PARTY PUNCH
32 calories per cup
- 2 quarts apple cider
- 1 11-ounce can apricot nectar
- 1¼ cups lemon juice
- 2 cups orange juice
- 2½ tablespoons Sucaryl solution (or to taste)
- 2 quarts non-caloric ginger ale
- orange slices

Combine cider, nectar, lemon juice, orange juice, and Sucaryl solution. Chill. Pour over ice in punch bowl. Just before serving add ginger ale. Garnish with orange slices. Makes about 50 punch-cup servings.

REDUCER'S PUNCH

25 calories per serving

1 envelope D-Zerta (any flavor)
1¼ cups hot water
1 teaspoon lemon juice
½ cup unsweetened pineapple juice

Dissolve D-Zerta in hot water. Add fruit juices. Chill slightly and pour into ice-filled glasses. This punch thickens if kept in refrigerator more than 6 hours. Makes 3 servings, each about ¾ cup.

KOOL-AID

An inexpensive soft-drink powder in several flavors to which a non-nutritive sweetener may be added instead of sugar. Mixed with cold plain or carbonated water or cold skim milk it makes a convenient summer drink.

Also see the electric blender and vegetable juice cocktails in the Anti-Appetizer section.

BEVERAGE SEASONINGS

Tea, hot or cold: Balm and Lemon Balm leaves, Bergamot, Borage leaves, Rose and other Geranium leaves, Lemon and Lime juice, Curly, Apple, Orange, Pepper, Spear, and other Mints, Lemon Thyme, Sage, Verbena, Wintergreen. Also see Herb Teas.

Coffee: Cardamom, Cinnamon, Lemon juice.*

Lemonade: Balm leaves, Borage leaves, Lime juice, Mint and Geranium leaves, Lemon Thyme, Lemon Verbena, 1 crushed leaf of Woodruff in bottom of glass for May Wine flavor.

Hot drinks: Cinnamon, Mace, Nutmeg.

Milk drinks: Mace, Nutmeg, Vanilla.

---

* Wolfe Kaufman, the Paris epicure, likes his coffee plain black, but kills whatever bitterness it may have with a few drops of lemon juice.

It is highly improbable that anyone on a reducing diet needs anything to sharpen his appetite at dinnertime. The problem is to blunt or dull the desire for food and this can be done with a number of low-calorie snacks, such as:

> celery or carrot sticks
> pineapple fingers, dusted with Sucaryl sweetening powder
> thin pieces of raw apple
> flowers of raw cauliflower
> scallions
> red radishes cut in rose shapes
> thin white or icicle radishes
> small Italian and little egg tomatoes
> cucumber spears
> shrimps or smoked clams
> mushrooms
> green and sweet red pepper slices

More and more hostesses are recognizing that quite a few of their guests must have this sort of cocktail snack or none at all, and that any guest will enjoy the change from the usual fattening pretzels, potato chips, and calorie-laden crackers.

However, you can prepare a number of interesting and unusual canapés and other hors d'oeuvre (*hors* means outside and *d'oeuvre* is the meal) which will not throw anyone off a thinning diet. In addition to the spreads that follow, you can use some of the different-seasoned cottage cheese mixtures in the Cheese, Pastas, and Combination Dishes section. Also see the Beverage section for Watermelon Frappé and additional pre-dinner cocktails.

HOMEMADE PATE

15 calories per teaspoon

1 pound calf's liver
1 medium onion
1 large or 2 small stalks celery
2 tablespoons lemon juice
salt and pepper to taste

Boil liver in water until tender. Remove skin, fibers, and "pipes." Grind in food chopper with onion and celery. Blend to a smooth paste and season to taste with lemon juice, salt, and pepper. Form into large mound and chill. Before serving, paté can be sprinkled with chopped hard-cooked egg yellows and whites; truffles may be added. Serves 6.

BLENDED LIVER PASTE

17 calories per tablespoon

½ pound beef liver
1 tablespoon butter or margarine
2 tablespoons chili sauce
1 tablespoon prepared mustard
1 tablespoon Low Calorie Mayonnaise (see page 196)
2 tablespoons water
1 small clove garlic
½ teaspoon salt
½ teaspoon rosemary

Trim off membrane, tissue, and "pipes" from liver and brown in fat, cooking over medium heat until done. Then put remaining ingredients, in order listed, into container of Hamilton Beach or other blender and mix at high speed. Drain liver and cut into ½-inch cubes and add to contents of blender, a few pieces at a time. Blend until smooth, stopping blender several times to scrape sides of container so that all of contents will be cut fine. Makes about 1½ cups.

EGG-PICKLE SPREAD

20 calories per tablespoon

¼ cup Low Calorie Mayonnaise (see page 196)
2 tablespoons evaporated milk
1 teaspoon prepared mustard
¼ cup low calorie sweet pickles, sliced
3 hard-cooked eggs, quartered

Put all ingredients in blender in order listed. Cover container. Blend on low speed about 10 seconds, or until pickles and egg whites are cut in medium-fine particles. Stop and start blender and stir down mixture once or twice during blending, if necessary. Makes ½ cup.

A.1. SPREAD

18 calories per tablespoon

6 ounces skim-milk cottage cheese
1 tablespoon fine-chopped chives
2 ounces fine-chopped smoked salmon
1 tablespoon A.1. Sauce

Blend chives into cottage cheese, then mix in salmon. Add sauce. Use immediately or store in refrigerator until needed. Makes 16 tablespoons—enough for 32 canapés. Using 5-calorie wafers, total per canapé is 14 calories.

YOGURT COTTAGE CHEESE SPREAD

14 calories per tablespoon

2 cups skim-milk cottage cheese
1 cup yogurt
1 hard-cooked egg, chopped fine
1 tablespoon chopped chives
1 teaspoon tomato catsup

Blend all ingredients thoroughly; cover and chill for at least 30 minutes before using. Enough for 40 crackers or cucumber slices.

ANCHOVY COTTAGE SPREAD

14 calories per tablespoon

6 ounces skim-milk cottage cheese
1 ounce anchovy paste or chopped anchovies
1 tablespoon lemon juice
1 teaspoon Lea & Perrins or other Worcestershire sauce
1 teaspoon minced onion, optional

Put cottage cheese through sieve and mix well with all other ingredients; chill to blend flavors. Use as a spread for 5-calorie whole-grain wafers. Makes 16 tablespoons.

SHRIMP CANAPE FILLING

12 calories per tablespoon

20 medium shrimp
3 tablespoons Low Calorie Mayonnaise (see page 196)
½ teaspoon Worcestershire sauce

Cook, peel, and clean shrimp. Canned or frozen may be used. Mash, then blend in other ingredients well to make a smooth paste. Makes approximately 20 tablespoons.

The next canapé is a favorite recipe of Fred Waring, after whom, incidentally, the Waring Blendor is named. These shrimp-filled celery appetizers are frequently served to guests at Waring's Shawnee Inn in eastern Pennsylvania.

SHRIMP PASTE

19 calories per tablespoon

2 tablespoons chili sauce
2 tablespoons Almost Mayonnaise
1 tablespoon lemon juice
⅛ teaspoon curry powder
5-ounce can shrimp, drained

Place all in glass container of blender and blend until smooth (about 30 seconds), stopping to stir down sides after 15 seconds. Serve spread in celery stalks. Makes ¾ cup paste.

TUNA SPREAD
15 calories per tablespoon

6 tablespoons tuna
1 hard-cooked egg
2 tablespoons minced green pepper
4 stuffed olives
2 tablespoons minced onion
dash Worcestershire sauce
4 tablespoons 999 Island Dressing
salt and pepper

Drain oil from tuna, and flake. Chop egg, pepper, and olives fine; then combine all with Worcestershire sauce and season to taste. Add 999 Island Dressing and mix well. Au gratin under low flame for 2 or 3 minutes and serve hot on 5-calorie wafer or slice of cucumber (1 calorie). Makes 18 tablespoons.

Also, see Shrimp Remoulade in Salad section. And almost any other salad, in smaller portions, can be used as a meal-starter.

CRAB COCKTAIL SPREAD
7 calories per tablespoon

8 tablespoons crab meat
1 stalk celery (5 inches)
1 tablespoon minced pimento
2 tablespoons Low Calorie Mayonnaise (see page 196)
salt and pepper

Flake crabmeat being careful to eliminate bones; chop celery fine and blend all ingredients to a smooth paste. Green pepper or sweet red pepper may be substituted for pimento. Salt and pepper to taste. Makes about 16 tablespoons.

LOBSTER STUFFING
10 calories per tablespoon

8 tablespoons lobster meat
1 hard-cooked egg
1 tablespoon green pepper
salt and pepper
2 tablespoons Low Calorie Mayonnaise (see page 196)

Flake lobster meat; chop egg and green pepper fine and season to taste. With a fork blend in Low Calorie Mayonnaise until mixture has consistency of paste for spreading on thin crackers or cucumber slices, etc. Makes about 20 tablespoons.

CLAMWICH SPREAD
7 calories per tablespoon

Meat from 1 4-ounce can minced clams
1 scallion, chopped fine
2 tablespoons minced green pepper
1 teaspoon minced parsley
1 teaspoon lemon juice
salt and pepper
5 tablespoons skim-milk cottage cheese

Combine everything but cheese, blending well. Put

cheese through sieve to remove lumps, then add to rest and blend into smooth paste. Makes about 20 tablespoons.

BROILED MUSHROOMS
Hardly any calories

Wash 12 large mushrooms; separate stems from caps; place on broiler pan or baking sheet. Brush with butter and put on a dash of Worcestershire, A-1 or Escoffier Diable Sauce. Place under medium flame for 10 minutes. Serve at once, skewering each piece with a toothpick. Since mushrooms are only about 60 calories to the pound, the caloric content of each piece is negligible. Makes 24 pieces.

MINCED MUSHROOM CANAPE
8 calories per tablespoon

8 tablespoons minced mushrooms

3 tablespoons minced green pepper

1 stalk celery, chopped fine

2 teaspoons butter

2 tablespoons Low Calorie Mayonnaise (see page 196)
salt and pepper

Put mushrooms, pepper, and celery into pan with butter and sauté until light brown. Remove, and blend with mayonnaise. Salt and pepper to taste, and serve. Makes about 16 tablespoons.

CAULIFLOWERETS
7 calories per ounce

Crisp, cold raw cauliflower makes a most delicious and low calorie appetizer. Select a fresh head of cauliflower; trim and soak in ice water and 1 tablespoon vinegar 1 hour. Drain thoroughly, break into flowerets, and serve on platter, either plain or with a low calorie cocktail dip.

STUFFED CELERY DIABLE
15 calories per piece

¼ pound skim-milk cottage cheese

2 teaspoons Escoffier Diable Sauce

12 medium stalks celery
caraway, sesame, or celery seed, chives or spices

Cream cheese to a smooth texture with the Diable Sauce well blended in. Either mix in seasoning or fill hollow of celery stalks and then sprinkle with seasoning. Or you can substitute Lawry's Seasoning Salt. Makes 12 pieces.

COCKTAIL CUCUMBER
4 calories per slice

1 medium cucumber (5 inches)

4 tablespoons skim-milk cottage cheese

1 tablespoon fine-chopped pimento
salt and cayenne pepper

Scoop out the center of the

cucumber with an apple corer. Scratch green skin with sharp fork into decorative pattern. Put cottage cheese through strainer to get smooth paste. Blend with pimento and season with salt and pepper. Stuff paste into center of cucumber and chill well. Just before serving, slice into ¼-inch slices. Makes 20 slices.

LITTLE PIGS IN BLANKETS
60 calories each

Wrap thin slices of bacon around large oysters and fasten them together with a toothpick. Place under a hot flame and broil, turning frequently, until crisp and brown. Serve immediately.

FROSTED PEAR APPETIZER
21 calories per serving

2 Diet Delight pear halves
½ tablespoon lemon juice
drop green food coloring
drop mint extract

Drain juice from pears and to it add lemon juice, green coloring, and mint extract. Turn into freezing tray and freeze until firm, stirring occasionally with fork. Heap frozen mixture ino chilled pear half and serve at once. Makes 2 servings.

Mabel Stegner is the foremost authority on electric blender recipes and here are the low calorie versions of 11 of her crazy, mixed-up cocktails, any of which makes a glamorous start for a meal.

To make any of these cocktails, place all the ingredients in the glass container of the electric blender in the order indicated. Cover container and turn on blender to high speed. Run until ingredients are smoothly blended—from 15 seconds to 1 minute. Serve immediately. Each recipe makes 4 small servings.

APRICOT NECTAR
65 calories per serving

½ cup drained unsweetened apricots
2 cups orange juice
3 tablespoons lemon juice
1 cup finely cracked ice
sweetener to taste

PEACH NECTAR
33 calories per serving

1 cup sliced unpeeled peaches
½ cup orange juice
3 Sucaryl tablets
1 cup finely cracked ice

CRANBERRY-PINEAPPLE COCKTAIL
40 calories per serving

1⅓ cups unsweetened Ocean Spray cranberry juice
2 tablespoons lemon juice
½ cup crushed raw or unsweetened pineapple
Sucaryl to taste

PEAR NECTAR
49 calories per serving
1 cup unsweetened pine-
   apple juice
1 cup canned pears
1 cup finely cracked ice

STRAWBERRY NECTAR
40 calories per serving
1 cup unsweetened
   orange juice
6 Sucaryl tablets
1 cup fresh strawberries
1 cup finely cracked ice

COTTAGE CHEESE COCKTAIL
40 calories per serving
1 cup chilled tomato
   juice
½ cup skim-milk cottage
   cheese
⅛ teaspoon celery salt
⅛ teaspoon onion salt

GRAPEGG NECTAR
83 calories per serving
1 cup grape juice
2 tablespoons lime or
   lemon juice
2 Sucaryl tablets
2 raw eggs

ORANGE EGGNOG
67 calories per serving
1⅓ cups orange juice
4 teaspoons lemon juice
3 Sucaryl tablets
2 eggs

CANTALOUPE COCKTAIL
53 calories per serving
1⅓ cups orange juice
2 teaspoons lemon juice
2 cups diced cantaloupe
1 cup finely cracked ice
   dash of salt

HONEYDEW NECTAR
40 calories per serving
1 cup orange juice
1 tablespoon lemon juice
1 cup diced honeydew
1 cup finely cracked ice

CARROT COCKTAIL
26 calories per serving
½ cup orange juice
1 tablespoon lemon juice
1 cup sliced raw carrots
½ cup finely cracked ice

WATER-CRESS COCKTAIL
37 calories per serving
1 cup unsweetened pine-
   apple juice
1 tablespoon lemon juice
½ bunch water-cress
1 cup finely cracked ice
   There also are vegetable
cocktails you can run up on
your electric blender. Below
are a number that are made
by simply placing all the
ingredients listed into the
glass container, covering,
and turning to high speed.
Run until the vegetables are
cut fine—from 1 to 3 min-
utes. Strain if desired, and
serve immediately. Each of
the recipes makes 4 servings.

CELERY COCKTAIL
69 calories per serving
2 cups apple juice
2 tablespoons lemon juice
1 cup celery leaves
2 cups finely cracked ice

PARSLEY COCKTAIL
65 calories per serving
2 cups pineapple juice
1 cup parsley leaves
2 cups finely cracked ice

CUCUMBER COCKTAIL
20 calories per serving

4 cups diced cucumber
½ cup water
2 tablespoons lemon juice
dash salt
2 cups finely cracked ice,
optional

ESCAROLE COCKTAIL
45 calories per serving

1 cup grapefruit juice
2 cups tightly packed
escarole
1½ cups finely cracked ice

GREEN PEPPER COCKTAIL
40 calories per serving

1¼ cup grapefruit juice
1 large green pepper,
seeded and diced
dash salt
2 cups finely cracked ice,
optional

VITAMINADE
77 calories per serving

4 tablespoons lemon juice
2 eggs
2 navel oranges, peeled
and in sections
6 Sucaryl tablets
2 cups finely cracked ice,
optional

CARROT JUICE
57 calories per serving

*Try flavoring an 8-ounce
portion of carrot juice with
1 teaspoon of lemon juice
and a dash of Worcester-
shire sauce for taste. Served
chilled. Serves 1.*

TOMATO JUICE COCKTAILS
25 calories per 4-ounce glass

*Because of their low-caloric
content and universal ac-
ceptance, tomato juice cocktails make one of the best
meal starters. Chill the juice
and season with any of the
following: salt, pepper, cayenne; celery, onion, or garlic salt; lemon or onion juice;
Worcestershire, Tabasco, or
soy sauce; savory herbs,
such as basil, chervil, parsley, lemon balm, lovage,
mint, tarragon, and thyme;
Mintit; mixed with sauer-
kraut juice; garnished with
lemon slices; and plain, frozen to a mush in the freezing tray of the refrigerator.*

SEASONINGS
FOR ANTI-APPETIZERS

Nasturtium leaves and little onions are appetizers in
themselves.

For decoration on or over
canapés: Aniseed, Poppy
seed, Sesame seed, Capers,
chopped Dill, Parsley, Water Cress.

Mixed with Cheeses:
Coriander, Cumin, Marjo-
ram, Red Pepper, Worces-
tershire sauce; mix skim-
milk cottage cheese with
Paprika and Celery seed as
a dip.

Stuffed Eggs: Cumin,
Tarragon, Worcestershire
sauce.

Liver Paté: Marjoram,
Summer Savory, Truffles.

Meat Spread: Marjoram.

Meat Balls: Orégano,
Sage.

Stuffed Mushrooms: Marjoram.

Cauliflowerets: dip in equal parts Mustard sauce and Basil vinegar.

All Juices: Basil, Lemon, Lime, the Mints.

Fruit and Cranberry: ground Cloves, Hyssop.

Vegetable: White Pepper, Rue, small sprig Summer Savory, Tarragon.

Tomato: ground Allspice, Celery salt, Garlic salt, Lovage, Thyme.

Sauerkraut: Celery salt.

SLIM SOUPS

The most universal form of food of all times and among all
civilized people is soup. Unfortunately many soups are
made with the most fattening ingredients. However, it is
possible to make very low-calorie soups. One of these,
served very hot, is a fine, appetite-blunting opening for any
dieter's meal, as it provides bulk and taste satisfaction and
slows down the diner's eager rush to get at the heavier
foods.

The usual garnishes for soup are also high in calorie
content. In place of croutons, slices of toast, whipped
cream, crackers, noodles, etc., try one of the following:

> bits of chopped pimento
> dices of low calorie custard or lemon gelatine
> thin slices of lemon, lime, or orange
> paper-thin, unpeeled cucumber slices
> thin slices of radish
> sprinkle or thin slices of hard-boiled egg
> slivers of raw celery, carrot

Also see herb and spice garnishes in Soup Seasonings at
the end of this section.

CLEAR SOUP
Calories negligible

1 pound meat (beef, veal, chicken, or mutton)
1 quart water
1 teaspoon salt
1 teaspoon chopped parsley
1 tablespoon minced chicken
1 teaspoon chopped celery
1 bay leaf

Cut meat in small cubes. Cover with the water and add the salt. Allow to stand ½ hour. Heat gradually, and bring to the boiling point. Add the remaining ingredients. Allow to simmer for 1 to 2 hours. Cool, remove fat, and strain. Makes 1 quart.

EGG IN BROTH
77 calories per cup

1 medium egg
1 cup Clear Soup

Put broth into saucepan, place over flame, and allow to simmer. After beating the egg lightly, pour it slowly into the broth, stirring all the time. Serve immediately. Serves 1.

See Breast of Chicken Petite Marmite in Poultry section for Chicken Soup and Beef Petite Marmite in Meat section for Beef Soup.

VEGETABLE SOUP
Calories negligible

1½ cups Clear Soup
½ cup parboiled vegetables (asparagus, green beans, cauliflower, leaf cabbage, celery, green pepper)

Place broth in a saucepan and add vegetables. Allow to simmer 5 to 10 minutes to improve flavor. Bouillon may be substituted, using 1 bouillon cube to each cup. If 1 ounce grated cheese is sprinkled over top, add 113 calories. Serves 1.

TOMATO SOUP
Calories negligible

¼ cup tomato juice
¾ cup Clear Soup

Mix and cook together. Season to taste. Small spice bag (bay leaf, cloves, peppercorns, etc.) may be used. Serves 1.

If you made the next two recipes with canned beef bouillon or chicken consommé or soup stock, the calorie count would be about 20 more per serving. Use either beef or chicken bouillon cubes.

TOMATO-BEEF CONSOMME
37 calories per serving

½ cup boiling water
3 bouillon cubes
1 cup water
1½ cups tomato juice
pinch of thyme
2 tablespoons sherry
4 teaspoons sour cream

Dissolve bouillon cubes in ½ cup boiling water, add 1 cup water, tomato juice, and thyme; bring to boil. Add sherry and serve, topping each cup with a teaspoon of sour cream. Serves 4.

MUSHROOM CONSOMME
19 calories per serving

2 cups boiling water
4 bouillon cubes
1½ cups minced mushrooms
2 tablespoons sherry

Dissolve bouillon cubes in water, add mushrooms, cover, and simmer until tender (mushrooms cook quickly). Take off fire and add sherry. Serves 4.

FRESH VEGETABLE SOUP WITH CHILI MEAT BALLS
33 calories per serving

2 pounds soup bones
2 quarts cold water
2 whole cloves
¾ teaspoon whole black pepper
3 tablespoons salt
3 cups diced fresh tomatoes
2 cups diced fresh carrots
1 cup shredded raw cabbage
1 cup cut-up fresh snap beans
1 cup chopped celery
1 cup chopped onion
3 Sucaryl tablets

Simmer soup bone, water, cloves, pepper, and salt together for 2 hours. Then add remaining ingredients and cook only until vegetables are tender. Serve with

meat balls. Makes 3 quarts or 12 8-ounce servings.

MEAT BALLS
43 calories per meat ball

2 pounds chopped lean beef
¼ cup dry bread crumbs
1 teaspoon salt
⅛ teaspoon ground dried pepper
¼ teaspoon poultry seasoning
¼ teaspoon celery salt
½ teaspoon chili powder
2 teaspoons grated onion
2 tablespoons milk

Combine all the ingredients and shape into ½-inch meat balls. Braise in skillet until brown. Serve with vegetable soup. Makes 35 to 40 meat balls.

Any desired leftover meat may be substituted for the meat balls. This includes meat loaf cut in cubes.

VEGETABLE GARDEN SOUP
26 calories per serving

2 cups tomatoes
1 cup diced carrot
1 cup sliced celery
2 tablespoons chopped onion
2½ cups water
1 teaspoon Worcestershire sauce
bit of bay leaf
1 cup spinach

Combine all ingredients except spinach, and cook slowly, covered, until vegetables are tender. Chop spinach fine and add to soup. Heat thoroughly. Makes about 7 cups.

OXTAIL VEGETABLE SOUP
104 calories per serving

2½ pounds oxtails
1 teaspoon salt
⅛ teaspoon pepper
½ bay leaf
2 sprigs parsley
2 quarts water
⅓ cup each diced celery, carrots and onion
1 teaspoon Worcestershire sauce

Wash oxtails and dry; brown with a minimum of hot fat in a deep, heavy utensil. Add salt, pepper, bay leaf, parsley, and water. Boil for 10 minutes; skim. Cover, and simmer over low heat 2 to 3 hours, or until meat is very tender. Remove oxtails; pick meat from bones and return meat to soup stock. Add vegetables, and simmer 30 minutes. Add Worcestershire sauce, and season to taste with salt and pepper. Makes about 2 quarts, or 8 servings.

The way to make real Italian minestrone is with macaroni and garbanzo peas or navy or kidney beans. Even without the added fattening power, it is still an interesting and appetizing

soup when made the following way:

THIN-ESTRONE
65 calories per serving

4 cups beef bouillon or 4 bouillon cubes and 4 cups boiling water
½ clove garlic
6 sprigs parsley leaves
½ cup coarsely cut onion
1 tablespoon catsup
1 cup coarsely cut cabbage
1 cup coarsely cut celery
1 cup canned or quick-frozen peas
1 cup canned or quick-frozen string beans

Put 2 cups of the bouillon in glass container of Waring or other blender, add the garlic, parsley, onion, and catsup and run at high speed until parsley is finely cut— about 15 seconds. Turn off, and add cabbage and celery. Take care to run only until cabbage and celery are cut as fine as desired—about 5 seconds. Pour mixture into saucepan, add remaining 2 cups of bouillon, bring to boil, and simmer 10 minutes. Add the peas and string beans and let cook until they are barely tender (about 5 minutes if frozen). Season to taste. Serves 4.

A cup of cooked and thin-sliced zucchini can be substituted for the string beans.

HOT BORSCHT
60 calories per serving

2 cups well-seasoned clear chicken broth
1 slice onion or 1 scallion, chopped
1 slice lemon, unpeeled
¼ cup celery tops
1 cup coarsely diced cabbage
1 cup coarsely diced raw beets

Mix broth, onion, lemon, and celery in electric mixer for 2 minutes. Stop; add cabbage and beets. Blend for about 3 seconds, until vegetables are barely chopped. Pour into saucepan and bring to boil. Let simmer 5 minutes. Serves 4.

If served topped with 1 tablespoon of sour cream, add 31 calories.

If served with 1 tablespoon of yogurt, add 11 calories.

YOGURT BORSCHT
51 calories per serving

6 medium beets
juice of ½ lemon
2 Sucaryl tablets
salt to taste
1 cup yogurt

Shred beets on medium shredder, cover with cold water, and bring to a boil. Remove scum that forms, add lemon juice, sweetening, and salt to taste, cover, and cook 20 minutes, or until beets are tender. Chill well. Place 4 tablespoons yogurt in a bowl, add a little clear beet soup, and blend well; add additional sweetening if desired. Soup should be slightly pungent in taste, but not predominantly sweet or sour. Add remaining beet soup and blend well. Top each soup plate with 2 tablespoons yogurt, and serve. Serves 6.

QUICK BORSCHT
44 calories per serving

1 No. 2 can (2½ cups) shredded beets
4½ cups bouillon
6 tablespoons lemon juice
½ teaspoon salt
few grains pepper
1 cup yogurt

Combine beets, beet liquor, and bouillon (or 4½ bouillon cubes dissolved in 4½ cups water); simmer 10 minutes; add lemon juice and seasonings. Serve hot or chilled, topped with a large spoonful of yogurt. Serves 8.

Cream, butter, and flour are the "heavies" in any cream soup for the dieter. Skim-milk powder is a calorie-saving substitute. Below are four "cream" soups that are mixed in electric blenders. If you do not have a blender, purée the solid vegetables through a sieve; use an egg beater to mix the liquid and milk powder and then blend in the purée.

CREAM OF GREEN BEAN SOUP
83 calories per serving

1 cup canned green beans
½ cup water
2 tablespoons dry skim milk
¼ teaspoon salt
1 cup whole milk
seasonings to taste

Blend beans and water in Oster or other high-speed blender for 5 minutes. Add salt and dry milk and blend 3 minutes more. Remove to saucepan, add milk, and heat, but do not boil. Serves 3.

Using skim milk instead of whole, each serving is only 57 calories.

CREAM OF PEA SOUP
122 calories per serving

Use frozen peas, parboiled, or canned peas in place of green beans in recipe above and liquid from either. Add water to make up 1 cup. Use ½ teaspoon salt. Otherwise proceed as above. Serves 3.

Using skim milk, calories per serving are 93. If young, immature peas are used, subtract 11 calories per serving.

Other cream soups can also be made using the Cream of Green Bean recipe.
Substitute 1 cup, drained, of:

cooked or canned asparagus for Cream of Asparagus Soup, 87 calories per serving.
cooked broccoli for Cream of Broccoli Soup, 89 calories per serving;
cooked cabbage for Cream of Cabbage Soup, 88 calories per serving;
diced cooked or canned carrots for Cream of Carrot Soup, 89 calories per serving;
cooked cauliflower for Cream of Cauliflower Soup, 84 calories per serving;
cooked celery for Cream of Celery Soup, 82 calories per serving;
cooked or canned spinach for Cream of Spinach Soup, 89 calories per serving.

CREAM OF TOMATO SOUP
77 calories per serving

1 medium tomato, quartered
½ cup tomato juice
2 tablespoons dry skim milk
¼ teaspoon salt
½ cup skim milk

Put tomato and tomato juice in Oster or other blender and run at high speed 5 minutes. Add dry milk and salt; blend for 3 minutes more. Remove to saucepan, add milk, heat, and serve. Serves 2.

QUICK THICK CREAM OF TOMATO SOUP

114 calories per serving

10½ ounces water
6 tablespoons dried skim milk
10½-ounce can tomato soup
⅛ teaspoon celery salt

Put water in mixing bowl or blender container, sprinkle milk on top, mix or blend until foamy; add tomato soup and celery salt; mix thoroughly. Pour into saucepan and heat but do not boil. Serves 4.

CREAM OF ONION SOUP

103 calories per serving

2½ cups finely sliced onions
1½ teaspoons salt
1 cup dry nonfat milk
1 tablespoon flour
4 cups liquid (cooking liquid from onions plus water)

Cover onions with boiling water. Add salt, and cook, covered, until tender. Drain, and measure liquid, adding water to make 4 cups. Add milk powder and flour to liquid and beat until smooth. Cook over low heat or in double boiler until slightly thickened—about 15 minutes—stirring as necessary to prevent sticking or lumps. Combine with onions, and reheat. Serves 6.

HOLLYWOOD SOUP

110 calories per serving

1 cup Diet Delight or other canned spinach
¼ cup finely chopped onion
1 tablespoon unsalted butter
2 cups skim milk
dash nutmeg

Force undrained spinach through a sieve or chop very fine. Cook onion slowly in butter until tender and golden. Add spinach and milk and heat to scalding. Blend in a dash of nutmeg. Serves 3.

FRUIT SOUP

20 calories per serving

2 tablespoons lemon juice
½ cup orange juice
½ cup pineapple juice
1 teaspoon Sucaryl solution
6 cups water
½ cup puréed peaches, canned without sugar
½ cup unsweetened applesauce

Combine all ingredients in saucepan; simmer 10 minutes. Serve hot or chilled, garnished with lemon slices and sprigs of mint. If Sucaryl-sweetened peaches are used, do not add Sucaryl.

Makes 10 servings.

Here is a thick version: Measure 1 cup cold soup; blend with 1 tablespoon cornstarch; add remaining soup. Cook, stirring over low heat, until thickened. Serves 10. 23 calories per serving.

_____

The authentic Spanish way of making this next zesty, spicy, cold red soup is to add at least a tablespoon of olive oil for each serving, but this, alone, brings each plateful up from 61 calories to 185! Which is why we have skipped that bit of authenticity in our Gazpacho (or Gaspacho) soup.

GAZPACHO

61 calories per serving

2 cloves garlic, minced
1 large onion, minced
3 tablespoons chopped parsley
1½ teaspoons salt
3 large tomatoes
1 cucumber
1 large green pepper shell
4 canned pimentos
3 tablespoons vinegar
1 teaspoon orégano dash Tabasco sauce ground pepper

Mash the garlic, onion, and parsley in a mortar with the salt. Chop the tomatoes, cucumber, green pepper, and pimentos into smallest size possible. Add the garlic-onion mixture and mash all together. Add the vinegar, orégano, Tabasco and pepper to taste. Mix well. If too thick, add 1 cup ice water. Season in refrigerator until ice cold, at least 1 hour. Serve "over the rocks" with ice cubes. Serves 4.

_____

Here are two filling cold soups, either of which can be eaten as the main course of a low calorie lunch on a hot day.

COOL GREEN SOUP

150 calories per serving

1 11-ounce can condensed asparagus soup
1½ cups Sealtest or other skim milk
1 tablespoon lemon juice
1 teaspoon horse-radish few drops Tabasco sauce
¾ teaspoon marjoram
1½ cups Sealtest or other skim-milk cottage cheese

Combine all ingredients except cottage cheese. Beat well. Chill until icy cold. Add cheese; beat with egg beater until well blended. Garnish with paper-thin lemon slices or finely chopped parsley or chives. Serves 5.

_____

COOL TOMATO SOUP

140 calories per serving

Substitute tomato soup for asparagus and basil for marjoram.

BUTTERMINT SOUP
70 calories per serving

1 small cucumber, sliced
3 cups buttermilk
½ teaspoon Mintit or 1 tablespoon finely chopped fresh mint
pinch of onion salt

Put all ingredients into electric blender and turn on high speed for 1 minute. Chill well. Serves 4.

COLD CHICKEN SOUP
140 calories per serving

6 cups chicken broth, strained
6 eggs, beaten
4 tablespoons lemon juice
½ teaspoon salt
¼ teaspoon pepper
3 tablespoons sherry wine
1 tablespoon curry powder

Bring chicken broth to a slow boil, then gradually pour in beaten eggs, to which the lemon juice has been added. Add salt and pepper. Add sherry and remove from fire. Stir in curry powder and place in refrigerator for several hours. Serve very cold. Serves 6.

JELLIED BEEF BOUILLON
7 calories per serving

1 envelope Knox or other unflavored gelatine
3 cups water
3 beef bouillon cubes
2 tablespoons strained lemon juice

Sprinkle gelatine on ½ cup cold water to soften. Simmer bouillon cubes in the remaining water until dissolved. Add softened gelatine and stir until dissolved. Stir in lemon juice. Serve hot, or chilled to soft jelly consistency. Serves 6.

JELLIED CONSOMME
9 calories per serving

Use reconstituted canned consommé instead of water, bouillon cubes, and lemon juice in previous recipe. Serves 6.

Another version is in the Poultry section under Breast of Chicken Petite Marmite.

JELLIED CHICKEN BOUILLON
6 calories per serving

Use chicken bouillon cubes instead of beef bouillon cubes. Season with ½ teaspoon salt, ¼ teaspoon each pepper and mace instead of lemon juice.

JELLIED CHICKEN BROTH
9 calories per serving

Use 3 cups clarified chicken broth instead of bouillon cubes and water. Season same as Jellied Chicken Bouillon. Serves 6.

JELLIED TOMATO BROTH
17 calories per serving

1 envelope Knox or other unflavored gelatine
1½ cups cold water
1½ cups tomato juice or canned tomatoes
½ teaspoon salt
2 teaspoons whole mixed spices

Sprinkle gelatine on ½ cup cold water to soften. Combine the remaining water, tomato juice, salt, and spices. Bring to a full boil. Strain to remove spices and solids, if canned tomatoes are used. (It is helpful to place whole spices in a bag or tea ball, so that they can be removed without straining the broth.) Stir in softened gelatine until thoroughly dissolved. Serve hot, or chilled to soft jelly consistency. Serves 6.

JELLIED TOMATO BEEF BOUILLON
15 calories per serving

1 envelope Knox or other unflavored gelatine
½ cup cold water
2 tablespoons minced onion
2 beef bouillon cubes and 1¾ cups water
1 cup tomatoes
1 tablespoon chopped parsley
  dash powdered cloves
½ teaspoon salt

Sprinkle gelatine on the cold water to soften. Simmer onion in bouillon with tomatoes, parsley, cloves, and salt until tender. Strain. Add softened gelatine and stir until thoroughly dissolved. Measure, and if necessary add very hot water to make 3 cups. Serve hot, or chilled to soft jelly consistency. Serves 6.

JELLIED TOMATO CHICKEN BOUILLON
14 calories per serving

1 envelope Knox or other unflavored gelatine
2 cups chicken broth or 2 chicken bouillon cubes and 2 cups water
1 cup strained tomatoes or tomato juice
½ teaspoon salt

Sprinkle gelatine on ½ cup cold broth to soften. Heat the remaining broth, tomato juice, and salt until very hot. Add softened gelatine and stir until thoroughly dissolved. Serve piping hot, or chilled to soft jelly consistency. Serves 6.

Using 2 chicken bouillon cubes plus 3 cups tomato juice instead of chicken broth and 1 cup tomatoes, each serving is 31 calories.

JELLIED MADRILENE
19 calories per serving

1 envelope Knox or other unflavored gelatine
3 bouillon cubes in 2½ cups water
1 medium tomato, fresh or canned
1½ tablespoons tomato paste
2 tablespoons tarragon vinegar
½ bay leaf
3 peppercorns
½ teaspoon salt
1 crushed eggshell

Sprinkle gelatine on ½ cup

cold bouillon to soften. Combine the remaining bouillon, tomato, tomato paste, vinegar, spices, salt, and eggshell. Heat to boiling, stirring constantly, over low heat. Remove from heat. Add softened gelatine and stir until thoroughly dissolved. Let stand 10 minutes. Strain through fine sieve covered with a damp cloth. Serve hot, or chilled to soft jelly consistency. Serves 4.

JELLIED ORANGE SOUP
93 calories per serving

- 4 envelopes unflavored gelatine
- 2¼ cups chicken bouillon
- 3 tablespoons fresh lime juice
- ½ teaspoon grated lime rind
- 1 teaspoon Sucaryl solution
- 3 cups fresh orange juice
- 1 cup orange pulp
- ½ teaspoon salt
- ⅛ teaspoon ground white pepper
  yellow vegetable coloring
  mint sprigs

Soften gelatine in ¼ cup of the chicken bouillon. Bring remaining bouillon to a boil. Add softened gelatine and stir until completely dissolved. Remove from fire and add lime juice, grated rind, Sucaryl, and orange juice. Cool. Place in refrigerator and let stand until syrupy. Remove from refrigerator and beat with rotary beater until light and fluffy. Add orange pulp, salt, and pepper. If the color is too pale, add a few drops of yellow coloring. Replace in refrigerator and let set. Break up with a fork and pile in chilled soup cups. Top with sprigs of mint. Garnish with slice of orange or lime if desired. Serves 6.

OYSTER STEW
190 calories per serving

- 1 cup skim milk
- 1 teaspoon butter
- 5 oysters
  salt and pepper to taste

Heat the milk in a double boiler. Place butter in small frying pan, and melt. Add oysters to butter after washing well and cook only until edges curl. Add salt and pepper. When ready to serve, add the oysters to the hot milk. Do not reheat because milk may curdle. Serves 1.

FISH CHOWDER
194 calories per serving

- 1 ounce cooked fish (cod or haddock)
- 1 teaspoon butter or margarine
- 1 sliced onion, chopped
- 1 small potato, sliced
- ½ cup water
- 1 cup skim milk
  salt and pepper to taste

Cook fish in lightly salted water. Melt the butter in a saucepan and brown the onion. Add the cooked fish and potato with the water, cover, and cook until the potato is tender. Add milk and seasonings, and reheat. Serve piping hot, sprinkling parsley on top if desired. Serves 1.

What started out as a pun—"what would you call the sea food version of Vichyssoise?"—has ended up as a most delicious new thick but low caloried soup.

FISHYSSOISE!

84 to 106 calories per serving*

1 cup raw lean fish, coarsely diced (⅓ lb.)
¼ cup onions, coarsely chopped
1 cup raw green peppers or carrots, diced
1¾ cups chicken broth or 2 chicken bouillon cubes dissolved in 1¾ cups hot water
½ teaspoon salt
pinch of celery salt
⅛ teaspoon ground pepper
1 cup whole milk
paprika or chopped chives

Put fish, onion, vegetables, and broth into saucepan. Bring to boil. Cover; simmer until tender—about 15 minutes. Pour slowly into glass container of electric blender. Add salt, celery salt, and pepper. Cover, and turn on high, running until smooth—about 30 seconds. Pour into bowl, stir in milk, place in refrigerator and chill thoroughly. Sprinkle with paprika if green peppers are used, with chopped chives if soup has been made with carrots. Can also be served piping hot. Serves 4.

CRAB-MEAT CHOWDER
89 calories per serving

½ cup water
1 thin slice onion
1 sprig parsley leaves
2 tablespoons diced celery
2 tablespoons diced carrot
½ cup skim milk
¼ teaspoon salt
3 tablespoons canned crab meat

Place water, onion, and parsley in high-speed mixer such as Waring Blendor. Blend 30 seconds. Add celery and carrot. Blend until finely cut, about 1 second longer. Pour into top of double boiler. Add milk, salt, and crab meat. Heat

---

* Calories depend on fish used; flounder, 84; cod, 86; haddock, 88; crab, lobster, shrimp, and perch, 91; swordfish, 103; bluefish, 105; halibut, 106.

thoroughly over boiling water—about 10 minutes. Serve, sprinkled with paprika. Makes 1 10-ounce serving.

If you have no blender, vegetables can be fine chopped by hand.

NEW ENGLAND OYSTER STEW
150 calories per serving

- 6 medium-sized oysters
- ½ cup water
- 1 teaspoon Dia-Mel gluten flour
- ½ cup skim milk
- 1 teaspoon butter
  salt and pepper

Heat the oysters in the water until the edges curl. Add the flour, milk, butter, salt and pepper. Reheat, and serve. Serves 1.

SOUP SEASONINGS

For almost any: whole Allspice, beef extract to add piquancy, ground Ginger, Lemon and Lime slices, Parsley or Borage chopped, Paprika, toasted Sesame seed as garnish. Also see Bouquets Garnis in Seasoning Blending.

Meat: Leek, ground or whole White and Black Pepper.

Bouillon: Celery leaves and seed, Lovage seed.

Chicken: chopped Dill before serving, Marjoram leaves, Rosemary, Saffron, Tarragon.

Broth: Coriander, Juniper berries.

Consommé: a few Cloves, Juniper Berries, Mace, Nutmeg, Savory, Tarragon.

Fish Soups and Chowders: Basil, Bay leaves, Curry powder, Marjoram, Saffron, Sage, Savory, Tarragon, chopped fresh Thyme leaves, Water Cress.

Oyster Stew: Mace, Nutmeg, Thyme.

Vegetable: fresh Anise leaves, Basil, crushed Bay leaf, chopped caraway leaves before serving, Hyssop leaves to sweeten, Leek, whole and ground Black and White Pepper, Sage, Savory, chopped fresh Thyme leaves, Water Cress.

Minestrone: Basil.

Asparagus: minced Balm leaves just before serving, Burnet, Chives.

Borscht: ground Cloves, Orégano, chopped fresh Thyme leaves.

Cabbage: chopped Caraway leaves before serving or ¼ teaspoon Caraway seed while cooking, Orégano.

Cauliflower: chopped Caraway leaves or seed, Chives.

Celery: Burnet, chopped fresh Thyme leaves.

Gumbo: Gumbo Filé, chopped fresh Thyme leaves.

Lettuce: Sesame seed.

Mushroom: Burnet, Tarragon.

Onion: Marjoram leaves, chopped fresh Thyme leaves.

Pea: Basil, ground Cardamom seed, chopped Dill just before serving, ½ teaspoon Peppermint or other Mint per serving as a garnish, Savory, chopped fresh Thyme leaves.

Sorrel: fresh Chervil leaves, Sesame seed.

Spinach: Basil, fresh Chervil leaves, Marjoram leaves, Rosemary.

Tomato: Basil, crushed Bay leaf, Celery leaves and seed, chopped Dill before serving, 1 teaspoon Curry powder, Lovage seed, Orégano, Sage, Tarragon.

Soup Stock: crushed Bay leaf, Fennel, Garlic, ½ teaspoon monosodium glutamate to quart.

Add ½ teaspoon monosodium glutamate to any can of soup.

Use different herb vinegars sparingly. Try 2 teaspoons of Basil Wine vinegar to 6 servings of Tomato, Pea, or Vegetable soup.

Eggs are important in low-calorie diets for a number of reasons. They are available at all times; they are inexpensive, rarely as high as 50 cents a pound, net; they furnish valuable protein, vitamins (A, D, thiamine, riboflavin) and minerals (iron, phosphorus, calcium), and have half the calories of most meats.

Also they can be prepared in a wide variety of ways and combine well with probably more different foods than any other. Their use is not confined to breakfast dishes. Have them at lunch or as a central ingredient of main dishes.

365 WAYS WITH EGGS

The writer has been able to prepare different versions of breakfast eggs almost daily for more than a year while writing this book without repeating the same combination. Using the sweet herbs as well as many other ingredients, a Sunbeam Electric Frypan or Egg Cooker-Poacher, and a Waring Blendor, he has soft and hard-cooked, grilled, poached (whole and beaten up), shirred or baked, scrambled and pancaked the following ingredients to 1 egg:

1 teaspoon fresh basil leaves or ⅛ teaspoon crushed dried

½ teaspoon caraway seed

2 teaspoons minced celery or ¼ teaspoon celery seed or ⅛ teaspoon celery salt

1 or 2 teaspoons chopped fresh chervil

1 teaspoon chopped chives

¼ teaspoon chili powder or curry powder

½ teaspoon chopped dill

pinch of crushed dried or powdered marjoram

1 to 2 teaspoons chopped mushrooms

¼ teaspoon dry mustard

chopped or thin-sliced onion, shallot, or scallion to taste

1 teaspoon minced parsley

⅛ teaspoon paprika

red, white, or black pepper to taste

1 to 2 teaspoons minced green or red pepper or pimento

½ teaspoon minced fresh rosemary

1 teaspoon minced fresh or ¼ teaspoon crushed dried summer savory

½ to 1 teaspoon sesame seed

1 tablespoon minced fresh sorrel

½ teaspoon sunflower seed

⅛ to ¼ teaspoon fresh minced tansey

½ teaspoon fresh minced tarragon, with 1 teaspoon minced parsley

light sprinkle of thyme or chili powder before serving

2 teaspoons minced water cress

1 teaspoon fresh minced or ¼ teaspoon crushed dried winter savory

pinch of blended pulverized thyme, summer savory, sweet marjoram, dried parsley, sage, celery seed, bay leaf

Also, a teaspoon of one of the following sauces for mixing with or over 1 egg: A.1., barbecue, chili, Escoffier Diable or Robert, H. P., tomato, Worcestershire or 101; catsup, tomato juice, V-8 or other vegetable combination; skim milk, skim-milk powder, buttermilk, yogurt, or just plain water. In addition, cooked, chopped artichoke hearts, asparagus, broccoli, olives, peas, bean sprouts, string beans, fresh stewed tomatoes, green tomatoes, water chestnuts; anchovies, kippers, lean fish and sea food such as crab meat, minced clams, oysters, shrimp; bacon, ham, chicken, chicken livers, turkey, beef, chipped and corned beef, tongue, hamburger, frankfurters, salami, leftover lamb and veal; 5-calorie Holgrain wafers, Ritz crackers, Venus wafers, Soya flakes, blueberries, low-calorie jelly, jam and marmalade, and almost any kind of cheese.

BUYING EGGS

It is best to purchase not more than a week's supply at a time. If the eggs you buy are United States graded, in cartons, the date of inspection is given, as well as the size, or weight, and the grade, or interior quality. When shopping, consider what you are getting in freshness, in quantity, and in quality—all in relation to the price.

Grade AA and Grade A are the top-quality eggs and can be used for all purposes but mainly for poaching, frying, cooking in shell, and shirring. Grade B and Grade C eggs are good where appearance and delicate flavor are not so important, as in scrambling, omelets, baking custards and hard-cooked eggs to be chopped.

Brown and white eggs are exactly alike inside the shell.

TO TELL HOW MUCH YOU ARE GETTING

United States Weight Classes	Minimum Number Ounces Per Dozen
Jumbo	30
Extra Large	27
Large	24
Medium	21
Small	18
Peewee	15

You can check weights on the grocer's scales, allowing 2 ounces for the carton.

TO TELL WHAT QUALITY YOU ARE GETTING

Grade	Area Covered	White	Yellow
AA	small	thick, stands high	firm and high
A	moderate	reasonably thick, stands fairly high	firm and high
B	wide	only small amount is thick	somewhat flattened and enlarged
C	very wide	thin and watery	flat, enlarged, breaks easily

CARE OF EGGS

Take care of your eggs after you buy them. Do not leave them in a hot car or kitchen; heat lowers egg quality quickly. As soon as they reach home, put them in a covered container, away from strong-smelling foods, in refrigerator. Take out only as needed.

Eggs with clean shells

keep best. Wipe off soiled spots with a damp cloth but don't wash eggs until just before you use them.

Keep leftover egg yellows or separated whites in refrigerator until they can be used. Place yellows in dish or cup and add just enough cold water to cover. Place whites in a jar or dish and cover tightly.

WHEN COOKING EGGS

Don't overcook.

Always cook eggs on low to moderate, even heat, to keep them from getting tough and leathery.

Water should be at least ¼ inch over the top of boiling eggs.

When eggs are separated and water is to be added, add it to the yellows.

For a whiter meringue, which cuts well, add lemon juice before beating.

Egg whites whip best at room temperature. They foam more if a pinch of salt is added before beating.

Add hot liquids or mixtures a little at a time to beaten eggs.

When combining beaten egg whites with other mixtures, fold, don't stir, the heavy mixture into the whites, not vice versa.

Professional chefs do not try to flip omelets like flapjacks. They either fold them in half, roll them, or au gratin the top. Au gratin does not mean "with cheese," it means "brown under broiler flame."

CODDLED EGGS
77 calories per egg

Bring water to a boil, take off heat, immerse eggs, and let stand 10 to 15 minutes. Break open and mix with one of Seasonings at end of this section.

POACHED EGGS
77 calories per egg

Heat salted water to boiling in a shallow pan. Add 1 tablespoon vinegar to keep egg white more compact. Break 1 egg at a time onto a saucer and slide carefully into boiling water. When all eggs have been added, cover pan and remove from heat. Let stand until eggs are set.

WINE-POACHED EGGS
100 calories per egg

Use a custard cup for each egg, rubbing inside first with garlic clove and filming with butter. Break egg into cup and sprinkle with salt and freshly ground black pepper, cayenne pepper or nutmeg. Pour 1 tablespoon dry white wine over and sprinkle with 1 teaspoon of grated Swiss cheese. Place in 350° oven for 6 to 12 minutes, accord-

ing to degree of hardness desired. Serve with a sprinkle of chopped chives or parsley.

SHIRRED EGGS IN SPINACH
92 calories per serving

2 cups hot cooked spinach
6 eggs
salt and pepper

Put spinach in greased baking dish, season with salt and pepper. Drop eggs on top and bake in moderate (350°) oven 20 25 minutes, or until eggs are firm. Serve at once. 6 servings.

BELL-BOTTOM EGGS
96 calories per serving

4 green pepper shells
4 eggs
salt and pepper to taste

Select peppers that will stand up, remove stem, seeds, and membrane. Parboil 5 minutes. Drain and drop an egg into each, or beat eggs and divide among peppers. Season to taste. Place on baking dish and put in hot oven until eggs are done to desired consistency. Serves 4.

EGGS AND TOMATOES
94 calories per serving

6 medium-ripe tomatoes
6 eggs
salt and pepper
grated cheese, optional

Wash tomatoes, cut off tops, and scoop out centers, making ample room for an egg. Break egg into each hollow, allowing room for top for expansion. Sprinkle with salt and pepper and bake in moderate (350°) oven 10 minutes, or until egg is almost set. Remove from oven and sprinkle with grated cheese, if desired (adding 19 calories), and return to oven for 5 minutes longer. Serves 6.

HARD-COOKED EGGS
77 calories per egg

Place eggs at room temperature in saucepan. Add enough cold water to cover tops completely. Cover; heat rapidly until water boils. Turn heat very low and let stand covered 15 to 20 minutes. Promptly cool eggs under running water until easy to handle. To remove shells, tap entire surface of each egg on work surface. Roll one at a time between hands to loosen shell. Then peel, starting at large end. Peeling under cold water helps to ease off shell.

SOFT-COOKED EGGS
77 calories per egg

Cook as above, allowing about 2 minutes for very soft eggs, 3½ minutes for medium-cooked eggs, and about 4 minutes for firmer cooked eggs.

DEVILED EGGS
44 calories per half

Hard cook as many eggs as you will need to serve. Slice each in half. Scoop out yellow. Mash up yellow, add salt and pepper, and prepared mustard. Tasti-Diet or other whipped dressing may be added also. Fill in dent in egg and sprinkle with paprika.

Try adding minced celery, parsley, lemon juice, and garlic salt to the yellow mixture. This will add very few calories.

PICKLED EGGS
78 calories per egg

½ teaspoon pickling spice (4 peppercorns, 1 clove, celery seed, mace, ginger root, etc.)
½ teaspoon salt
3 Sucaryl tablets
1 small onion, sliced
1 cup mild white vinegar
6 to 8 hard-cooked eggs, peeled

Add spices, seasonings, and onion to vinegar and simmer 8 minutes. Place eggs in mason jar and pour hot mixture over. Seal and let stand several hours or longer before using.

Other flavors: use sprig of dill, or a few caraway seeds, or a slice of garlic added to the brine. Leftover beet juice can also be used to pickle and color the eggs.

HAM AND EGGS
137 calories per serving

1 egg
salt, pepper, seasonings
1 ounce ham, a thin-sliced round

The least caloric way of having your ham and eggs is to use a thin slice of ham as the basis for the dish, either in a frying pan or grill without added fat or in a baking ramekin. Over this put your egg, either unshelled or beaten lightly and seasoned to taste. Usually there is sufficient natural fat on the ham to keep it from sticking to the bottom of the utensil. Serves 1.

FRIED EGGS
110 calories per egg

Have eggs at room temperature and break carefully into saucer. Slip gently into hot buttered frying pan at low heat and fry slowly, using 1 teaspoon of butter per egg.

SCRAMBLED EGGS
83 calories per egg

4 eggs
¼ cup skim milk
¼ teaspoon salt
few grains pepper

Beat eggs slightly in top of double boiler. Stir in milk, salt, and pepper. Cook over boiling water, stirring constantly, until eggs turn firm —about 5 minutes. Serve at once. Serves 4.

See Crisp Lamb Dices and Scrambled Eggs in Combination Dishes.

OMELETS

There are flat omelets and foamy or fluffy ones, plain, filled, mixed, blended, and shortcake omelets, as well as dessert omelets. The pancake type are the flat ones. Using the same ingredients, you arrive at a foamy or fluffy omelet by separating the eggs and beating the yellows thoroughly, adding a tablespoon of milk or water for each egg, then beating the whites until stiff but not dry. Fold the yellows into the whites and cook in frying pan over low heat.

Filled omelets have mushroom, tomato, or Spanish sauce, etc., on top or folded in the middle after cooking is done. Mixed omelets have this added ingredient folded in the mixture with the yellows before cooking. The blended kind requires an electric blender to fine-cut and mix the other food with the eggs.

SHORTCAKE OMELET
93 calories per serving without filling

6 eggs whites
¾ teaspoon salt
6 egg yolks
¼ teaspoon pepper

1 tablespoon grated onion
3 tablespoons flour
2 tablespoons minced parsley
2 cups filling (creamed spinach, chicken, shrimp, cheese, etc.)

While oven is heating to 350°, grease 2 8-inch layer pans and heat. Beat egg whites with salt until stiff but still glossy. Then beat yellows until well mixed; add pepper, onion, flour, and parsley; beat until thick and completely blended, then fold into egg whites. Spread mixture in hot pans and bake 15 minutes, or until knife inserted in center comes out clean.

Invert 1 layer onto serving dish; spread top with half of filling. Invert second layer on top. In serving, tear apart with 2 forks. Serves 6.

PUFFY SPANISH OMELET
115 calories per serving

½ cup chopped onion
1 small green pepper, chopped
½ cup chopped celery
4 eggs, separated
1 teaspoon salt
½ cup drained canned or cooked tomatoes
½ cup dry skim milk
1 tablespoon butter or fat pepper, orégano

Combine onion, green peppers, and celery. Cook in small amount boiling water until tender. Drain, if any liquid remains. To the egg yellows add salt, tomatoes, and milk powder. Beat well. Beat egg whites until stiff but not dry. Gradually fold in the beaten egg yellow mixture and then the cooked vegetables. Pour into hot frying pan in which butter or fat has been melted. Sprinkle with spices. Cook over low heat until lightly brown on bottom—about 10 minutes. Bake in a moderate (350°) oven until brown on top—10 to 15 minutes. Crease omelet through the center, fold over, and roll onto a hot platter. Serves 6.

FLUFFY CHEESE OMELET
142 calories per serving

- 2 eggs, separated
- ¼ teaspoon salt
- ½ teaspoon butter or margarine
- ¼ cup fresh grated American cheese

Beat egg yellows; add salt. Beat egg whites until stiff. Fold into yellows gradually. Heat skillet and melt butter or margarine. Add egg mixture. Spread evenly, and cook over low heat for 5 or 6 minutes, till bottom is brown. Place omelet under broiler for about 2 minutes until top is dry. Then sprinkle grated cheese over half of omelet. Fold carefully, and serve. Serves 2.

SAILOR'S OMELET

Add 1 teaspoon of anchovy paste and 1 of minced parsley to egg yellows when making a fluffy omelet. Sprinkle with paprika when ready to serve. Add 15 calories.

Here is a Western Omelet for those people who do not like onions, or with whom onions do not agree.

TENDERFOOT OMELET
193 calories per serving

- 4 eggs
- 4 tablespoons skim milk or buttermilk
- ⅛ teaspoon pepper
- 1 tablespoon butter or margarine
- 4 tablespoons chopped green pepper
- ⅓ cup minced cooked ham

Beat eggs slightly. Add milk and pepper. Melt butter or margarine in skillet and sauté the green pepper lightly. Then add chopped ham and cook 1 minute longer. Add egg mixture and cook over low heat, moving the cooked portion occasionally to allow uncooked to run underneath. When omelet is set, increase heat slightly to brown undersurface. Crease omelet through the center, fold over, and roll onto a hot platter. Serve immediately. Serves 4.

For the regular Western

Omelet add 4 tablespoons of chopped onions to the recipe and 4 calories to each serving.

ASPARAGUS PANCAKE
88 calories per serving

3 medium or 4 small stalks cooked or canned asparagus

1 egg

2 dashes celery salt

Put ingredients in Waring or other blender, turn on at high speed until contents become smooth and creamy —2 to 3 minutes. Pour in frying pan lightly smeared with butter; cook one side until done, turn over or brown under broiler. When ready, serve on warmed plate. Serves 1.

If you usually have 2 eggs for breakfast, try the following recipe some morning, since it only contains about 3 more calories and comes out a very toothsome "almost blintz."

BREAKFAST BLINTZ
157 calories per serving

1 egg
   pinch salt

4 Hol-Grain Wafer-ets or Devonsheer protein wafers

1 tablespoon buttermilk

2 tablespoons skim-milk cottage cheese with herbs

Put egg, salt, crumbled wafers, and buttermilk into Waring or other high-speed electric blender and run for several minutes— long enough for wafers to absorb moisture. Heat Sunbeam or other controlled-heat electric frying pan to 380°. Frying pan needs little or no butter if it has been used and wiped clean. If just washed, wipe with buttered paper. Pour batter onto pan; grill until both sides are brown; remove to warmed plate and spread seasoned cottage cheese over. Can be rolled, folded over twice, or served flat. Serves 1.

In communities with Italian food stores you can get a delicious version of cottage cheese called Ricotta, very rich and creamy. A skim-milk Ricotta has been introduced which has about the caloric value of skim-milk cottage cheese and if you succeed in locating a source of supply you will find it has been worth the effort.

For other egg dishes, see Souffles in Cheese, Pastas and Combination Dishes section.

SEASONINGS FOR EGGS

Interesting with eggs in any form: Cayenne, Celery salt, Chili powder, Chives, Curry powder, Fennel seed, Garlic and Garlic salt, Onion and Onion salt, Parsley,

Sesame seed, Water Cress, Worcestershire sauce.

For omelets and soufflés: Basil, Chervil, Dill, Marjoram, Orégano (for Spanish omelets), Rosemary, Summer and Winter Savory, minced Tansy.

In Scrambled: Marjoram, Orégano, Rosemary, Winter Savory, minced Tansy.

Shirred: Thyme.
Boiled: Orégano.
Stuffed: Cumin seed, Summer Savory.

Pickled: herb vinegars.
Curried: Turmeric, to sweeten Curry powder.

VEGETABLES

There are more different low-calorie vegetables than any other type of food. And vegetables provide valuable vitamin and mineral nutrients, as well as the bulk needed to feel satisfied after eating. But in most cases the nutrients that vegetables contain are extremely perishable. Vegetables should be fresh when purchased, stored where cool, used quickly, and prepared with the least possible amount of water and heat. Also for dieters, with the least possible amount of fat, bread crumbs, and rich sauces.

Use cooking pans with straight sides, flat bottom, tight-fitting lid, and designed to hold heat and distribute it evenly. Overcooking will make vegetables mushy, washed out in color, and boiled out in flavor. When done, the vegetables should have a crisp, tender texture. To achieve this, here are a few rules:

Cook without added water wherever possible, or with a minimum.
Cook vegetables as close to serving time as possible and for a minimum of time.
Simmer, below the boiling point.
Steam rather than boil.
Avoid bruising vegetables.
Keep in cold or cool place until used.
Try not to remove cover while cooking.
Do not use soda.
Avoid chipped, worn utensils or those with copper alloys.
Do not clean vegetables with copper scouring pads. Use plastic or stiff brush.

BOILED VEGETABLES

Fresh. Boil green vegetables in lightly salted water—½ teaspoon salt and ½ to 1 cup water (depending on cooking time) are usually enough for 4 servings. Bring water to boil, add vegetables, and put cover on pan. When the water boils again, reduce heat, and begin to count cooking time.

Frozen. You can boil most frozen vegetables without thawing them first. See directions on package.

Greens cook more evenly if thawed enough to separate the leaves. Use ½ cup water for each pint of frozen vegetables and proceed with cooking as for fresh vegetables. You may need to separate the pieces as they cook to insure even cooking.

Canned. Heat commercially canned green vegetables in their own liquid. When you combine canned vegetables with fresh, add the canned ones when the fresh ones are almost done.

BOILING TIME FOR FRESH VEGETABLES

Remember that vegetables may call for shorter or longer cooking time than given, depending on quality and variety. The altitude at which you live also affects boiling times.

Vegetable	Minutes	Vegetable	Minutes
Asparagus	10–20	Greens	
Beans,		Beets, young	5–15
snap, 1-inch pieces	15–30	Dandelion	10–20
Beets		Kale	10–25
young, whole	30–45	Turnip	15–30
older, whole	45–90	Kohlrabi, sliced	20–25
Broccoli, separated	10–20	Okra,	
Brussels sprouts	10–20	whole or sliced	10–20
Cabbage		Onions,	
shredded	3–10	whole or half	20–40
quartered	10–15	Parsnips, whole	20–40
Carrots		Peas	8–20
young, whole	15–25	Rutabagas,	
older, sliced	15–25	pared, cut up	20–30
Cauliflower		Spinach, whole	3–10
separated	8–15	Squash	
whole	20–30	Summer, sliced	10–20
Celery, cut up	15–20	Winter, cut up	20–40
Collards, whole	10–20	Swiss chard	10–20
		Tomatoes, cut up	7–15
		Turnips, cut up	15–20

BOILED ARTICHOKES
51 calories apiece

Wash artichokes in salted water and turn upside down to drain. Remove the tough outside leaves at the base and clip off the ends of the other leaves if they are sharp or coarse. Place in a saucepan. Cover with water. Add 1 teaspoon salt and cook 25 to 30 minutes, or until tender. Drain well by holding upside down.

COOKED ASPARAGUS
18 calories per serving

Two pounds of asparagus will make from 6 to 8 servings. Wash thoroughly. Cut off stems and retie in a bundle. Use just enough water to cover the thick part of the stalk of the asparagus and stand upright in the pan; use a double boiler or pan that has a cover that will fit over the asparagus without crushing, if you have one. This will catch the steam and helps make asparagus tender. Add 1 teaspoon salt to the water and boil 10 minutes, or until stalks are tender. Then place bundle so the tips of the asparagus are in water also and cook 5 minutes longer. Season with salt and pepper.

ASPARAGUS VINAIGRETTE
50 calories per serving

16 cooked or canned asparagus spears
salad greens
1 teaspoon grated onion
2 teaspoons chopped green pepper
2 teaspoons fine-chopped pimento
1 tablespoon salad oil
2 tablespoons vinegar
dash black pepper

Arrange asparagus on salad greens. Combine remaining ingredients and pour over asparagus. Serves 4.

Cooked broccoli can be served the same way.

Clementine Paddleford has a favorite lunch that is simple to make and easy on the calorie count.

ASPARAGUS LUNCH
150 calories per serving

1 pound asparagus
salt
4 eggs
4 pats butter
2 tablespoons chopped parsley

Cut asparagus into 1-inch pieces, saving out the tips. Cover pieces with boiling salted water and cook 10 minutes, then add tips and cook 5 minutes more, or until just tender. Meanwhile, soft-cook the eggs. Drain asparagus, divide into 4 portions, serve each with an egg and pat of butter, so that each person can break own egg, mix with butter and parsley, and pour freshmade sauce over asparagus. Serves 4.

BOILED GREEN OR WAX BEANS
20 calories per serving

Wash 1 pound of beans and remove ends and strings with sharp knife. Cover with boiling water; add ½ teaspoon salt. Cook in an uncovered pot until tender —about 20 to 30 minutes. Serves 4 to 6.

Green or wax beans may be cut lengthwise in slender long slivers (frenched) before cooking, or cut in half crosswise. In either case, allow about 5 minutes less for cooking time.

SPANISH SNAP BEANS
34 calories per serving

1 teaspoon fat
1 tablespoon chopped onion
⅓ cup chopped green pepper
1 cup cooked or canned tomatoes
1½ cups cooked or canned snap beans
salt and pepper

Heat the fat and brown the onion and green pepper in it. Add tomatoes and cook slowly about 15 minutes. Add beans and season to taste with salt and pepper. Heat thoroughly. Serves 4.

GREEN BEANS HONGROISE
50 calories per serving

1 4-ounce can button mushrooms
1 tablespoon butter or margarine
4 cups drained cooked green beans
½ pint yogurt
½ teaspoon salt
few grains pepper
½ teaspoon nutmeg

Cook mushrooms in butter or margarine until golden brown. Add green beans, yogurt, and seasonings. Heat thoroughly. Serves 6.

BOILED BEETS
47 calories per serving

Pare and dice 1 pound of beets and add to ½ cup boiling water and ¼ teaspoon salt. Cover pan and bring to a boil. Reduce heat and simmer for from 25 to 40 minutes depending on the age and size of beets. Drain, and serve with salt and pepper. Serves 4.

CREAMED BEETS
42 calories per serving

2 cups grated raw beets
4 tablespoons yogurt
3 tablespoons water
1 teaspoon honey
salt

Put grated beets in saucepan and add about 3 tablespoons water. Cook 10 minutes; salt to taste, and serve at once. Add honey to yogurt, and pour over beets. Serves 4.

Using ½ Sucaryl tablet, dissolved, for the honey,

servings are 37 calories apiece.

The next recipe is the favorite dish of a niece of the author, and coincidentally her hair matches the color of the orange sauce.

BEETS A LA JUDY
63 calories per serving

1 tablespoon butter
1½ tablespoons flour
¾ cup orange juice
1 teaspoon grated orange rind
1½ teaspoons Sucaryl solution
 salt and pepper
2½ cups diced cooked beets

Melt butter in top of double boiler. Add mixture of flour, orange juice, rind, and Sucaryl. Cook until thick, stirring constantly. Add seasonings and beets. Heat thoroughly. Serves 6.

PICKLED BEETS
40 calories per serving

1 pound canned or cooked beets
¼ cup vinegar
½ teaspoon salt
4 whole cloves
1 bay leaf
½ teaspoon Sucaryl solution
 pinch of allspice and cinnamon

Drain liquid from beets into saucepan; add remaining ingredients and bring to boil. Slice beets. Pour boiling liquid over beets. Chill 6 hours. Serve cold or reheat. Serves 4.

COOKED BROCCOLI
22 calories per serving

Wash 1½ pounds broccoli and split any heads that are particularly thick. Fill pan half full of water and bring to a boil with 1 teaspoon salt. Place broccoli, ends down, in the pan with heads out of water and cook uncovered 10 to 20 minutes. Then place broccoli heads in water also, and cook 5 minutes longer. Drain and serve, seasoned. Serves 6.

BROCCOLI WITH MOCK TARTAR SAUCE
93 calories per serving

2 pounds broccoli
1 cup yogurt
1 large dill pickle, chopped fine
1 anchovy filet or ring, chopped fine
½ teaspoon prepared horse-radish
 salt and pepper to taste
2 tablespoons grated cheese

While broccoli is cooking (see recipe above), blend all seasonings into yogurt, and mix well. Put broccoli on preheated serving dish. Spoon or pour about ½ of yogurt sauce over upper part of broccoli. Sprinkle each portion with 1 tea-

spoon of cheese. Pass rest of sauce in separate dish with spoon. Serves 6.

SPICED RED CABBAGE
42 calories per serving

4 cups shredded red cabbage
¼ cup vinegar
¾ cup water
1½ teaspoons Sucaryl solution
½ teaspoon ground cloves
2 tart apples, diced small
1 teaspoon salt

Combine all ingredients and cook at low temperatures until cabbage and apples are tender—about 20 minutes. Serves 6.

COOKED CARROTS
36 calories per serving

Wash and scrape 1 pound of carrots. Cut in slices or strips if desired. Heat ½ to 1 cup of water to boiling point. Add ½ teaspoon salt and carrots. Cover and bring to a boil again. Reduce heat and simmer carrots 20 to 30 minutes, or until tender. Drain, and serve with salt and pepper. Serves 4.

PINEAPPLE GLAZED CARROTS
43 calories per serving

½ cup unsweetened crushed pineapple
½ cup water
1 teaspoon Sucaryl solution
2 teaspoons cornstarch
¼ teaspoon salt
1 teaspoon butter

1 pound carrots, freshly cooked fresh mint, Mintit, or parsley

Put pineapple and water in saucepan. Stir in Sucaryl, cornstarch, and salt. Cook over high heat until mixture boils, about 3 minutes, stirring constantly. Add butter. Combine with carrots a few minutes before serving. Garnish with mint, a few dashes of Mintit, or parsley. Serves 4.

This Pineapple Sauce may also be served with ham patties or baked ham.

STEWED CELERY
30 calories per serving

4 stalks celery, split lengthwise
½ cup boiling water
1 chicken bouillon cube
⅛ teaspoon dried basil

Place all in large skillet or pan, cover, and simmer about 20 minutes. Serves 1.

Mary Anderson Gregg, formerly the dietician at the Beverly Hills Clinic in California, recommends this next dish.

BRAISED CELERY
60 calories per serving

2 bunches celery
1 tablespoon butter
⅛ teaspoon salt
⅛ teaspoon fresh-ground pepper
⅛ teaspoon dried basil
1 bouillon cube
½ cup boiling water

Trim tough outer stalks and leaves of celery. Split bunches lengthwise once through middle, unless bunches are very large, then into quarters. Wash thoroughly. Heat butter in large skillet over low flame; add celery and seasonings. Brown lightly, then add bouillon cube that has been dissolved in boiling water. Cover tightly and simmer gently until celery is tender but not mushy—about 25 minutes. Serve hot in own juice. Serves 4.

STEWED CUCUMBERS
8 calories per serving

2 medium cucumbers
1 tablespoon vinegar
    ice water, salted
    salt and pepper
½ cup consommé or ½ bouillon cube dissolved in ½ cup water

Peel cucumbers and slice into ¼-inch thick rounds. Put in a bowl of salted ice water with vinegar and soak ½ hour. Drain and season. Place in saucepan with hot consommé and simmer 15 minutes. Serve with consommé. Serves 4.

OVEN-FRIED OR BROILED EGGPLANT
41 calories per serving

1 eggplant (1 pound)
1½ tablespoons cooking oil

Peel eggplant, slice thin, and let stand ½ hour in salted water. Oil each piece thinly, place in baking dish, and brown in slow oven.

Eggplant can also be broiled under flame in oven after thin film of oil has been brushed over cut surface. Serves 6.

BAKED EGGPLANT SCALOPPINI
154 calories per serving

1 small eggplant, peeled and cut into cubes
1 teaspoon minced onion
½ teaspoon chopped parsley
½ teaspoon chopped green pepper
    salt and pepper
1½ teaspoons grated American cheese
1 tablespoon Diamel Soyrina breakfast food (optional)

Cook eggplant in boiling water until tender, then drain. Butter a frying pan and mix cooked eggplant with onion, parsley, and green pepper. Season with salt and pepper. Heat all the ingredients and transfer to small shallow baking dish and sprinkle with American cheese and Soyrina. Brown in moderate (350°) oven 15 minutes, or until cheese is melted. Serves 1.

The Spaniards serve this stuffed eggplant as a separate course. Unless it is sprinkled with oil or melted butter before baking it is very low caloried for the size of the portion.

EGGPLANT ANDALUSIAN
62 calories per serving

3 large eggplants
1 chopped green pepper
1 chopped sweet red pepper
¼ cup chopped mushrooms
½ teaspoon chopped chives
½ teaspoon chopped parsley salt, pepper, paprika
6 ½-inch thick tomato slices

Cut the eggplants in halves lengthwise. Scoop out the green part with plastic or stainless steel spoon, so that only shells remain. Chop the flesh fine and combine with peppers, mushrooms, chives, and parsley. Season with salt, pepper, and paprika to taste, and return mixture to shells and place in baking dish. Cover each eggplant half with a tomato slice and bake for 1 hour. Serves 6.

MUSHROOMS
51 calories per pound

Aside from dill or sour pickles (49 calories per pound), the mushroom has the lowest food value of anything we can eat and enjoy. It is an appetite-teaser for other foods and it can be prepared quite simply without the butter and cream with which it is so frequently associated.

Don't peel fresh mushrooms. Wipe them with a damp cloth, snap off stems and, either whole or sliced, put them in a heavy pan with a tight lid. Sprinkle with salt and pepper and mono-sodium glutamate and cook over the barest minimum of heat—without water—until they are steaming in their own juice. This will not take long. When they are tender but still plump, and before they start to shrink very much, take off fire.

They can also be baked or broiled in a hot (400°) oven.

STEWED OKRA AND TOMATOES
81 calories per serving

2 teaspoons bacon drippings or other fat
1 small onion, chopped
2 cups sliced okra
2 cups cooked or canned tomatoes
½ teaspoon salt
pepper

Melt fat in frying pan. Brown onion and okra slightly, stirring as they cook. Add tomatoes and salt. Cook over moderate heat until vegetables are tender and mixture is thick—about 20 minutes. Stir occasionally to prevent sticking. Season with pepper and more salt, if needed. Serves 4.

BAKED ONIONS

42 calories each half

Peel medium-size sweet onions; cut in half crosswise. Place in baking dish, sprinkle with salt and pepper, and dot with ½ teaspoon butter. Add enough water to cover bottom of dish. Cover, and bake in a moderate (375°) oven 30 minutes. Uncover, and bake 15 to 20 minutes longer—until onions are tender.

FRENCH PEAS

90 calories per serving

1½ tablespoons butter or margarine
2 tablespoons water
½ cup thinly sliced mushrooms
1½ cups fresh peas or one 10-ounce package frozen peas
1 small onion, thinly sliced
½ teaspoon salt

Melt butter or margarine in pan; add the other ingredients. Cover tightly and cook over moderate heat, shaking the pan occasionally to prevent sticking. Cook fresh peas until tender—8 to 20 minutes. For frozen peas, start timing when steam begins to escape. Cook 5 to 10 minutes. Serves 4, about ½ cup each.

The following dish makes an excellent replacement for mashed potatoes in planked steak or fish dinners.

CREAMED SPINACH

51 calories per serving

1½ pounds of spinach, fresh, canned, or frozen
¾ cup Thin White Sauce, hot (see Sauces)
1 pinch nutmeg
salt and pepper

Clean fresh spinach; cook, covered, using water clinging to spinach or very little added until steaming; turn down heat and continue cooking for total of 10 minutes. Heat canned spinach. Cook frozen spinach according to directions on package. Chop or purée cooked spinach; add hot sauce and blend well over slow fire. Add seasonings to taste. Serves 6.

SPINACH CUSTARD

118 calories per portion

1 cup chopped cooked spinach, drained
1 teaspoon butter or margarine
¼ cup hot skim milk
½ teaspoon salt
pepper
2 eggs, beaten
2 hard-cooked eggs, finely chopped

Blend spinach, fat, and seasonings with milk. Stir this mixture into the beaten eggs. Add the hard-cooked eggs, stirring them carefully through the mixture. Pour into a greased shallow bak-

ing dish. Set the dish in a pan of hot water. Bake in moderate (350°) oven until set—35 to 40 minutes. Allow stand 5 minutes before unmolding. Two ounces of grated cheese can be substituted for the hard-cooked eggs. Serves 4.

BOILED BRUSSELS SPROUTS
53 calories per serving

Remove wilted leaves from 1 pound of sprouts. Wash, and allow to stand in cold water 15 minutes. Drain, and place sprouts in pan. Cover with boiling water and add ½ teaspoon salt. Cook uncovered 10 to 20 minutes. Drain, season, and serve. Serves 4.

BAKED SQUASH
54 calories per 4-ounce serving

Carefully clean banana or other winter squash and cut into pieces 3 inches square. Steam until half done (approximately 10 minutes). Brush lightly with melted butter, sprinkle with paprika and salt, and bake in pan in moderate oven 20 minutes.

BAKED SUMMER SQUASH
31 calories per serving

1 pound (12 to 15 small) summer squash
1 tablespoon olive oil
    salt to taste
    chopped fresh parsley

Wash squash and cut off stem and blossom ends. Leave whole and parboil in small amount of water 5 minutes. Drain, and put in baking dish. (Water can be saved for soup or gravy.) Add olive oil and salt to taste. Bake 15 minutes in moderate (350°) oven. Serve hot, sprinkled with parsley. Serves 6.

Baked without the olive oil, this is only 12 calories per serving.

STEWED TOMATOES
30 calories per serving

Remove stem ends and quarter 6 medium-sized ripe or green tomatoes (peel ripe tomatoes if preferred). Add 1 tablespoon minced onion for flavor if desired. Cover, and cook until tender—10 to 20 minutes for ripe tomatoes, 20 to 35 for green. Add a little water to green tomatoes, if needed. Season with 1 teaspoon salt and a little pepper; sweeten, if desired—½ Sucaryl tablet for ripe tomatoes, ¼ teaspoon Sucaryl solution for green. Serves 6.

Season canned tomatoes in the same way as fresh ripe, and heat (if onion is added, cook until onion is tender).

With onions or celery: Cook chopped ripe tomatoes with half as much sliced onion or chopped celery. Season as above. Cook covered until onion or celery is tender—about 20 minutes. This is an excellent way to use the outer stalks of celery that are less desirable for eating raw. With celery, calories remain the same; with onions, add ⅓ more.

BAKED TOMATOES
30 calories each

Wash medium-sized tomatoes, ripe or green, and cut off stem ends. Place tomatoes in a baking dish; sprinkle with salt and pepper. Add just enough water to cover bottom of dish. Cover and bake at 375° until tomatoes are soft—about 30 minutes for ripe tomatoes, 45 minutes for green.

SAVORY TOMATOES

Another way to bake tomatoes is to cut them in two, through the equator, and spread cut side of each half with thin coating of prepared mustard, then topping with ½ teaspoon minced onion, over which is poured ¼ teaspoon A.1. sauce, then a dash of Sucaryl solution and a sprinkle of salt. Proceed with baking as above or broil 15 minutes under low heat.

BROILED TOMATOES
15 calories per half

Wash medium-sized tomatoes, ripe or green, and remove stem ends. Cut tomatoes in two, and place cut side up in shallow pan or on broiling pan. Sprinkle with chopped chives, thyme, salt and pepper. Place under direct heat with top of tomatoes about 3 inches below the tip of medium flame or broiler unit. Broil until tender—10 to 15 minutes for ripe tomatoes, 15 to 25 for green.

Adding ½ teaspoon butter with salt and pepper adds 17 calories. One teaspoon bread crumbs (7 calories) or grated cheese (9 calories) can be sprinkled over each half during the last few minutes of broiling.

Try a sprinkle of curry powder on each half after salting.

Here is a luncheon or dinner vegetable dish that contains four of the most available and enjoyable vegetables in the lowest calorie group.

V-4 CHOWDER
36 calories per serving

2 cups diced green and /or sweet red peppers
1 cup sliced or diced mushrooms
1 cup chopped celery
1 cup tomato juice
  salt and pepper
  pinch of ground allspice

Mix ingredients together. Can be stewed in saucepan, baked in oven, or broiled under flame in about 15 minutes. Serves 4.

Jerry Colonna occasionally dons a white apron and presides at a backyard barbecue in his Fryman Canyon home near Hollywood. This is one of his specialties.

ZUCCHINI COLONNA
83 calories per serving

1 pound zucchini
2 tablespoons butter or olive oil
1 tablespoon chopped green onions
2 medium tomatoes
   dash garlic salt
   salt and pepper

Wash and drain zucchini; cut crosswise into thin slices. Heat butter or oil in skillet; add zucchini and stir briskly until slices are lightly browned. Add onions, tomatoes that have been peeled and diced, and garlic salt. Season with salt and pepper then cover skillet and place on slow fire about 5 minutes. Serve in casserole dish. Serves 4.

SEASONINGS FOR VEGETABLES

Ground Allspice adds new interest to vegetables.

Garnishes: Chives, chopped Cress, Lemon and Lime slices, chopped Parsley and Marjoram, and Sesame seed. Add Savory for vegetables cooked in their own juices.

For boiled or steamed vegetables: Basil, ¼ teaspoon crushed Bay leaves in cooking water, Marjoram leaves, ¼ teaspoon monosodium glutamate to cooking water of sweet vegetables.

Baked vegetables: Cinnamon, ground Clove, Mace, Nutmeg, Paprika, ground or fresh crushed White and Black Pepper.

Artichoke: Bay leaf, Tarragon.

Asparagus: add Caraway leaves to canned asparagus before heating, Marjoram leaves, Summer or Winter Savory.

Beets: Bay leaves, Caraway leaves, Chervil, add Cloves to water before boiling, Dill, 1 teaspoon Mixed Pickling spices, Tarragon, Thyme. Sprinkle boiled beets before serving with 1 teaspoon Mustard seed, or when almost done add 1 teaspoon wine vinegar for 4 servings.

Beet Tops: Tarragon, Thyme, mix tops with ½ Borage.

String Beans: Borage leaves, add Cloves to cooking water, Marjoram leaves, Orégano in water when cooking, Paprika, Rosemary, Sage, fresh or dried Summer or Winter Savory, chopped Water Cress before serving.

Cabbage: Caraway leaves, Coriander, Cumin, Fennel seeds, 1 teaspoon Mixed Pickling spices, 1 teaspoon Mustard seed to water before boiling, Orégano, Paprika, fresh or dried Summer or Winter Savory leaves.

Carrots: Bay leaves, Marjoram leaves, Mint, Peppermint, Thyme, chopped Water Cress before serving.

Cauliflower: Caraway leaves, Paprika, Rosemary, chopped Water Cress before serving.

Celery: Tarragon.

Cucumbers: Summer or Winter Savory.

Eggplant: Chervil, Dill, 1 fresh Sage leaf before baking or in water for boiling, Summer and Winter Savory, Thyme.

Kale: Paprika.

Leek: Orégano, Rosemary.

Braised Lettuce: Celery salt and seed, Tarragon.

Mushrooms: Dill, Tarragon, Thyme.

Onions: Bay leaf, Orégano in water for boiling, Sage for scalloped onions, Thyme.

Parsnips: Dill.

Peas: Borage leaves, Marjoram leaves, Onions, Orégano, sprinkle of Poppy seed before serving, Rosemary, 1 fresh or dried Savory leaf, 1 Sage leaf in cooking water, Thyme.

Spinach: cook with Borage, Cress, or Water Cress in equal proportions, Chervil, Fennel, Marjoram, Orég-ano, Peppermint, Rosemary, Tarragon, add 1 teaspoon wine vinegar per pound when almost cooked.

Squash: Basil for baked squash, Cloves to water when boiling, Orégano, Summer or Winter Savory.

Turnips: Paprika, sprinkle with Poppy seed before serving.

Tomatoes: Marjoram leaves, Orégano, 1 teaspoon crushed Red Pepper, Tarragon, sprinkle sliced raw tomatoes with Basil or Thyme then put in refrigerator for 2 hours and serve on Water Cress with low calorie French dressing and chopped Dill or Chives.

Scalloped tomatoes: Curry powder, Dill.

Stewed tomatoes: Bay leaf, Sage.

Zucchini: Marjoram leaves, Mace, Nutmeg, Peppermint, Paprika.

Use Mint with all green vegetables. Boiled or steamed Sorrel mixes well with other greens. Try Onions or Shallots in sweet vegetables. When using Garlic, don't mince. Cut clove lengthwise and run toothpick through each half. Cook just long enough to give flavor, then remove while still whole.

FISH AND SEA FOOD

Lean fish provides excellent food for the dieter in a number of ways. It is an inexpensive change from meat and just as rich in protein content although lower in calories. It is readily available in fresh or frozen form. It can be cooked in a variety of styles and by itself it can be prepared quickly for serving. Though butter, cream, and stuffings are frequently associated with fish dishes, we have included a number of different methods of fixing the leaner fish while keeping the calories to a minimum.

The Fish and Wildlife Service of the United States Department of the Interior made analyses of almost 200 different fish dishes. Thirty-six of the dishes are listed below as examples of fish and sea-food preparations that have been found well suited for dieters seeking to cut their calorie intake.

APPROXIMATE CALORIES OF FISH AND SEA-FOOD DISHES

Fish	Dish	Size of Portion	Calories
Cod fillets baked in Spanish sauce		⅛ pound	150
Flounder fillets boiled with egg sauce		⅛ pound	170
Groundfish loaf		5 ounces	160

Fish Dish	Size of Portion	Calories
Haddock fillets		
fried	⅕ pound	135
fried in mustard sauce	¼ pound	140
oven-fried	⅕ pound	140
Ocean perch fillets		
baked	4½ ounces	175
baked in Spanish sauce	⅓ pound	145
kabobs	⅕ pound	125
kabobs with mushrooms	¼ pound	123
Pollock		
creamed	4½ ounces	155
loaf	¼ pound	140
Rockfish		
baked stuffed fillets	¼ pound	140
oven-steamed fillets	¼ pound	115
cocktail	2 ounces	50
Shad		
broiled roe	¼ pound	135
Tilefish steaks		
boiled	¼ pound	150
boiled with egg sauce	¼ pound	148
Crab meat		
baked	⅕ pound	148
jambalaya	¼ pound	110
ravigote	⅕ pound	110
salad in tomato aspic ring	¼ pound	108
stew	¼ pound	106
quick casserole	5 ounces	160

Fish	Dish	Size of Portion	Calories
Clams			
	New England chowder	¼ pound	75
Lobster			
	salad	¼ pound	117
Scallops			
	kabobs with pineapple	⅕ pound	100
	kabobs with tomato	3 ounces	63
Shrimp			
	French fried, in batter	⅙ pound	150
	stuffed in green pepper	⅓ pound	135
	Creole	¼ pound	105
	in tomato aspic	4½ ounces	80
	jambalaya	¼ pound	100
	salad	3½ ounces	130
	sauce	3 ounces	95
	stuffed in tomato	5 ounces	112

There are 160 different species of fish marketed in the United States, although only about a dozen are used in large volume. About half of the more popular ones are fat fish and should be avoided by reducing dieters. These include tuna, salmon, catfish, whitefish, brook and lake trout, mackerel, pompano, shad, sea herring and, as you might suspect, butterfish.

However, this leaves a great many other fish—and all of the shellfish—that are classified as lean.

In buying fresh fish, look for eyes bright and bulging, gills reddish in color, scales shiny and tight to the skin.

When thawing frozen fish, remember that the more juices retained the more flavor the fish will have, so when the outside surface loses its icy rigidity, begin cooking. A quick searing in pan or broiler retains the flavor-giving moisture in fish flesh. Allow a slightly longer cooking time, with lower heat, after initial searing.

Fish flesh is naturally tender. Cooking coagulates the protein and develops flavor at the same time. Overcooking dries and toughens any fish, and the longer it is stored after leaving the water, the weaker the flavor becomes.

LEAN FISH, A BUYING GUIDE

(INFORMATION FROM FISH & WILDLIFE SERVICE, U.S. DEPT. OF THE INTERIOR)

Species	Usual Market Range of Whole Fish in Pounds	Usual Market Forms*	Main Market Areas†
SALT WATER			
Bluefish	1–7	Whole, drawn	Mid and South Atlantic
Cod	3–20	Drawn, dressed, steaks, fillets	Entire U.S.
Croaker	½–2½	Whole, dressed, fillets	Mid and South Atlantic; Gulf
Flounder	¼–5	Whole, dressed, fillets	Entire U.S.
Grouper	5–15	Whole, drawn, dressed, steaks, fillets	South Atlantic; Gulf
Haddock	1½–7	Drawn, fillets	Entire U.S.
Hake	2–5	Whole, drawn, dressed, fillets	North and Mid Atlantic; Midwest
Halibut	8–75	Dressed, steaks	Entire U.S.
Lingcod	5–20	Dressed, steaks, fillets	Pacific
Mullet	½–3	Whole	Mid and So. Atlantic; Gulf; Midwest
Pollock	3–14	Drawn, dressed, steaks, fillets	Entire U.S., except Pacific
Rockfish	2–5	Dressed, fillets	Pacific and Midwest; Gulf
Rosefish	½–1¼	Fillets	Entire U.S.
Scup (Porgy)	½–2	Whole, dressed	Mid and South Atlantic
Sea bass	¼–4	Whole, dressed, fillets	Mid and South Atlantic; Pacific
Sea trout	1–6	Whole, drawn, dressed, fillets	Mid and South Atlantic; Gulf
Snapper, red	2–15	Drawn, dressed, steaks, fillets	Mid and South Atlantic; Gulf

Spot	¼–1¼	Whole, dressed	Mid and South Atlantic
Whiting	½–1½	Whole, drawn, dressed, fillets	Entire U.S., except Pacific
FRESH WATER			
Buffalofish	5–15	Whole, drawn, dressed, steaks	Midwest
Carp	2–8	Whole, fillets	Midwest, Mid Atlantic
Lake herring	⅓–1	Whole, drawn, fillets	Midwest
Sheepshead	½–1	Whole, drawn, dressed, fillets	Midwest
Suckers	½–4	Whole, drawn, dressed, fillets	Midwest
Yellow perch	¼–1	Whole, fillets	Midwest
Yellow pike	1½–10	Whole, dressed, fillets	Midwest
SHELLFISH			
Clams		In the shell, shucked	Entire U.S.
Crabs		Live, cooked meat	Entire U.S., except Midwest
Lobsters		Live, cooked meat	No. and Mid Atlantic; Midwest; Pacific
Oysters		In the shell, shucked	Entire U.S.
Shrimp		Headless, cooked meat	Entire U.S.

* Whole or round fish are those marketed just as they come from the water. Drawn fish are marketed with only the entrails removed. Dressed fish are scaled and eviscerated, usually with the head, tail and fins removed. Steaks are cross-section slices of the larger sizes of dressed fish. The sides of the fish, cut lengthwise away from the backbone, are called fillets.

† North Atlantic area includes the coastal states from Maine to Connecticut; Middle Atlantic area, New York to Virginia; South Atlantic area, North Carolina to Florida; Gulf area, Alabama to Texas; Pacific area, Washington to California; and Midwest area, central and inland states.

TIME AND TEMPERATURE CHARTS AND INSTRUCTIONS

FOR PREPARING FISH DISHES

(FROM THE FISHERY COUNCIL)

BROILING FISH FILLETS

Broiled fish fillets take between 5 and 10 minutes to cook, depending on the variety of fish. Never turn fillets while broiling them. Baste as prescribed below. Using aluminum foil boats will save cleaning up later and also will add flavor by retaining fish juices around the fillet during cooking period.

Fresh Fillets: Wipe fillet dry with damp cloth. It is important to preheat broiling compartment and pan under full heat (550°) for 10 minutes, or follow directions of range manufacturer for preheating. Place fillet on preheated broiling pan 2 inches from source of heat. Baste evenly with minimum of butter, margarine, shortening, or oil. Broil fillet length of time indicated.

Frozen fillets: Cook them frozen but allow a little more cooking time, and place them 3 inches from the source of heat. Be sure to baste evenly over the entire surface of the fish.

Fish	Thickness of Fillets	Baste while Broiling	Broiling Time
Bluefish	¼— ¾ inch	once	6 min.
Carp	¼—1¼ inch	once	8—10 min.
Cisco (Lake herring)	¼—1½ inch	once	5— 7 min.
Cod	½—1 inch	twice	8—10 min.
Flounder	¼— ½ inch	once	5— 7 min.
Fluke	¼— ⅔ inch	twice	5— 8 min.
Haddock	⅓— ⅔ inch	twice	5— 8 min.
Hake	¼— ½ inch	twice	6— 8 min.
Mullet	¼— ¾ inch	twice	6— 8 min.
Pike	¼— ⅔ inch	once	6— 8 min.
Pollock	½—1 inch	twice	6— 8 min.
Porgy	¼— ⅝ inch	twice	6 min.
Sea bass	¼— ½ inch	twice	5 min.
Sole—lemon	¼— ¾ inch	twice	5— 8 min.
Sole—gray	usually ¼ inch	once	5 min.
Weakfish	¼— ¾ inch	twice	6 min.
Whiting	¼— ¾ inch	twice	5 min.

BROILING FISH STEAKS

Steaks may be cut to any desired thickness. Average thickness will vary from ½ to 1 inch. Wipe steak dry with damp cloth. Preheat broiling pan and compartment at full heat (550°) for 10 minutes or follow instructions of range manufacturer for preheating. Place steak on preheated broiler pan.

Brush top of steak evenly with thin film butter, margarine, shortening, or oil. Make sure steak is 2 inches from source of heat. Broil according to chart below. Place still-frozen steaks 3 inches from heat and cook slightly longer.

Fish steaks are best broiled a shorter period of time on the first side. Thus the second side, or side that will be served up, will be a rich golden brown. Fish steaks take between 6 and 10 minutes of broiling, depending on the variety of fish and thickness of the steaks. Use aluminum foil boats to save flavor and cleaning up later.

	Fish Thickness	Time on 1st Side	Time on 2nd Side	Extra Bastings
Cod	½ inch	3 min.	5 min.	1
	1 inch	5 min.	5 min.	1
Swordfish	½ inch	3 min.	3 min.	
	1 inch	3 min.	5 min.	
Halibut	½ inch	3 min.	3 min.	1
	1 inch	4 min.	5 min.	1
Striped bass	½ inch	3 min.	3 min.	1
	1 inch	4 min.	4 min.	1

BROILING WHOLE DRESSED FISH

Whole dressed fish, like steaks, must be broiled on both sides. Only fluke and flounders are not turned while broiling. Preheat broiling compartment and pan at full heat (550°) for 10 minutes, or follow range manufacturer's directions. Wipe fish with damp cloth. Brush top side of the whole fish evenly with minimum of butter, margarine, shortening, or oil. Place fish, basted side up, on preheated broiling pan distance from heat specified on chart below. Broil first side according to chart. Season, and turn. Baste second side evenly. Broil second side for time specified on chart. Use aluminum foil boat to keep juices around fish while broiling.

Fish	Inches from Flame	Time on 1st Side	Time on 2nd Side
Bluefish	3	4 min.	5 min.
Carp (up to 3 lbs.)	6	12 min.	14 min.
Cisco (Lake herring)	6	4 min.	5 min.
Croaker	6	5 min.	8 min.
Flounder	3	10 min.	white side up— don't turn
Fluke	3	8 min.	white side up— don't turn
Mullet	6	5 min.	9 min.
Pike	6	5 min.	8 min.
Porgy	6	3 min.	6 min.
Sea bass	6	5 min.	6 min.
Sea squab tails	3	5 min.	6 min.
Weakfish	6	3 min.	5 min.
Whiting	6	4 min.	5 min.

BROILING SPLIT FISH

Any fish weighing less than 4 pounds may be split for broiling. Split fish, cooked with bone left in, is juicier and has more flavor. You may have the fish split where you buy it or do it yourself at home. Slit the underside of the fish all the way down to the tail. Then, keeping the knife pressed against the backbone, slice the fish in two along its entire length.

Preheat broiling pan and compartment at full heat (550°) for 10 minutes or follow directions given by range manufacturer. Place split fish on preheated broiler rack as specified on chart below. Baste surface evenly with small amount of butter, margarine, shortening, or oil. Broil split fish length of time required according to chart. Use aluminum foil for more flavor and less work later.

Fish	Inches from Flame	Thickness of Fish	Broiling Time
Bluefish	3	¾ in.	8 min.
Bonito Mackerel	3	½–1½ in.	10 min.
Croaker	2	¾ in.	8 min.
*Carp	6	½–1½ in.	12–14 min.
Cisco (Lake herring)	3	¼–1 in.	9–11 min.
Hake	3	1 in.	6– 8 min.
Mullet	3	¼–1 in.	10–12 min.
*Pike	3	¼–1¼ in.	8–10 min.
Porgy	3	½–1 in.	6– 8 min.
Sea bass	3	½–1 in.	6– 8 min.
Weakfish	2	½–¾ in.	6– 8 min.
Whiting	3	¼–½ in.	6– 8 min.

* Carp and pike should be basted twice during the broiling period instead of the single basting recommended for the other varieties.

BAKING FISH

Fish take less time to bake than any other meat. Therefore, you must know the exact weight because this determines oven time—and flavor of the fish, too. For if it is not cooked the proper time, taste will suffer. Fish should be baked with the head on. It may be removed before serving. When the head is off, the flesh at the cut end dries and toughens. Leaving the head on during baking seals in flavor and juices—and shortens cooking time.

Douse fish quickly in cold salted water. Dry it with damp cloth or drain it on absorbent paper. All fish should be placed on aluminum foil in the baking pan to aid in removing it from pan without breaking when it is done. This also eliminates scrubbing the baking pan later.

Oven should be heated moderately hot (400°) before putting in fish. If your oven does not have thermostatic control, use an oven thermometer to check and keep proper temperature.

Fish should not be slashed to hasten cooking time. Juices and flavor will be lost and the fish will be drier. Bastings with white wine dress up fish and add piquancy to its flavor. For something different try marinating fish in low calorie French dressing for a couple of hours prior to baking.

Fish Thickness		Baking Time Head on	Baking Time Head off
SMALL FISH			
Bluefish	1½ in.	1½ min. per oz.	2 min. per oz.
Croaker	½ in.	3 min. per oz.	
Flounder	1 in.	2 min. per oz.	
Herring	1 in.	1½ min. per oz.	2 min. per oz.
Pike	2¼ in.	1¼ min. per oz.	1 min. per oz.
Porgy	2 in.	1 min. per oz.	1¼ min. per oz.
Sea bass	1½ in.	1⅔ min. per oz.	2 min. per oz.
Mullet	2 in.	1½ min. per oz.	2 min. per oz.
Weakfish	1½ in.	1⅔ min. per oz.	2 min. per oz.
Whiting	2 in.	1¼ min. per oz.	1½ min. per oz.
LARGE FISH OR PIECES			
Carp	2½ in.	12 min. per lb.	16 min. per lb.
Cod	2¾ in.	9 min. per lb.	12 min. per lb.
Haddock	3¼ in.	10 min. per lb.	14 min. per lb.
Halibut	2¾ in.		11 min. per lb.
Spotted sea trout	3½ in.	14 min. per lb.	15 min. per lb.
Striped bass	2½ in.	12 min. per lb.	16 min. per lb.

STEAMING

The secret of perfectly steamed fish is this—use very little water, cover the pot tightly, and steam fish exactly the right length of time. Juices and flavor stay in the fish entirely when it is cooked with most heat.

Use a deep pan with a tightly fitted cover. Fill pan with 1½ to 2 inches of water. Place metal rack in bottom of pan. Any support may be used that will keep the fish higher than the water level. Know the exact weight of the fish as it is ready for steaming. Wrap fish in cheesecloth or muslin so it can be lifted out easily without breaking when it is done. When water is boiling, place fish on rack and cover pot tightly.

Cooking time: For steaming fish, a chart of times and temperatures is not necessary. Simply remember this: Fish less than 2 inches thick require 1 minute of steaming for each ounce of weight. That is why knowing the exact weight of the fish is so important.

Fish more than 2 inches thick require different times, depending on the variety. However, since fish thickness always may be reduced to less than 2 inches with a knife, this presents no problem.

Do not add salt or vinegar to steamed fish until after cooking is completed. Other seasonings, such as a clove of garlic, cup of wine, parsley, celery, or onion, should be added to the pan at the beginning of the cooking period so that the flavors will have a chance to blend. Steamed fish calls for a mild sauce.

BOILED FISH
100 to 140 calories per serving
2 pounds lean fish fillets
2 quarts water
3 tablespoons salt

Cut fillets into serving-size portions. Boil water and salt. Place fish in a wire basket or on a plate. The plate if used, should be tied in a piece of cheesecloth to facilitate handling when hot. Lower the fish into the salted boiling water and simmer (never boil) about 10 minutes, or until fish flakes easily when tested with a fork. Remove fish carefully to a hot platter. Garnish, and serve hot with a bright-colored sauce. Serves 6.

BAKED FISH CREOLE
168 to 284 calories per serving*
2 cups stewed tomatoes
4 tablespoons thin-sliced onions

4 tablespoons chopped green peppers
4 tablespoons chopped mushrooms
1 tablespoon lemon juice or vinegar
½ teaspoon monosodium glutamate
¼ teaspoon Sucaryl solution
  pinch of orégano
⅛ teaspoon mustard
  salt and pepper to taste
2 pounds fish fillets or steaks

Put all ingredients except fish in saucepan and simmer, stirring occasionally, until vegetables are tender. Grease shallow baking dish, season fish with salt and pepper, place in dish, and pour sauce over. Bake in moderate (350°) oven about 30 minutes. Serves 4.

Mabel Stegner, who pioneered the preparation of foods with electric blenders, is responsible for this soufflé.

DANISH FISH PUDDING
139 calories per serving
1½ cups undiluted evaporated milk
1 teaspoon salt
1½ pounds boneless cod
2 egg whites, beaten stiff

Place half of milk, salt, and fish in glass container of electric blender. Cover, and

* Depending on fish used. Haddock is 190 calories per serving; halibut, 284; flounder, 168; perch, 206; swordfish, 268.

turn on. Blend 30 seconds. Stop and scrape down sides with spatula. Blend until smooth—about 30 seconds longer. Pour into mixing bowl. Repeat blending process with remaining milk, salt, and fish. Lightly fold in egg whites with rotary egg beater or mixer. Pile lightly into a greased 1-quart baking dish and bake in slow (325°) oven until pudding is set—about 1 hour. Serves 6.

Using haddock fillets instead of cod adds 8 calories per serving.

Serve with warmed Mushroom Catsup.

etables. Pour into 1½-quart casserole. Season and bake in moderate (350°) oven 30 minutes. Serves 6.

Potato Crust

If you wish to add 41 calories per serving, reserve 2 tablespoons of the milk powder before mixing with fish stock. Blend powder with 3 medium potatoes, cooked and mashed; mix in ¼ teaspoon salt and dash of pepper and top casserole with this as a crust or pile in 6 mounds. Bake as before, but from 30 to 40 minutes, until potato crust is nicely browned.

FISH CASSEROLE
122 calories per serving

1 pound lean fish fillets
4 carrots, sliced
1 medium onion, cut in rings
⅖ cup Starlac or other instant skim milk powder
1 teaspoon salt
2 eggs

Cook fish in 2 cups boiling salted water. Reserve ¾ cup of the fish stock. Flake fish. Cook carrots and onion together in boiling salted water. Pour ¾ cup fish stock in bowl and sprinkle milk powder and 1 teaspoon salt over. Beat with rotary beater until blended. Add eggs; beat until well blended. Fold in flaked fish and veg-

FISH RINGS
82 calories per ring

1½ pounds flounder or sole fillets
salt and pepper
1½ tablespoons butter or margarine
1 cup chopped mushrooms
1 tablespoon minced onion
1 tablespoon flour
⅔ cup skim milk
1 tablespoon fine-chopped parsley

Dry fillets; cut 8 1-inch strips; season with salt and pepper. Grease an 8-muffin tin lightly with butter and roll a strip of fish into each hole to make a ring. Chop remainder of fish fine. Sauté mushrooms and onion in butter for about 3 minutes; blend in flour, add milk, and cook until thickened, stirring constantly. Add the chopped fish, salt and pepper, and parsley. Blend. Divide mixture in fish rings and bake in moderate (400°) oven 15 minutes, or until filling is firm and rings are tender. Remove, and serve 2 to a portion. Serves 4.

Serve with lemon slices and Tartar Sauce.

LEMON-POACHED FISH
126 calories per serving

- 1 pound sliced fresh or frozen halibut (or cod, salmon, perch, bass*)
- 1 teaspoon salt
- 1 tablespoon fresh lemon juice

Cut fish into individual-sized servings. Put enough water in a pan barely to cover fish; add salt and lemon juice; bring to a boil. Place the fish in the water, cover, and cook below boiling point 8 to 10 minutes. Carefully remove fish from water and serve immediately with Tartar Sauce. Serves 4.

TARTAR SAUCE
14 calories per teaspoon

- 1 cup Cooked Salad dressing
- ¼ teaspoon grated onion
- 1 tablespoon chopped sweet pickle
- 1 teaspoon chopped pimento

Combine all ingredients and mix well. May be stored in covered jar in the refrigerator and used as needed. Makes 1 cup.

FISH MOUSSE
108 calories per serving

- 1 envelope lemon or lime Glow or other low-calorie gelatine*
- ½ cup boiling water
- 4 ounces cold flaked boiled cod or haddock
- 1 teaspoon onion juice
- 1 teaspoon lemon juice
- 1 tablespoon Lowmay or other low calorie mayonnaise
- ½ teaspoon salt

Dissolve gelatine in water and chill until syrupy. Mix other ingredients together and fold into chilled gelatine. Pour into ½-pint mold or small bowl and chill until firm. Unmold on salad greens. Serve with coleslaw, as a main dish. Serves 1.

The next way to eat your fish and have your figure, too, was a favorite of Jim and Marian Jordan of Encino, California, otherwise

---

* Other calories per serving: cod, 77; salmon, 292; perch, 97; bass, 288.

* Using enough for single portion.

known as Fibber McGee and Molly of Wistful Vista.

PLANKED FISH

Calories depend on fish and vegetables used

3- to 4-pound fish, dressed
1½ teaspoons salt
⅛ teaspoon fresh-ground pepper
1 tablespoon butter or margarine
Creamed Spinach for 6
2 other cooked vegetables
parsley
lemon wedges

If hardwood plank is used, oil well and place in a cold oven and heat thoroughly as oven preheats.

Clean, wash, and dry fish. Sprinkle inside and out with salt and pepper. Brush with butter or margarine. Place fish on the hot oiled plank or on a greased oven-glass or metal platter. Bake at 400° 35 to 45 minutes, or until fish will flake easily when tested with a fork. Remove from oven and arrange a border of hot Creamed Spinach (51 calories per serving) and 2 other hot vegetables around fish (French Peas, 90 calories per serving; Cooked Asparagus, 18 calories per serving; Cooked Carrots, 36 calories per serving; Boiled Beans, 20 calories per serv-ing; Boiled Brussels Sprouts, 53 calories per serving, etc. See Vegetable section). Garnish with parsley and lemon. Serve immediately on the plank. Serves 6.

CODFISH EGGS

190 calories per serving

10 ounces (1 can) cod-fish cakes prepared
4 eggs
salt and pepper

Divide codfish into 4 portions and shape into round cakes with deep dimple in top of each large enough for egg. Place in baking pan and break one egg into each dimple. Season to taste and bake in 400° oven until eggs have reached desired doneness. Serves 4.

CODFISH PROVENCALE

161 calories per serving

2 teaspoons butter
1 cup sliced mushrooms
4 slices codfish (1 pound)
salt and pepper
1 small onion, minced
1 tablespoon minced parsley
1 tomato, peeled and chopped
pinch marjoram
1 cup dry sauterne

Melt the butter in a Farberware or other even-heat frying pan; sauté mushrooms. Place fish on top of the mushrooms; sprinkle with salt and pepper. Top with vegetables and marjoram. Add wine and bring to a boil. Cover, and simmer until fish is tender—about 12 minutes. Remove fish to a hot platter. Quickly cook sauce, reducing liquid to ½ the amount. Pour over fish and serve. Serves 4.

The Stockholm Restaurant in New York is noted for its smörgåsbord table and its fish specialties. One of these is cod in the Swedish style.

POACHED COD
A LA STOCKHOLM

192 calories per serving

1 3-pound cod
1 large onion, halved
3 carrots, sliced
2 teaspoons salt

The fish should be cleaned without removing the head. The liver should be saved. Wrap fish and liver in cheesecloth, arrange in a pan, and cover with water. Add onion, carrots, and salt. Bring to a boil slowly, reduce heat, and simmer until the fish flakes easily when pierced with a fork. Allow about 20 to 25 minutes. Transfer fish to hot platter. Garnish with carrots and onion. Serves 6.

Serve with fresh-grated horse-radish or Vinaigrette sauce.

FINNAN HADDIE
177 calories per serving

1 quart water
1 cup milk
1 pound finnan haddie
1 lemon, halved
1 tablespoon minced parsley

Heat water and milk in a heavy kettle; add fish. Cover, and cook until well done—about 20 minutes. Place on napkin, bone, and remove skin. Serve at once on warmed dish with lemon and parsley as garnish. Serves 2.

BROILED HALIBUT EPICUREAN
195 calories per serving

3 tablespoons tomato juice
1 teaspoon rosemary leaves
2 tablespoons white vinegar
2 pound halibut steaks
1 teaspoon salt
dash pepper

Add rosemary and vinegar to the tomato juice; shake well, and let stand at room temperature for an hour or longer; strain. Sprinkle both sides of steaks with salt and pepper. Dip fish in tomato juice mixture and place on a preheated greased broiler pan about 2 inches from the heat. Broil 5 to 8 minutes, or until slightly brown. Baste with mixture, and turn carefully. Brush other side with mixture, and cook 5 to 8 minutes more, or until fish flakes easily when tested with a fork. Serve immediately. Any lean fish steaks may be used. Serves 6.

Unknown to the consumer before 1935, ocean perch now ranks ahead of all other New England species in volume of catch. Dorothy M. Robey and Rose G. Kerr, home economists of the Interior Department, have written a pamphlet on how to cook the No. 1 star of the fish box office and here is one of their recipes, a fish kabob.

OCEAN PERCH KABOBS

202 calories per serving

2 pounds ocean perch fillets
1 teaspoon salt
dash of pepper
6 slices bacon
4 medium tomatoes
¼ cup low calorie French dressing

Cut fillets into strips about 1 inch wide and 4 inches long. Sprinkle with salt and pepper; roll. Cut bacon into squares and tomatoes into eighths. Using long skewers, alternate a roll of fish, square of bacon, and tomato section, until skewers are filled. Brush with one of the low calorie French dressings (see Salad Dressings). Place on a preheated greased broiler pan about 3 inches from source of heat. Broil 6 minutes, turn, and brush with French dressing; continue broiling 5 to 6 minutes longer, or until brown. Can be broiled on a rotary grill, stopping to baste with French dressing. Serves 6.

PORGY WITH TOMATO SAUCE

181 calories per serving

2½ pounds of porgies, dressed
3 tablespoons fine-chopped onion
3 tablespoons chopped parsley
2 cups water
1 tablespoon fat or oil
1 4-ounce can tomato purée
½ teaspoon salt
¼ teaspoon pepper
½ bay leaf

Cut porgies into serving pieces. Brown onion and parsley in hot fat. Add tomato purée or paste, water, and seasonings, and blend well. Add porgies. Place pan in moderately hot (350°) oven 30 to 35 minutes. Remove to warm serving platter, garnish with water cress or parsley, and serve immediately. Serves 4.

FILLET OF RAINBOW TROUT EN PAPILLOTE

145 calories per serving

Substitute filleted boned trout for sole.

POACHED SHAD ROE
140 calories per ¼-pound serving

Place roe in cold water, add 1 tablespoon lemon juice and 1 teaspoon salt. Bring to boil, and cook 15 minutes. Remove skin and serve immediately.

BROILED SHAD ROE
170 calories per ¼-pound serving

Proceed as above but cook only 10 minutes. Remove roe, dry with damp cloth, or drain on absorbent paper. Sprinkle with 1 teaspoon flour and baste with 1 teaspoon butter or margarine. Preheat broiling compartment to 550° and place roe 2 inches from source of heat. Broil 3 minutes on one side, turn, and broil 5 minutes on other. Garnish, and serve immediately.

FILLET OF SOLE MARGUERY
177 calories per serving

Follow directions for Fillet of Sole Bonne Femme, only add 12 small shrimp, oysters, or mussels, or 4 of each,, when sauce or juice is almost reduced. Without butter or flour, each portion is 145 calories. Serves 4.

Fish *en papillote*, or in paper, is eye-filling as well as appetizing, and the use of Reynolds Wrap or another aluminum foil adds to the effect—and safety— of the dish, since it won't burn.

FILLET OF SOLE EN PAPILLOTE
120 calories per serving

8 small or 4 large fillets of lemon sole or flounder (2 pounds)
½ pound mushrooms
1 tablespoon chopped onions
¼ teaspoon basil
1 teaspoon fine chopped chives
1 tablespoon butter or margarine
½ cup white wine
1 medium tomato, peeled and chopped fine
1 teaspoon Worcestershire sauce
juice of ½ lemon
salt
1 teaspoon *beurre manié*
4 slices peeled lemon

Tear from roll of aluminum foil 4 pieces, each 14 by 12 inches. Rinse and dry the fish and arrange enough for 1 portion in center of each piece of foil. Chop the stems of the mushrooms and sauté stems and caps with onions, basil, and chives in skillet in which butter has been heated until lightly browned. If more butter is needed, pour off excess after mixture is cooked, as 2½ tablespoons of butter contain as many calories as the 2 pounds of fish. Add wine to skillet and reduce by ⅓. Add tomato, Worcestershire sauce, and lemon juice. Salt to taste and bring to gentle boil 4 minutes more. Thicken with beurre manié (½ teaspoon butter mixed with ½ teaspoon flour) and divide sauce over the portions of fish. Put a slice of peeled lemon on top of each serving. Bring foil together up over fish and seal all edges so a tight package is formed. Place the 4 packages on cookie sheet and bake in a hot (425°) oven 40 minutes.

To serve, place each package on serving plate and, at the table, snip through foil with scissors to form crisscross on top. Turn back foil and eat right from package. Serves 4.

FILLET OF SOLE BONNE FEMME
147 calories per serving

4 fillets (1 pound) flat lean fish, preferably sole
6 ounces dry white wine
1 small onion, chopped
¼ pound mushrooms, sliced
1 teaspoon chopped parsley
1 tablespoon butter
1 tablespoon flour
salt and pepper

Lay fillets in a small, thinly buttered pan. Pour wine, onion, mushrooms, and parsley over, and marinate 1 hour. Then put in preheated oven set at 325° and bake 20 minutes. Lift fillets out carefully. In a saucepan melt the butter, add flour, and stir. Slowly add juice from fish and simmer until thick. Season fillets with salt and pepper and pour sauce over. Serves 4.

Of course to make our bonne femme (good wife) really thinner, just reduce the juice by simmering and skip the butter and flour. This cuts each portion to 115 calories.

Here is a new way to cook fish, using a red wine vinegar to give it a different color and a different flavor. In the recipe below, water can be used if fish stock is not available, and a cup of Burgundy wine instead of the white wine, if white vinegar is used.

POACHED BLUE RAINBOW TROUT

3 cups fish stock
1 cup white wine
½ cup wine vinegar
1 bay leaf
12 black peppercorns
½ onion, sliced
1 sprig parsley
1 small carrot, sliced
1 tablespoon salt
1 opund very fresh trout, whole and cleaned

Boil sharply for 5 minutes all ingredients except trout; then submerge trout in hot bouillon and simmer 12 minutes. Remove to heated casserole and add 1⅓ cups of the strained bouillon. Serves 2.

TIPS ON COOKING SHRIMP

One pound of fresh shrimp will serve 3 persons. Keep shrimp tightly wrapped in refrigerator or on ice until ready to cook. If shrimp is not to be eaten immediately, keep them in the stock in which they were cooked and store them, covered tightly, in the refrigerator to have them plump and juicy. In cooking, shrimp should always be simmered in a covered saucepan not longer than 5 minutes. Do not boil shrimp.

To simmer 1 pound of shrimp, use 1 cup of water, 1 teaspoon of salt, and ½ stalk celery. Simmer the stock 5 minutes before adding shrimp. Cooking time should be reckoned from time stock returns to simmer after shrimp have been added. To cut down cooking odor given off by shrimp with excessive iodine content, shell before cooking. Always remove sand veins and wash. There are several types of tools available that shell and devein shrimp at the same time.

SPICED SHRIMP

141 calories per serving

1½ pounds shrimp, fresh or frozen
1 bunch celery tops
1 bunch parsley
1½ teaspoons crushed bay leaves
1½ teaspoons whole all-spice
1½ teaspoons whole red peppers
1½ teaspoons whole black peppers
¾ teaspoon whole cloves
2 quarts boiling water
1 cup vinegar
¼ cup salt

Wash shrimp but do not remove shells. Tie celery, parsley, and spices in a piece of cheesecloth. To the water add vinegar, salt, and bag of seasonings. Cover, and simmer 45 minutes. Add shrimp, cover, and return to boiling point; simmer 5 minutes. Drain shrimp, peel, and remove sand veins. Serve with cocktail sauce. Serves 6.

See Shrimp Remoulade in Salad section.

TO BOIL LOBSTER

The simplest way to prepare lobster in the kitchen is to thrust the lobster head first into boiling water (3 quarts of water and 3 tablespoons of salt for a 1-pounder). Cover, and boil 10 minutes for 1 pound, and 3 minutes for each additional pound. Don't overcook. As soon as lobster is cool enough to handle after boiling, split it down the front from head to tail. Force the 2 halves apart with the fingers. Take out the intestinal vein that runs the length of the tail. The green liver may be removed or not, depending on individual taste. Some remove it for mixing with bread crumbs, salt, and pepper as an added delicacy. If it's a female lobster, a red roe may be found in the stomach cavity. This is edible and is favored by some lobster lovers.

ROCK LOBSTER TAILS

Rock lobster tails are imported from Australia, Cuba, New Zealand, and South Africa. They range in size from 4-ouncers to 1-pound ers and over. The over 1-pound size are split in halves lengthwise and marketed as "splits." An 8-ounce tail makes a normal serving.

For boiling tails, defrost and allow 5 minutes for 4-ounce tails, 6 minutes for 5-ounce tails, etc. In broiling, split thin underside lengthwise and place tails, shell side up, 4 to 5 inches below flame. Broil all sizes for 5 minutes, shell side up. Then turn tails and broil, flesh or underside up, 6 minutes for 4-, 5-, and 6-ounce tails; 7 minutes for 7- and 8-ounce tails. For tails up to 1 pound allow 8 to 9 minutes broiling with the flesh side up. A tip for added juiciness and tenderness is to place a little water in the bottom of the broiling pan.

BALTIMORE DEVILED CRAB MEAT
160 calories per serving

1 pound fresh crab meat, or 2 8-ounce cans
2 cups Thin White Sauce
½ teaspoon salt
2 tablespoons minced celery
2 tablespoons finely minced green peppers
⅛ teaspoon Tabasco sauce
¼ teaspoon dry mustard
2 tablespoons lemon juice

Flake the crab meat and remove shell bits. Prepare White Sauce, add all seasonings except lemon juice, and simmer 2 or 3 minutes. Remove from heat and add lemon juice and crab meat. Spoon into large cupcake pans lined with Reynolds Wrap or other aluminum foil or into foil cups made by molding 2 thicknesses of foil over bottom of water tumbler and then double folding edges for a firm brim. Bake in hot (400°) oven 20 to 25 minutes. Transfer foil cups to plates and frill the edges of foil attractively. Serves 6.

OYSTERS

Oysters have been a luxury food since ancient times, and when the first settlers came to America they knew that this was a rich land, indeed, by the size and excellence of the oysters that abounded in the surrounding waters.

Oysters also contribute to a balanced diet, being an excellent source of proteins, iron, copper, calcium, magnesium, phosphorus, vitamin A, thiamine, riboflavin, and niacin.

Never cook oysters too long—just enough to heat them through and leave them plump and tender.

The entire oyster is edible once removed from the shell. It can be served raw or cooked in stews and chowders, broiled, fried, scalloped or baked, or with cheese, bacon, spinach, broccoli, or a combination of minced celery, shallots, fresh chervil, and tarragon, with Tabasco sauce. Some recipe detectives believe they have detected the last combination among the 18 ingredients alleged to make up Oysters Rockefeller.

Oysters Rockefeller was created at Antoine's in New Orleans, where they were given that name because of their richness. The butter and bread crumbs in the dish furnish the caloric extravagance, but by eliminating them, a serving of the United States test kitchen version can be cut from 212 calories to 84.

OYSTERS POOR ROCKEFELLER
84 calories per serving

36 shell oysters
2 cups spinach, cooked
4 tablespoons onion
2 bay leaves
1 tablespoon parsley
½ teaspoon celery salt
½ teaspoon salt
6 drops Tabasco sauce
   lemon slices

Shuck and drain oysters; place on deep half of shells. Put spinach, onion, bay leaves, and parsley through food grinder. Add seasonings, and cook over hot water 5 minutes. Spread mixture over oysters and bake in hot (400°) oven about 10 minutes. Garnish with lemon slices. Serves 6.

If shell oysters are not available, use 1½ pints select oysters. Drain oysters, arrange on a shallow buttered baking dish, and proceed as above.

Also, see Oyster Stew in Soup section.

MUSSELS MARINIERE
237 calories per serving

20 mussels well cleaned
1 pint water
1 young carrot, chopped
1 sprig parsley, chopped
1 large Spanish onion, chopped
   spice bag containing 1 bay leaf, ¼ teaspoon thyme
   salt and pepper
   paprika

Wash mussels in several changes of water, using small knife and brush to make sure they are perfectly clean. Place mussels in large saucepan the sides of which has been rubbed with garlic; add water, carrot, parsley, onion, spice bag, salt and pepper, and paprika. Cook over hot fire until mussels open. Remove them to hot dish and continue cooking liquid until carrot and onion are done. Remove spice bag. Serve mussels either with liquid and vegetables, or liquid strained through cloth or fine sieve. Serves 2.

STEAMED CLAMS BORDELAISE

150 calories per serving

- 36 medium-sized steamer, razor, or Coo-Coo clams
- 4 beads shallots, chopped fine
- 2 tablespoons chopped celery
- ½ cup white wine
- 1 cup fish stock or water
- 1 teaspoon celery salt
- 1 tablespoon chopped parsley
- 1 lemon, cut in thirds

Clean clams thoroughly, place in heavy kettle. Add shallots, celery, wine, fish stock, celery salt, and parsley. Cover pot securely; allow to steam until all clams are open. Remove clams to very hot deep dish. Strain broth through cloth or fine sieve. Serve broth from a heated tureen or in heated cup, with clams on side with lemon. Serves 3.

GARNISHES FOR FISH

A dash of color or a touch of garnish can turn a plain dish into an attractive and appetizing one. The most popular garnishes are listed below, together with suggested methods of preparation.

Beets, cooked whole or sliced; carrots, tops, sticks, curls, or shredded; celery, tops, hearts, sticks, curls; cucumbers, slices or sticks; green peppers, sticks or rings; hard-cooked eggs, slices, wedges, deviled, or grated yellows; lemons, slices or wedges; lettuce, leaves or shredded; paprika, sprinkled sparingly; parsley, sprigs and chopped; pickles, whole, sliced, or chopped; radishes, whole, sliced, or roses; sweet red peppers, strips or rings; water cress, sprigs or chopped.

SEASONINGS FOR FISH AND SEA FOOD

Add ½ teaspoon monosodium glutamate to the pound of fish or pint of fish stock when cooking. Other flavors for any fish or sea food: whole Allspice, Cayenne, Celery seed and salt, Garlic (split and speared on tooth-picks for early and easy removal), Horse-radish, Lemon and Lime juice, Mint, Red and White Pepper, Soy and Tabasco sauces, minced Water Cress, Worcestershire sauce. As a garnish, try chopped Angelica leaves, Cress, Paprika, Summer Savory.

FISH

Broiled: sprinkle with fine chopped Chervil and Marjoram before serving, Fennel seed or leaves before putting on the fire, Summer Savory, Thyme.

Boiled: Marjoram, Parsley.

Baked: Angelica, ground Clove and Marjoram before serving, Mace, Nutmeg, Orégano, Thyme, Summer Savory, Tansy leaves.

Scalloped: Mace, Nutmeg.

Stew: Basil, fresh chopped Hyssop leaves, Marigold petals.

Bouillabaise: Bay, Saffron.

Chowder: Lovage or Celery, Marigold petals, Onions.

Salt Cod: Sage, Summer Savory, chopped Parsley.

Halibut: Dill, Rosemary, Saffron.

Sole: Basil, Saffron.

Sea Trout: Dill.

Fish balls: Thyme.

Fish roe: Should first be parboiled in boiling water with 1 tablespoon wine vinegar and 1 teaspoon salt per quart.

SEA FOOD

Boiled: fresh Anise leaves, Basil, 1 dozen Fennel seed, Rosemary leaves, Sage, Summer Savory.

Broiled: sprinkle with Red Pepper before.

Shrimp: Curry powder, Orégano.

Lobster: Curry powder, Orégano, for broiling use fresh or dried Tarragon leaves before putting on the fire.

Shellfish stews: Saffron.

The only excuse for including rice and pasta dishes in a low-calorie cookbook is that the basic seven foods necessary for balanced nutrition include some cereals each day. The recipes that follow furnish far fewer calories than other versions bearing the same names and among the macaroni dishes, especially, there are far fewer of the starchy calories. Rice is included to give an idea of the calorie count of a dinner dish in which rice is the predominant ingredient. Aside from cottage, pot, or farmer's cheese made from skim milk, cheese is a highly concentrated food, rich in food fuel (calories). If you plan to indulge in a cheese soufflé or the family demands a Welsh rabbit, make sure that you cut out your regular portion of milk in other form that day.

COTTAGE CHEESE FLAVORS   108 calories per ½ cup serving

Chive cottage cheese has become a popular dairy item, but there are many more herbs, spices, and condiments that can be used to pep up the bland, monotonous taste of farmer's or pot cheese or skim-milk cottage cheese. These flavors add everything except calories to the cheese and are not only good as luncheon main dishes, but as canapé spreads and dips for cocktail parties or as dinner appetizers.

Try blending ½ cup (4 ounces) of cheese with one of the following:

> ½ to 1 teaspoon anise seed
> 1 teaspoon pickled capers
> 1 teaspoon chopped fresh
>   caraway leaves or ½ to
>   1 teaspoon seed

⅛ teaspoon cayenne pepper

1 tablespoon minced celery or ½ teaspoon seed or salt

1 teaspoon chopped fresh chervil

1 teaspoon chopped chives or powder

¼ teaspoon ground coriander

½ teaspoon cumin seed

¼ to ½ teaspoon curry powder or salt

2 teaspoons finely minced fresh dill leaves and tender stems or 1 teaspoon crushed seed

½ teaspoon fennel seed

1 teaspoon fresh-chopped mint leaves

2 teaspoons chopped tender nasturtium leaves

¼ to ½ teaspoon onion juice, minced onion, powder or salt

½ teaspoon paprika

1 teaspoon minced parsley or salt

⅛ teaspoon red pepper sprinkle with poppy seed

1 teaspoon finely minced fresh rue leaves (allow mixture to stand 1 hour)

2 fresh sage leaves, minced

1 teaspoon toasted sesame seed

½ teaspoon dried thyme

4 sprigs minced water cress

Different combinations of any of above

Any of the following sauces: A.1.; chili; Escoffier Diable or Robert; H.P.; O. K.; Worcestershire; 101.

Catsup

French dressing

Pickles

WELSH RABBIT
283 calories per serving

¾ tablespoon soft butter

½ pound sharp Cheddar cheese, diced

1 egg

½ tablespoon Worcestershire sauce

½ teaspoon dry mustard

½ teaspoon salt
    dash of Tabasco sauce or cayenne

¾ cup (6 ounces) stale beer or ale

Make sure beer or ale has lost all its bubbles and is flat. First put all other ingredients in Waring or other blender container and blend about 1 minute, until smooth. Then add beer or ale and blend thoroughly. Place mixture in top of double boiler over hot, but not boiling, water and stir constantly until it is hot and smoothly thick—about 5 minutes. Last step can also be done in chafing dish. Serves 4.

If blender is not available, grate cheese and use rotary beater.

RINK-TUM-DIDDY RABBIT
309 calories per serving

2 cups grated Cheddar cheese (½ pound)
½ teaspoon salt
1 can (10½ ounces) condensed tomato soup
3 tablespoons water
1 tablespoon Lea & Perrins or other Worcestershire sauce

Place cheese in top of double boiler over hot water, stirring until melted. Add salt, soup, water, and Worcestershire, and heat, stirring constantly, until thick and bubbly. Serve over toasted Hol-grain (5 calorie), Devonsheer (5 calorie) wafers or Slim Krisp (9 calorie) melba toast. Serves 4.

SWISS FONDUE
223 calories per serving

cut clove garlic
½ cup dry white wine or French vermouth
½ pound shredded Swiss cheese
salt
fresh-ground pepper or nutmeg

Rub chafing dish, earthenware casserole, or top of double boiler with garlic; pour in wine and set over very low flame. When wine is just below boiling point, add cheese and stir until blended. Add seasonings, and serve over half slices of fresh white toast (30 calories), pumpernickel bread

(35 calories), or whole slices of party rye toast (37 calories). Serves 4.

TOMATO-CHEESE SOUFFLE
145 calories per serving

1 can condensed tomato soup
¾ cup grated sharp Cheddar cheese
4 eggs, separated
½ teaspoon orégano or marjoram

Place soup and cheese in top of double boiler, stirring until cheese is melted. Beat yellows and whites of eggs separately. Add yellows to soup-cheese mixture and cool slightly. Fold in stiffly-beaten egg whites, add seasoning, and bake in 1½-quart ungreased casserole in 375° oven 20 to 25 minutes. Serves 6.

VEGETABLE SOUFFLE
94 calories per serving

1 tablespoon minced onion
1 tablespoon fine-chopped green pepper
2 tablespoons fine-chopped celery
1 tablespoon fat, melted
1 tablespoon flour
¾ cup skim milk
3 large eggs, separated
1 cup diced cooked vegetables
¼ cup fine, dry bread crumbs
¾ teaspoon salt
pepper to taste

Brown onion, green pepper, and celery lightly in the melted fat. Blend in flour and add milk. Cook over low heat, stirring constantly, until thickened. Beat egg yellows. Add the sauce, then the vegetables, crumbs, salt, and pepper. Beat egg whites until stiff but not dry. Fold in the vegetable mixture. Pour into a greased baking dish and bake in a moderate (325°) oven 50 to 60 minutes, or until set. Serves 6.

CHEESE SOUFFLE
150 calories per serving

Omit vegetables and bread crumbs and add 1 cup grated cheese.

CHEESE-SPINACH CASSEROLES
219 calories per serving

- 3 eggs
- ¼ teaspoon salt
- ⅛ teaspoon pepper
- ¼ teaspoon onion salt
- ⅛ teaspoon nutmeg
- 2 cups cooked spinach, chopped
- ½ cup Thin White Sauce
- 1 pound skim-milk cottage cheese
  pimento strips

Beat eggs and seasonings together in bowl. Add spinach, White Sauce, and cottage cheese (try Breakstone's in New York area). When thoroughly mixed, divide into 4 lightly buttered individual casseroles or ramekins. Decorate tops with strips of pimento. Set casseroles in pan of hot water and bake in 350° oven 45 minutes. Serves 4.

HIGH-PROTEIN PASTAS

Regular macaroni and spaghetti contain 678 calories per pound, cooked. It is from 75 to 80 per cent carbohydrate, or starch, and less than 13 per cent protein. There are pastas that have higher protein content and less starch, as well as from 10 to 20 per cent fewer calories.

Among these is the Buitoni 20-per-cent Protein Special Dietetic Macaroni. It is made with high-protein flour, Semolina, wheat gluten, and wheat germ and has from 65 to 66 per cent starch.

The increase in proteins and lowering of starch are important to all dieters and are vital for diabetics who must limit their intake of starches. Therefore, the Buitoni and other high-protein pastas are particularly welcome in low-carbohydrate diets.

However, remember that the caloric difference is not too great and "pasta," after all, means a flour paste.

Regular macaroni or spaghetti: 678 calories per pound, cooked.

Buitoni 20-per-cent Protein: 560 calories per pound, cooked.

Pastas come in a great variety of forms, sizes, and names, but these do not indicate any difference in ingredients or calories. A pound of 20-per-cent spaghettini (very fine spaghetti) and a pound of 20-per-cent flat macaroni or of elbow macaroni are all made from exactly the same materials.

For a simple way to prepare one serving of Italian spaghetti try the following:

SPAGHETTI AND MEAT SAUCE
306 calories per serving

¾ teaspoon oil
3 ounces ground round steak
2 tablespoons chopped onion
3 ounces (⅜ cup) canned tomatoes
½ cup hot water
1 ounce raw high-protein spaghetti (about ¼ cup, broken)
½ teaspoon salt
¼ teaspoon chili powder

Heat oil in skillet and brown beef. Add onion when meat is almost browned. Continue until both are seared. Add tomatoes, hot water, spaghetti, and seasonings. Cover tightly, and simmer 20 to 30 minutes. Serves 1.

SPAGHETTINI WITH CLAM SAUCE
278 calories per serving

1 clove garlic
1 tablespoon olive oil
4 ounces canned clams and liquid
1 8-ounce can of Buitoni Marinara sauce or 1 cup Brazilian or tomato sauce
salt and pepper
1 8-ounce package Buitoni or other 20-percent protein spaghettini

Split garlic lengthwise and brown in oil heated in skillet. Remove garlic and add clams, including juice, sauce, and seasonings. Simmer over low flame. Meanwhile, cook spaghettini according to directions on box. Drain; place on hot platter; pour hot sauce over. Serve immediately. Serves 4.

ANCHOVIES WITH SPINACH MACARONI
295 calories per serving

2 tablespoons butter or margarine
1 clove garlic, split
12 anchovy fillets
few grains fresh-cracked black pepper
1 8-ounce package Buitoni 20-per-cent or other high-protein spinach macaroni
1 ounce Buitoni or other grated Parmesan cheese

Heat butter in skillet; sauté garlic about 5 minutes; remove garlic. If anchovy fillets are salted, rinse in cold water. Cut anchovies in ½-inch pieces; add to butter, and cook 2 minutes, stirring constantly. Add pepper. Meanwhile, cook spinach macaroni according to directions on package. Drain, and serve on hot platter with the anchovy sauce and grated cheese. Serves 4.

NOODLES

Egg noodles, when cooked, have about half of the calories of even the high-protein spaghetti or macaroni (Noodles, 302 per pound; other, 618). This is because dry noodles absorb 80 per cent water as against 60 per cent for the other pastas.

Therefore they provide more bulk per calorie for those dieters who crave paste dishes. An 8-ounce package of noodles will give almost 8 1-cup servings of 108 calories each when cooked plain.

SESAME SEED NOODLES
129 calories per serving

1 8-ounce package egg noodles
1 tablespoon butter
2 teaspoons sesame seeds

Cook noodles as directed on package, rinse, and drain. Melt butter in pan. Add sesame seeds, and toast over low heat. Mix well with drained noodles. Makes 8 servings.

NOODLES AND CHEESE
228 calories per serving

2 ounces Cheddar cheese, cubed
½ cup drained canned green beans
¼ cup skim milk
½ cup cooked noodles
salt and pepper
paprika

Melt cheese in milk in small saucepan over low heat; blend until smooth. Combine with beans, noodles, salt and pepper. Place in individual casserole; sprinkle with paprika. Bake in moderate (350°) oven 20 minutes, or until brown. Serves 1.

Spinach may be substituted for beans with no change in calories.

COMBINATION DISHES
CABBAGE SCALLOP
111 calories per serving

4 cups raw cabbage
1 cup canned tomatoes
salt and pepper to taste
1 cup grated cheese, American, Parmesan, or Swiss

Shred cabbage and cook in small amount of boiling salted water in covered pan 5 to 10 minutes. Drain. Grease baking dish lightly; place cabbage and tomatoes in layers; season. Sprinkle with cheese and top with layer of cheese. Bake in moderate

(350°) oven 30 minutes, or heat thoroughly over water until cheese is melted. Makes 6 servings.

GREEN BEAN RINGS
134 calories per serving

- 1¾ cups cooked cut green beans, in 1-inch pieces
- 1 teaspoon salad oil
- 2 teaspoons vinegar
- ½ teaspoon garlic salt salt and pepper
- 1⅛ cups Sealtest or other skim-milk cottage cheese
- 3 strips cooked, finely chopped bacon

Drain beans; add oil, vinegar, garlic salt, salt and pepper to taste. Toss together to blend well. Press lightly into 4 small ring molds. Chill 1 hour. Run knife around edges to loosen. Unmold on greens. Spoon cottage cheese into centers. Sprinkle bacon over beans. Serves 4.

STRING BEANS AND HAMBURGER
118 calories per serving

- ½ pound ground round steak
- 5 cups string beans, cooked in small amount water
- 1 cup condensed tomato soup
- ½ teaspoon dry mustard Worcestershire sauce to taste
- Salt and pepper

Season beef with salt and pepper, shape into 6 patties, and brown on both sides under broiler. Drain string beans, add tomato soup, mustard, Worcestershire, and more pepper to taste. Blend well. Put in baking dish. Top with hamburgers. Bake 20 minutes at 400°. Serves 6.

GREEN PEPPER SANDWICHES
150 calories per patty

- 1 pound ground round steak
- ¼ cup skim milk
- 1½ teaspoons salt
- ¼ teaspoon fresh-ground black pepper
- ½ cup chopped green pepper
- 1 teaspoon fat

Mix together beef, milk, and seasonings, and shape into 12 thin patties about ¼-inch thick. Brown the chopped green pepper in fat and make sandwiches by placing pepper between 2 meat patties. Brown double patties in heavy skillet until done. Makes 6 patties.

CRISP LAMB DICES AND SCRAMBLED EGGS
325 calories per serving

- 1 pound boned lean lamb breast
- salt and pepper
- 4 eggs, beaten
- ¼ cup skim milk

Cut meat into 1-inch squares. Brown meat slowly

in a frying pan. Season. Cover, and cook slowly 45 minutes, until tender. Remove cover the last few minutes of cooking so meat will become crisp. Scramble eggs to which milk has been added. Serve on hot platter surrounded with lamb. Serves 4.

STUFFED PEPPERS

221 calories per serving

4 small green peppers
1½ teaspoons shortening
¾ cup lean ground round steak
2 tablespoons fine-cut onions
⅓ cup crumbs (6 Ry-Krisp or other low calorie wafers)
3 tablespoons fine-cut celery
⅓ cup drained canned tomatoes
½ teaspoon salt

Remove top, seeds, and membrane from peppers. Cover with boiling water. Cook 5 minutes. Drain. Brown meat in hot shortening. Add onions, crumbs, celery, tomatoes, and salt. Heat. Stuff peppers with meat mixture. Stand peppers upright in baking dish with 1 inch of hot water in bottom. Cover, and bake in moderate (350°) oven 1 hour. Serves 4.

RICE DINNER

332 calories per portion

1½ tablespoons butter or margarine
1 onion, finely chopped
½ green pepper, finely chopped
½ pound fresh mushrooms, sliced
1 cup diced raw celery
1 pound rice, washed well
2 teaspoons salt
⅛ teaspoon white pepper
2 cups canned tomatoes
1½ cups water
2 tablespoons chopped parsley

Melt butter in bottom of Sunbeam or other electric cooker with dial set at 300°. Add onion, green pepper, mushrooms, and celery at once. Cook, stirring until partially tender—about 5 minutes. Add rice, salt, pepper, tomatoes, and water. Stir until well blended. Bring to boiling point, then set dial at "simmer," and stir again. Cover, and simmer without stirring until rice has absorbed all the liquid and is tender—about 45 minutes. Let stand for 10 minutes longer. Sprinkle with chopped parsley just before serving. Serves 6.

Can be cooked in large saucepan or top of double boiler over gas or electric heat until boiling point is reached and then simmered over water, or at simmer position of electric range or lowest flame of gas stove. A wire trivet that holds the pot ¼ inch above electric element will also keep rice from sticking.

Also, see Vegetable Soup With Chili Meat Balls in Soup section.

SEASONINGS

With Welsh Rabbit: Basil, Mace, Paprika, Worcestershire sauce.

For cottage and other soft cheeses: Garlic salt, Marjoram, Saffron, Tarragon. See Cottage Cheese Spreads.

Pastas: Cayenne Pepper, Marjoram, Parsley, Pimento, Orégano.

Rice: Saffron, Marigold powder, Turmeric.

CHICKEN AND TURKEY

CHICKEN

It has happened so gradually that few people realize we have had a revolution in chicken. Not too long ago chicken was the extra-special Sunday dish—an infrequent treat. Now the production has gone up, the price has come down, and we eat it as a matter of meat course all the time. The same thing is now happening with turkey.

Formerly springers came along in the spring, fryers in summer, roasters in the fall, and turkeys only at Thanksgiving. New breeds, new marketing methods, new convenient packaging have changed this, and now you can buy your poultry in a dozen different forms during a dozen different months.

From the viewpoint of nutrition this is fortunate for dieters, since chicken and turkey are excellent sources of protein and provide the entire group of essential amino acids, the building blocks of protein.

In purchasing chicken, remember that the younger the bird the more tender—also the leaner and lower in calories. And white meat has fewer calories than dark.

Chickens come fresh or quick-frozen either whole, cut up, or by the piece. They may be ready-to-cook or bled and feather-dressed only (dressed chicken). Chicken is also available in cans whole, as fricassee, boned, à la king, etc. Or you can buy only the parts you like—frozen or fresh breasts, thighs, drumsticks, livers, etc.

But the whole bird remains the most popular form in which poultry is purchased. Size, age, and sex determine the method of preparation, the price, and the caloric content.

Squab broilers, from ¾ to 1½ pounds, are the smallest, most tender, lowest in fat content.

Then come broilers and fryers, 1½ to 3 pounds, usually 10 to 16 weeks old, tender meated, with a small amount of fat. Fryer white meat contains 472 calories per net pound and the dark meat 507. Regular broilers are about 685 calories to the net pound.

A roaster is a chicken of either sex up to 5 pounds, usually under 8 months of age, still tender, but fatter. An edible pound from a roaster gives off 909 calories.

A stewing hen is a mature chicken, female, 2½ to 5 pounds, usually more than 10 months old. It is less tender, fatter, contains 1,372 calories per edible pound.

Then there is the capon, a young unsexed male with tender flesh and a large proportion of white meat. It is only slightly lower in calories than the stewing hen.

The calorie figures above do not take into consideration anything except edible portions of the chicken: flesh, fat, skin, and giblets. In purchasing, figure as follows:

HOW MUCH TO BUY PER SERVING*

If ready to cook—	
For broiling	¼ to ½ bird
For frying	⅔ to ¾ lb.
For roasting	⅔ to ¾ lb.
For stewing	¼ to ⅔ lb.†
If dressed—	
For broiling	¼ to ½ bird
For frying	¾ to 1 lb.
For roasting	¾ to 1 lb.
For stewing	⅓ to ¾ lb.†

ROAST CHICKEN

342 calories per 4-ounce boneless serving

Clean chicken. Remove pin feathers. Singe, and wipe well. Chicken may be roasted without stuffing, using a sprig of parsley and thyme in the cavity while roasting. Sew up chicken, truss and rub with oil, butter, or lemon juice. Heat oven to 400° and roast chicken, basting often, allowing 15 to 18 minutes per pound. Chicken may also be cooked in a slow (300°) oven without basting, allowing 25 minutes per pound.

* This means per serving, not per person. Some people take more than one serving.

† Smaller amount is suggested if you serve vegetables or other foods.

BREAST OF CHICKEN
PETITE MARMITE
214 calories per serving

From Chicken in the Pot recipe (above) take the following:

1 breast of chicken, cut in 2 pieces
6 carrots
1 medium-sized onion
1 quart chicken broth

Add:

1 medium tomato, chopped fine
½ cup cooked peas
½ cup cooked string beans
2 teaspoons chives

Place chicken in 1-quart casserole. Add carrots, onion, tomato, peas, and string beans. Cover with chicken broth, sprinkle with chives, bring to a boil, and serve. Serves 2.

Or serve separately as Chicken Soup and Boiled Chicken and Vegetables.

The soup can be served piping hot or as Jellied Consommé. Concentrated broth from young birds will usually contain enough gelatine of its own, but that from older birds will probably require from ½ to 1 tablespoon of Knox or other unflavored gelatine to 1 pint of liquid.

JELLIED CHICKEN
74 calories per serving

1 pint clear broth gelatine

1½ cups cooked chicken, chopped
1 cup fine-cut celery
2 tablespoons chopped pimento
2 tablespoons chopped parsley
½ teaspoon grated onion
salt to taste

Follow directions for Jellied Consommé. When it begins to set, fold in the other ingredients. Pour mixture into single 1½-quart mold that has been rinsed with cold water, or 6 individual molds. When thoroughly stiffened, turn out on crisp lettuce. Serves 6.

EASY FRICASSEE
335 calories per portion

3½ ounces cooked chicken
salt and pepper
small piece of red pepper
½ carrot, sliced
4 teaspoons minced onion
1 small stalk celery, chopped
1 teaspoon Dia-Mel gluten flour

Cut chicken into small pieces and season with salt and pepper. Add other ingredients. Cover with boiling water and simmer until vegetables are tender. Serves 1.

The fricassee recipe of Mrs. Earl Warren is the

favorite chicken dish of the Chief Justice of the United States. Here is a version that cuts down on the fat and flour in the gravy and doesn't even mention Mrs. Warren's baking-powder dumplings

CHICKEN FRICASSEE
270 calories per serving

1 3-pound young chicken
¾ teaspoon salt
⅛ teaspoon pepper
½ cup onion
½ cup carrot
½ cup celery
1 bay leaf
1 tablespoon chicken fat or butter
1 tablespoon flour
2 tablespoons lemon juice
½ cup mushrooms
1 tablespoon minced parsley

Disjoint and cut chicken into serving pieces. Add salt and pepper and place in heavy kettle. Cover with 1 quart boiling water and cook slowly 1 hour. Add vegetables and bay leaf and continue cooking until chicken is almost tender—30 to 45 minutes longer. Remove chicken. Strain broth and skim off any fat.
Make gravy by blending fat with flour and slowly adding 1½ cups lukewarm chicken broth. Cook until smooth, stirring constantly. Simmer 5 minutes, add lemon juice, mushrooms, and parsley.

Season to taste with salt and pepper. Replace chicken in the gravy and heat to simmer. Serves 6.

CURRIED CHICKEN
Prepare Chicken Fricassee recipe above but in making gravy use 2 tablespoons of flour instead of 1; eliminate mushrooms and add 1 teaspoon of curry powder and either 1 Sucaryl tablet, dissolved, or ⅛ teaspoon Sucaryl solution. Serve with such curry condiments as chopped bell peppers, small sharp, sour, pickled peppers. chopped eggs, capers, and anchovies and, if available, Bombay Duck (actually a dried salted fish called the bummaloti).

This is chicken with orange juice and herbs.

POULET A L'ORANGE
197 calories per serving

¼ cup lemon juice
1 cup orange juice
1 teaspoon Sucaryl solution
1 tablespoon grated orange peel
½ teaspoon caraway seed
¼ teaspoon marjoram
¼ teaspoon rosemary
1 tablespoon cornstarch
1⅓ pounds boned fryer breast (8 slices)
1 tablespoon chopped parsley

Combine juices. Place Su-

caryl, orange peel, caraway seed, herbs, and cornstarch in saucepan. Make a paste with small amount of juice. Add rest of juice. Cook over low heat, stirring constantly, until slightly thickened. Place chicken slices in casserole; spoon sauce over them. Bake in moderate (350°) oven 15 minutes. Before serving, garnish with chopped parsley, if you like parsley. Serves 4.

CHICKEN CACCIATORE
325 calories per serving

1 2-pound broiler or fryer, cut up
2 medium tomatoes, diced
1 clove garlic, chopped fine
⅓ cup dry wine
⅓ cup water

Put all ingredients in pot with tight lid and simmer slowly 1¾ to 2 hours. Remove from flame, let cool, and after 15 minutes skim off all fat. Add

4 small onions
4 carrots, cut up

6 pieces of celery, cut up
1 green pepper, cut up

Return to simmering; cook 15 minutes more. Then add

8 to 12 mushroom caps chili or curry powder to taste (optional)
¼ to ½ teaspoon Worcestershire sauce

Return to simmering; cook another 15 minutes. Serves 4.

BROCHETTE OF CHICKEN LIVER
191 calories per portion

1 pound raw chicken livers
½ pound mushroom caps
1 tablespoon butter
salt, pepper, onion salt

Alternate sections of liver with mushroom caps on metal skewers. Brush lightly with butter. Broil on a rack in the broiler pan about 3 inches from source of heat. Turn to brown evenly—about 10 minutes in all. Season, and serve hot. Serves 4.

Serve plain, or with a hot tomato sauce or hot tomato juice.

BARBECUED POULTRY

Barbecuing, the second-oldest way of cooking, has been making a great comeback since World War II. It is an especially delicious way to prepare chicken and turkey and, if little or not fat is used in basting, especially recommended for reducing dieters.

Equipment can range from the simplest, a rack from the kitchen oven, supported by 4 bricks over a low bed of coals, to the most elaborate patios equipped with running hot and cold chefs.

Roaster-fryer turkeys of from 4 to 7 pounds require about 1¾ hours to cook. Young chickens, 1¾ to 3 pounds, take 1 to 1½ hours' cooking time outdoors.

The ever-increasing popularity of the rotary electric broiler as an article of common household equipment has brought the barbecue indoors for all-year use, and with it has come an interest in seasoning with herbs and spices. Experimenting with different barbecue sauces can be fun, and creating your own version is an achievement to warm the heart and palate of every do-it-yourself chef.

Keep fowl well chilled until ready, brush with sauce or marinade, and use either 2 forks or a fork and a spoon to handle and turn the bird. Avoid piercing meat, as juices will drain away through holes. Use brush, spoon, or a green stick with a clean cloth "mop" at one end to daub the sauce on and keep the meat moist. Heat should be very low so birds will not scorch or cook too quickly. Outdoors, watch closely to prevent burning, keeping a pail of water handy in case fat drippings ignite. Douse quickly, and if coals are at right stage this will not kill fire.

Diet cranberry sauce, coleslaw, and green salads are especially good with barbecued poultry.

BARBECUED CHICKEN WITH HOT BARBECUE SAUCE

2 3-pound chickens, halved or quartered
Hot Barbecue Sauce

Place chickens, skin side up, on a grill over bed of slow-burning charcoal after rubbing with monosodium glutamate, salt, and pepper. Turn to cook uniformly. When meat appears dry, baste all sides with water. And when it is half-done, begin basting at 10-minute intervals with Hot Barbecue Sauce. If done before ready to serve, put chicken in a pan, baste with sauce, and set in warm place until serving time. Serves 6 to 12.

HOT BARBECUE SAUCE
159 calories for entire recipe

½ cup lemon juice
⅓ cup cider vinegar
¼ cup tomato juice
¼ cup cold water
1 teaspoon salt
1 teaspoon dry mustard
1 teaspoon paprika
3 Sucaryl tablets or ⅛ teaspoon Sucaryl solution
½ teaspoon fresh-ground pepper
½ teaspoon red pepper
½ teaspoon onion powder
⅛ teaspoon garlic powder
1 teaspoon Tabasco sauce
1 tablespoon butter or margarine

Combine all ingredients in saucepan. Heat to boiling point. Makes 1½ cups.

Same sauce can be used for barbecuing turkey, veal, beef, or lamb.

Also see Basting Barbecue Sauce. Barbecue Sauce, and Hurry-up Barbecue Sauce in Sauce Section.

TURKEY

Preparing turkey is no longer the all-day chore it was not very long ago, since the bird is now available in sizes from 4 to 24 pounds, in halves, and in favorite pieces; fresh or quick frozen, ready to cook, or dressed.

A fryer or roaster is a young, immature turkey of either sex, weighing from 4 to 8 pounds, usually under 16 weeks old, tender, and lean-meated.

Young hen and young tom turkeys are usually under 8 months old and weigh from 8 to 24 pounds. The fully-mature birds, older, fatter, and less tender, are rarely found in consumer markets.

Where roasting was formerly the only method of preparing turkey, now other ways are becoming popular—broiling, simmering, or stewing and poaching. Turkeys are also fried and braised, but this means using generous amounts of cooking oil (110 calories per tablespoon).

BROILING

Use fryers or roasters for broiling over, under, or revolving around electric element, gas flame, or hot coals, either whole or in pieces. Rub with monosodium glutamate, herbs, or spices before oiling with minimum amount of butter, margarine, or fat. Or marinate in a barbecue sauce 1 to 3 hours. Drain, boil, and baste with the sauce. Or just baste with lemon juice during broiling. Allow about 1 pound per serving of ready-to-cook bird.

STEWING OR SIMMERING

This means slow cooking in a medium-to-large quantity of moist heat (water) and is the choice for less-tender birds. However, this method may be used for any type bird when the meat is for slicing, salads, etc. The turkey may be cooked whole, halved, quartered, or cut up. Place bird in heavy kettle with tight lid. Add ½ cup water and ½ teaspoon salt for each pound ready-to-cook weight. Add 1 small carrot, 1 small onion, 3 stalks celery, 1 clove, and

3 peppercorns in a cheese-cloth bag. Bring water to rapid boil. Skim any froth from surface and reduce heat to simmer. Cook gently until thickest pieces are tender to fork—2 to 3 hours. Remove turkey from broth and cool both. Refrigerate promptly unless preparing for immediate use.

POACHING

A variation of simmering or stewing, poaching is cooking in a very small quantity of water. An excellent method when original shape and maximum flavor are to be retained. Breast, wing, and thighs are good choices.

Arrange meat, skin side up, in heavy kettle or pan. Place thigh and wing on bottom, breast on top. For each 6 pounds sprinkle 1 tablespoon salt and 1 teaspoon white pepper over the meat. Add just enough broth or water to cover bottom of pan. Bring to simmer, cover kettle tightly. Start counting cooking time, and simmer 2 to 2½ hours, until meat is tender to fork. Remove from broth and cool both.

ROAST TURKEY

Season with salt, pepper, and monosodium glutamate rubbed into skin. Rub cavity with salt. Bind legs and wings to body. Close openings with skewers and cord. Place bird, breast up, in a level rack at least ½ inch high in a shallow open pan. If using a V-rack, place turkey breast down.

Take a piece of aluminum foil 4 to 5 inches longer than the turkey and lay it over. Then pinch the foil at the drumstick and breast ends, pressing at ends to anchor it. Leave this cap loose over top and at sides. This helps in uniform browning. No basting necessary.

Put in preheated slow (325°) oven. Do not sear. Do not add water. Do not cover further. When turkey is ⅔ done, cut the cord holding drumstick ends to tail, releasing legs and permitting heat to cook inside thigh thoroughly.

About 20 minutes before turkey is done (see timetable), move drumstick up and down. It should move readily or twist out of the joint. Or test fleshy part of drumstick with protected fingers. Meat should feel very soft. Remove turkey from oven when done.

ROASTING HALF OR QUARTER TURKEY

Rub cut side with salt. Skewer skin to meat along cut edges to prevent it from shrinking from meat. Tie leg to tail. Lay wing flat over white meat and tie cord around breast to hold wing down. Place on rack in shallow pan, skin side down. Cover with aluminum foil. Continue as directed for whole turkey, then turn skin side up when about ¾ done.

Test as for whole turkey. If the breast quarter alone is roasted, meat in thickest area should be soft.

TURKEY ROASTING TIMETABLE

IN A SLOW (325°) OVEN

These are approximate times for unstuffed ready-to-cook birds. If stuffing is used, add 5 minutes per pound longer. If you buy a dressed turkey, subtract 15 to 20 per cent to get approximate ready-to-cook weight.

Pounds, Whole Birds	Total Time, Hours and Minutes	Number of Servings
4– 6	2:40–3:15	4– 6
6– 8	3:00–3:45	6–10
8–12	3:20–4:00	10–20
12–16	4:00–4:40	20–32
16–20	4:40–5:50	32–40
20–24	5:50–7:00	40–50
Half or Quarter Turkey		
3½– 5	3:00–3:30	3– 6
5 – 8	3:30–4:00	6–10
8 –12	4:00–5:00	10–20

Use meat thermometer to tell if turkey is done, placing it in center of inside thigh muscle or thickest part of breast. Turkey is done when thermometer registers between 190 and 195°.

SERVING

Plan schedule so that turkey is out of oven 20 or 30 minutes before it is to be served. This gives the meat a chance to absorb the juices and makes the turkey easier to carve.

QUICK ROAST TURKEY IN FOIL

To cut down the time, especially on the larger birds, and keep the interior of the oven spotless, turkey can be cooked in a very hot (450°) oven if securely wrapped in aluminum foil and following these directions.

Use medium-weight foil

(the kind called "Heavy Duty") and an 18-inch width. For a large turkey, lay 2 lengths on a smooth, flat surface and join together at sides with a double lock fold.

Tie turkey drumsticks to tail, press wings to body, place bird in center of foil, bring sides up and join in lap fold. Press foil at ends down, fold over, bring ends up and mold against top and sides. There should be no chance of drippings escaping into the pan, as they would brown quickly, burn, and smoke.

Place turkey, breast up, in bottom—not rack—of a shallow pan. Put pan into a preheated 450° oven and cook to within 20 minutes of the total cooking time given in timetable below.

Remove from oven, quickly fold foil back away from the bird to the edges of the pan. Return to oven at same heat and turkey will now roast to golden brown during last 20 minutes. Apply the same tests for doneness as for other method.

FOIL-ROASTING TIMETABLE

Pounds	Total Time, Hours and Minutes
8–10	2:15–2:30
10–12	2:45–3:00
14–16	3:00–3:15
18–20	3:15–3:30
22–24	3:15–3:45

Turkey meat becomes quite tender and falls away from the bone when foil-roasted. Care should be taken that the skin does not tear.

PRESSED TURKEY

131 calories per serving

1 envelope unflavored
    gelatine
¼ cup cold water
2 cups boiling turkey
    broth
    salt and pepper
4 hard-cooked eggs
2 cups fine-chopped
    cooked turkey
1 cup fine-diced celery
¼ cup fine-chopped green
    pepper

Soften gelatine in cold water. Add softened gelatine to boiling broth and stir until it is thoroughly dissolved. Season to taste. Cool. Chop egg yellows and white separately. Arrange solid ingredients in greased loaf pan (approximately 8 x 4½ x 3) in following order:

half the turkey
egg whites
celery and green pepper
    mixed together
egg yellows
remaining turkey

Season egg and celery layers with salt and pepper. Pour the broth in carefully and do not disturb the layers. Cover, and chill overnight.

Unmold, and slice to serve.
Makes 10 servings.

Chicken may be used instead of turkey.

POULTRY SEASONINGS

Season any fowl with: Costmary, Curry powder, Garlic*, Ginger, Lemon juice, Lime juice, Parsley, Paprika, Saffron, Sage (sparingly), Sesame seed as garnish, Soy and Tabasco sauces, Tarragon leaves.

CHICKEN

Broiled: Shallots, minced Tarragon just before serving, sprinkle of Turmeric, rub with monosodium glutamate.

Roast: 1 Bay leaf in bottom of pan, Dill rubbed inside, Marjoram, Red Pepper rubbed over before roasting, fresh or dried Rosemary leaves inside, Tarragon leaves rubbed over, Thyme, monosodium glutamate rubbed over.

Stewed: 1 Bay leaf in bottom of pan, Pennyroyal, Red and White Pepper, Rosemary leaves, Tarragon, herb or wine vinegar, Rue, ½ teaspoon monosodium glutamate per pound in water.

Fricassee: 1 Bay leaf in bottom of pan, Rosemary, Thyme.

Croquettes: Winter and Summer Savory.

Minced Chicken and Mushrooms: Rue.

TURKEY

Roast: Basil, Marjoram, Mushrooms, Savory, Thyme, Water Cress.

* Instead of mincing Garlic, cut a clove in halves lengthwise and pierce each half with toothpick. Cook ½ hour, then remove while still whole.

There is no use pretending that meat isn't packed with calories. It has been known for this ever since the prodigal son returned, skinny and hungry, and his father trotted out the fatted calf in an effort to restore him to the ideal weight.

However, meat is our ideal food, in flavor, complete protein content, and appetite and stomach satisfaction if we select the leaner cuts and cut off all visible fat.

Because of its appearance, aroma, and flavor, a properly cooked meat dish has universal appetite appeal. It stimulates the flow of digestive juices, aids digestion, and has many other plus properties. It is important as a supplier of vitamins and minerals as well as essential amino acids to aid in keeping internal organs in good health as weight is reduced; because of its effect on our metabolism, it can increase weight loss by its dynamic action; and it continues to renew muscle tone as the fat stores are reduced.

And meat has a very high satiety value, giving a feeling of well-being and delaying the next hunger longer than any other food.

In the recipes that follow the leaner meats have been indicated wherever possible. Although these are the highest caloried recipes in the book, we should make our greatest expenditures of calories on meat protein, for which there are no adequate lower substitutes.

In most cases these recipes furnish generous portions and the dieter can further restrict calorie intake by cutting the size of servings.

Cook meat at low temperatures (300 to 325°) for tender, juicy results and less shrinkage

Meat shrinks approximately 25 per cent when cooked, and when your physician indicates amounts of meat on your diet, usually in ounces or fractions of a pound, he means cooked ,ready to eat.

Veal and pork must be cooked well done.

When cooking meat in liquid, the ordinary method is to first dredge in flour and sear in fat. However, where practical, grill or broil quickly, without either flour or fat, in skillet or under flame to seal in the juices.

In addition to the seasonings for meats suggested at the end of this section, try mixing your own blend of seasoning salt to have on hand for steaks and other meats. Here is an example:

**DO-IT-YOURSELF
SEASONING SALT**

no calories

2 tablespoons salt
2 tablespoons paprika
1 teaspoon fresh-ground black pepper
1 teaspoon onion salt
1½ teaspoons monosodium glutamate
1 teaspoon celery salt
1 teaspoon garlic salt (optional)
1 teaspoon smoked salt

Mix together and put in properly labeled canister.

HOW MUCH MEAT TO BUY

Boneless meat: allow ¼ pound per serving for boneless round steak, cutlets, liver, stew meats, ground meat, and rolled roasts.

Meat with average amount of bone: allow ⅓ to ½ pound per serving for bone-in roasts, steaks, ham.

Meat with larger amount of bone and gristle: allow ⅔ to ¾ pound per serving for short ribs, spareribs, oxtails, etc.

HOW TO ROAST MEATS

The modern method of roasting meats at low temperature does away with spattered ovens, cuts down shrinkage, and gives you more and juicier servings per pound. ("Baking" is the term usually applied to roasting smoked and picnic hams.)

1. Sprinkle meat with salt and pepper.

2. If you have a meat thermometer, insert through the outside fat into thickest part of muscle, so point does not rest on fat or bone.

3. Roast in slow (325°) oven. Use this same temperature throughout cooking period. Do not add water, do not sear meat, do not cover pan, do not baste.

4. Remove from oven when meat thermometer registers desired degree of doneness, or follow this time schedule:

TIMETABLE FOR ROASTING

Cut	Minutes Per Pound	Meat Thermometer
BEEF		
Rib Roast		
Rare	22–26	140°
Medium	26–30	160°
Well Done	33–35	170°
Rolled Ribs		
Rare	30–34	140°
Medium	33–37	160°
Well done	38–41	170°
Standing Rump	25–30	150–170°
Rolled Rump	25–30	150–170°
LAMB		
Leg	30–35	175–180°
Shoulder, bone-in	30–35	180°
Shoulder, boneless	40–45	180°
PORK		
Loin	35–40	185°
Shoulder Butt	45–50	185°
Whole Ham (smoked)	18–20	160°
Half Ham	25	160°

(Cooked ready-to-eat hams require only 10 to 12 minutes per pound heating time—internal temperature of 130°.)

Cut	Minutes Per Pound	Meat Thermometer
VEAL		
Leg or Loin	30–35	180°
Shoulder, bone-in	35–40	180°
Shoulder, boneless	40–45	180°

Allow the longer number of minutes per pound for smaller roasts. Add approximately 10 minutes per pound for boneless roasts.

HOW TO BROIL

Broiling a steak or a chop depends on a lot of things—the thickness, your preference for rare, medium, or well done, and the fact that there are so many different makes and models of stoves. However, here are some general rules to follow.

GENERAL RULES

1. To keep steaks, chops, and ham slices from "cupping" while broiling, slash through outside fat covering at 1-inch intervals.

2. Broiling is not recommended for veal or pork. The only exceptions are smoked ham steaks and bacon.

3. Meats may be broiled in the frozen state, or partially or completely thawed.

BROILING IN A STOVE

1. Set regulator at 550° or "broil."

2. Put meat on broiler rack and place under broiling unit so that top surface of meat is about 2 inches from heat (greater distance for very thick chops or steaks).

3. Broil with door closed if using a gas range; leave door slightly ajar if broiling by electricity.

4. Broil until meat is well browned, season with salt and pepper.

5. Turn and brown other side. Only 1 turning is necessary.

6. Serve broiled meats immediately on hot platter "to save the sizzle."

BROILING OVER CHARCOAL

1. Build a big enough fire to have a good bed of coals. Give it plenty of time for all flames to die down to a glowing bed of embers before starting to cook the meat.

2. Trim excess fat from meat. Have grill far enough from coals so that when fat from meat drips and flares up, flames do not char the meat.

HOW TO PAN BROIL

1. Preheat your heaviest cast-aluminum or iron skillet or griddle. Do not add fat. (If you're afraid of meat sticking, rub pan lightly with piece of suet or other fat.)

2. When pan is very hot, put in meat; brown quickly on both sides. Do not cover pan.

3. Reduce heat and cook slowly until done. If fat collects in pan, pour it off. Season before serving.

4. For hamburgers with a charcoal flavor, cover bottom of skillet with very thin sprinkling of salt. Place over high heat until salt is very hot, then put hamburgers, in thick patties, in pan and cook each side until crisp

crust is formed and meat reaches desired doneness.

HOW TO BRAISE

Braising is a method of moist-heat cookery in which the meat is browned in a minimum of fat, then cooked slowly in a covered utensil, usually with a small amount of added liquid. (Examples: pot roast, Swiss steak.)

1. Season meat with salt and pepper.

2. Brown meat slowly on all sides in a little hot fat.

3. Add small amount of liquid. As liquid cooks away, a little more may be added.

4. Cover tightly. Cook over low heat at simmering temperature on top of range or in moderately low (325°) oven until meat is tender. (2 to 3½ hours for a pot roast, 1½ to 2½ hours for Swiss steak.)

5. Vegetables may be added 30 to 45 minutes before meat is done. Continue cooking until meat and vegetables are tender.

HOW TO MAKE A STEW

1. Have beef, veal, or lamb cut into uniform pieces, 1 to 2 inches square. Season with salt and pepper.

2. Brown on all sides in hot lard. You can also brown sliced chopped onions along with the meat.

3. Barely cover meat with hot water, stock, or other liquid. (To make a quick meat stock, dissolve a bouillon cube or 1 teaspoon of beef extract in a cup of hot water or liquid from cooked vegetables.)

4. Cover kettle tightly; cook slowly until meat is tender. Simmer; do not boil. Add extra liquid if necessary.

5. Add vegetables just long enough before meat is tender to be done but not overcooked.

COOKING MEATS IN WATER

This is a method often used for cooking cuts such as corned beef, fresh brisket, hocks, ham shank, smoked tongue. "Boiled" meats should never be cooked at the boiling point.

1. Cover meat with hot water.

2. Season with salt and pepper, unless cooking cured or smoked meats such as corned beef, ham, or smoked tongue. Add a peeled onion and herbs or spices, if desired.

3. Cover, and cook over low heat at simmering temperature (just below the boiling point) until done. (40 to 50 minutes per pound for fresh or corned beef, 35 to 40 minutes per pound for smoked pork, 50 minutes per pound for tongue.)

4. If vegetables are to be

cooked with the meat, add them 30 to 45 minutes before meat is done.

BEEF

BUTTERFLY MINUTE STEAK
579 calories per serving

8 ounces well-trimmed New York cut sirloin steak
salt and pepper

To butterfly the steak, split it from the lean side. Care should be taken not to cut all the way through. It should be split to resemble an open book. Flatten out with mallet. Salt and pepper the steak and broil on fast fire or over very hot charcoal. This steak usually cooks medium in about 1½ minutes on each side. Serves 1.

TENDER ROUND-STEAK BROIL
283 calories per serving

1 tablespoon Lea & Perrins Worcestershire sauce
⅛ cup lemon juice or vinegar
2 teaspoons onion juice
1 pound round steak 1-inch thick

Mix first 3 ingredients, pour over steak, and allow to remain overnight. When ready to cook, wipe steak dry and broil each side (about 10 minutes over all for medium rare). Season to taste. Serves 3.

SWISS STEAK
460 calories per serving

3 pounds round steak about 1½ inches thick
1 clove garlic
2 teaspoons salt
⅛ teaspoon pepper
1 tablespoon fat
1 onion, sliced
2 cups hot tomato juice

Place steak on a board and rub well with garlic clove cut in half. Combine the salt and pepper and pound into the meat on both sides with a meat tenderer or the edge of a heavy saucer. Put fat in frying pan and sauté onion until brown. Then brown meat on both sides. Meat may be cut in individual portions if desired. Combine meat and onion in heavy skillet. Add additional salt and pepper if necessary and pour the hot tomato juice over. Cover, and simmer 2 or 3 hours, or until meat is well done. Serves 6.

STANDING RIB ROAST
80 calories per ounce, without bone

2- or 3-rib beef roast
salt and pepper

Have the butcher remove chine to make carving easier. Season. Place fat side up on rack in open roasting pan. Insert meat thermometer so the bulb reaches the center of the thickest part, being sure that the bulb doesn't rest in fat or on bone. Do not add water. Do not cover. Roast in slow oven (300°) to the desired degree of doneness. Allow 18 to 20 minutes a pound for cooking a rare roast, 22 to 25 minutes for medium, and 27 to 30 minutes for well done. Remove from oven when meat thermometer reads 140° for rare, 160° for medium, and 170° for well done.

It takes 5 days to make Sauerbraten the authentic way, and modern science has not yet found a method of speeding up the process.

SAUERBRATEN
604 calories per serving

4 pounds chuck rump or round beef
salt and pepper
1 pint vinegar
water
whole peppercorn
4 bay leaves
4 cloves
1 bunch carrots, cut in strips
6 onions, sliced
3 Sucaryl tablets
6 gingersnaps

Wipe meat with damp cloth and then sprinkle thoroughly with salt and pepper. Place meat in an earthen dish and add vinegar and enough water to cover. Add the peppercorn, bay leaves, and cloves, and let stand tightly covered for 5 days in a cool place. Remove meat and place in a Dutch oven and brown well on all sides. Add the carrots and onions and 1 cup of the spiced vinegar. Cover tightly and cook over low flame about 3 hours, or until meat is tender. When done, add the Sucaryl and gingersnaps and cook for 10 minutes. If necessary, more of the spiced vinegar may be added during cooking. Serves 8.

Now, here is a 24-hour version.

SPICED POT ROAST
514 calories per serving

5 pounds boneless chuck beef
salt and pepper
1 onion, sliced
3 bay leaves
1 teaspoon whole pepper
vinegar
water

Rub the meat thoroughly with the salt and pepper and put in an earthen dish. Add the onion, bay leaves, and whole pepper. Pour over enough equal parts of vinegar and water to cover the meat. Let stand in this liquid for 24 hours. Put meat in a roasting pan and sear well in a 400° oven. When well browned, add a little of the spiced vinegar mixture. Cover pan tightly and cook slowly for 3½ hours, or until meat is tender. Add more of the vinegar if necessary. When cooked, remove meat to a platter and use liquid as gravy. Serves 10.

Mrs. Katie Louchheim, Director of Women's Activities of the Democratic National Committee, serves this at family dinner in her attractive Georgetown home.

SELF-TENDING POT ROAST
275 calories per 3-ounce serving

4- to 5-pound chuck roast
1 stalk celery, with leaves, cut up
2 carrots, cut in quarters
2 medium onions, quartered (optional)
salt and pepper
crumbled bay leaf
herb seasoning

Tear off enough heavy-duty Reynolds Wrap or other aluminum foil to wrap the roast in; place on cookie sheet or pan. Put meat in center and fold foil up around but not over, pan fashion. Season the meat. Place under broiler flame or unit 3 inches from heat, and brown, turning the meat once or twice until all sides are browned. While meat is browning, prepare and add the vegetables so they will brown a little also. Turn down heat and set for "low" (300°). Close the foil, seal-ing all edges with a tight double fold to make an air-tight package. Place meat in oven in usual roasting position. Bake 2½ to 3 hours, or for 4 hours at 250°. When done, remove roast and open foil. Transfer meat to hot platter, arrange vegetables around, and pour juices in foil into saucepan. Skim off fat, heat, and serve. Gravy should be so good it won't need thickening. Makes 10 servings.

If rump roast is used, a serving is about 330 calories. Heel of round, as a roast, comes only to 207 calories and crosscut lean beef shanks, cooked as a baby pot roast, are about the same per serving.

CORNED BEEF
53 calories per ounce

Soak a 3-pound brisket of corned beef in cold water overnight. Remove and place in pot with new cold water, 1 whole onion, 2 or 3 carrots, and 2 branches of celery. Boil over very slow fire until tender (approximately 3½ to 4½ hours). Keep covered with plenty of water at all times. After the brisket is tender (when it can be easily pierced with a fork), lift out carefully, preferably by placing a pan under it. Place in 300° oven 25 minutes. Remove to slic-ing board and trim off ex-

cess fat. Serve with steamed cabbage. Serves 6 to 9.

Here is a traditional French double-dish, soup and meat, out of the same pot.

BEEF PETITE MARMITE
544 calories per serving

4 pounds brisket of beef
1 pound marrow bones
1 onion split and burned
8 medium-sized carrots
1 leek
4 branches celery, diced
2 medium-sized tomatoes, peeled and cut in squares
1 bay leaf
8 black peppercorns
3 sprigs parsley
    salt and pepper
¼ head cabbage

Be sure brisket of beef is very lean. Place in heavy kettle with marrow bones, cover with cold water, and bring to quick boil. Remove water and wash brisket. Return to kettle. Add onion that has been split crosswise and on cut side burned under open flame. Also add carrots, leek, celery, tomatoes, bay leaf, peppercorns, parsley, and salt and pepper to taste. Cover with water and simmer 2½ to 3 hours. Add cabbage and continue simmering 10 to 15 minutes. To serve: cut brisket in thick slices. Arrange in casserole. For every serving place one or two marrow bones in casserole, also add all vegetables that have been cooking with brisket. Cover with the broth and serve with horseradish (add 8 calories per tablespoon.) This dish may also be served separately as soup and meat, the soup as a broth or with the vegetables chopped; the meat as brisket with horseradish or mustard sauce. Serves 8.

And here is another, simpler version.

POT AU FEU
384 calories per serving

1½ pounds plate of beef, with bone
2 quarts water
1 teaspoon salt
½ teaspoon black pepper
2 or 4 carrots, cut in pieces
4 white turnips, cut in pieces
2 leeks
    few sprigs parsley
    salt and pepper

Boil beef in water, skimming off scum till it no longer appears. Add salt and pepper, cut-up carrots and turnips, whole leeks with the outside and some of the green removed, and parsley. Simmer 2 hours. Remove meat, leeks, and some of the vegetables and serve the soup first. Beef, *leeks, and vegetables may be served either hot or cold. Serves 4.*

———

BEEF GOULASH

236 calories per serving

1 pound round steak cut in ½-inch cubes
1 tablespoon fat
fresh-cracked black pepper to taste
salt to taste
1 medium onion, sliced thin
2 bay leaves
1 teaspoon caraway seeds
2 cups water
3 Sucaryl tablets, crushed
1 or 2 tablespoons flour
1 tablespoon paprika
¼ cup cold water
1 tablespoon vinegar

Brown beef lightly in hot fat, using heavy skillet. Season with salt and pepper. Add onion, bay leaves, caraway seeds, and cover with 2 cups of water. Dissolve Sucaryl in liquid. Put cover on skillet and simmer 1½ hours. Remove bay leaves and stir into skillet combined flour, paprika, water, and vinegar, using only enough flour to give desired thickness. Stir, and cook about 10 minutes to thicken. Makes 4 generous servings.

BEEF STEW

333 calories per serving

1½ pounds beef stew meat, cut in squares
1 tablespoon fat
1½ teaspoons salt
¼ teaspoon pepper
1 stalk parsley
1 bay leaf
beef stock or water, hot
6 medium-sized onions
6 small carrots

Brown meat pieces in the melted fat until all sides are browned. Add the seasoning. Add barely enough hot stock or water to cover; put tight lid on kettle and simmer until tender, adding extra liquid if necessary. Add vegetables just long enough before meat is done to cook crisply—20 to 30 minutes. Entire cooking time about 1½ to 2 hours. Remove parsley and bay leaf. Serves 6. Try adding 2 teaspoons Worcestershire sauce, 1 clove garlic, 1 teaspoon lemon juice, ¼ teaspoon paprika, and a dash of Sucaryl solution to seasonings for a richer flavor. Does not increase calories.

This is a slim version of Chili con Carne and skips the 2 cups of cooked red beans that contribute another 460 calories to the recipe.

MEXICAN BEEF

188 calories per serving

1 tablespoon fat
1 pound ground round steak
⅓ cup chopped onion
½ cup minced green pepper
¾ teaspoon salt
⅛ teaspoon pepper
1 teaspoon chili powder
1 10½-ounce can tomato soup
⅔ cup water

Preheat Nesco Cookryte or other controlled-heat electric skillet to 300°. Melt fat. Add beef and onion, and cook, stirring frequently, until lightly browned. Add remaining ingredients. Reduce heat to 225° and cook, covered, 30 minutes, stirring occasionally. Serves 6.

By substituting 1⅛ cups tomato juice for the soup, calorie count per serving drops to 157.

If you do not have an electric frying pan, use heavy iron skillet and heat under usual frying flame, then reduce to simmer when adding remaining ingredients.

STUFFED BEEF ROLLS

220 calories per serving

1 pound round steak, cut ¼-inch thick
¾ cup drained Diet Delight or other canned spinach
⅛ teaspoon nutmeg
¼ cup chopped onion
1 cup Diet Delight or other tomatoes
tip of bay leaf
2 tablespoons chopped green sweet pepper
¼ teaspoon dried basil

Trim fat from meat and cut into 4 equal-size pieces. Flatten meat with potato masher or side of cleaver. Drain spinach thoroughly and chop. Mix with nutmeg and 2 tablespoons onion and divide among meat servings. Roll meat around spinach and fasten with wooden picks. Heat to boiling the tomatoes, remainder of onion, bay leaf, green pepper, and basil. Add meat rolls. Cover, and bake in slow (325°) oven about 1½ to 2 hours, until meat is tender. Serves 4.

STUFFED GROUND ROUND STEAK WITH CHEDDAR CHEESE

520 calories per serving

12 ounces lean ground round steak
salt and pepper
4 ounces chopped Cheddar cheese

Salt and pepper the ground round to taste; mold in 4

equal patties. Divide the cheese on 2 of the patties. Use the 2 remaining patties to cover the cheese and mold together. Broil under flame to desired doneness, about 20 minutes, turning once. Serves 2.

HAMBURGER STEAK

295 calories per serving

2 pounds lean ground round steak
1 egg
1 teaspoon English mustard
2 tablespoons Worcestershire sauce
salt and pepper to taste
1 cup cold chicken broth or consommé

Mix meat, egg, and seasonings thoroughly. Add consommé gradually, blending well. Shape into 6 patties. Sear quickly in a hot skillet or on an oiled grill. Finish cooking over low heat. Serves 6.

Here is a different version:

BARBECUED HAMBURGER STEAK

295 calories per serving

1 egg
¼ cup celery, finely chopped
¼ cup onion, finely chopped
½ teaspoon chili powder
1½ teaspoons Worcestershire sauce
½ teaspoon English mustard
salt and pepper

1 small peeled tomato, finely chopped
2 pounds ground lean round steak

Mix egg, celery, onion, chili powder, Worcestershire sauce, mustard, salt and pepper, and tomato; add meat and blend well. Mold into desired size and shape. Barbecue on an oiled grill or over charcoal. Serves 6.

Hilda Terry, the "Teena" cartoonist, serves these unusual burgers to her group of Campfire Girls.

HERBED HAMBURGERS

234 calories per serving

1 pound lean chopped beef
⅛ teaspoon ground marjoram leaves
⅛ teaspoon ground basil leaves
¼ teaspoon rubbed thyme leaves
¼ teaspoon garlic powder
2 tablespoons fresh lemon juice
1 teaspoon grated lemon rind
1 egg
1 cup skim milk

Combine all ingredients. Form into cakes and broil over coals or in oven. Serves 4.

A roll or bun will add about 87 calories.

BROILED DEVILED HAMBURGERS

226 calories per serving

1 pound lean ground beef
4 tablespoons catsup
1½ teaspoons prepared mustard
2 teaspoons horse-radish
2 teaspoons minced onion
1½ teaspoons Worcestershire sauce
1 teaspoon salt
dash of pepper

Combine all ingredients and blend well. Place under broiler and broil with meat surface about 3 inches from flame, for about 6 minutes, 3 to a side. Serves 4.

WINE MEAT LOAF

332 calories per serving

2½ pounds ground lean meat
6 tablespoons claret or other red wine
1 teaspoon paprika
¼ teaspoon Tabasco sauce
2 teaspoons salt
½ teaspoon pepper

Blend meat and other ingredients thoroughly in bowl. Pack loosely into meat-loaf pan. Bake 1 hour at 350°. Serves 6.

Here is a meat loaf from author Alice Richardson that only just takes a quarter of an hour cooking time.

MEAT BALLS

124 Calories per serving

2 ounces very lean chopped round steak
1 teaspoon Diamel gluten flour
2 tablespoons water
1 teaspoon chopped onion
salt and pepper

Add the flour, water, and onion to the round steak. Salt and pepper to taste. Shape into balls, cover with water, and cook slowly at 350° 40 minutes, or until gravy thickens. Serve hot. Serves 1.

QUICK MEAT LOAF

280 calories per serving

1 pound ground round beef
1 teaspoon salt
pinch of pepper
2 tablespoons minced green pepper
1⅓ cups tomato juice
1 tablespoon chopped onion (optional)
½ teaspoon Sucaryl solution
pinch orégano
¼ teaspoon Worcestershire sauce

Mix well together the beef, salt, pepper, green pepper, ⅓ cup of tomato juice, and onion, if used. Pack into baking dish that has been lightly greased. Bake on lowest shelf in hot (425°) oven 10 minutes. Take out, place under broiler, and broil 5 minutes longer. Meanwhile, combine remainder of tomato juice, Sucaryl, orégano, and Worcestershire sauce in pan and simmer 3 minutes. Remove meat, cut into portions and pour sauce between and on top. Serves 4.

BARBECUED MEAT BALLS
219 calories per serving

1 pound twice-ground lean beef
1 teaspoon salt
½ teaspoon pepper
½ cup catsup
⅛ teaspoon Sucaryl solution or 1 Sucaryl tablet, dissolved
1 teaspoon vinegar
1 teaspoon powdered mustard
1 teaspoon Worcestershire sauce

Season beef with salt and pepper. Form into balls and grill until brown in skillet. Add seasonings and bring almost to a boil. Serves 4.

If made with tomato juice instead of catsup, cook long enough to reduce sauce and subtract 27 calories per portion.

SWEET-AND-SOUR MEAT BALLS
185 calories per serving

3 green peppers
1 pound ground lean beef
1 teaspoon salt
¼ teaspoon pepper
1 tablespoon shortening
1 cup chicken stock or bouillon

No. 1 or 303 can Diet Delight apricots
1 teaspoon soy sauce
¼ cup vinegar

Cut green peppers into eighths; season beef and form into small balls the size of English walnuts; heat shortening in frying pan over medium heat and brown meat balls on all sides. Remove from pan. Place ⅓ cup of chicken stock, apricots with liquid, and green peppers in frying pan; cover, and simmer 10 minutes. Blend soy sauce and vinegar with remaining chicken stock. Add to apricot mixture. Cook slowly, stirring constantly, until thicker. Return meat balls to sauce, and heat. Serves 6.

Also, see Vegetable Soup with Chili Meat Balls in Soup section.

BOILED OX TONGUE
79 calories per ounce

1 ox tongue
½ onion, diced
1 leek, diced
2 carrots, diced
1 bay leaf
4 cloves
1 clove garlic, optional
salt and pepper to taste

Blanch tongue by placing in heavy kettle, covering it with cold water, bringing to a brisk boil, draining, and washing. Return tongue to kettle and add remaining ingredients. Cover with water and cook until done—about 50 minutes to the pound. The best way to determine is to test the tip of the tongue for tenderness. When done, allow to cool slightly before peeling and trimming root ends. If tongue is salted and smoked, no vegetables or seasonings are necessary. Cook in plenty of water. Serve 4 ounce portions .

LIVER

Liver is a natural storehouse of nutritious elements, being rich in protein, vitamin A, niacin, the various complex vitamin Bs and B12 and iron. It is also, for meat, low in calories:

Pork liver
608 calories per pound
Beef liver
618 " " "
Sheep liver
618 " " "
Lamb liver
618 " " "
Chicken liver
638 " " "
Calf liver
639 " " "

Liver is concentrated food, with practically no waste. It should be cooked quickly, otherwise it becomes tough and leathery.

BROILED LIVER
40 calories per ounce

Use baby beef, calf, or lamb liver, and have it sliced to ½ or ¾ inch thick. Broil at moderate temperature until meat changes color, about 3 minutes to each side. Serve immediately.

CALF'S LIVER SUPREME
228 calories per serving

½ pound calf's liver, cut in very thin slices
1 tablespoon fat
  clove garlic
1 teaspoon butter
1 teaspoon Lea & Perrins Worcestershire sauce

Rub frying pan with cut clove of garlic. Melt fat. Cook liver 1½ minutes on each side. Remove liver, add butter and Worcestershire to pan. Stir, and cook 1 minute. Pour over liver. Serves 2.

VEAL

Veal is the leanest and therefore lowest-caloried meat. As with chicken, the youngest of any animal has the least fat.

VEAL SHOULDER ROLL
312 calories per serving

3 pound lean shoulder roll
  salt and pepper

Season meat and place on rack in open roasting pan. Insert the meat thermometer so that the dial reaches the center of the roast. Do not add water. Do not cover. Roast in slow (300°) oven until the thermometer *reaches 120°, or from 2 to 2½ hours, allowing about 40 minutes per pound for roasting. Serves 6.*

SPICED VEAL CHOPS
236 calories per serving

6 loin veal chops
1 tablespoon flour
1 teaspoon salt
1 teaspoon red pepper
⅛ teaspoon thyme
1 clove garlic, split
1 tablespoon oil or shortening
1 teaspoon Worcestershire sauce
1 bay leaf
½ cup water
1 lemon cut in 6 wedges

Have veal chops cut about ¾-inch thick. Dredge in flour that has been mixed with the salt, red pepper, and thyme. Rub skillet with garlic clove. Add oil, and heat. Brown chops in heated oil on both sides. Add water, Worcestershire sauce, and bay leaf. Cover, and simmer 1½ hours. Remove bay leaf and serve chops garnished with lemon. Serves 6.

VEAL CHOPS ZINGARA
282 calories per serving

2 teaspoons fat
4 thick veal chops
1 medium onion, chopped
1 clove garlic, minced
3 carrots, sliced
2 medium tomatoes, peeled and chopped

1 teaspoon salt
⅛ teaspoon pepper
¼ teaspoon rosemary
⅓ cup dry white wine
1 can sliced mushrooms, drained

Melt fat in a Farberware or other evenheat frying pan; sauté chops until brown on both sides. Add vegetables, seasonings, and wine. Cover, and simmer until chops are tender—about 40 minutes. Add mushrooms to heat. Serves 4.

VICTORIAN VEAL STEW
190 calories per serving

1 3½-ounce slice veal cutlet or steak
boiling water
salt and pepper
¼ cup sliced carrots
2 tablespoons peas
¼ cup chopped celery
1 teaspoon minced onion

Cut veal into small pieces and cover with boiling water. Season with salt and pepper. Cook slowly until nearly done. Then add the carrots, peas, celery, and onion. Cook until vegetables are tender. When ready to serve, pour into a serving dish. Serves 1.

Try 1 tablespoon Dia-Mel Soyrina breakfast food sprinkled over the top of the stew. (Adds 38 calories.)

VEAL SCALOPPINI
294 calories per serving

1½ pounds veal cutlet
1 teaspoon salt
⅛ teaspoon pepper
1 tablespoon flour
1 tablespoon butter
¼ cup bouillon
3 tablespoons sherry
1 tablespoon chopped
   parsley

Flatten thin slices of cutlet. Season and sprinkle sparingly with flour, then brown on both sides in hot butter in frying pan until done. Take out cutlets, pour bouillon and wine into pan, cook 3 to 4 minutes, then pour sauce over cutlets. Garnish with parsley. Serves 4.

PAPRIKA SCHNITZEL
340 calories per serving

1 slice bacon, chopped
   fine
½ pound veal cutlet in 2
   thin slices
2 tablespoons chopped
   onions
1 tablespoon Hungarian
   paprika
   salt to taste
1 cup yogurt
½ cup tomato juice

Fry the bacon until crisp; add veal, pounded flat. Brown in hot bacon fat. Add onions, and brown; season well with paprika and salt; stir in yogurt and tomato juice. Cover pan and cook about 20 minutes.

Serve covered with the sauce. Serves 2.

According to Joseph Wechsberg, author of *Blue Trout and Black Truffles*, the test of a schnitzel in Vienna was to sit on it. If it was so tender and so dry that an officer could sit on it without getting a fat stain on his dress trousers, then it was perfect. It is possible, with the following recipe, to come off with flying colors.

WIENER SCHNITZEL
276 calories per serving

1 tablespoon butter
   (or less)
1 pound veal steak, ½
   inch thick
   salt and pepper
1 egg, slightly beaten
1 tablespoon water
½ cup fine bread crumbs
½ cup hot tomato juice
4 lemon slices
   capers
   chives
4 anchovies

Heat butter in heavy skillet. Cut veal into 4 pieces. Season with salt and pepper. Dip pieces in the egg mixed with the water, then into crumbs. Brown in hot butter on both sides for about 10 minutes. Turn down heat, cover, and cook slowly until tender—about 30 minutes. Garnish with round slices of lemon decorated with pap-

rika and fine-chopped chives, and place on top of each a rolled anchovy with capers in center. Serve hot tomato juice as sauce. Serves 4.

Wiener Schnitzel Holstein is served with a fried egg (add 77 calories) between cutlet and lemon slice.

_____

VEAL KLOPPS
269 calories per serving

2 cups (1 pound) finely minced cooked veal
juice of 1 small onion
salt and paprika
1 tablespoon grated lemon rind
unbeaten whites of 3 eggs

Add onion juice, seasonings, and lemon rind to the veal. Form a paste of the seasoned meat with the whites of the eggs. Shape into small balls and drop a few at a time into boiling salted water. Cook 5 minutes. Serve plain or with tomato sauce (add 28 calories per serving). Serves 4.

_____

JELLIED VEAL RING
208 calories per serving

1 veal knuckle
2 pounds veal shoulder, diced
1 bay leaf
2 cloves
2 teaspoons salt
¼ teaspoon pepper
3 quarts hot water
1 slice onion
1 stalk celery
2 teaspoons Worcestershire sauce

Have knuckle cut in 3 or 4 places. Combine knuckle, veal, bay leaf, cloves, salt and pepper in a large heavy kettle. Add hot water, bring to a boil, reduce heat, and simmer, covered, 2 hours, or until meat falls from bone. Remove from heat. Remove bay leaf, veal knuckle, and veal. Strain broth from meat, and hold. Put meat through medium blade of food chopper with onion and celery. Cook down meat broth until it measures about 2 cups. Blend with veal and Worcestershire sauce. Grease a 10-inch ring mold slightly. Pack meat mixture into mold and chill until firm. Serves 6.

_____

VEAL OR LAMB CURRY
425 calories per serving

1½ pounds lamb or veal stew meat
½ cup chopped onion
1 tart apple pared and cored
1½ teaspoons salt
⅛ teaspoon pepper
1 teaspoon curry powder
½ teaspoon ginger
1 Sucaryl tablet, dissolved
2 cups bouillon or water

Brown or sear meat on grill or in skillet. Place in pot,

add all other ingredients, cover, and cook gently until done (approximately 1 to 1¼ hours). Serves 4.

LAMB
ROAST LEG OF LAMB
490 calories per serving

Do not have the fell removed from a 6-pound leg of lamb. Season. Place skin side down on rack in open roasting pan. Insert meat thermometer so the bulb reaches the center of the thickest part of the leg, being sure the bulb does not rest in fat or on bone. Do not add water. Do not cover. Roast in a slow (300°) oven to the desired degree of doneness. The meat thermometer will register 175° for medium-done; 180° for well-done lamb. Allow 30 to 35 minutes per pound for roasting. Serves 12.

CROWN ROAST WITH CAULIFLOWER AND PEAS
496 calories per serving

1 3-pound crown roast of lamb
    salt and pepper
1 head cauliflower, broken into flowerettes
1 12-ounce package frozen peas

Place roast with rib ends down on rack in open roasting pan. Season. Roast in slow (300°) oven 1 hour. Turn placing roast rib ends up. Continue roasting until done, allowing 35 minutes per pound. Meanwhile cook cauliflower and peas. Season. Place paper frills on rib ends. Serve roast with center filled with peas and cauliflower flowerettes. Serves 8.

BROILED LAMB CHOPS
313 calories per 4-ounce chop

Have rib, loin, or shoulder chops cut 1 to 2 inches thick. Set regulator to broil. Place chops on broiler rack. Insert broiler pan and rack so the top of 1-inch chops is 2 inches from the heat and 2-inch chops are 3 inches from the heat. When one side is browned, season, turn, and finish cooking on the second side. Season second side. Chops cut 1-inch thick require 10 to 12 minutes. Chops cut 2 inches thick require 20 to 22 minutes.

SKEWERED LAMB, HAWAIIAN
427 calories per serving

2 pounds boneless lamb leg or shoulder
1 No. 1 can unsweetened pineapple cubes
6 slices bacon
    salt and pepper

Have lamb leg steaks or shoulder chops cut into 1-inch cubes. Place lamb on 6 skewers, alternating a cube of lamb then one of pineapple and a square of bacon, and place on broiler rack. Allow 2 inches between heat and surface of meat. Broil on one side until brown—about 8 to 10 minutes. Season, turn, and brown on second side. Season and serve. Serves 6.

SHISH KABOBS
305 calories per serving

- 1½ pounds lean lamb shoulder
- 1 teaspoon garlic salt
- ¼ teaspoon ground black pepper
- ½ teaspoon powdered dry mustard
- ½ teaspoon chili powder
- ¼ cup cider vinegar
- 2 tablespoons tomato sauce
- 2 tablespoons salad oil
- 15 small parboiled onions or 15 onion slices

Cut lamb into 1½-inch cubes. Combine spices, vinegar, tomato sauce, and oil. Pour over the lamb. Marinate 4 to 5 hours or overnight, turning 3 to 4 times. Alternate on skewers with onions. Broil (over a charcoal fire, if possible) 25 to 30 minutes, or until done, turning to cook uniformly on all sides. Serves 6.

Here is a quicker way to fix barbecued lamb.

BARBECUED LAMB
270 calories per serving

- 2 pounds leg of lamb, skin and fat removed, in strips ½ inch thick and 1 inch square

- ¼ teaspoon orégano
  salt
- 8 whole peppercorns, crushed
- 1 clove garlic
- 2 tomatoes, quartered
- 1 pound small onions, peeled
- 1 eggplant, cut like lamb

Place pieces of lamb in cold water with a little salt. Bring to brisk boil and remove. Wash well. Rub lamb with orégano, salt, pepper, and garlic. Arrange meat and vegetables on brochette needles in following order: piece of lamb, tomato, onion, eggplant; repeat until brochette is full. Barbecue (on medium charcoal fire, if possible). Serves 6.

Tender beef or veal can also be barbecued in the above manner.

Shanks of lamb look something like turkey drumsticks and make a fine, inexpensive dinner dish. They are usually from 1 to 2 pounds apiece and are about half bone.

LAMB SHANKS WITH VEGETABLES
558 calories per serving

- 6 small lamb shanks
- 3 tablespoons Worcestershire sauce
  juice of 1 lemon
  salt and pepper
- 6 medium-sized carrots
- 6 medium-sized onions

Remove any fat and sear

shanks in hot skillet or under broiler. Sprinkle with Worcestershire sauce and lemon juice. Season, and cover with water. Cover tightly, and simmer 1 hour (or bake in a moderate—350°—oven 1 hour), then add carrots and onions. Cover, and cook (or bake) until vegetables are tender and the shanks are done—about 1 hour more. Arrange lamb shanks and vegetables on a large platter. Serves 6.

This is the low-calorie version of a famous Brown Derby Restaurant specialty.

THIN IRISH LAMB STEW
405 calories per serving

2 pounds lean leg or shoulder of lamb
spice bag consisting of 1 bay leaf, 10 peppercorns, ¼ teaspoon nutmeg, 1 sprig thyme, and 1 clove of garlic
1 medium-sized white cabbage
18 small white onions, peeled
12 small carrots, scraped
12 1-inch pieces of celery salt and pepper
6 sprigs parsley
1½ cups cooked peas

Remove all fat from meat and cut into 1-inch squares. Place in heavy kettle and blanch by covering with cold water and bringing to a rolling boil. Remove from water and wash meat lightly. Prepare spice bag. Cover bottom of a medium-sized kettle with blanched lamb and on top of meat place some of the cabbage, a few onions, a few carrots, and celery pieces. Repeat this procedure until all meat and vegetables are used. Cover meat and vegetables with water, add salt, pepper, and spice bag. Cover tightly and simmer 1 hour. Skim stew every 20 minutes. After 1 hour of gentle cooking, add parsley. Cover tightly again and continue to simmer until meat is well done—¾ to 1 hour. Serve stew in heated casserole; sprinkle cooked peas over all. Serves 6.

Below is a recipe which was originally called Parsley Lamb Patties.

LAMBURGERS
160 calories per patty

1 pound ground lamb
1 teaspoon salt
¼ teaspoon pepper
½ cup chopped parsley
1 teaspoon allspice

Combine ingredients, form into 4 patties, and broil. Serves 4.

Also, see Lamb Dices and Scrambled Eggs in Cheese, Pasta and Combination Dishes section.

LAMB ASPIC
273 calories per serving

2 envelopes lemon Jel-ex or 4 envelopes D-Zerta
2 cups hot water
2 cups cold water
30 stuffed green olives, sliced
4 cups diced cooked lamb
½ cup chopped green pepper
¼ cup vinegar
¼ cup prepared horse-radish, drained
3 teaspoons salt
½ teaspoon Worcester-shire sauce

Dissolve gelatine in hot water. Add cold water. With some of the olives, make a stuffed-olive design in bottom of a 5 x 9-inch loaf pan. Cover with a thin layer of gelatine and place in refrigerator until set. Chill remaining gelatine until it begins to congeal. Add lamb, green pepper, seasonings, and the remaining sliced olives. Pour over design in loaf pan. Chill until firm. Unmold on lettuce. Garnish with tomato slices, if desired. Serves 10.

PORK

There are very few recipes for pork in this book.

Several of the most revered authorities on gastronomy have indicated that there is no place in a fine cuisine for pork dishes.

Pork is the fattest of meats and it is not unusual to find double the calories in a cut of pork compared with a similar cut of another meat.

That is why there are very few recipes for pork in this book.

SPARERIBS
516 calories per serving

3 pounds pork spareribs cut in pieces
1 lemon, sliced
1 large onion, sliced
1 cup catsup
⅓ cup Worcestershire sauce
1 teaspoon chili powder
1 teaspoon salt
2 dashes Tabasco sauce
2 cups water

Place ribs in shallow pan, meat side up. Garnish with slices of unpeeled lemon and thin slices of onion, fastening with toothpicks. Roast in hot oven (450°) 30 minutes. Combine remaining ingredients in a saucepan. Heat to boiling and pour over ribs. Continue baking in moderate oven (350°) until tender—about 1 hour. Baste ribs with the sauce every 15 minutes. If sauce gets too thick, add more water. Serves 6.

HAM IN COLA

Ham may be baked or boiled in any of the low- or no-calorie colas or ginger ales, giving it an unusual taste. Put a 10- to 12-pound cured ham in a deep vessel and pour in enough cola to half cover it. Set over a low flame, cover, and boil until ham is tender—approximately 15 minutes per pound. Or bake the ham using 325° oven. Test by sticking long tines of fork into meat. As liquid boils out, add more cola. When tender, take out, skin, and slice either hot or cold. It will have a sweet flavor, but no calories are added to the ham, which is 110 calories per ounce, without bone.

BAKED HAM SLICE WITH MUSTARD SAUCE

520 calories per serving

1 teaspoon Sucaryl solution
½ teaspoon mustard
½ teaspoon Worcestershire sauce
¼ cup water
1 cup unsweetened pineapple juice
¼ teaspoon salt
¼ teaspoon paprika
1 center slice tenderized ham about 1¼ inches thick (about 2 pounds)

Combine all seasonings, and blend. Pour over ham slice. Bake in moderate oven 30 to 40 minutes. Serves 4.

SEASONINGS FOR MEATS

Like salt, but to a greater degree, monosodium glutamate (Ac'cent) brings out the flavor of meat. Use 1 teaspoon per pound for any meat dish and sprinkle or rub on roasts, chops, steaks, etc. Seasonings that go well with all meats include Cayenne and Paprika pepper, as well as Black peppercorns and ground White pepper; Cumin seeds, Lemon and Lime juice, Tarragon, Onion, Parsley, Tabasco sauce, Cress and Water Cress as garnish. Try Mace and Nutmeg with meats.

FOR BEEF

Marjoram and Summer and Winter Savory go well with any cut of beef.

Braised Beef: Fennel seed, Garlic and Garlic salt, Juniper berries. Lovage seed, pulverized Marigold.

Boiled Beef: Horse-radish, fresh Thyme leaves, a few Cloves.

Roast Beef: Basil, minced Chervil just before serving, ground Coriander, Costmary, fresh and dried Dill leaves, Rosemary, fresh Thyme leaves, herb and other vinegars, Worcestershire sauce.

Beefsteak: Chervil just before serving, fresh and dried Dill leaves, Garlic and Garlic salt, Shallots, Soy sauce, Worcestershire sauce.

Hamburger: Allspice berries, Chili powder, Celery salt, Cloves, Costmary, ground Ginger, whole Mustard seed, Onion salt, brush with Mustard sauce before broiling, or mix 1 teaspoon Garlic Wine vinegar, and ½ teaspoon Mustard Sauce to the pound of meat before cooking.

Meat Loaf: Allspice berries, Basil, ground Cloves, ground Ginger, Poultry Seasoning Blends, Sausage Seasoning.

Pot Roast: Allspice berries, Bay leaves, ground Coriander, Garlic and Garlic salt, ground Ginger, Juniper berries, pulverized Marigold, fresh Thyme leaves, Garlic Red Wine vinegar.

Beef Stew: Half teaspoon Aniseed in bag, Balm leaves, Basil, Bay (or Myrtle) leaves, Bouquet Garni, Borage (or Parsley), Caraway leaves or seeds in bag, fresh or dried Chervil leaves, Chili powder, Celery salt, Cloves, ground Ginger, Juniper berries, Leek, Lovage leaves and seed (as Celery is used), Mint, Mixed Pickling Blend in bag, dry Mustard, Orégano, Pennyroyal, Rosemary, Rue, powdered Sage, Shallots (for Onions), Tansy, fresh Thyme leaves, Basil and Tarragon vinegar.

Beef Casseroles: Sprinkle of Sesame seed, Tarragon Wine vinegar, Worcestershire sauce.

Kidneys: Garlic and Garlic salt, Hysop, Shallots before broiling, Thyme, Rue in stews.

Liver: Basil, Basil Wine vinegar, Thyme.

Meat Pies: Basil, Lovage seed, 1 leaf Tansy in bottom, or fresh leaf minced.

Hash: Basil.

Oxtail: Bay leaves.

Goulash: Caraway leaves.

Tongue: Cloves, Thyme, Bay leaves, Basil Wine vinegar.

Corned Beef: Juniper berries, Bay leaves.

Blend, for roast or broiled beef: Dill, Marjoram, Thyme and/or Parsley with lemon juice.

For stews and meat loaf: small quantities of 2 or more: Thyme, Marjoram, Summer Savory, Celery, Parsley, Chervil.

FOR LAMB

Mint leaves of almost all flavors go with every lamb dish.

Roast Lamb: Rub with Balm leaves, Curry powder, ground Fennel seed, Garlic and Garlic salt, Orégano, Rosemary, fresh Thyme leaves, Juniper berries in pan, baste with Tarragon, Garlic or Basil vinegars.

Lamb Chops: chopped Basil leaves, fresh and dried Chervil leaves, fresh and dried Dill leaves, Shallots.

Shish Kabob: Bay leaves, Lovage seed.

Lamb and Mutton Stew: Curry powder, Caraway seed, Bay or Myrtle leaves, fresh and dried Chervil leaves, Celery salt, ground Cinnamon, Cloves, Hyssop, Juniper berries, Leek, Lovage leaves or seed (instead of Celery), bag of Mixed Pickling spices, dry Mustard, Pennyroyal, Rosemary, Rue, Shallots for Onions, Sage powder, Tansy, fresh Thyme leaves, Basil or Garlic Wine vinegar.

Broiled Lamb: fresh and dried Dill leaves.

Try blending various combinations of Garlic, Marjoram, Parsley, Onion, and Thyme.

FOR VEAL

The following seasonings blend well with any veal dish: Peppermint, Saffron, Summer Savory, Soy sauce.

Roast Veal: Basil, Bay, Curry powder, Marjoram, Tarragon Red Wine vinegar, Mixed Herb vinegar.

Veal Stew: Bay or Myrtle leaves, fresh or dried Chervil leaves, Celery salt and seed, Cloves, Curry powder, Garlic and Garlic seed, Juniper berries, Leek, Lovage seed and leaves, Sage powder, Shallots instead of Onions, fresh and dried Thyme leaves, Tarragon Red Wine and Basil White Wine vinegar.

Braised Veal: Lovage seed, Shallots before cooking.

Veal Birds: Sausage Seasoning.

Blend for Veal dishes: Thyme or Marjoram with either Summer Savory or Chervil or both.

FOR PORK

Summer and Winter Savory and fresh Thyme leaves are seasonings that do well as flavoring for all pork dishes.

Roast Pork: Basil, Caraway leaves, Rosemary, Sage, rub Orégano on before roasting, Tarragon Red Wine vinegar.

Pork Spareribs: try Paprika along with the usual salt and pepper.

Ham: Cinnamon stick, Cloves, Coriander seed, Nutmeg, Mace.

Ham Loaf: Rosemary.

OTHERS

Vension: Basil, Bay or Myrtle leaves, Thyme.

Game: Allspice and Juniper berries, Basil, Orégano, Rosemary.

If you are reducing, sauces are rarely recommended by your doctor, since they are essentially flour, butter, and milk with various flavorings. However, if you will cut your daily allowance of the high-calorie ingredients from other meals, an occasional sauce can enliven a dish that might be dull or flat without it.

In an effort to cut down non-protein calories, the use of butter and oil has been cut to a minimum and to make the reducer more conscious of the richness of sauces, their caloric value is given here in tablespoons. Use them sparingly. Or . . . spare the sauce and save the shape.

The basis of many standard sauces is White Sauce. Here we have thin, medium, and thick versions, saving 80 calories a cup by using skim milk instead of whole.

WHITE SAUCE

Ingredients	Thin	Medium	Thick
Skim milk _____cup	1	1	1
or skim-milk powder _____cup	¼	¼	¼
and water _____cup	1	1	1
Flour _____ tablespoons	1	2	3
Salt _____ teaspoon	¼	¼	¼
Butter or fat _____ tablespoons	1	2	3
Calories per tablespoon _____	15	23	31
Calories per cup _____	237	366	495

Pour liquid in pan, add dry ingredients, and beat until smooth. Add fat, and cook over low heat or boiling water until thickened, stirring constantly. Makes 1 cup.

CHEESE SAUCE

Add ½ cup grated cheese to 1 cup White Sauce after it is cooked. Stir until cheese is melted. Adds 223 calories, increase bulk ¼.

EGG SAUCE

Add 1 or 2 hard-cooked eggs, coarsely chopped, to 1 cup White Sauce. Adds 77 calories and increases bulk ⅛ per egg.

HERB WHITE SAUCE

Make thin or medium White Sauce with following variations: Add a pinch of marjoram or thyme to the flour. Cook 2 teaspoons chopped chives and 2 teaspoons chopped parsley in fat before combining with other ingredients. No change in calories.

HORSE-RADISH SAUCE

Add ⅓ cup fresh grated horse-radish to 1 cup, preferably thick, White Sauce. If bottled horse-radish is used, drain well. Adds 150 calories and ⅓ to bulk.

MUSTARD SAUCE

Stir 2 teaspoons prepared mustard into thin or medium White Sauce after cooking.

QUICK CURRY SAUCE

Mix ½ teaspoon curry powder with small amount of White Sauce, add remainder of 1 cup of sauce. Stir over hot water to blend.

PARSLEY SAUCE

Add 2 or more tablespoons fine-chopped parsley and season with a few drops of onion juice to 1 cup White Sauce. No change in calories.

PICKLE SAUCE

Mix 2 or 3 tablespoons fine-chopped pickles and more salt to 1 cup White Sauce. Does not add enough calories to count, unless sugar-sweetened pickles are used. Then add 13 calories per tablespoon.

PIMENTO SAUCE

Add 2 tablespoons chopped pimento and dash of pepper to 1 cup thin or medium White Sauce.

BROWN MUSHROOM SAUCE

2 calories per tablespoon

1 bouillon or consommé cube
1 cup boiling water
½ cup mushrooms, chopped coarsely
1 teaspoon flour
  salt and fresh-ground black pepper
¼ teaspoon Worcestershire sauce

Dissolve cube or meat extract equivalent in water; simmer mushrooms 5 minutes if raw, until warmed if cooked or canned. Add flour that has been moistened into a paste with cold water. Season with salt, pepper, and Worcestershire sauce. Makes about 1½ cups.

Miss Llewellyn Miller, the peripatetic author of the *Reducing Cook Book*, created a sauce base that is smooth as cream, thick as medium White Sauce, and lower in calories. It contains no fat or flour.

CREAMY SAUCE BASE
16 calories per tablespoon

1 cup double-strength skim milk
2 egg yellows, well beaten
dash of cayenne
½ teaspoon salt or less to taste

Blend together. Double-strength skim milk contains 6 tablespoons of milk powder per cup instead of 3. Either cook the sauce in a double boiler, stirring constantly until thickened, or in a small pan over very low heat, stirring briskly and constantly. In either case, keep over warm (not boiling) water until served. Unless stirred constantly while cooking and kept below boiling point, this sauce will curdle. Makes 18 tablespoons.

WHITE MUSHROOM SAUCE
10 calories per tablespoon

½ cup canned or cooked mushrooms
¼ teaspoon Worcestershire sauce

1 cup thin White Sauce
salt and pepper

Chop mushrooms coarsely, add Worcestershire and White sauces, season, and simmer 5 minutes. Makes about 1½ cups.

VELOUTE SAUCE
10 calories per tablespoon

Makes as above, except use undiluted canned bouillon instead of milk and omit salt and pepper.

For vegetable or fish dishes.

SAUCE AUX FINES HERBES No. 1
10 calories per tablespoon

4 teaspoons butter
1 tablespoon chopped onion
2 teaspoons flour
1 cup stock (vegetable or fish, depending on dish)
1 teaspoon parsley, minced
½ teaspoon tarragon, minced
¼ teaspoon basil, minced
¼ teaspoon marjoram, minced
few drops basil or tarragon vinegar

Heat half the butter in heavy skillet. Add onion, and cook, stirring constantly, until onion begins to color. Stir in flour and blend well. Gradually add stock and stir constantly 4 minutes. Add fresh seasonings (or ¼ as much dried) and cook 4 minutes more. Then add remainder of butter and vinegar. Makes 18 tablespoons.

A hot sauce for meats or fowl.

SAUCE AUX FINES HERBES No. 2
8 calories per tablespoon

- 4 teaspoons butter
- 1 tablespoon chopped onion
- 4 teaspoons minced celery
- 1 teaspoon parsley, minced
- ½ teaspoon marjoram, minced
- ½ teaspoon fresh sage, minced
- ½ teaspoon chervil, minced
- ½ teaspoon fennel, minced
- ½ cup cider vinegar
- ½ cup water

Heat half the butter in heavy skillet. Add onion, and cook, stirring constantly, until onion begins to color. Add all the seasonings and mix well. Add vinegar and water and allow to simmer 10 minutes. Salt and pepper can be added to taste. Add remainder of butter, and stir well. Serve hot. Makes about 18 tablespoons.

TOMATO SAUCE
9 calories per tablespoon

- ¼ cup sliced onions
- 1 tablespoon fat
- ¼ cup skim-milk powder
- 2 tablespoons flour
- 2 cups cooked or canned tomatoes, with juice
- salt and pepper

Cook onions in fat until very tender. Mix milk powder and flour thoroughly; add tomatoes (chopped or put through sieve, if desired) gradually, stirring until smooth. Add mixture to onions and cook over low heat or boiling water until it thickens, stirring constantly. Season to taste. Makes 2½ cups.

Add water if a thinner sauce is desired.

QUICK TOMATO SAUCE
10 calories per tablespoon

- 1 can condensed tomato soup, undiluted
- 1 bay leaf
- ½ teaspon thyme
- pinch of rosemary
- parsley flakes

Heat soup with bay leaf, thyme, and rosemary. Remove bay leaf and serve, garnishing with parsley flakes. Makes more than 20 tablespoons.

KING CRAB COCKTAIL SAUCE
30 calories per serving

- 2 tablespoons Low-Calorie Mayonnaise
- 1 tablespoon chili sauce
- 1 teaspoon lemon juice

Mix all ingredients together. Use for crab, lobster, shrimp, meat. Serves 1.

This is a cold sauce for sea-food cocktails or with pan-fried, sautéed, or broiled fish. And try it as a salad dressing also.

LOUIS SAUCE
10 calories per tablespoon

- 1 cup Low-Calorie Mayonnaise
- ¼ cup Low-Calorie French dressing
- ¼ cup catsup
- 1½ teaspoons Lea & Perrins Worcestershire sauce
- ¼ teaspoon each salt and pepper

Mix well and chill. Makes 24 tablespoons.

SEA-FOOD COCKTAIL SAUCE No. 1
13 calories per tablespoon

- ½ cup catsup
- 2 tablespoons lemon juice or vinegar
- 1 tablespoon grated onion orie Mayonnaise or salad dressing
- 1 teaspoon Worcestershire sauce
- 2 tablespoons Low Calorie
- ¼ teaspoon salt dash pepper or Tabasco sauce

Combine all ingredients and chill. Makes 13 tablespoons.

SEA-FOOD COCKTAIL SAUCE No. 2
12 calories per tablespoon

- ¾ cup chili sauce
- ¼ cup finely chopped celery

- 1 tablespoon lemon juice or vinegar
- 1 tablespoon horse-radish
- ½ teaspoon salt

Combine all ingredients and chill. Makes 18 tablespoons.

OYSTER COCKTAIL SAUCE
28 calories per serving

- juice ½ lemon
- ½ teaspoon vinegar
- 1 tablespoon tomato catsup several drops Tabasco
- ½ teaspoon grated horse-radish
- ½ teaspoon Worcestershire sauce

Mix well. Serves 1. Use tomato juice and cut calories to half.

LEMON-CUCUMBER SAUCE
5 calories per tablespoon

- ½ lemon, peeled
- 1 cucumber, peeled
- 1 small onion, peeled
- 1 cup Almost Mayonnaise
- ½ teaspoon salt
- ¼ teaspoon dry mustard
- ¼ teaspoon Worcestershire sauce pinch of thyme and cayenne pepper

Put lemon, cucumber, and onion through coarse blade of food grinder. Combine with the other ingredients and chill. For fish and fried sea food. Makes 45 tablespoons.

Another version of this sauce, with a more bland taste, follows.

CUCUMBER COLD FISH SAUCE
5 calories per tablespoon

1 cup diced unpeeled cucumber
2 tablespoons lemon juice
1 teaspoon onion salt
¼ teaspoon celery salt

Place everything in blender or fast mixer for about 30 seconds, until cucumber is smooth, with fine flecks of green. Then take

⅓ cup yogurt
⅓ cup Low Calorie Mayonnaise

Mix together in bowl, then combine with cucumber mixture and chill. Makes about 1½ cups.

For Poached Cod à la Stockholm and other fish dishes try this sharp sauce.

VINAIGRETTE SAUCE
2 calories per tablespoon

1 tablespoon cucumber or low calorie sweet pickles, chopped
1 tablespoon green pepper, chopped
2 teaspoons capers, chopped
2 teaspoons fine-chopped parsley
1 teaspoon prepared mustard
2 tablespoons cider vinegar

1 tablespoon tarragon vinegar
1 teaspoon salt
few grains pepper
3 tablespoons water

Combine all ingredients. Mix well. Heat if desired. Makes more than ½ cup.

Also see Tartar Sauce in Fish section.

QUICK CHEESE SAUCE
64 calories per serving

This sauce needs no cooking. Blend ½ cup grated cheese (preferably Cheddar type) with 1 cup yogurt and ½ teaspoon white pepper. Serves 6 (4 tablespoons each).

For Spanish omelets or over pastas.

BRAZILIAN SAUCE
7 calories per tablespoon

¼ cup water
1 cup quartered tomatoes
1 green pepper, coarsely diced
1 small onion, sliced
1 teaspoon salt
½ cup coarsely diced celery
1 tablespoon butter
1 tablespoon Worcestershire sauce

Put everything except Worcestershire sauce into Hollywood Liquefier or other electric blender and run at high speed 20 seconds. Pour into saucepan and simmer 20 minutes. Add Worcestershire sauce. Makes 2 cups.

ONION-CELERY SAUCE
14 calories per tablespoon

1 medium-size onion
½ cup diced celery
½ cup water
⅓ cup Starlac or other
  skim-milk powder
1 tablespoon flour
½ teaspoon salt
  dash of pepper

Slice onion; separate into rings. Cook onion rings and celery together in boiling water until tender—about 10 minutes. Drain thoroughly. Pour water into top of double boiler. Combine milk powder, flour, salt, and pepper. Sprinkle over surface of water. Beat with rotary beater until blended and smooth. Stir in cooked onions and celery. Place over hot water and cook, stirring constantly, until mixture has thickened. Makes 1 cup.

For barbecuing hamburgers, chicken, and frankfurters.

BARBECUE SAUCE
12 calories per tablespoon

1 saccharin or Sucaryl
  tablet
3 tablespoons cider vinegar
3 tablespoons butter or
  margarine
1 tablespoon grated
  onion
1½ teaspoons mashed
  garlic

3 tablespoons Worcestershire sauce
¾ teaspoon salt
½ cup water
½ teaspoon paprika
½ cup tomato purée
½ teaspoon chili powder
3 drops Tabasco sauce
1 tablespoon prepared
  mustard

Mix ingredients in quart saucepan, then cook, stirring until mixture boils. Lower heat, and cook 5 minutes longer. Makes about 2 cups.

To use as a marinade for soaking meats or to dip into just before barbecuing, as well as for basting, here is a sauce with very little fat.

BASTING BARBECUE SAUCE
10 calories per tablespoon

1 medium onion, chopped
1 tablespoon butter, margarine, or cooking oil
¾ teaspoon Sucaryl solution
4 tablespoons lemon juice
  or vinegar
½ cup chopped celery
1 cup canned or cooked
  tomatoes
1 tablespoon Worcestershire sauce
1 teaspoon chili powder
½ teaspoon dry mustard
  dash of cayenne pepper
½ cup water

Simmer all the ingredients together over a low flame 30 minutes. Makes 1½ cups.

HURRY-UP BARBECUE SAUCE
5 calories per tablespoon

1 cup tomato purée
1 cup tomato juice
juice of 1 lemon
2 teaspoons prepared mustard
1 teaspoon dry mustard
½ cup fine-chopped scallions
1 teaspoon tarragon
2 crushed garlic cloves
1½ teaspoons salt
1 teaspoon fresh-ground black pepper

Combine ingredients, shake vigorously, and use. Makes 2½ cups.

Substituting tomato catsup for purée increases calories to 9 per tablespoon.

Also, see Hot Barbecue Sauce in Poultry section.

QUICK MINT SAUCE
2 calories per tablespoon

½ teaspoon salt
4 teaspoons Mintit
½ cup cider vinegar
½ teaspoon Sucaryl solution

Dissolve salt in other ingredients; mix well in saucepan. Heat to boiling point, remove, and serve hot with hot dishes, cool with cold meats. Makes 8 tablespoons.

DRIED MINT SAUCE
2 calories per tablespoon

¼ cup water
3 tablespoons cider or distilled vinegar
⅔ teaspoon Sucaryl solution or 6 tablets dissolved
3 tablespoons dried mint leaves

Heat water in small saucepan, add vinegar and Sucaryl, and bring to boil. Add dried mint leaves and turn flame out, leaving pan over burner. Cover tightly and steep leaves 12 minutes. Makes 8 tablespoons.

FRESH MINT SAUCE
2 calories per tablespoon

¼ cup fresh mint leaves
½ cup cider vinegar
⅓ teaspoon Sucaryl solution or 3 tablets

Wash leaves well, remove stems, chop with sharp knife, and put in small saucepan. Mix vinegar and Sucaryl, pour over mint leaves, and keep heated barely lukewarm for about 1 hour. Cool. Serve cold. Makes 10 to 12 teaspoons.

If the following raisin sauce were made with sugar it would have 3 times the calories. For poultry or ham.

RAISIN SAUCE DE LUXE
34 calories per serving

1 tablespoon cornstarch
¼ teaspoon cinnamon
⅛ teaspoon cloves
1½ cups water
2 teaspoons Sucaryl solution
1 tablespoon vinegar
½ cup seedless raisins

Place cornstarch, cinnamon,

and cloves in saucepan. Combine water, Sucaryl, and vinegar; add a small amount to the cornstarch mixture to make a smooth paste. Gradually add remaining liquid. Cook over low heat, stirring constantly, until mixture thickens. Remove from heat and add raisins. Let stand 10 minutes. Reheat over low flame, stirring constantly. Makes 8 servings 2 ounces each.

For puddings and custards, either served hot or cold.

SWEET SPICED SAUCE
2 calories per teaspoon

⅛ teaspoon cinnamon
⅛ teaspoon allspice
⅛ teaspoon nutmeg
⅛ teaspoon mace
2 teaspoons flour
1 cup boiling water
1½ tablespoons Sucaryl solution
1 teaspoon vanilla extract

Blend all dry ingredients in top section of double boiler. Place over hot water. Make a paste by adding small quantity of the boiling water, then gradually stir in remainder, a little at a time. Add Sucaryl, and blend well. Cook until sauce thickens— 8 to 10 minutes. Add vanilla. If serving cold, cool sauce before adding vanilla. Makes about 10 tablespoons.

This is a distinctive topping over fresh or canned fruits and on puddings.

DANNON'S SHERRY SAUCE
13 calories per tablespoon

4 egg yellows, slightly beaten
Sucaryl or other non-caloric sweetener to taste
¼ teaspoon salt
1 cup skim milk
1 jar Dannon or other yogurt (1 cup)
6 tablespoons California sherry
nutmeg

Combine eggs, Sucaryl, and salt in the top part of double boiler. Stir in the milk and place over hot water, not boiling, and cook, stirring constantly, until mixture coats the spoon. Cool. Add yogurt and sherry. Beat with a rotary beater until well blended. Chill and serve, adding a sprinkle of nutmeg. Makes 42 tablespoons.

QUICK STRAWBERRY SAUCE
6 calories per tablespoon

1 pint fresh strawberries, hulls removed
1 tablespoon Sucaryl solution

Place in Waring or other blender and blend until nearly smooth—about 5 seconds. Chill in refrigerator until ready to use. Makes 1 cup.

PINEAPPLE SAUCE
6 calories per tablespoon

½ cup unsweetened crushed pineapple
½ cup water
1 teaspoon Sucaryl solution
2 teaspoons cornstarch
¼ teaspoon salt
1 teaspoon butter

Put pineapple and water in saucepan. Stir in Sucaryl, cornstarch, and salt. Cook over high heat until mixture boils, about 3 minutes, stirring constantly. Add buter. Excellent with baked ham. Makes 1 cup.

See Pineapple Glazed Carrots in Vegetable section for another pineapple sauce recipe.

_____

Maple syrup contains about 28 calories per tablespoon. Here's a sauce that answers the purpose and has only 3 calories per tablespoon.

MAPLE-FLAVORED SAUCE
3 calories per tablespoon

2 tablespoons cornstarch
¼ teaspoon salt
1 teaspoon Sucaryl solution
1 cup water
1½ teaspoons maple flavoring

Combine the cornstarch and salt in the top of a double boiler. Mix Sucaryl with the water and maple flavoring. Add a small amount of the liquid to the cornstarch to make a paste, then add rest of liquid. Cook and stir over boiling water until thickened. Serve warm over baked custard, ice cream, etc. (Sauce becomes very thick when cool.) Makes 16 tablespoons.

Store in refrigerator. Do not keep more than a few days.

_____

CRANBERRY SAUCE
3 calories per tablespoon

2 cups cranberries
½ cup water
1½ tablespoons Sucaryl solution

Select ripe cranberries and wash well. Boil water, then add Sucaryl and cranberries. Cover par and cook until cranberries stop popping —about 10 minutes. Skim off top if necessary. Pour into dish and let cool before serving. Makes about 32 tablespoons.

_____

Now a quick way to fix cranberries without cooking.

CRANBERRY RELISH
4½ calories per tablespoon

1 pound cranberries
1 orange, unpeeled
1 apple, unpeeled
1½ tablespoons Sucaryl solution

Grind all the fruit together. Add the Sucaryl and mix thoroughly. Serve as a sauce to garnish holiday meats. Makes 5 cups.

DIET WHIPPED CREAM
5 calories per tablespoon
½ cup water
1 teaspoon Sucaryl solution or 2 teaspoons Sacrose
½ teaspoon vanilla
1 tablespoon lemon juice
½ cup nonfat dry milk

Combine water, sweetener, vanilla, and lemon juice in 1-quart bowl. Sprinkle dry milk over top. Beat with rotary or electric beater until stiff — about 15 minutes. Chill. Whips up into 2½ cups.

LOW-FAT WHIPPED TOPPING
8 calories per tablespoon
2 saccharin or Sucaryl tablets
¼ cup evaporated milk
1½ teaspoons lemon juice
¼ teaspoon grated lemon rind

Dissolve the sweetener in a little of the milk, heated; mix into remainder of milk; put in ice tray of refrigerator. Chill until ice crystals begin to form around edges. Put milk into small, cold bowl and whip with chilled rotary beater or electric mixer at high speed until fluffy. Then add lemon juice and rind and continue whipping until stiff. Serve as topping on fruit gelatines or puddings or other desserts that blend with lemon flavor of topping. Makes about ¾ cup.

Also see Whipped Topping with Orange Cheese Pie in Cakes, Cookies, Pies, and Breads chapter.

Also see Chili Sauce in Preserves section; Custard Sauce in Puddings and Custards section; Soft Custard Sauce in Dessert section.

PREPARED SAUCES

The world's greatest chef within living memory was Auguste Escoffier (1846-1934) who created Peach Melba, Cherries Jubilee, and a number of other dishes, as well as the Escoffier sauces. The three favorites among these are Sauce Diable, Sauce Robert, and Sauce Melba. Although they are expensive and not low in calories, they are so concentrated that a little will add a great deal of flavor to prosaic foods. The Robert is 21 calories per tablespoon and is equally good with fish and meat. The Diable, 22 calories per tablespoon, is for steaks, chops, and poultry. Sauce Melba, 38 calories per tablespoon, is for desserts and should be served only on great occasions, as when the dieter discovers for the first time that the desired weight has been reached.

SAUCE SEASONINGS

In addition to the usual spices in your sauces here

are more suggestions: Balm leaves, Cayenne, Curry powder, Garlic, Lemon and Lime juice, Mint, dry Mustard, Paprika, sweet, vinegar and Dill Pickles, Poppy and Sesame seed, Thyme, Worcestershire sauce.

Sauces for Meats: Bay leaves, Capers, Ginger, Horse-radish, Rosemary, Sage, fresh or dried Tansy, Turmeric, Basil vinegar.

Sauces for Beef: Juniper berries.

Sauces for Veal and Poultry: Summer and Winter Savory.

For Barbecue Sauces: Caraway.

Sauces for Fish: Capers, Dill seed, Horse-radish, Mace, fresh or dried Tansy, Turmeric.

For Sea-food Cocktails: Basil, Chili powder, Horse-radish.

Tartar Sauce: Dill, Mustard, Parsley.

Sauces for Vegetables: Rosemary.

Spaghetti Sauce: Basil, Orégano.

Vinaigrette: Shallots.

Tomato Sauce: ground Allspice gives it pep, Basil, Bay leaves, Marjoram, a dash of Orégano, crushed or ground Red Pepper.

Chili Sauce: ground Cloves.

Mushroom Sauce: Marjoram, Orégano.

GRAVY SEASONINGS

Whole Allspice, Beef Extract adds piquancy, Worcestershire sauce.

Pan Gravy: add a pinch of crushed or ground Red Pepper.

Curries: Saffron, Turmeric, pulverized Marigold in addition to Curry powder.

Ground Cloves combine well with Bay, Thyme, and Lemon in sauces and gravies.

The big problem here is to avoid the use of oil (110 calories to the tablespoon) in all dressings and flour, cream, and sour cream in the mayonnaise and other creamy types. Fortunately it is possible to solve this problem, as the large variety of dressings that follows can prove.

One warning—do not use mineral oil in salad dressings. This was a practice among dieters for some years, until it was learned that mineral oil, while free of calories, was harmful from a nutritional view, because as it passed through, it robbed the body of valuable vitamins.

The four main components in reducing diet dressings are vinegar, tomatoes, seasonings, and yogurt. Caloric calculations for the yogurt are at the old figure of 160 per cup. If the skim-milk variety, like Dannon yogurt in New York, is available, the calorie count is 120 per cup.

SIMPLE SALAD DRESSING   3 calories per tablespoon

½ cup tomato juice
4 tablespoons wine vinegar
1 tablespoon finely minced onion
salt and pepper

Combine and shake well. Keep refrigerated. For variations add either 1 tablespoon finely minced green pepper, 1 tablespoon finely minced leek or mustard or Worcestershire sauce. Makes 13 tablespoons.

JIFFY SALAD DRESSING
1½ calories per teaspoon

clove of garlic
pinch of salt and paprika
¼ teaspoon dry mustard
2 tablespoons vinegar
1 teaspoon tomato catsup
(or walnut or Worcestershire sauce)
1 teaspoon chopped chives or parsley

Rub salad bowl with garlic. Mix salt, paprika, and mustard together. Add vinegar, catsup, and chives, blending thoroughly. Makes 8 teaspoons.

Since this dressing contains cheese, it will not keep like a commercial product. Make only enough for 2 or 3 days' use and store in refrigerator.

LOW-CALORIE DRESSING
8 calories per tablespoon

1 cup skim-milk cottage cheese
1 cucumber, 7 to 8 inches long
3 tablespoons fresh lemon juice
⅓ cup skim milk
½ teaspoon salt
⅛ teaspoon freshly ground black pepper

Press cottage cheese through sieve. Peel, seed, and chop cucumber very fine. Add remaining ingredients. This

dressing may be mixed entirely in an electric blender. Chill. Shake before serving. Makes more than 1 pint.

GOLDEN SALAD DRESSING
2 calories per tablespoon

1 teaspoon tomato catsup
½ teaspoon onion juice
¼ teaspoon paprika
1 tablet saccharin
pinch black pepper
¼ teaspoon salt
½ cup cider vinegar
¼ cup water
5 drops orange food color

You may vary saccharin to taste or substitute Sucaryl. Mix all ingredients in stoppered container and shake vigorously. Preserve in refrigerator in tightly covered jar. Shake well before using. Makes 13 tablespoons.

TANGY DRESSING
4 calories per tablespoon

2 tablespoons diced onion
½ cup tomato juice
1 teaspoon Worcestershire sauce
3 tablespoons lemon juice
½ teaspoon celery salt

Place ingredients in glass container of Waring or other electric blender. Blend until smooth—about 15 seconds. Makes ¾ cup.

FRENCH DRESSING SUBSTITUTE
2 calories per tablespoon

1 cup vinegar
½ teaspoon paprika
½ teaspoon salt
½ teaspoon prepared mustard
⅛ teaspoon cayenne
1 Sucaryl tablets, dissolved

Combine all ingredients and shake well. Try this dressing over hot vegetables as well as with vegetable salad. Makes 1 cup.

VINAIGRETTE DRESSING
4 calories per tablespoon

To the above dressing add the following:

1 teaspoon capers
1 teaspoon minced parsley
1 teaspoon minced chives
1 teaspoon minced dill pickle
1 teaspoon minced green pepper
1 tablespoon minced pimento
1 hard-cooked egg white, chopped

SPICE SEED DRESSING
2 calories per tablespoon

To the French Dressing Substitute above add any of the following or a combination.

Anise seed
Caraway seed
Celery seed
Cumin seed
Dill seed
Light mustard seed

Try soaking the seeds overnight or for several days in the vinegar.

FRENCH HERB DRESSING
2 calories per tablespoon

Add to the French Dressing Substitute the following:

1 teaspoon minced parsley
pinch of orégano
pinch of basil
pinch of thyme

FRUIT JUICE FRENCH DRESSING
2 calories per tablespoon

¼ cup pineapple juice
¼ cup orange juice
1 tablespoon lemon juice
3 tablespoons vinegar
⅛ teaspoon ground clove
3 drops Sucaryl (or other liquid sweetener)
pinch of salt

Place all ingredients in jar with tight-fitting lid and shake well. Keep under refrigeration. Always shake before using. Makes ¾ cup.

MINT FRENCH DRESSING
5 calories per tablespoon

½ cup pineapple juice
¼ cup lemon juice
¼ cup vinegar
1 teaspoon chopped mint leaves or 3 drops Mintit
5 drops Sucaryl (or other liquid sweetener)
⅛ teaspoon dry mustard
pinch salt

Place all ingredients in jar, and shake well. Keep refrigerated. Always shake before using. Makes 1 cup.

Combine all ingredients and shake in jar with tight-fitting lid. Keep refrigerated. Shake before using. Makes 1 cup.

SOUR FRENCH DRESSING
4 calories per tablespoon

⅛ teaspoon dry mustard
⅛ teaspoon salt
   pepper to taste
2 tablespoons vinegar
1 tablespoon lemon juice
¾ cup tomato juice
1 teaspoon Worcestershire sauce
5 drops Sucaryl (or other liquid sweetener)
2 tablespoons very cold skim milk

Combine mustard, salt, and pepper with vinegar and lemon juice; add tomato juice, Worcestershire sauce, and liquid sweetener and mix well. Add milk, a few drops at a time, stirring continuously until well blended. Pour into jar and shake well. Keep under refrigeration. Always shake well before using. Makes 1 cup.

TOMATO FRENCH DRESSING
3 calories per tablespoon

½ cup tomato juice
½ cup vinegar
¼ teaspoon dry mustard
   pinch orégano
⅛ teaspoon garlic powder
6 drops Sucaryl (or other liquid sweetener)
   salt and pepper to taste

TOMATO SOUP FRENCH DRESSING
9 calories per tablespoon

1 clove garlic, crushed
½ teaspoon salt
1 can condensed tomato soup (11 ounces)
¼ teaspoon rosemary
1 bay leaf, crushed
6 tablespoons lemon juice

Combine garlic and salt; add to tomato soup. Add rosemary and bay leaf. Thin soup to desired consistency with lemon juice. An excellent dressing for green salads. Makes 1¾ cups.

FIVE-CALORIE FRENCH DRESSING
5 calories per tablespoon

2 tablespoons fresh lemon juice
2 tablespoons grapefruit juice
½ teaspoon paprika
½ teaspoon salt
¼ teaspoon dry mustard
2 Sucaryl tablets, dissolved
2 drops Mintit

Combine all ingredients and shake well. Makes 4 tablespoons.

NO-CAL SALAD DRESSING

9 calories per tablespoon

½ cup condensed tomato soup

½ cup No-Cal or other non-caloric ginger ale

¼ teaspoon salt

¾ tablespoon grated onion

⅛ teaspoon pepper

3 tablespoons cider vinegar

1 teaspoon dry mustard

⅛ teaspoon Worcestershire sauce

⅛ teaspoon garlic salt

Blend all ingredients together. Serve with fruit, vegetable, or gelatine salads. Makes 20 tablespoons.

WHIRLING WARING TOMATO DRESSING

3 calories per tablespoon

⅔ cup diced, peeled, and seeded tomatoes

1 small clove garlic (optional)

½ teaspoon salt

⅛ teaspoon pepper

⅛ teaspoon dry mustard

2 tablespoons lemon juice

2 leaves fresh basil, tarragon, or parsley

Place all ingredients in glass container of Waring Blendor. Cover, and blend until smooth—about 30 seconds. Makes about ¾ cup.

Real mayonnaise contains 92 calories per tablespoon.

ALMOST-MAYONNAISE DRESSING

8½ calories per tablespoon

½ teaspoon dry mustard

½ teaspoon salt

1 tablespoon flour

½ teaspoon celery seed

½ cup skim milk

1 clove garlic (optional)

1 egg yellow, beaten

3 tablespoons vinegar

2 drops Sucaryl (or other liquid sweetener)

pinch of Ac'cent (monosodium glutamate)

Combine mustard, salt, flour, and celery seed in top of double boiler. Add milk slowly, while stirring, until thickened. Add clove of garlic if desired, cover, and cook 8 minutes. Add egg yellow and cook 3 minutes, stirring continuously. Remove from heat and take out clove of garlic. Stir in vinegar, sweetener, and Ac'cent. Stir well. Chill before using. Keep in refrigerator. Makes slightly less than 1 cup.

COOKED SALAD DRESSING

10 calories per tablespoon

2 tablespoons flour

¾ teaspoon Sucaryl solution

1 teaspoon prepared mustard

1¼ teaspoons salt

dash of cayenne pepper (optional)

1 cup water

6 tablespoons lemon juice

2 eggs, slightly beaten

Combine flour, Sucaryl, mustard, salt, cayenne pepper,

and water in top of double boiler. Cook over boiling water, stirring constantly, until thickened — about 20 minutes. Remove from heat. Gradually stir lemon juice into the beaten eggs. Then gradually add the lemon-egg mixture to the cooked ingredients, stirring constantly. Return to heat, and cook, while stirring, over hot but not boiling water, until thickened, about 20 minutes. Remove from heat, and cool. Store, covered, in refrigerator and use as needed. Makes 1½ cups dressing.

FRENCH MUSTARD DRESSING
2¼ calories per tablespoon

1¼ cups water
2 tablespoons cornstarch
½ cup vinegar
1 tablespoon dry French mustard
½ teaspoon celery salt
¼ teaspoon salt

Add water slowly to cornstarch. Blend until smooth. Cook over low heat until thickened, stirring constantly. Add remaining ingredients. Beat well with rotary beater. Refrigerate in jar with tight-fitting cover. Shake well before using. Makes about 2 cups.

HERB SALAD DRESSING
4 calories per tablespoon

1 egg
2 tablespoons flour

1 tablespoon dry mustard
¼ tablespoon marjoram
¼ tablespoon rosemary
1½ cups water
½ cup vinegar
1½ teaspoons Sucaryl solution (12 tablets, dissolved)

Beat egg thoroughly. Combine dry ingredients; add to beaten egg. Add water, vinegar, and Sucaryl solution, beating well. Cook over low heat, stirring constantly, until mixture comes to a boil. Remove from heat. Cool. Makes 32 tablespoons.

LOW-CALORIE MAYONNAISE
5 calories per tablespoon

1 teaspoon plain gelatine
1 teaspoon salt
½ teaspoon paprika
¼ teaspoon dry mustard
⅛ teaspoon cayenne
¾ cup cold skim milk
2 tablespoons lemon juice

Soften gelatine in ⅛ cup cold water and dissolve over hot water. Combine all ingredients and chill until half thick. Then beat until fluffy with a wire whisk beater. Jell until quite firm; then beat again, and store in refrigerator until needed. Just before serving, stir vigorously, thinning with milk or lemon according to taste. Makes 1 cup.

A different way to make this type of dressing follows.

LOW-CALORIE MAYONNAISE WITH EGG

13 calories per tablespoon

½ teaspoon salt
¼ teaspoon paprika
¼ teaspoon dry mustard
⅛ teaspoon cayenne
2 tablespoons vinegar
¼ cup skim milk
1 egg, beaten

Put all the ingredients together in a thick mixing bowl about 6 inches wide. Put the mixing bowl in an iron skillet filled with hot water. While beating constantly with a wire rotary whisk beater, bring the water just to a boil. The dressing will thicken after about 4 minutes of constant beating over hot water. Pour it immediately into a jar, cover, and chill. When cold, it will be quite thick. Use the same day. Makes ½ cup.

If this dressing is too sharp, use 1 tablespoon vinegar and 5 tablespoons milk. Or use lemon juice instead of vinegar.

Or whip in ¼ cup yogurt after the dressing is chilled. Makes ¾ cup and calories remain the same.

For old-fashioned "sweet-and-sour" taste, add ¼ teaspoon Sucaryl solution.

A DOZEN YOGURT DRESSINGS

Creamy lower-calorie salad toppings can be made with yogurt in a variety of different flavors. Here are 12, each one different in character.

___

YOGURTAISE DRESSING

11 calories per tablespoon

1 egg yellow
¾ cup yogurt
½ teaspoon dry mustard
¼ teaspoon salt
   pinch cayenne pepper
   pinch paprika
1 tablespoon vinegar
1 drop Sucaryl solution or Sweeta

Beat egg yellow well. Combine with other ingredients and mix well. Chill before using. Keep in refrigerator. Makes almost 1 cup.

___

999 ISLAND DRESSING

14 calories per tablespoon

1 cup Yogurtaise (see above)
1 hard-cooked egg, chopped
1 teaspoon chopped pimento
1 teaspoon minced onion
2 tablespoons chili sauce

Combine all ingredients and mix well. Chill before serving. Makes 1⅜ cups.

MOCK MUSTARD MAYONNAISE
14 calories per tablespoon

Blend 1 cup yogurt with 3 tablespoons prepared mustard and a dash of Worcestershire sauce. Excellent with meat or cooked vegetable salads. Makes 18 tablespoons.

TASTY SALAD DRESSING
10 calories per serving

1 cup yogurt
¼ teaspoon each of garlic powder, paprika, chopped caraway
½ teaspoon chopped parsley
salt and pepper to taste

Mix seasonings into yogurt and blend very well. Cover jar tightly and chill for at least 8 hours before use. Covered and stored in upper part of refrigerator, it will keep 1 week. Makes 16 tablespoons.

Next a similar but sweeter mixture.

CREAMY SALAD DRESSING
11 calories per tablespoon

1 cup yogurt
¼ teaspoon honey
¼ teaspoon each of paprika, basil, marjoram
salt to taste
Same directions as above.

SNAPPY LOW-FAT SALAD DRESSING
13 calories per tablespoon

½ pint yogurt (1 cup)
½ cup chili sauce

1 tablespoon prepared horse-radish
1 tablespoon grated onion
1 teaspoon prepared mustard
few drops Tabasco sauce
1 teaspoon Worcestershire sauce
1 Sucaryl tablet, disolved

Combine all ingredients. Mix thoroughly. Chill. For mixed greens, vegetable, meat, or fish salads. Makes 1½ cups.

This next one is a favorite of Earl Wilson.

WHIPPED YOGURT DRESSING
8 calories per tablespoon

¼ cup coarsely diced onion
½ clove garlic (optional)
¼ cup celery leaves
¼ cup parsley leaves
1 teaspoon salt
¼ teaspoon Sucaryl solution
1 tablespoon tomato paste
1 cup yogurt

Place all ingredients in glass container of Waring or other electric blender in order indicated. Cover container and run until smoothly blended — about 1 minute. Pour over crisp salad greens and toss lightly. Makes 1½ cups.

Now, one in which the other ingredients are first cooked.

YOGURT DRESSING
10 calories per serving

1 teaspoon salt
¼ teaspoon paprika
¼ teaspoon dry mustard
¼ cup skim milk
2 tablespoons vinegar
1 egg yellow
   dash of Tabasco sauce
½ cup yogurt

Cook all ingredients with the exception of the yogurt in the top of a double boiler, stirring constantly, until the dressing thickens. Chill. When cold, stir in the yogurt. Makes 1 cup.

PIQUANT CHEESE DRESSING
15 calories per tablespoon

1 cup yogurt
½ cup tomato juice
2 tablespoons scraped onion
1 tablespoon lemon juice
½ teaspoon salt
   dash Worcestershire sauce
3 tablespoons Roquefort or other sharp cheese, crumbled

Combine all ingredients except cheese and beat until well blended. Add the cheese. Serve with vegetables, eggs, fish, or meat. Makes 1½ cups.

CLARET SALAD DRESSING
15 calories per serving

½ clove garlic
1 teaspoon salt
1 teaspoon paprika
   dash Tabasco sauce
1½ tablespoons California claret wine
1 jar Dannon or other yogurt (½ pint)
1 tablespoon salad oil

Rub inside of mixing bowl with garlic. Add rest of ingredients and beat with a fork thoroughly to blend the flavors. Makes 1¼ cups.

CRANBERRY-YOGURT SALAD DRESSING
4 calories per tablespoon

½ cup fresh cranberries
½ small lemon
   Sucaryl solution to taste
1 cup yogurt

Put cranberries and lemon through food chopper. Blend in sweetener. Fold cranberry mixture into yogurt. Chill in refrigerator. Serve as dressing with fruit and other salads. Makes 26 tablespoons.

CREAM FRUIT DRESSING
9 calories per tablespoon

Blend 1 cup yogurt with 2 or 3 tablespoons fruit juice (pineapple, orange, or other fruit juice); season to taste with Sucaryl or other noncaloric sweetener, ¼ teaspoon cinnamon, and ⅛ teaspoon mace. Makes 18 tablespoons.

Here are 3 vinegar dressings that are particularly suitable for tossed green salads.

VINEGAR SALAD DRESSING
2 calories per tablespoon

1 cup vinegar
saccharin, Sugarine, or
Sucaryl to taste
½ teaspoon dry mustard
½ teaspoon salt
½ teaspoon paprika

Dissolve sweetener in vinegar and add other ingredients. Place in jar and shake well. Makes 1 cup.

SOY-VINEGAR DRESSING
5 calories per tablespoon

½ cup garlic vinegar
¼ teaspoon soy sauce
1 teaspoon olive oil
¼ teaspoon paprika
salt and pepper

Combine soy sauce with vinegar and stir well. Stir in olive oil. Add Paprika, salt and pepper to taste. Pour in jar and shake well. Keep refrigerated. Shake before using. Makes ½ cup.

SHARP SALAD DRESSING
3 calories per tablespoon

½ cup cider vinegar
¼ teaspoon paprika
Sucaryl or saccharin to taste
½ teaspoon salt
1 clove garlic, grated
1 tablespoon onion, grated

Shake well together. Makes 9 tablespoons.

ROYAL SALAD DRESSING
5 calories per tablespoon

1 tablespoon minced parsley
1 tablespoon minced pimento
½ cup skim milk
¼ teaspoon paprika
1 tablespoon lemon juice
1 teaspoon onion juice

Place all ingredients in stoppered container and shake vigorously. Must be prepared fresh each time. Makes 12 tablespoons.

FRUIT SALAD DRESSING
5 calories per tablespoon

1 clove minced garlic
¼ cup cider vinegar
½ cup unstrained orange juice
¼ teaspoon paprika
saccharin or Sucaryl to taste
½ teaspoon salt
1 teaspoon black pepper

Let garlic stand in vinegar for 1 hour. Strain. Add rest of ingredients. Shake or beat well. Chill. Shake each time before using. Makes 12 tablespoons.

ORANGE SALAD DRESSING
12 calories per tablespoon

2 tablespoons flour
½ teaspoon salt
¼ teaspoon dry mustard
1 cup orange juice
¼ cup lemon juice
2 teaspoons Sucaryl solution
2 egg yellows, beaten

Combine flour, salt, and mustard in top of double boiler. Combine orange juice, lemon juice, Sucaryl, and egg yellows; add gradually to the flour mixture. Cook over boiling water, stirring constantly, until mixture thickens. Remove from heat; cool. Makes 24 tablespoons.

PREPARED DRESSINGS

Commercial salad dressings mixed especially for the low-calorie dieter are gaining in number and distribution constantly. A list of 21 varieties appears in the Dietetic and Low-Calorie Food Products section.

In addition, the Good Seasons Salad Dressing Mixes may be utilized for very low-calorie dressings by using, instead of the 5 ounces of oil called for, such substitutes as tomato and V-8 juice, apricot and pear nectar, apple or pineapple juice.

And lemon juice can be used in place of vinegar to give another change in flavor.

See Sauce section for fish sauces which may be used as dressings for sea-food and fish salads.

SEASONINGS FOR SALAD DRESSINGS

Balm leaves, Basil, Cayenne, Celery seed and salt, Chives, Dill, Garlic and Garlic salt, Horse-radish, Lemon and Lime juice, dry Mustard, Paprika, sweet, Dill, and vinegar Pickles, Sesame seed, any of the herb vinegars.

With French dressings: Chervil, Coriander, Curry powder, dried Tarragon, Tarragon vinegar, Turmeric.

With Low Calorie Mayonnaise and other dressings for fruit salad: Bay, Mace, Nutmeg.

When the early Romans tossed salt on their lettuce, the word "salad" ("sal" is Latin for salt) got its start. Today the salad is the dieter's best friend, being versatile enough for use as a meal starter, a side vegetable, the main course, or dessert.

Since fresh, crisp, dry vegetables and ripe, juicy fruits are the principal components, salads can be inviting, appetizing, and provide satisfying bulk at a low-calorie cost.

And here is a dish where the imagination and invention of the salad mixer is the only limit.

Good equipment helps greatly in the salad department. Most gourmets use a wooden bowl and wooden spoon and fork. Or, if you prefer, there are wood composition sets, also attractive ones in plastic and glass, or china and pottery.

A pepper grinder for fresh-crushed black pepper is another essential. Some people can't do without a little garlic press and others swear by rubbing the bowl with a cut clove of garlic.

There are handy shredders and grinders on the market that reduce the task of slicing or chopping to an easy operation. (See Appliance list.) A little egg-slicer from the 5-and-10 gives you a dozen slices with one operation.

The right dressing is very important to salads, but more important is the right amount. Soggy greens on a salad plate are worse than on a golf course.

If you live on the Pacific coast, where salads are part of everyday eating, you'll probably have your salad before the main course. Back East it serves as a light layer between main course and dessert. You toss your salad and you take your choice.

Henry of the Fairmont in San Francisco is fast becoming the successor to the late Oscar of the Waldorf as the most distinguished *maître d'* in America. However, Henry, unlike Oscar, is very tall and very slender. He attributes his thinness to one of the Fairmont's famous salads.

COQUETTE SALAD
151 calories per serving

shredded lettuce
1 slice unsweetened pineapple
1 tiny artichoke
1 small strip turkey, white meat
4 slices green pepper
4 wedges tomato
2 slices hard-cooked egg

Put thin layer of shredded lettuce on large dinner plate, then place pineapple in center. Wrap turkey white meat slice around small button artichoke and place in center of pineapple. Decorate with green pepper and tomato and garnish with egg. Serves 1.

TOMATO SURPRISE
43 calories per serving

Scoop out the pulp of a medium-sized tomato and mix the pulp with 1 table-spoon chopped celery and 1 tablespoon of cream-type low calorie dressing. Add salt and pepper. Refill the tomato shell with the mixture and serve on crisp lettuce leaves. Serves 1.

STUFFED TOMATO SALAD
48 calories per serving

6 medium-sized tomatoes
½ cup cottage cheese
½ cup grated fresh carrots
2 teaspoons chopped chives
½ teaspoon salt
⅛ teaspoon ground black pepper
lettuce or water cress
parsley for garnish

Wash tomatoes. Scoop out centers (save ¼ cup to mix with the cottage cheese) and drain. Combine cottage cheese, the ¼ cup tomato pulp, carrots, chives, salt, and black pepper. Fill the tomatoes with cheese mixture. Serve on bed of lettuce or water cress. Garnish with a sprig of parsley. Makes 6 servings.

TOMATO CHEESE ROSETTE
101 calories per serving

Peel tomato. Remove stem end. Place tomato upright on cutting board. Cut into 8 wedges, but not all the way through to the bottom. Place on salad greens. Spread wedges apart gently. Spoon ⅓ cup Sealtest or other skim-milk cottage cheese into cen-

ter. Garnish with strip of green pepper. Serves 1.

FLUFFY CARROT RING
48 calories per serving

6 large carrots, grated (about 3 cups)
1 teaspoon lemon juice
1 cup yogurt
   celery salt to taste
1 bunch water cress

Sprinkle carrots with lemon juice. Blend celery salt into yogurt, reserving 2 tablespoons for later garnishing. Fold yogurt into carrots with a light hand, and pile in center of glass platter. Garnish with a ring of water cress, and top salad with remaining yogurt. Serves 6.

HUNGARIAN CUCUMBER SALAD
52 calories per serving

3 small firm cucumbers
2 green peppers
2 medium firm tomatoes
1 teaspoon poppy seeds
1 cup yogurt
½ teaspoon salt
½ teaspoon paprika

Peel cucumbers only if skin is tough; slice cucumbers and peppers; quarter or cube tomatoes. Place all vegetables in salad bowl. Blend yogurt with seasonings, and mix into vegetables. Chill for at least 15 minutes before serving. Serves 6.

FRESH CUCUMBERS IN YOGURT
56 calories per serving

6 medium-sized cucumbers
1 tablespoon cooking salt
1½ cups yogurt
   salt and pepper
1 tablespoon chives, finely chopped

Peel cucumbers, split lengthwise, scoop out seeds with small spoon, slice as thin as possible. Place in chilled bowl, sprinkle with salt, and blend well. Stand in refrigerator 1 hour. Place cucumbers between dry towels and press firmly until free of water. Return to chilled bowl; add yogurt along with salt and pepper to taste. Blend well. Sprinkle with chives. Serves 6.

RAW VEGETABLES AND YOGURT
186 calories per serving

2 medium-sized cucumbers
6 medium-sized carrots
8 radishes
1½ cups yogurt
   juice of ½ lemon (2 tablespoons)
   salt and pepper

Peel cucumbers, split lengthwise; remove seeds with small spoon; slice as thin as possible. Shred carrots through fine shredder, slice radishes as thin as possible. Place vegetables in chilled salad bowl. Add yogurt, lemon juice, salt and pepper

to taste. Mix well. Serves
2 as main dish. As a side
salad, serving 6, it contains
62 calories per portion.

WAGON-WHEEL SALAD
100 calories per serving

1½ cups skim-milk cottage
  cheese
1 cup coarsely grated
  carrot
¼ cup finely chopped
  celery
½ teaspoon celery salt
1 tablespoon finely
  chopped water cress
  salt, onion salt
4 slices tomato
  water cress sprigs

Fold together cottage cheese,
carrot, celery, celery salt,
and chopped water cress.
Season to taste with salt and
onion salt. Place a tomato
slice on each salad plate,
surrounding it with cottage-
cheese mixture. Garnish with
sprigs of water cress. Serves
4.

If you like the manner in
which French restaurants
serve lettuce as a salad and
would like to fix it that way
at home, try the method
used at the Brown Derby
restaurants in California.

WILTED LETTUCE OR
OTHER GREENS
67 calories per portion

4 strips fine-chopped
  bacon
2 tablespoons vinegar
1 dash celery salt

1 tablespoon chopped
  green onions or chives
  juice of 1 lemon
1 Sucaryl tablet
1 pound lettuce, torn in
  small pieces

Sauté bacon in skillet until
brown and crisp. "Stop"
sautéing with vinegar and
keep over heat, adding celery salt, onions, lemon juice,
and Sucaryl. Stir well and
bring to boil. Put well-
drained lettuce in bowl and
pour boiling sauce over.
Cover with plate and allow
to steam 5 to 6 minutes. Remove cover, toss lettuce,
and serve. Serves 4.

Spinach, collards, kale, endive, escarole, beet greens,
mustard greens, turnip
greens, chard, cornsalad
(lamb's lettuce, lamb's quarter), cress, etc., may be
used in place of lettuce.
Soak water cress in cold
water for several hours to
remove bitter taste.

SPRING SALAD BOWL
68 calories per serving

Mix one cup of vegetables
(asparagus tips, celery, cabbage, string beans, or other
non-fattening vegetables)
with 1 tablespoon Low Calorie Mayonnaise. Salt and
pepper to taste. Serve on
crisp lettuce leaves. Serves
1.

GREEN SALAD WITH HERB DRESSING

130 calories

1 clove garlic
salad greens
1 tablespoon olive oil
2 tablespoons garlic vinegar
1 teaspoon grated lemon rind
1 tablespoon chopped parsley
1 teaspoon celery salt
⅛ teaspoon ground black pepper
¼ teaspoon powdered dry mustard
1 teaspoon minced onion
½ teaspoon minced fennel

Rub bowl with garlic. Add salad greens. Add oil and toss 1 to 2 minutes until all greens are thoroughly coated. Add remaining ingredients. Toss again gently until blended. Serves 1.

GROUND GARDEN SALAD

41 calories per serving

1 medium carrot
¼ green pepper
¼ peeled cucumber
2 stalks celery
dash of Mintit (optional)

Run all vegetables through coarse ring of Grind-O-Mat or other food chopper. Mix in several drops of Mintit to give extra-fresh taste. Serves 1.

Add 3 tablespoons Vinegar Salad Dressing, 6 calories, (See page 200) and mix well.

COLESLAW

54 calories per serving

1 small head cabbage
2 carrots
½ cup grated unsweetened pineapple
1 cup yogurt
2 tablespoons garlic vinegar
salt to taste

Shred cabbage on medium shredder; chop carrots. Mix with pineapple, yogurt, vinegar, and salt to taste. Toss lightly. Serves 6.

Here is another way to prepare it.

COLESLAW WITH YOGURT DRESSING

46 calories per serving

3 cups shredded cabbage
2 carrots, shredded
1 cup yogurt
¼ teaspoon salt
¼ teaspoon rosemary
¼ teaspoon onion juice
⅛ teaspoon basil
dash of chili powder

Place cabbage in dry towel and beat well with something heavy (rolling pin, wooden mallet, or milk bottle); this makes cabbage very tender. Blend with shredded carrots. Blend all seasonings into yogurt, and mix well; if desired, the yogurt dressing may be prepared ahead of time and stored, covered, in refrigerator. Mix dressing with cabbage and toss lightly. Serves 6.

SPICY SNAP-BEAN SALAD
95 calories per serving

- 3 cups sliced snap beans, cooked or canned
- 1 cup yogurt
- 2 tablespoons chopped black olives
- 1 canned pimento, chopped
- 1 tablespoon prepared mustard
- 1 teaspoon capers, chopped
- ½ teaspoon salt or garlic salt
- ¼ teaspoon marjoram
- 3 hard-cooked eggs, if desired

Drain beans and blend with all ingredients except eggs. Marinate for at least 30 minutes, then garnish with quartered eggs. Without the eggs, each serving is only 71 calories. Serves 6.

CHEF'S SALAD
217 calories per serving

- 4 cups mixed greens (lettuce, romaine, chicory, escarole, water cress)
- ½ cup diced celery
- ½ cup diced baked ham
- 1 hard-cooked egg, chopped fine
- 1 tablespoon finely chopped parsley

- 1½ tomatoes, cut in quarters
- ½ cup French-type low-calorie dressing

Toss mixed salad greens in a medium-sized ice-cold salad bowl. On top of them sprinkle celery, ham, egg, and parsley. On sides of bowl lay tomatoes. Serve in the bowl with the dressing. Serves 2.

TASTY MEAT SALAD
228 calories per serving

- 3 cups cooked leftover meat (lean beef, poultry)
- 1 cup yogurt
- 1 tablespoon prepared horse-radish
- 1 teaspoon mustard
- ¼ teaspoon marjoram or orégano lettuce cups

Have all ingredients well chilled. Place meat in deep bowl; blend seasonings into yogurt. Mix into meat, and toss. Serve on lettuce cups. Serves 6.

PICNIC SALAD BOWL
163 calories per serving

- 1 cup cooked meat (veal, ham, beef, etc.)
- ⅔ cup grated carrots
- ⅔ cup grated cabbage
- ⅔ cup chopped celery
- ⅓ cup chopped raw apple salt to taste
- 2 tablespoons Low-Calorie French dressing
- 3 tablespoons Low-Calorie Mayonnaise pickle slices

Combine meat and vegetables. Season. Chill in refrigerator. Combine French dressing with mayonnaise and toss with salad just before serving. Serve on lettuce garnished with pickle slices. Serves 4.

TUNA SALAD
198 calories per serving

- 1 6½-ounce can tuna
- 1 tablespoon minced celery
- 1 tablespoon minced dill pickle
  dash of lemon juice
  salt and pepper
- 2 tablespoons Low-Calorie Mayonnaise
- 1 tablespoon minced green pepper
- 1 tablespoon grated carrot

Drain off all excess oil from can of tuna. Break up, and add celery, pickle, lemon juice, and salt and pepper, and mix well with the whipped dressing desired. Garnish with pepper and carrot. Serves 2.

Above goes well in a tomato for luncheon.

ROCK LOBSTER SALAD
90 calories per serving

- 1 cup yogurt
- 5 chopped ripe olives
- ¼ teaspoon red paprika
- ¼ teaspoon salt
  dash Tabasco sauce
- 1 6½-ounce can rock lobster

Blend seasonings into yogurt and mix well. Cut rock lobster into bite-size pieces and toss lightly into dressing. Cover. Chill for at least 3 hours before serving. Serves 4.

CRABMEAT SALAD FRENCH STYLE
132 calories per serving

- 3 cups cooked, diced crab meat
- 1 teaspoon lemon juice
- ⅓ cup diced celery
- ½ teaspoon curry powder
- 1 cup yogurt

Have all ingredients well chilled. Blend lightly before serving. Serves 6.

SHRIMP REMOULADE
206 calories per serving

- ½ cup Sylph or other low-calorie French-type dressing
- 1 tablespoon cornstarch
- 1 teaspoon paprika
- 1 teaspoon House of Herbs Tomato Teasoning
- ¼ teaspoon parsley
- 5 tablespoons water
- 2 hard-cooked egg yellows
- 1 teaspoon horse-radish
- 1 pound cooked shrimp

Put Sylph in porcelain or Pyrex saucepan and simmer 5 minutes. Add cornstarch, and stir until smooth. Remove from heat and add paprika, Tomato Teasoning

*(if not available, use cat-
sup), parsley, and water.
When mixture is cool, stir
in horse-radish and egg. Put
through fine sieve. Chill.
Pour over shrimp. Place in
refrigerator 3 or 4 hours.
Stir several times to insure
complete coating of shrimp.
Serve on bed of shredded
lettuce. Serves 4 as main
dish.*

As an appetizer, cut
shrimp in halves and serve
on toothpicks.

FISH SALAD
110 to 150 calories per serving*

2 cups cooked flaked
    lean fish
½ cup Low-Calorie May-
    onnaise or salad dress-
    ing
½ cup celery, diced
½ cup cooked string
    beans cut in 1-inch
    pieces
2 tablespoons sweet pic-
    kle, chopped
2 tablespoons onion,
    chopped (optional)
3 hard-cooked eggs,
    diced
    lettuce

*Combine all ingredients ex-
cept the lettuce, being careful not to break the fish into
too small pieces. Serve on
lettuce cup. Serves 6.*

See Garnishes for Fish.

* Depending on fish used.

As may be expected, the
California Fresh Peach
Board has the salad below
quite frequently at its meet-
ings in Los Angeles or San
Francisco.

PEACH BOARD SALAD
70 calories per serving

6 fresh peach halves,
    peeled and pitted
    salad greens
6 tablespoons fresh
    raspberries
12 tablespoons skim-milk
    cottage cheese

*Place peach halves in circle
on salad plate filled with
salad greens. Fill centers of
peaches with raspberries
that may be dusted with
Sucaryl powder, and pile
cottage cheese in center of
plate. Makes 6 servings.*

SLIM JIM SALAD
100 calories per serving

2 Diet Delight or other
    dietetic peach halves
¼ cup skim-milk cottage
    cheese
1 tablespoon chopped
    celery
1 tablespoon grated car-
    rot
½ teaspoon finely chop-
    ped green onion (op-
    tional)
    lettuce

*Drain peaches thoroughly.
Mix cottage cheese, celery,*

carrot, and onion and spoon into peach halves. Place peaches on lettuce-garnished salad plate. Serves 1.

PEACH-PEAR SALAD
188 calories per serving

1½ cups Sealtest or other skim-milk cottage cheese
¼ pound American processed or Cheddar cheese, cut in small cubes
5 large peach halves
5 large pear halves
salad greens

Combine two cheeses lightly with a fork. Pile on peach halves, packing well, then press a pear half against cheese. Place on greens. Serves 5.

WALDORF SALAD
123 calories per serving

3 medium-tart apples
4 stalks green celery, chopped fine
8 ripe olives, chopped
½ cup nut meats
1 cup yogurt
1 tablespoon cottage cheese
salt, red pepper, and nutmeg
lettuce leaves

Quarter and core apples, and slice crosswise; do not peel. Blend celery with apples, olives, nut meats, and

yogurt; add seasonings to taste, and chill for at least 30 minutes. Serve on lettuce leaves. Serves 6.

If you can do without the nuts, each serving is only 69 calories.

CRISP CRANBERRY SLAW
55 calories per salad serving

4 cups shredded cabbage, crisped and dried
1 tablespoon minced onion
1 cup Cranberry-Orange Relish, well drained
1 teaspoon salt
1 cup yogurt

Mix ingredients lightly together with a fork. Chill in refrigerator ½ hour or more before serving. Makes 10 (33 calories each) to 12 (28 calories) relish servings; 6 salad servings.

CRANBERRY-ORANGE RELISH
44 calories per serving

2 cups fresh cranberries
1 orange, quartered and seeded
Sucaryl solution to taste

Put cranberries and orange quarters through food chopper. Add Sucaryl to taste. Chill before using. Makes 2 cups.

Also see Cranberry Salad Mould in Fruit section.

GELATINE SALADS
AND ASPICS

CARROT-CABBAGE SALAD
16 calories per serving

2 packages lemon-flavored diet gelatine
2 cups hot water
⅔ cup skim milk
½ cup shredded carrot
¾ cup shredded cabbage
2 tablespoons vinegar
1 tablespoon finely chopped onion
salad greens

Dissolve gelatine in boiling water. Chill until syrupy. Beat with eggbeater until foamy. Add milk gradually, beating with eggbeater after each addition until well mixed. Pour a little of this mixture into a 1¼-quart ring mold, just enough to cover the bottom. Sprinkle with ¼ cup carrot. Fold cabbage, vinegar, onion, and remaining ¼ cup carrot into remaining gelatine mixture. Pour into mold. Chill until set. Unmold and garnish with greens. Serves 8.

SUNSET SALAD
35 calories per serving

1 envelope orange D-Zerta
1 cup hot water
dash of salt
1½ teaspoons vinegar
⅓ cup coarsely grated carrot

2 tablespoons drained, diced unsweetened pineapple
salad greens

Dissolve D-Zerta in hot water. Add salt and vinegar. Chill. When thickened but not yet set, blend in carrot and pineapple. Divide evenly to fill 2 molds. Chill until firm. Unmold and serve on salad greens. Serves 2.

CUCUMBER JELLY
30 calories per serving

1 envelope unflavored gelatine
¼ cup cold water
¼ cup concentrated quick-frozen orange juice
2 tablespoons lemon juice
2 cups sliced unpeeled cucumber
½ small white onion
4 sprigs parsley
1 teaspoon salt, or to taste

Soften gelatine in cold water for 5 minutes. Then dissolve gelatine over hot water or low heat. Place orange juice and lemon juice in glass container of Waring or other cutting mixer. Add dissolved gelatine and the remaining ingredients in the order indicated. Cover container and turn on blender; run until contents are thoroughly blended—about 3 minutes. *Chill until begin-ning to thicken. Stir well and pour into 6 lightly oiled 4-ounce salad molds. Chill until firm. Serves 6.*

MOLDED SHREDDED CUCUMBER SALAD

21 calories per serving

2 envelopes unflavored gelatine
½ cup fresh lemon juice
1 cup cold water
1 tablespoon Sucaryl solution
¼ teaspoon salt
¼ teaspoon ground black pepper
⅛ teaspoon garlic powder
½ teaspoon grated lemon rind
2 teaspoons grated onion
1 teaspoon horse-radish
¼ cup chopped green pepper
½ cup diced celery
3 cups shredded raw cucumbers
thinly sliced cucumber and green or red pepper strips for garnish

Soften gelatine in lemon juice. Dissolve over hot wa-ter. Add next 11 ingredi-ents, mixing well. Chill un-til mixture begins to thick-en. Rinse a 9 x 5 x 3-inch pan in cold water. Arrange a garnish of sliced cucum-bers and green or red pep-per strips on bottom. Pour gelatine mixture over gar-nish, being careful not to dis-turb the design. Chill until

firm. *Unmold onto salad plate. Decorate with crisp water cress and lettuce. Serve in 1-inch slices top-ped with Low-Calorie May-onnaise. Serves 8.*

FRESH TOMATO ASPIC

21 calories per serving

1 pound tomatoes
1 small onion
¾ cup cold water
1 envelope unflavored gelatine
1½ teaspoons salt
1 tablespoon lime juice
½ teaspoon Worcester-shire sauce

Wash tomatoes and remove stem ends. Slice tomatoes and onion into saucepan. Add ½ cup of the water. Cover, and bring to boil; let cook 3 minutes. Pour into glass container of War-ing Blendor. Run until to-matoes are smoothly blend-ed—about 10 seconds. Strain out seeds. Soften gelatine in remaining ¼ cup water for 5 minutes; then dissolve over low heat. Add to to-mato liquid. Add salt, lime juice, and Worcestershire sauce. Mix well and pour into lightly oiled 3-cup ring mold or 6 individual ring molds. Chill until firm. Un-mold on crisp salad green. Serves 6.

This can be accompanied by one of the spiced cottage cheeses.

TOMATO ASPIC

31 calories per serving

1 cup unsweetened
   tomato juice
   dash of salt
   dash of celery salt
1 teaspoon chopped
   onion
1 whole clove
   small piece bay leaf
1 teaspoon vinegar
1 envelope lemon
   D-Zerta

Combine tomato juice and all seasonings in saucepan. Cover, and bring to a boil. Remove from heat and pour over D-Zerta, stirring until D-Zerta is dissolved. Cover, and let stand 5 minutes. Strain. Divide evenly in 2 molds or rings. Chill until firm. Unmold. Serves 2, each ½ cup.

PERFECTION SALAD

37 calories per serving

2 envelopes unflavored
   gelatine
½ cup cold water
2 cups hot water
½ cup lemon juice
3 teaspoons Sucaryl so-
   lution (or to taste)
1 teaspoon salt
1 cup finely diced celery
1 cup finely shredded
   cabbage
1 cup finely grated
   carrots

2 pimentos, finely
   chopped
   salad greens

Soften gelatine in cold water, add hot water and stir until gelatine is dissolved. Add lemon juice, sweetener, and salt. Cool until the mixture becomes syrupy. Fold in celery, cabbage, carrots, and pimentos. Pour into a 2-quart mold and chill until firm. Unmold on crisp salad greens and serve with Cooked Salad Dressing. Without dressing this is 25 calories per serving. Serves 8.

SPRING SALAD

15 calories per serving

1 envelope lime
   D-Zerta
½ teaspoon salt
1 cup hot water
1½ teaspoons vinegar
⅓ cup finely diced
   cucumber
¼ cup finely diced
   celery
2 tablespoons finely cut
   green onions

Dissolve D-Zerta and salt in hot water. Add vinegar. Chill until slightly thickened. Add cucumber, celery, and onions. Divide evenly in 2 cups or molds. Chill until firm. Unmold. Serves 2, each about ⅔ cup.

Any sugarless lime gelatine can be substituted.

GARDEN SALAD RING
20 calories per serving
1 envelope unflavored gelatine
¼ cup cold water
2 cups boiling water
1 teaspoon salt
¼ cup lime juice
1½ teaspoons Sucaryl solution
green food coloring
1 cup diced peeled cucumber
1 cup sliced radishes
¼ cup sliced scallions

Sprinkle gelatine on cold water; dissolve in boiling water. Add salt, lime juice, Sucaryl, and enough food coloring to tint mint green. Chill to consistency of unbeaten egg white. Fold in remaining ingredients. Spoon into lightly oiled 5-cup ring mold. Chill until set. Unmold. Fill center with crisp salad greens. Serves 6.

SEA-FOOD SALAD
38 calories per serving
1 envelope lemon D-Zerta
½ teaspoon salt
1 cup hot water
1 teaspoon vinegar
1 tablespoon chopped celery
1 tablespoon chopped green pepper
1 teaspoon chopped onion
½ cup flaked crab meat or shrimp

Dissolve D-Zerta and salt in hot water. Add vinegar. Chill until slightly thickened. Add celery, green pepper, onion, and sea food. Divide evenly in 2 cups or molds. Chill until firm. Unmold. Serves 2, about ⅔ cup each.

SEA-FOOD TOMATO SALAD
50 calories per serving
Use the above Sea-food Salad recipe, but dissolve D-Zerta and salt in only ½ cup hot water. Add ½ cup unsweetened tomato juice, dash of pepper, 2 teaspoons horse-radish, ⅛ teaspoon Worcestershire sauce, and 2 drops Tabasco sauce. Use 2 tablespoons chopped green pepper and onion.

JELLIED TUNA SALAD
123 calories per serving
Use recipe for Sea-food Salad, but substitute ½ cup flaked tuna. Prepare as directed. Serves 2, about ⅔ cup each.

Here is another jellied tuna recipe created by the Waring Blendor kitchen staff.

TUNA SALAD MOLD
72 calories per serving
1 package lime D-Zerta
1 cup boiling water
1 cup cold water
1 cup diced cabbage
½ cup diced carrots
½ cup diced celery
1 6½-ounce can grated tuna fish

Place D-Zerta in glass container of Waring Blendor or other high-speed mixer. Add boiling water. Cover container, and blend about 3 seconds. Stop blender and add remaining ingredients in order given. Cover container, and blend just until vegetables are coarsely cut —about 3 seconds. Chill until beginning to thicken. Pour into lightly oiled ring mold or 6 individual molds. Chill until firm. Serve, unmolded, on crisp salad greens. Serves 6.

This is a salad that has been enthusiastically received by many women dieters.

CHICKEN SALAD
207 calories per serving

1 envelope lemon D-Zerta
½ teaspoon salt
1 cup hot chicken broth
1 cup finely diced chicken
2 tablespoons finely diced cooked mushrooms
1 teaspoon minced onion

Dissolve D-Zerta and salt in hot broth. Chill until slightly thickened. Add the chicken, mushrooms, and onion. Divide evenly into cups or molds. Chill until firm. Unmold. Serve on salad greens. Serves 2, ⅔ cup each.

Also see Jellied Chicken and Pressed Turkey in Chicken and Turkey section.

PINEAPPLE COTTAGE MOLD
36 calories per serving

1 envelope unflavored gelatine
2 cups water
1½ teaspoons Sucaryl solution
4 ounces cottage cheese
juice of 2 lemons
½ cup grated pineapple
cucumber slices
water cress

Soften gelatine in ¼ cup cold water. Heat remaining water with Sucaryl; add to gelatine. Stir until gelatine dissolves. Add cottage cheese and pineapple. Beat with rotary beater until well blended. A few drops of green vegetable coloring may be added. Pour into a 5-cup oiled mold. Chill until firm. Unmold. Garnish with cucumber slices and water cress. Serves 6.

ORANGE MINCE SALAD
96 calories per serving

1 envelope unflavored gelatine
¼ cup cold water
1 cup boiling water
½ cup orange juice
¼ teaspoon salt
2 teaspoons Sucaryl solution, or to taste
1 cup prepared mincemeat

Soften gelatine in cold water and dissolve in the boiling water. Mix Sucaryl with orange juice; add with salt to the gelatine. Chill until almost firm. Fold in the mincemeat. Spoon into 6 individual molds rinsed with cold water. Chill until firm. Serves 6.

SPRINGTIME SALAD

40 calories per serving

1 cup Diet Delight fruit cocktail
½ cup boiling water
1 teabag
½ tablespoon plain gelatine
1 tablespoon lemon juice
1 teaspoon chopped fresh mint
salad greens

Drain fruit cocktail thoroughly, reserving ½ cup juice. Pour boiling water over teabag and allow to stand 3 or 4 minutes. Remove teabag. Soften gelatine in lemon juice and dissolve in hot tea. Stir in the ½ cup of juice from fruit cocktail. Cool until slightly thickened. Stir in mint and fruit cocktail. Spoon into individual molds and chill until firm. Unmold on salad greens. Serves 3.

Also see Fruit Cocktail Whip in Gelatine Dessert Chapter.

SALAD SEASONINGS

Garnishes: Capers, Celery seed Parsley, Paprika, chopped Pickles, Poppy seed, Tansy, Water Cress minced or sprigs.

Mixed Green: Angelica fresh leaves and stems, Anise leaves, fresh chopped Balm leaves, Basil, Bergamot, toss Burnet with other greens, Caraway seed as garnish, fresh Chervil leaves, Chives, Coriander seed, blend with Cress, Fennel leaves as garnish, Marjoram leaves, Mustard greens and seed, Nasturtium flowers and leaves, Onion, Parsley, Peppermint and other mints, crushed Black Pepper, chopped Savory leaves, Sesame seed sprinkled through, Sorrel, fresh or dried Tarragon leaves.

Mixed Vegetable: Anise leaves, Burnet, Chives, chopped Dill, Hyssop leaves as garnish, Nasturtium flowers and leaves, Onion, all Peppers, ½ teaspoon chopped Rue added to dressing, chopped Savory leaves, Sesame seed scattered through.

Beet: fresh Chervil leaves, chopped Savory leaves.

Cabbage: Caraway seed as garnish.

Coleslaw: Caraway seed, Dill seed, Mustard seed, Peppermint, Garlic and Basil vinegar in dressing.

Cucumber: Anise leaves,

fresh Chervil leaves, Chives.

Green Pepper, Marjoram leaves.

Spinach: half and half with Borage or Bergamot, with French Mustard dressing.

Tomato salad and Surprise: Basil, fresh Chervil leaves, chopped Savory leaves, Thyme.

Fruit: 1 or 2 chopped fresh Angelica, Anise, or Balm leaves, Cardamon, Cress as garnish, Mace, Sesame seed as garnish, Verbena and Lemon Verbena leaves.

Apple: sprinkle with chopped Anise leaves.

Orange: Peppermint leaves as garnish.

Pear: garnish with chopped Mint leaves.

Meat: Orégano, Thyme.

Chicken: Marjoram leaves, Orégano, ½ teaspoon minced Rue in dressing, fresh or dried Tarragon leaves, Thyme.

Egg: Marjoram leaves.

Fish and Sea Food: Basil, Chives, all Peppers, Saffron, fresh or dried Tarragon leaves, Thyme.

Use Lovage or Fennel as you would Celery.

Garlic in Green Salads: Rub a crust of dried bread with a clove of Garlic and toss the bread with the salad as you dress it. Remove bread before serving. This distributes the flavor evenly.

For an unusual taste, rub the salad bowl with crushed fresh Lovage leaves.

Different herb vinegars can be used as straight salad dressings and contain only 2 calories per tablespoon.

Vegetable Aspics: Basil, Thyme, herb vinegars.

Cucumber Aspic: Tarragon, herb vinegars.

Tomato Aspic: Orégano, herb vinegars.

Sea-food Aspic: 1 crushed Bay leaf, herb vinegars.

People who hate desserts rarely need reducing diets. And since a rich, delicious dessert can give you as many calories as the rest of the meal that preceded, the determined dieter must choose between the agony of no dessert and replacing the fattening one with something that will be toothsome and satisfying without lingering on the hips the rest of the life.

Fortunately there are a great many different lower-calorie desserts from which the dieter can choose. Here you will find 150 different low-calorie sweets—the largest collection, to our knowledge, ever assembled in one cookbook. But in spite of this extensive array, don't make dessert (from the French *desservir*, to remove from table) the main feature or big event of the meal. As Jane Nickerson, the food oracle of *The New York Times* has written, "plan your dessert in relation to the rest of the meal, light if preceding courses have been heavy and vice versa. Appeal to the eye. Conform with the season."

SEASONINGS FOR DESSERTS

Allspice, Angelica, Anise, Cardamom, Clove, Cinnamon, Coriander, the Geraniums, Ginger, Lavender, Lemon, Licorice, Lime, Mace, the Mints, Nutmeg.

For Dessert Gelatines: Lemon and Lime rind and juice, Almond and Vanilla extract.

For Puddings: ground Allspice, ground Cassia, and Cinnamon (especially for Chocolate pudding), Ginger, Lovage seed, Licorice, ground Mace and Nutmeg, Tansy, Almond and Vanilla extract.

Custard: Bay leaf, Mace and Nutmeg, Rose Geranium leaf, Ginger.

"Junket": ground Clove and Cinnamon.

FRUITS

Fruits seem such a natural choice as dessert for dieters that people are inclined to overlook one fact. Sugar is still sugar, still pure carbohydrate, whether in fruit or a sugar bowl. So keep portions small, even when eating raw fruit or fruit stewed with a noncaloric sweetener and spices.

For instance, don't be misled by the fact that watermelon is very low in calories. A 2-pound slice has about 1 pound of rind and waste and there are 126 calories in the edible portion, which is primarily water (92 per cent) and sugar (7 per cent). The sugar amounts to almost exactly 8 teaspoons—a fact to be kept in mind during the watermelon season.

Raw fruits are tastiest when chilled in the refrigerator (except bananas) before serving. Bananas are mostly starch, avocados mainly fat, and all fruits are predominantly sugar.

Lowest in calories are:

Raw Fruit	Calories per edible pound
Rhubarb	72
Lemons	88
Honeydew melon	92
Cantaloupe	93
Peaches	123
Watermelon	126
Limes	126
Pumpkin	140
Tangerines	144
Oranges	147
Strawberries	160
Gooseberries	178
Papayas	178
Plums	195
Apricots	216
Cranberries	218
Apples	232
Pears	236
Pineapple	240

In the recipes given, the methods used to prepare a dessert with one fruit will apply or be adaptable to another; such as Applesauce and Pear Sauce, Apricot Whip and Peach Whip, etc. Also each of the fruits can be used in many different forms, as demonstrated by the quartet of recipes that follow.

Here are four different ways to serve the popular and low-calorie cranberry —as a gelatine, an ice, a pudding, and a salad.

CRANBERRY JEL
22 calories per serving

4 cups fresh cranberries
1½ cups water
4 teaspoons Sucaryl solution
1 envelope unflavored gelatine
¼ cup cold water

Combine cranberries, water,

and Sucaryl in a large sauce-pan. Bring to a boil; lower heat and simmer gently 10 minutes, or until cranberries pop open. Sprinkle gelatine in cold water; dissolve in hot cranberry mixture. Pour into individual molds and chill until set. Serves 10.

CRANBERRY SHERBET
28 calories per serving

1 7-ounce jar Ocean Spray dietetic cranber-ries
2 teaspoons lemon juice
1 teaspoon lemon rind
2 stiffly beaten egg whites

Combine the cranberries with the lemon juice and rind. Freeze until firm. Beat to a mush. Fold in stiffly beaten egg whites. Return to freezing tray and freeze until firm. Serves 2.

CRANBERRY SALAD MOLD
37 calories per serving

2 envelopes unflavored gelatine
½ cup cold water
2 7-ounce jars Ocean Spray dietetic cranber-ries
½ cup orange juice
½ cup diced celery
¼ cup diced apple

Soften gelatine in cold wa-ter 2 minutes; dissolve over hot water. Add cranberries. Stir until mixed. Add orange juice. Chill until slightly

thickened. Add diced celery and apple. Pour into 1 large mold or 6 individual molds. Chill until firm. Unmold in-to lettuce cups. Serves 6.

CRANBERRY MOUSSE
45 calories per serving

½ cup nonfat dry milk powder
½ cup cold water
2 7-ounce jars Ocean Spray dietetic cranber-ries
1 teaspoon almond extract
1 tablespoon lemon juice

Sprinkle dry milk powder over cold water; beat until thick and slightly stiff. Beat in cranberries, almond ex-tract, and lemon juice. Pour into freezing tray and freeze until creamy firm. Serves 6.

BAKED APPLES
132 calories per serving

4 medium-sized tart, firm apples
½ cup coarse soft bread crumbs
1 teaspoon Sucaryl solu-tion
½ teaspoon cinnamon
¾ cup water
¼ cup orange juice

Core apples; pare ¼ way down. Place in greased bak-ing pan, pared side up. Thor-oughly mix bread crumbs, Sucaryl, and cinnamon. Fill cavities of apples with crumb mixture. Combine water and orange juice and pour over apples. Sprinkle any remaining crumbs over apples. Bake in moderate 375° oven 1 hour, or until easily pierced with a fork. Spoon liquid from pan over apples several times during baking. Makes 4 servings.

By eliminating bread crumbs each apple has only 84 calories.

By substituting chopped fresh cranberries or crushed unsweetened pineapple each apple has 92 calories.

BAKED APPLE-CREAM APPLES
135 calories per apple

6 medium-sized cooking apples
2 teaspoons Sucaryl solution
3 tablespoons cornstarch
3 cups skim milk
1 teaspoon vanilla

Core apples. Remove extra pulp and leave a hollow from 1 to 2 inches in diameter, depending upon the size and shape of the apples. Pare about 1 inch down from top of apples and place in baking pan pared side up. Put cores, parings, and pulp in saucepan with water to cover; cook until soft. Strain, reserving liquid. Put cooked sauce through food mill or sieve; reserve. Bake cored apples with the apple liquid with 1 teaspoon Sucaryl so-lution added in moderate (350°) oven about 45 minutes, or until tender. Meanwhile, combine cornstarch, remaining Sucaryl solution, and ½ cup of the milk. Scald remaining milk; add slowly to cornstarch mixture. Cook over hot water, stirring, until mixture thickens. Cover and cook 15 minutes longer. Add sieved apple; cook 5 minutes longer. Cool. Add vanilla, and pour into centers of cooled baked apples, filling to brim. Chill thoroughly. Use remaining apple-cream for sauce. Serves 6.

APPLESAUCE
58 calories per serving

1¼ pounds cooking apples
water
1½ teaspoons Sucaryl solution
¼ teaspoon nutmeg
¼ teaspoon cinnamon
1 teaspoon lemon juice

Wash apples. Remove cores and cut into quarters. Barely cover with water and cook until almost soft. Add Sucaryl, nutmeg, and cinnamon, and cook a few minutes longer. Add lemon juice. Put through a strainer if fine applesauce is desired. Cool. Serves 5.

For a quick single portion of applesauce, using a high-speed mixer, try the following:

BLENDED APPLESAUCE

58 calories per serving

1 diced, unpeeled, small red-skinned apple (¼ pound)
½ cup water
Sucaryl solution to taste

Place apple and water in Waring Blendor. Blend 20 seconds, then pour into saucepan. Cover, and bring to boil. Cook 2 minutes. Cool slightly. Sweeten to taste with Sucaryl. Makes about ½ cup.

Mrs. Ezra Dolan of Rye, N.Y., has added a new trick to applesauce which gives it a memorable taste, and adds only 7 calories.

VIVIAN'S APPLESAUCE

65 calories per serving

2½ pounds cooking apples
1 lemon
water
1 package strawberry Jel-ex or other low-calorie gelatine dissolved in 8 ounces boiling water

Wash, core, and quarter apples. Cut up lemon. Mix in pot and use only enough water to keep from burning. Cover tightly and simmer until apples are mushy—15 to 20 minutes. Stir occasionally; add water to keep fruit from sticking. Put through medium sieve. Stir in Jelex, mixing thoroughly. Allow to cool. Makes 10 servings.

OLD-FASHIONED APPLE SNOW WITH SOFT CUSTARD SAUCE

97 calories per serving

1 pound cooking apples (McIntosh, Baldwin, Greening, etc.)
water
1 tablespoon grated lemon rind
1 ½-inch cinnamon stick
1 tablespoon cold water
¼ teaspoon Sweeta
2 egg whites
½ cup soft Custard Sauce (½ of recipe)
⅛ teaspoon grated nutmeg

Wash, pare, core, and chop apples. Put in saucepan. Add enough water barely to cover. Add lemon rind and cinnamon stick. Cover, and simmer 15 to 20 minutes, or until apples are tender. Stir occasionally, adding water if necessary to prevent scorching. Remove cinnamon stick. Mash apples with fork or rotary beater. Cool applesauce. Stir Sweeta in 1 tablespoon cold water; add to applesauce and blend well. Chill thoroughly. Shortly before serving beat egg whites until stiff; fold into applesauce; blend lightly until fluffy. Place in 4 individual serving dishes. Top with Custard Sauce. Sprinkle with grated nutmeg. Serve at once. Serves 4.

SOFT CUSTARD SAUCE
25 calories per serving

1 cup skim milk
2 egg yellows
⅛ teaspoon salt
⅛ teaspoon (12 drops) Sweeta
½ teaspoon vanilla flavoring

Make sauce several hours in advance, if possible, and chill thoroughly before serving. Heat milk in top part of double boiler over boiling water until tiny bubbles appear around edge. In medium bowl beat egg yellows with salt; slowly add milk, stirring constantly. Pour mixture back in top part of double boiler. Cook over hot, not boiling, water until mixture "coats" the spoon, stirring constantly. Remove custard at once from warm water, pour into cold bowl, and allow to cool. Add Sweeta and flavoring, or rum or sherry flavoring to taste can be used instead of vanilla. Cover, and chill. Makes 1 cup. Serves 8, 2 tablespoons each.

BANANA WHIP
58 calories per serving

1 ripe banana, sliced
1 teaspoon lemon juice
1 egg white, unbeaten
dash of salt
12 drops Sweeta
½ teaspoon vanilla flavoring
dash of cinnamon or nutmeg

Mash banana with lemon juice; add remaining ingredients except cinnamon or nutmeg. Beat in electric mixer until light and fluffy. Divide into 2 sherbet glasses and sprinkle with cinnamon or nutmeg. Serve at once. Serves 2.

WHITE BERRIES
124 calories per serving

2 cups fresh strawberries
2 cups yogurt
6 teaspoons chopped almonds or other unsalted nuts
Sucaryl sweetening powder, if desired

Blend berries with yogurt and arrange in large glass bowl or individual dishes; sprinkle with chopped nuts and with Sucaryl, if desired. Serves 6.

If you substitute blueberries, add 11 calories per portion.

If you skip the nuts, subtract 30 calories per portion.

FROSTY MELON BALLS
24 calories per serving

1 pint non-caloric ginger ale
2 cups melon balls
salt

Pour ginger ale into freezing tray of refrigerator and

*set control for freezing ice
cream. Freeze to mush, stirring once. Remove, sprinkle
melon balls with salt, and
fold into ginger ale. Serves
4.*

SPICED FRUIT COMPOTE
54 calories per serving

1 No. 2 can unsweetened
   peach halves
1 No. 2 can unsweetened
   fruit cocktail
1 tablespoon Sucaryl
   solution
8 whole cloves
1 tablespoon broken stick
   cinnamon
¼ teaspoon nutmeg

*Drain peach halves and
fruit cocktail, saving liquid.
Arrange 1 or 2 peach halves
in each dessert dish; top
with fruit cocktail. Mix Sucaryl and combined liquids
in saucepan; add spices;
simmer 15 minutes. Strain.
Cool. Pour over fruits, and
chill. Serves 4.*

If fruits have been pack-
ed in noncaloric sweetener,
omit Sucaryl.

JELLIED MELON BALLS
20 calories per serving

1 envelope lime D-Zerta
   or other non-caloric
   gelatine
   dash of salt
1 cup hot water
½ cup (8 to 10 medium
   sized) melon balls

Dissolve D-Zerta and salt in
*hot water. Chill until slight-
ly thickened, then fold in
melon balls. Divide evenly
into molds. Chill until firm.
Unmold. Serve plain or garnish with mint. Serves 2.*

BAKED STUFFED PEACHES
52 calories per serving

4 Diet Delight peach
   halves
2 teaspoons seedless
   raisins
½ cup juice from peaches
½ teaspoon cornstarch
¼ teaspoon grated lemon
   rind

*For each serving put 2
peach halves together with
1 teaspoon raisins. Fasten
together with picks and
place in small shallow baking dish. Heat juice to boiling with cornstarch and
lemon rind. Pour over peaches. Bake in moderate (350°)
oven 15 to 20 minutes until
heated. Serve warm. Serves
2.*

Use same amount of pears
or 12 apricot halves for variations with same calories.

PEARS IN WHITE SHIRTS
91 calories per serving

1 cup yogurt
¼ cup skim-milk cottage
   cheese
¼ teaspoon nutmeg
1 No. 2 can diet-pack
   Bartlett pears
   Sucaryl or other non-
   caloric sweetening, if
   desired

Mix yogurt with cottage cheese and nutmeg, and chill for at least 10 minutes. Drain pears and arrange in glass bowl. Cover with yogurt mixture. Use sweetening, if desired. Serves 4.

Also served as a salad.

GINGER PEAR HALVES
48 calories per portion

- ½ cup liquid drained from diet-pack pears
- 1 Sucaryl tablet
- ¼ teaspoon ginger
- 2 diet-pack pear halves, drained

Combine liquid, Sucaryl, and ginger. Heat to boiling. Pour over pear halves. Cover, and let stand in hot liquid for at least half an hour. Serve hot or chilled. Serves 1.

PRUNE WHIP
60 calories per serving

- 4 large dried prunes
- 1 tablespoon lemon juice
- 1 unbeaten egg white dash of salt
- ⅛ teaspoon (12 drops) Sweeta

Cook prunes according to package directions without sugar; remove pit and mash with fork. Cool. Add lemon juice, egg white, salt, and Sweeta. Beat with electric mixer until light and fluffy.

Pour into 2 sherbet glasses and serve at once. Serves 2.

APRICOT WHIP
67 calories per serving

Substitute 10 dried apricot halves for prunes in above recipe. Add 1 more egg white and leave out salt. Sprinkle with cinnamon and garnish with sprig of mint.

JELLIED STRAWBERRIES AND RHUBARB
17 calories per serving

- 1 envelope unflavored gelatine
- ¼ cup cold water
- 2 cups boiling water
- 1 tablespoon lemon juice
- 1 tablespoon Sucaryl solution
  red food coloring
- 1 cup cooked unsweetened rhubarb
- 1 cup sliced unsweetened strawberries

Sprinkle gelatine on cold water. Add lemon juice, water; dissolve in boiling Sucaryl, and enough food coloring to tint deep pink. Chill to consistency of unbeaten egg white. Meanwhile, combine rhubarb and strawberries. Mix well. Fold fruits into chilled gelatine. Spoon into lightly greased individual molds. Chill until set. Unmold and garnish with whole strawberries. Serves 6.

THE FAVORITE FRUIT BOWL
117 calories per serving

1 orange, peeled and diced
1 apple, diced
¼ cup fresh berries
Sucaryl to taste
dash of lemon juice
½ cup yogurt

Combine fruit with Sucaryl to taste; sprinkle with lemon juice. Pile fruit into individual bowls and top with yogurt. Serves 2.

FRUIT SEASONINGS

With any fruit: Lemon juice and rind, Almond extract.

Fresh Fruit Cup: leaves of Balm, Rose Geranium, any Mint, Rosemary, Verbena, Woodruff (1 leaf just before serving).

Stewed Fruit Compote: Anise, Basil, Cardamom, Cassia buds, Cinnamon, Coriander (sparingly), Ginger (also adds zest to canned fruits), Lovage seed, Rosemary.

Baked Apples: Anise, Caraway, Cardamom, Cinnamon, Cloves, Fennel seed, Rose Geranium.

Applesauce: Ginger, Cinnamon, Mace blades, ground Nutmeg.

Broiled Pineapple or Grapefruit: Cinnamon.

Stewed Pears: Rose geranium leaf in pan, Savory.

Stewed Peaches: Rose Geranium leaf in pan.

Stewed Cherries: Mace or Nutmeg.

GELATINE DESSERTS

This book could be filled with nothing but recipes for gelatine desserts, for in the campaign to replace sugar-laden last courses with something just as sweet and attractive, but much lower in calorie content, the jells have been a logical and successful substitute and hundreds of variations have been concocted.

In addition to straight, clear gelatines there are those broken up, whipped, combined with fruit juices and other flavors, and made into whips, fluffs, sponge, snow, mousse, mold, Spanish cream, and Bavarian.

However, remember that you must use either unflavored gelatine or artificially sweetened flavored powders such as D-Zerta, Jelex, Glow, etc. For the regular brands of gelatine powder are ⅞ sugar and ⅛ gelatine. Gelatine, by itself, is almost pure protein, and is sometimes recommended by physicians in water as a supplement to reducing diets. It is extracted from animal cartilage, tissues, and bones by boiling. That is why you can make Jellied Consommé from the soup of a young chicken without adding any outside jelling agent.

Not only can you use these gelatines for very low calorie desserts, but many of the same ones can serve as salads (also see large selection of Gelatine Salads in Salad section) or as extra vegetable dishes (Tomato Aspic), fish or meat main courses (Fish Mousse, Lamb Aspic), and in jellied soups. Other desserts include gelatine, too, such as the fruits, sherbets, and ice cream.

HOW TO USE PLAIN GELATINE
4 calories per serving

Most widely available and popular unflavored gelatine is Knox's. It comes already measured in envelopes and one envelope will jell up to 2 cups of liquid, or 4 servings.

1. Soften by sprinkling gelatine into ½ cup cold liquid. Let stand about 5 minutes.

1A. If the liquid is cold milk, stir the gelatine into milk.

2. Dissolve softened gelatine by stirring into hot liquid called for in recipe. Or place over hot water and stir until dissolved.

3. Use only canned pineapple or fresh or frozen that has been cooked.

4. Quick chilling of gelatine mixture can be done by filling lower half of double boiler with ice and water and setting mixture in top part over the ice and stirring frequently. Or use two bowls.

5. When beaten egg whites are used in recipe, any low-calorie sweetener indicated should be folded in when whites are beaten stiff but not dry.

6. Gelatine desserts with eggs are perishable and should be used the same day or the next day.

7. Use sherbet or parfait glasses so that desserts can chill evenly on all sides.

HOW TO MAKE D-ZERTA
12 calories per serving

Pour D-Zerta from envelope into small bowl. Add 1 cup hot water (use 8-ounce measuring cup) and stir until D-Zerta is completely dissolved. Pour into 2 sherbet glasses or molds. Chill until firm. Serves 2.

D-Zerta may be combined with 2 or 3 tablespoons of unsweetened fruits or vegetables for each serving.

JELEX
10 calories per serving

Each ½-ounce envelope, when mixed with 1 pint (2 cups) of hot water, will make 5 servings.

Quick method: mix envelope with ½ pint hot water, stir until thoroughly dissolved, then add ½ pint cold water.

To whip: cool until slightly thickened and whip with rotary egg beater until gelatine is fluffy and thick.

To unmold: dip mold quickly into hot water (do not allow water to come over top). Loosen from sides of mold with knife; place serving dish over top. Quickly turn upside down. Remove mold.

To add fruit: fresh or canned fruit (drained well) can be added after gelatine begins to thicken. (Always cook fresh pineapple before adding.)

GINGER GEL

4 calories per serving

1 envelope Knox unflavored gelatine
½ cup cold water
1½ cups non-caloric ginger ale

Sprinkle gelatine on cold water in top of double boiler. Stir over hot water until gelatine is thoroughly dissolved. Remove from heat. Add beverage, and blend. Pour into 1 large mold (2 cups) or 4 individual molds. Chill until firm. Serves 4.

Any other flavor of non-caloric carbonated beverage can be used.

SINK AND SWIM

Some fruits sink and others float in gelatine. This makes it easy to make decorative molds with two layers of fruit.

Pour gelatine into mold, add a layer of heavier fruit, distributing pieces as evenly as possible, then add a layer of floating fruit.

Fruits That Sink	*Fruits That Float*
Canned (Sucaryl or saccharin sweetened)	Fresh
Royal Anne cherries	Apple cubes
Apricots, peaches, or pears	Grapefruit sections
Pineapple, raspberries	Peach slices
Fresh	Pear slices
Orange sections, grapes	Raspberries
Cooked	Strawberry halves
Prunes or plums	

GRAPE MOLD

79 calories per serving

1½ envelopes unflavored
  gelatine
1½ pints unsweetened
  grape juice
1 teaspoon Sucaryl so-
  lution or 8 Sucaryl
  tablets, crushed

*Soften gelatine in ¼ cup
grape juice. Heat remaining
grape juice with Sucaryl.
Add hot grape-juice mixture
to gelatine; stir until dissolved. Pour into 1-quart
mold or 6 individual molds.
Chill until firm. Unmold.
Serves 6.*

GRAPE JELLY

19 calories per tablespoon

*Proceed as above, but use
only 1 envelope of the gelatine. Keep refrigerated.*

GRAPE COOLER

29 calories per serving

1 envelope strawberry or
  raspberry D-Zerta
¾ cup hot water
¼ cup unsweetened
  grape juice

*Dissolve D-Zerta in hot wa-
ter. Add grape juice. Pour
into cups or molds and chill
until firm. Unmold. Serves
2, about ½ cup each.*

FRUIT GELATINE

32 calories per serving

1 envelope unflavored
  gelatine

¼ cup cold water
1 1-pound can water-
  packed fruit salad
2 tablespoons lemon
  juice
2 teaspoons Sucaryl
  solution
  food coloring, as
  desired

*Soften gelatine in cold water
and dissolve over boiling
water. Drain fruit and measure juice; add enough water
to make 1½ cups of liquid.
Mix together fruit juice, lemon juice, and Sucaryl. Add
food coloring, if desired.
Stir in dissolved gelatine,
mixing thoroughly. Cool.
When partially thickened,
add fruit. Pour into 6 individual molds or a 1-quart
mold rinsed in cold water.
Chill until set. If Sucaryl-
sweetened fruit is used,
leave out Sucaryl in recipe.
Serves 6.*

ORANGE JEWELS

23 calories per serving

1 envelope orange
  D-Zerta
1 cup hot water
6 sections orange

*Dissolve contents of enve-
lope in hot water. Turn into
pan or bowl and chill until
firm. Using fork, break into
flakes or "jewels." Divide
into 2 sherbet glasses and
garnish each with 3 sections
of orange. Serves 2.*

ORANGE COOLER
30 calories per serving

1 envelope orange, lemon, or lime D-Zerta
½ cup hot water
½ cup orange juice

Dissolve D-Zerta in hot water, then add orange juice. Pour into cups or molds. Chill until firm. Unmold. Serves 2.

SPICED PEAR MOLD
18 calories per serving

1 envelope cherry D-Zerta
    dash each salt, ginger, and cinnamon
1 cup hot water
⅓ cup diced unsweetened pears

Combine D-Zerta and seasonings. Add hot water and stir until D-Zerta is dissolved. Chill until slightly thickened and then fold in pears. Divide evenly in 2 individual molds. Chill until firm. Unmold. Serves 2, ⅔ cup each.

Duke Ellington, the composer-conductor, is a man of size and capacity with a well-earned reputation as an eater of quality and quantity. He has rather unorthodox ideas on eating, and the author of this book once asked him why he began his dinner with a large dish filled with apple pie, ice cream, and gelatine dessert. "It's simple," he replied with a bland smile. "If I wait until I've eaten everything else I'm going to have, I may not have room."

Below is one of the gelatine desserts the Duke favors.

CHERRY GELATINE DELIGHT
38 calories per serving

1 teaspoon unflavored gelatine
1 tablespoon cold water
½ cup boiling water or hot liquid from cherries
1 tablespoon lemon juice
3 Sucaryl tablets
⅓ cup drained dietpack dark cherries

Sprinkle gelatine over cold water. Let stand 5 minutes. Add boiling water; stir until dissolved. Add lemon juice and Sucaryl. Chill until mixture begins to set. Beat until fluffy with rotary beater. Fold in cherries. Chill until firm. Serves 1.

LEMON COLA SNOW
8 calories per serving

1 tablespoon unflavored gelatine
½ cup water
1 cup non-fattening cola drink
1 teaspoon grated lemon rind
¼ cup lemon juice
1 tablespoon Sucaryl solution
1 egg white, beaten

Soften gelatine in cold water; dissolve over hot water. Combine cola, lemon rind, juice, and Sucaryl. Chill until consistency of unbeaten egg white; whip until light. Add beaten egg white. Set in bowl of ice water and continue beating until mixture begins to hold its shape. Chill until firm. Serves 8.

LEMON SPONGE

29 calories per piece

2 tablespoons gelatine
3 cups water
2 tablespoons Sucaryl solution
½ teaspoon grated lemon rind
¾ cup lemon juice
2 egg whites, beaten stiff
12 graham crackers, crushed

Soften gelatine in ½ cup cold water; heat remaining water and add Sucaryl, lemon rind, and juice. Add gelatine. Stir until gelatine is dissolved. Chill until thickened. Place in large mixer bowl and beat until frothy, then fold in egg whites. Pour into a lightly oiled 9-inch square cake pan and chill until firm. Before serving, cut into squares and coat with crushed graham crackers. Makes 16 servings.

FRUIT COCKTAIL WHIP

23 calories per serving

1 teaspoon unflavored gelatine

2 tablespoons cold water
½ cup boiling water
1 tablespoon lemon juice
3 Sucaryl tablets, or to taste
½ cup drained diet-pack fruit cocktail

Sprinkle gelatine over cold water. Let stand 5 minutes. Add boiling water. Stir until dissolved. Add lemon juice and Sucaryl. Chill until mixture begins to set. Beat until fluffy with rotary beater. Fold in fruit cocktail. Chill until firm. Other diet-pack fruit may be substituted for fruit cocktail, and instead of the boiling water, the liquid drained from the fruit may be brought to a boil and used. Serves 2.

For Jellied Fruit Salad, omit beating.

APPLESAUCE WHIP

40 calories per serving

1 envelope Knox unflavored gelatine
½ cup cold water
½ cup very hot water
2 tablespoons lemon juice
5 non-caloric sweetening tablets or equivalent
2 cups cold, unsweetened applesauce

Sprinkle gelatine on cold water to soften. Stir the softened gelatine into very hot water until thoroughly dissolved. Add lemon juice

*and noncaloric sweetener.
Blend in cold applesauce.
Chill thoroughly until thickened but not jellied. Whip
with rotary beater until
light. Chill again. Heap into serving dishes. Serves 6.*

APPLE WHIP

62 calories per serving

1 envelope unflavored
   gelatine
¼ cup cold water
1¼ cups apple juice
2 teaspoons Sucaryl
   solution
⅓ cup water
1 tablespoon lemon juice
⅓ cup Instant Starlac or
   other dry skim milk

*Soften gelatine in cold wa-
ter. Let stand 5 minutes.
Heat apple juice to boiling
point. Add Sucaryl and softened gelatine; stir until gelatine dissolves. Chill mixture until slightly thickened.
Pour ⅓ cup water and lemon
juice into 1-quart bowl;
sprinkle dry milk over surface of water. Beat with rotary beater or electric mixer
until stiff—8 to 10 minutes.
Fold whipped milk into
slightly thickened gelatine
mixture. Pour into molds or
individual serving dishes.
Chill until firm. Serves 6.*

A non-fattening recipe for
an old, reliable dessert.

BLANC MANGE

47 calories per serving

1 envelope unflavored
   gelatine
¼ cup cold skim milk
1½ cups skim milk
4 Crystallose crystals or
   Sucaryl or saccharin
   tablets
½ teaspoon salt
1 teaspoon vanilla or
   mint extract or ¼ tea-
   spoon Mintit

*Soften gelatine in cold milk
5 minutes. Scald skim milk
and add Crystallose and
salt; stir until thoroughly
dissolved. Add to softened
gelatine and stir until dissolved and mixed. Chill until thick as unbeaten egg
whites. Add vanilla or mint
extract and beat until frothy.
Pour into serving dish or
mold, and chill until set.
Serves 4.*

STRAWBERRY FLUFF

25 calories per serving

1 envelope strawberry
   low calorie gelatine
1 cup hot water
1 cup Sealtest or other
   skim milk

*Dissolve gelatine in hot wa-
ter. Chill until almost set
and quivery. Whip with rotary hand beater or electric
mixer until very light and
foamy. Add milk gradually,
beating constantly. Pour into dessert glasses. Chill until set. Serves 6.*

PINEAPPLE FLUFF
39 calories per serving

1 envelope lemon
  D-Zerta
1 cup hot water and liq-
  uid from canned pine-
  apple
1 Sucaryl tablet
3 tablespoons non-fat dry
  milk
3 tablespoons ice water
1½ teaspoons lemon juice
½ cup drained, canned,
  cut unsweetened pine-
  apple

Dissolve D-Zerta in liquid that has been heated; add sweetener. Chill. Meanwhile sprinkle dry milk over ice water and lemon juice. Beat with egg beater until consistency of whipped cream. Fold in thickened D-Zerta and then the pineapple. Divide evenly into sherbet glasses and chill. Serves 4, about ½ cup each.

ORANGE OR LEMON FLUFF
35 calories per serving

1 envelope Dia-Mel
  lemon or orange gela-
  tine dessert
½ cup boiling water
2 tablespoons skim-milk
  cottage cheese
⅛ teaspoon powdered
  nutmeg
  non-caloric sweetener
  to taste

Dissolve gelatine in boiling water. Chill until syrup is thick. Whip with egg beater until fluffy. Mix the cottage cheese, nutmeg, and sweetener together. Stir into gelatine. Chill and serve. Serves 2.

SPANISH CREAM
62 calories per serving

1 envelope unflavored
  gelatine
¼ cup cold water
1½ teaspoons Sucaryl
  solution
1½ cups skim milk
3 eggs, separated
½ teaspoon salt
2 teaspoons grated
  orange rind
1 teaspoon vanilla

Soften gelatine in cold water. Mix Sucaryl with milk; scald in top of double boiler. Beat egg yellows slightly; beat in salt, orange rind, and softened gelatine. Slowly stir in hot milk until well blended. Return to top of double boiler and cook, stirring constantly, until mixture coats spoon. Cool slightly. Add vanilla. Chill until cold and slightly thickened. Beat egg whites until stiff but not dry; fold into chilled custard. Spoon into large mold or individual sherbet glasses, if desired. Chill until firm. Serves 6.

PEACH SPANISH CREAM
122 calories per serving

3 cups skim milk
2 teaspoons Sucaryl solution
2 envelopes unflavored gelatine
3 eggs, separated
1 teaspoon vanilla
1 No. 303 can dietetic sliced peaches sweetened with Sucaryl

Pour milk into top of double boiler; add Sucaryl. Sprinkle gelatine over top of milk and allow to soften thoroughly. Cook over hot water, stirring until gelatine dissolves. Beat egg yellows. Add small amount of milk mixture to egg. Stir egg-yellow mixture into milk mixture. Cook until mixture coats spoon. Add vanilla. Chill until consistency of unbeaten egg white. Beat egg whites until stiff; fold into gelatine mixture. Fill 6 individual dessert glasses; chill until firm. Top with sliced peaches. Serves 6.

PEACH WHIP
103 calories per serving

1 tablespoon unflavored gelatine
2 tablespoons cold water
1 egg, separated
½ pint Dannon or other yogurt
½ teaspoon Sucaryl solution

few drops almond extract
½ cup diced peaches canned without sugar

Soften gelatine in cold water; dissolve over hot water. Beat egg yellow; add yogurt, sweetener, almond flavoring, and dissolved gelatine; mix well. Chill until mixture begins to set. Beat egg white stiff; fold in with peaches. Pour into individual molds. Chill until well set. Serves 3.

STRAWBERRY YOGURT FLUFF
41 calories per serving

1 package low-calorie strawberry gelatine
1 cup hot water
1 cup cold water
1 cup Dannon strawberry yogurt, or yogurt with strawberry preserves

Dissolve gelatine in hot water. Add cold water, and chill until slightly thickened. Reserve ⅓ cup mixture for garnish. Place remaining gelatine in bowl over ice and water and whip with rotary egg beater until fluffy and thick, like whipped cream. Add well-blended yogurt, and mix lightly. Turn into serving bowl. Garnish with slightly thickened (⅓ cup) gelatine. Serves 6.

More than half the calories have been removed from the usual Bavarian recipe by using skim milk and Sucaryl.

APRICOT BAVARIAN
41 calories per serving

4 teaspoons unflavored
gelatine

¼ cup cold water

1 1-pound can dietetic
apricots

1 tablespoon lemon juice

2 teaspoons Sucaryl

1 cup nonfat dry-milk
solids

1 cup ice water

Soften gelatine in cold water; dissolve over boiling water. Cook apricots to soft mush; strain. Add with lemon juice and Sucaryl to gelatine. Cook 5 minutes. Chill until consistency of unbeaten egg whites. Beat dry-milk solids with ice water until stiff. Fold into gelatine. Chill in an 8-cup mold. Divide into 15 servings.

Any other fruit or fruit cocktail can be used.

APRICOLA WHIP
36 calories per serving

1 tablespoon unflavored
gelatine

1 cup nonfat carbonated
cola

10 halves unsweetened
apricots

4 tablespoons apricot
juice

1 tablespoon lemon juice

½ teaspoon liquid no-
calorie sweetener, or
to taste

2 egg whites
dash of salt

Soften gelatine in ½ cup of cola, and dissolve over low heat. Place in electric blender. Add remaining ½ cup cola, apricots and juice, lemon juice, and sweetener; blend until smooth—about 10 seconds. Cool until mixture begins to thicken. Beat egg whites with salt until stiff but not dry. Fold apricot mixture into beaten egg whites. Pile in serving dishes and chill. Serves 6.

CHOCO-COLA WHIP
44 calories per serving

1 tablespoon unflavored
gelatine

1 cup skim milk

1 ounce unsweetened
chocolate

1 cup Streamliner or
other low-calorie cola
drink

¼ teaspoon vanilla

½ teaspoon Sucaryl solu-
tion

Soften gelatine in milk in top of double boiler; add chocolate. Place over hot water and stir until chocolate is melted and gelatine is dissolved. Beat with rotary beater, if necessary, to blend. Add cola, vanilla, and Sucaryl. Chill until consistency of unbeaten egg whites. Whip with rotary or electric blender until fluffy. Chill until set. Serve with Whipped Topping. Serves 6.

COFFEE-COLA SPONGE
29 calories per serving

1 tablespoon unflavored gelatine
¼ cup cold water
½ cup strong coffee
2 teaspoons Sucaryl solution, or to taste
dash of salt
2 eggs, separated
1 cup low-calorie carbonated cola drink

Soften gelatine in water. Combine coffee, sweetener, salt, and egg yellows. Cook over low heat until slightly thickened. Add gelatine. Stir until dissolved. Add cola. Chill until partly set. Beat egg whites until stiff but not dry. Fold in gelatine mixture. Pile in sherbet glasses. Chill. Serves 6.

Use this the same day it is made.

COFFEE ALMOND WHIP
11 calories per serving

1 teaspoon unflavored gelatine
2 tablespoons cold water
½ cup boiling water
3 Sucaryl tablets
½ cup hot coffee
⅛ teaspoon nutmeg
¼ teaspoon almond extract

Sprinkle gelatine over cold water. Let stand 5 minutes. Add boiling water. Stir until dissolved. Add remaining ingredients and blend. Chill until mixture begins to set. Beat until fluffy with rotary beater. Chill until firm. Serves 1.

COFFEE WHIP
6 calories per serving

1 tablespoon unflavored gelatine
¼ cup cold water
2 cups strong hot coffee
2 teaspoons Sucaryl solution

Soften gelatine in cold water; dissolve in hot coffee with Sucaryl. Pour about ¼ of this mixture into small shallow pan to depth of ½ inch. Chill until firm jelly. Cut into ½-inch cubes. Chill remaining mixture until syrupy. Beat with rotary egg beater until light and fluffy. Spoon into sherbet glasses. Chill until firm. Garnish with the ½-inch cubes of coffee jelly. Serves 6.

COFFEE AND CREAM PUDDING
56 calories per serving

1 envelope unflavored gelatine
¼ cup cold water
2½ teaspoons Sucaryl solution
1 square 1-ounce unsweetened chocolate
1 cup skim milk
½ cup cold strong coffee
2 eggs, separated
1 teaspoon vanilla
¼ cup evaporated milk, whipped

Soften gelatine in cold water. Mix Sucaryl, chocolate, milk, and coffee in saucepan; stir over low heat until chocolate melts. Bring mixture to boiling point. Beat egg yellows. Stir hot mixture into beaten egg yellows. Return mixture to saucepan. Cook over low heat, stirring constantly, 1 minute. Remove from heat; add softened gelatine and vanilla.

Mix thoroughly. Cool. When cold and beginning to set, fold in stiffly beaten egg whites and whipped evaporated milk. (To whip evaporated milk, chill in freezer until ice crystals form around edge, then beat with rotary beater until stiff.) Spoon into sherbet dishes. Chill. Serves 9.

Also see Cranberry Jel in Fruit section.

SHERBETS AND OTHER FROZEN DESSERTS

APPLE ALMOND SHERBET

43 calories per serving

- 1 cup cold unsweetened applesauce
  juice of ½ lemon or lime
- ¼ teaspoon Sweeta
- ¼ cup cottage cheese
- 1 tablespoon skim milk
- 6 drops Sweeta
- ⅛ teaspoon almond flavoring
- 1 egg white
- ⅛ teaspoon grated orange rind, if desired
- ⅛ teaspoon cinnamon, if desired

Blend applesauce with lemon or lime juice and ¼ teaspoon Sweeta. Put in cold refrigerator tray and freeze (with refrigerator turned to coldest position) until applesauce is frozen to about ½ inch around edges. Put applesauce in chilled bowl and beat with rotary beater or mixer until mushy. Meanwhile, cream cottage cheese with fork until smooth. Blend milk with Sweeta and almond flavoring; mix thoroughly. Add to cheese and blend again. Beat egg white until stiff and fold into cheese mixture. Mix with applesauce; add orange rind, if desired; blend well and return to chilled tray. Freeze mixture until firm. Sprinkle with cinnamon before serving, if desired. Serves 8, ¼ cup each.

APRICOT GLACE

46 calories per serving

- 4 cups unsweetened apricot purée
- 1 tablespoon unsweetened orange juice
- 1 cup unsweetened grapefruit juice
- 3 tablespoons lemon juice artificial sweetener to taste

Make purée by draining apricots and putting them through a coarse sieve. Then mix liquid from apricots with purée. Add all other ingredients. Mix thoroughly and freeze in refrigerator tray. Serve immediately after removing from refrigerator. Makes 2½ cups. Serves 8.

APRICOT SHERBET

27 calories per serving

¾ cup Diet Delight apricots

1 teaspoon unflavored gelatine

½ teaspoon lemon juice

¼ teaspoon grated orange rind

¼ teaspoon grated lemon rind

Drain juice from apricots; measure ½ cup and heat. Soften gelatine in lemon juice and dissolve in hot apricot juice. Force apricots through sieve. Stir in gelatine mixture and rinds. Turn into refrigerator tray and place in freezing compartment with control set at lowest temperature. Freeze 1 hour, or until thick layer of mixture on bottom and sides of tray is firm. Turn into chilled bowl and beat with rotary beater until smooth and fluffy. Return to freezing compartment and freeze to desired consistency. Reset temperature control to normal. Serves 3.

FROZEN COFFEE WHIP

38 calories per serving

½ cup ice water

½ cup nonfat dry milk

2 teaspoons Sucaryl

2 teaspoons instant coffee powder

1 egg white, unbeaten

Put ice water and dry milk in small mixing bowl of electric mixer; beat at low speed 1 minute to blend. Add Sucaryl mixed with coffee. Beat at high speed 5 minutes until light and fluffy. Add unbeaten egg white and beat 1 minute longer. Spoon mixture into 6 ½-cup molds. Freeze until firm—about 4 hours, or overnight. To unmold, loosen with edge of knife and tap mold. Serves 6.

QUICK COFFEE SHERBET

43 calories per serving

¼ cup instant coffee

1 tablespoon Sucaryl solution

½ cup evaporated milk

2 cups liquefied nonfat dry milk, or skim milk

Combine all ingredients, mixing thoroughly. Pour into freezing tray and freeze until almost firm. Loosen from tray and put into a large chilled mixing bowl. Break into small pieces with fork, then beat on low speed until creamy. Return to tray or freezer carton at once. Freeze until firm. Serves 8.

FRUIT MOUSSE

72 calories per serving

1 cup nonfat dry milk powder
1 cup cold water
1 6-ounce can undiluted quick-frozen concentrated fruit juice (orange, grapefruit, grape, tangerine, etc.)
1½ teaspoons Sucaryl solution

Sprinkle dry milk over cold water; beat with rotary egg beater or electric mixer until stiff. Beat in partially defrosted fruit juice and Sucaryl solution. Pour into refrigerator freezing tray and freeze until creamy firm. Serves 12, ½ cup each.

Also see Cranberry Sherbet and Cranberry Mousse in Fruit section.

If it is made with sugar, this frozen custard contains 169 calories.

CREAMY FROZEN CUSTARD

72 calories per serving

4 teaspoons cornstarch
¼ teaspoon salt
1½ cups skim milk
2 eggs, separated
2 teaspoons Sucaryl solution
2 teaspoons vanilla
½ teaspoon nutmeg
4 drops yellow food coloring
⅓ cup evaporated milk

Put cornstarch and salt in top of double boiler. Add skim milk; stir until cornstarch dissolves. Blend in beaten egg yellows and Sucaryl. Cook over hot water until mixture thickens—6 to 8 minutes—stirring constantly. Add vanilla, nutmeg, yellow coloring, and evaporated milk. Cool. Fold stiffly beaten egg whites into cooled custard. Pour into freezing tray and freeze. When firm, remove to chilled mixer bowl and beat on slow speed until creamy. Return to tray at once. Freeze until firm. Serves 6.

KOOL-AID SHERBET

44 calories per serving

1 package Kool-Aid, any flavor
3 cups skim milk
2 tablespoons Sucaryl solution

Dissolve Kool-Aid in milk; add Sucaryl. Pour into freezing tray of refrigerator and set control at coldest. When mixture is almost firm, spoon into cold bowl and beat with rotary beater until smooth but not melted. Return to tray and freeze until firm. Serves 6.

Another easy-to-make ice is this one.

NO-CAL MILK SHERBET

43 calories per serving

¾ cup evaporated milk
1½ teaspoons Sucaryl solution
1 16-ounce bottle No-Cal Orange or other diet beverage

Combine all ingredients; mix thoroughly. Pour into refrigerator tray; freeze to mush. Turn into chilled bowl; beat rapidly until smooth and creamy. Return to tray; freeze until firm. Serves 6.

———

Here is the quickest and simplest method of making lemon water ice—it can be done in about 2 minutes from start to finish, and it has only 30 calories for the whole quart.

LEMON WATER ICE

8 calories per cup

½ cup water
1 package Marvel lemon crystals
1 tablespoon Sucaryl solution or 24 Sucaryl tablets
8 crushed ice cubes

Put water, lemon crystals, and Sucaryl in Waring or other blender and mix until all is dissolved. Add crushed ice to fill glass container and switch to high. Makes 1 quart. Serve immediately. Serves 4.

Juice of 6 medium-size lemons can be used in place of Marvel crystals.

———

Made with sugar, this would be 189 calories for the same size serving.

FRESH LIME SHERBET

45 calories per serving

½ cup hot water
1 teaspoon finely grated lime rind
2 teaspoons Sucaryl solution
¼ cup lime juice
1 cup cold water
¼ teaspoon green food coloring
1 cup evaporated milk

To hot water in saucepan add lime rind and Sucaryl. Cover, and simmer over low heat 3 minutes. Remove from heat and add lime juice, cold water, and coloring. Blend in milk, stirring gently. (Mixture will curdle slightly.) Strain to remove rind, and freeze in freezing tray until almost firm. Loosen from tray and put into a large chilled mixer bowl. Break into small pieces with a fork, then beat on low speed until creamy. Return to tray or freezer carton at once. Freeze until firm. Serves 8.

Sherbet can be topped with melon balls or other fresh fruits and sprigs of mint.

FROZEN MAPLE CREAM
48 calories per serving

2 tablespoons flour
¼ teaspoon salt
1 cup liquefied nonfat dry milk or skim milk
2 teaspoons Sucaryl solution
2 eggs, separated
1 teaspoon maple flavoring

Put flour and salt in top of double boiler. Stir in a small amount of milk to make a smooth paste. Add remaining milk and Sucaryl. Cook over boiling water until thick (5 minutes), stirring constantly. Slowly pour hot mixture over beaten egg yellows in small mixer bowl. Beat at high speed until blended. Return mixture to top of double boiler. Cook, and stir, over gently bubbling water, until mixture mounds when dropped from a spoon (about 5 minutes). Add flavoring. Cool over ice cubes. Beat egg whites until they stand in soft peaks. Fold cold mixture into whites. Spoon into 6 ⅓-cup molds. Freeze until firm— about 2 hours. Unmold in sherbet glasses. Serves 6.

ORANGE ICE
40 calories per serving

1 envelope orange D-Zerta
½ cup hot water
1 cup orange juice
½ teaspoon grated orange rind
6 Sucaryl tablets

Dissolve D-Zerta in hot water. Add orange juice, rind, and sweetener. Freeze in freezing tray until almost firm, then beat until creamy. Return to refrigerator and freeze until firm. Serves 3, about ½ cup each.

ORANGE SHERBET
47 calories per serving

Use above recipe; beat until creamy. Fold into 1 egg white beaten until stiff. Freeze. Serves 2.

ORANGE POPSICLES

Use either of above recipes. Beat until creamy. Pour into ice cube tray. Insert a stick into each cube. Freeze until firm. Remove like ice cubes.

PEACH SHERBET
20 calories per serving

1 cup chopped unsweetened peaches
1 cup water
3 teaspoons Sucaryl solution
1 teaspoon grated lemon rind
⅓ cup orange juice
1 tablespoon lemon juice
2 egg whites, stiffly beaten

Combine peaches, water, and Sucaryl solution; add lemon rind, orange and lemon juice. Freeze firm. Beat to a mush; fold in egg whites. Return to freezing tray and freeze firm again. Serves 6.

___

PINEAPPLE SHERBET
66 calories per serving

- 1 lemon
- ¼ cup lemon juice
- ¾ cup water
- 8½ teaspoons Sucaryl solution
- 1 cup unsweetened crushed pineapple
- 2 cups buttermilk

Use only thin yellow of rind from lemon. Place in glass container of Waring Blendor and add lemon juice, water, and Sucaryl. Cover container and turn on blender. Run until rind looks finely grated—about 1 minute. Add pineapple and a few drops of green coloring, if desired. Blend 15 seconds longer. Pour blended mixture into mixing bowl containing buttermilk. Stir to mix well. Pour into freezing tray of refrigerator and freeze quickly. Serve when just frozen. Makes more than a quart. Serves 4.

___

Next comes a reducing dessert composed by the famous entertainer of the organ.

ETHEL SMITH FREEZE
48 calories per serving

- 1 package cherry diet gelatine

- 2 tablespoons skim-milk powder
- 1 8-ounce can apricot nectar
- 1 cup water

Put all ingredients into electric blender or bowl and mix thoroughly. Pour into freezer tray with motor-driven paddle and freeze. Or into regular tray, and freeze until ice crystals form, then take out, break pieces with wooden spoon in bowl, and beat with rotary beater or electric mixer until smooth. Return to tray, and freeze. Serve in sherbet glasses. Serves 4.

___

FRIGITEA
No calories

Sweeten fresh-brewed tea with Sucaryl to taste. Cool. Put in refrigerator tray and freeze until it is flaky. Serve in sherbet glasses with a slice of lemon for squeezing over.

___

VANILLA ICE CREAM
49 calories per serving

- 1½ cups skim milk
- 1 tablespoon Sucaryl solution
- 2 eggs, separated
- 1 teaspoon unflavored gelatine
- 2 teaspoons vanilla
- pinch of salt

Scald ¾ cup skim milk; add Sucaryl solution; pour over beaten egg yellows. Sprinkle gelatine over remaining milk.

Combine with hot milk mixture; stir until dissolved. Cool. Add vanilla and salt. Pour into freezing tray and freeze firm. Remove from tray to chilled bowl. Break up with wooden spoon. Beat

with electric mixer or rotary egg beater until free from lumps but crumbly. Fold in stiffly beaten egg whites. Return to tray and freeze firm. Serves 6.

PUDDINGS, CUSTARDS, ETC.

Puddings are desserts thickened with cornstarch or tapioca; custards are combinations of egg and milk that jell when cooked or baked slowly; "Junket" probably would be far more popular if it were not saddled with the least attractive name in modern advertising. It is a custardlike dessert that results from the action of a rennet tablet on milk.

Using skim milk and the least caloric ingredients available, here are some fine-tasting, filling sweets to end your dinner. Compare their calories with a ⅙ section of mince pie: 400 calories.

CHERRY FLUMMERY
48 calories per serving

1 No. 303 can Diet Delight or other unsugared cherries, drained
2 cups water
3 tablespoons cornstarch
1 tablespoon lemon juice
  few drops red vegetable coloring

Cut and pit cherries; combine with 1 cup of water and cook until soft. Mix cornstarch and 1 cup of water over low heat and cook until thickened, stirring constantly. Add to cherries slowly, continuing to stir. Bring to boiling point and cook 5 minutes. Remove from heat and add lemon juice and coloring. Serve with sauce made with liquid from drained cherries thickened with 1 tablespoon cornstarch and sweetened additionally with Sucaryl if desired. Serve hot or cold. Serves 4.

APPLE MERINGUE
126 calories per serving

2 cups stewed apples, hot
3 teaspoons Sucaryl solution
2 tablespoons butter
1 tablespoon lemon juice
½ teaspoon nutmeg
½ teaspoon cinnamon
3 eggs, separated
1 teaspoon vanilla

Combine stewed apples, half the Sucaryl, butter, lemon

juice, spices, and mix well. Beat the egg yellows and add to apple mixture. Beat until light. Pour into a buttered baking dish and bake in a hot (400°) oven about 15 minutes. Remove from oven and cover with a meringue made by beating the egg whites together with the rest of the Sucaryl and vanilla. Return to a moderately slow (325°) oven to brown the meringue. Serves 5.

Here is a low-caloried way of satisfying that longing for a piece of lemon meringue pie. The crust is missing but then many people never eat that part. If made altogether with sugar, it would be twice as rich in calories.

LEMON MERINGUE DESSERT
89 calories per serving

- 3 tablespoons cornstarch
- 1 tablespoon grated lemon peel
- 1½ cups water
- 6 tablespoons lemon juice
- 2 teaspoons Sucaryl solution
- 3 eggs, separated
- 1 tablespoon butter
- ½ teaspoon cream of tartar
- 2 tablespoons sugar
- ¼ teaspoon Sucaryl solution

Place cornstarch and lemon peel in a 1-quart saucepan. Blend water, lemon juice, Sucaryl, and egg yellows. Gradually add to the cornstarch mixture to make a smooth paste. Cook over a low heat, stirring constantly until mixture becomes quite thick. Stir in butter. Spoon into 6 6-ounce custard cups.

Meringue

Beat the egg whites until foamy. Add cream of tartar and beat until stiff. Gradually add sugar and the ¼ teaspoon Sucaryl solution. Spoon over lemon mixture. Place in a hot (400°) oven for about 5 minutes, or until meringue begins to brown. Serves 6.

One of the pleasantest ways to take your daily fat. egg, cereal, and milk is this pudding which, although higher than most desserts in this section, is still ⅓ lower than if made with sugar.

LEMON CHIFFON PUDDING
154 calories per serving

- 3 tablespoons softened butter or margarine
- 3 eggs, separated
- 2 teaspoons Sucaryl solution
- ¼ cup lemon juice
- 5 tablespoons flour
- ¼ teaspoon salt
- 1 cup skim milk
- 1 tablespoon grated lemon rind

Beat together butter or margarine and egg yellows. Mix Sucaryl with lemon juice; add to remaining ingredients, except egg whites, mixing well. Continue beating until mixture is very smooth and creamy. Beat egg whites stiff; fold into egg mixture. Pour into 1-quart casserole; place casserole in pan of warm water and bake in moderate (375°) oven 45 minutes, or until top is firm to the touch. Serve warm. Serves 5.

CHOCOLATE PUDDING

94 calories per serving

1 teaspoon unflavored gelatine
1 tablespoon water
1 tablespoon cornstarch
2 tablespoons cocoa
⅛ teaspoon salt
2 tablespoons water
2 cups liquefied nonfat dry milk, or skim milk
2 teaspoons Sucaryl solution
2 egg yellows, beaten
2 teaspoons vanilla

Mix gelatine with 1 tablespoon water. Set aside. Mix cornstarch, cocoa, salt, and 2 tablespoons of water to a smooth paste in a saucepan. Add milk and Sucaryl. Cook over medium heat until mixture boils—8 minutes—stirring constantly. Remove from heat. Stir in gelatine until dissolved. Pour a small amount of the hot mixture over beaten egg yellows. Blend with rest and return to saucepan. Cook 2 minutes longer over low heat, stirring constantly. (Mixture will thicken when chilled.) Cool slightly; add vanilla. Strain into 4 ½-cup molds or sherbet glasses. Chill until set. Serves 4.

If above recipe is made with sugar, it will add 96 calories to each portion.

TWO-TONE CHOCOLATE PUDDING

73 calories per serving

2 eggs
1½ teaspoons Sucaryl solution
¼ teaspoon salt (optional)
2½ cups skim milk
3 tablespoons breakfast cocoa
1 teaspoon vanilla

Beat eggs until frothy; add Sucaryl and salt. Blend cocoa with ½ cup cold milk; add remaining milk. Add vanilla. Pour into 6 custard cups. Set in pan of warm water. Bake in slow (300°) oven 1 hour, or until inserted knife comes out clean. Serves 6. Top with following:

Skim Milk Topping

Place 2 tablespoons water in a bowl with ¼ teaspoon Sucaryl solution, few drops lemon juice, and few drops of vanilla. Sprinkle 2 tablespoons dry skim milk over mixture and beat with rotary beater until stiff.

FRUIT PUDDING GLORIOSO
72 calories per serving

- 4 teaspoons cornstarch
- 2 cups unsweetened orange juice
- 1 medium-size ripe banana, mashed
- 1 cup canned dietetic pineapple, chopped fine
- 2 teaspoons Sucaryl solution
- 1 teaspoon lemon juice
- 1 teaspoon vanilla
  cinnamon
  nutmeg

Blend cornstarch with ¼ cup orange juice. Combine banana, pineapple, remaining orange juice, and Sucaryl in saucepan and bring to a boil. Add cornstarch solution, stirring constantly, until thickened to soft custard consistency. Cool. Add lemon juice, blending well; add vanilla, blending well. Pour into 6 individual dessert dishes. Dust top with cinnamon and nutmeg. Serves 6.

ALMOND AND COFFEE PUDDING
66 calories per serving

- 1½ cups skim milk
- 3 tablespoons cornstarch
- 4 teaspoons instant coffee powder
- ½ cup cold skim milk
- ¼ cup Sweeta, or 1½ teaspoons Sucaryl solution
- ¼ teaspoon almond flavoring

Scald 1½ cups milk in top of double boiler over boiling water. Meanwhile, mix cornstarch and coffee in small bowl; slowly stir in ½ cup cold milk and blend well. Slowly stir this mixture into scalded milk. Cook until smooth and thickened, stirring constantly. Cover. Cook 15 to 20 minutes, stirring often. Remove; cool. Add Sweeta and almond flavoring; blend well. Turn into 4 sherbet glasses. Chill. Serves 4.

If topped with 2 tablespoons of Soft Custard Pudding per portion, add 25 calories, making 91 for each serving.

CHOCOLATE SOUFFLE
87 calories per serving

- 1½ tablespoons butter or margarine, melted
- 2 teaspoons Sucaryl solution
- 1½ tablespoons flour
- ½ cup skim milk
- 3 tablespoons cocoa
- 3 eggs, separated
- 1½ teaspoons vanilla
- ¼ teaspoon cream of tartar

Combine butter or margarine and Sucaryl; set over low heat until butter is melted; blend in flour. Add milk; stir over medium heat until thickened. Add cocoa; mix well. Set aside and beat egg yellows until thick; add vanilla. Now add hot cocoa sauce very slowly. Add cream of tartar to egg whites; beat until stiff. Fold into egg-yolk mixture. Pour into ungreased 1-quart baking dish. Set in pan of hot water. Bake in moderate (350°) oven 45 minutes, or until firm. Serve with Fruit Sauce. Serves 6.

Fruit Sauce
7 calories per serving
Thicken 1 cupful orange juice with 1 teaspoon cornstarch and sweeten to taste with Sucaryl.

FRUIT SOUFFLE
105 calories per serving
- 1 cup skim milk
- 1 teaspoon vanilla
- 1 tablespoon flour
- 1 tablespoon water
- 3 egg yellows, beaten
- 3 egg whites, beaten stiff
- 1 cup (8-ounce can) Diet Delight or other sugarless fruit cocktail, drained

Scald milk and vanilla. Mix flour with 1 tablespoon cold water and add to milk solution; bring to a boil; cook 2 minutes. Remove from heat and allow to cool. Add egg yellows slowly and then fold in egg whites carefully. Butter a 1-quart mold and place drained fruit in bottom; pour batter over fruit, sprinkle top with cinnamon, if desired, and bake at 375°

40 minutes. Serve at once with fruit sauce made from liquid that was drained from fruit cocktail thickened with 1 tablespoon of cornstarch over low heat. Serves 4.

APRICOT TAPIOCA PARFAIT
106 calories per serving
- 1 egg, separated
- 2 cups milk
- 3 tablespoons quick-cooking tapioca
- 2¼ teaspoons Sucaryl solution
- ⅛ teaspoon salt
- ½ teaspoon vanilla
- 24 unsweetened apricot halves

Beat egg white stiff but not dry. Mix egg yellow with small amount of milk in a saucepan; add tapioca, Sucaryl, remaining milk, and salt. Cook over medium heat, stirring constantly, until mixture comes to a boil —5 to 8 minutes. Pour small amount of hot mixture into egg white, and blend. Add remaining mixture, stirring constantly. Add vanilla. Cool. Stir once after 15 minutes. Chill. Arrange alternate layers of tapioca and apricot halves in parfait glasses, using 4 apricot halves to a serving. Serves 6.

PINEAPPLE TAPIOCA PARFAIT

82 calories per serving

1 egg, separated
2 cups skim milk
3 tablespoons quick-cooking tapioca
2 teaspoons Sucaryl solution
⅛ teaspoon salt
½ teaspoon vanilla
1 8-ounce can dietetic pineapple, crushed

Beat egg white stiff but not dry. Mix egg yellow with small amount of milk in top of double boiler. Add tapioca, Sucaryl, remaining milk, and salt. Cook over boiling water, stirring constantly, until mixture thickens. Pour small amount of hot mixture into egg white; blend. Add remaining mixture, stirring constantly. Add vanilla. Chill. Drain pineapple, saving the juice for the sauce. Arrange alternate layers of tapioca and pineapple in 6 parfait glasses, using 1/6 of the Pineapple Sauce in each glass. Serves 6.

Pineapple sauce

pineapple juice from above
½ teaspoon Sucaryl solution
½ teaspoon cornstarch

Add Sucaryl and cornstarch to juice. Cook over low heat until thickened. Chill. Serve over parfait above.

COLA PUDDING

24 calories per serving

4 tablespoons quick-cooking tapioca
dash salt
2½ cups non-caloric cola beverage
Sucaryl solution, to taste
1 tablespoon lemon juice

Combine tapioca, salt, and cola; bring to a boil. Add lemon juice and sweetener to taste. Cool. Cover, and chill well. Serves 6.

Serve with Whipped Topping, see page 256.

BAKED CUSTARD

65 calories per serving

2 cups skim milk
2 eggs
1¼ teaspoons Sucaryl solution
¼ teaspoon salt
1 teaspoon vanilla
nutmeg or cinnamon

Scald milk in top of double boiler over simmering water. Beat eggs frothy; stir in Sucaryl, salt, and vanilla. Add hot milk and mix well. Strain into individual custard cups; sprinkle with spice. Set the filled cups in pan of hot water, having water within ½ inch of top of cups. Bake in slow (300°) oven 1 hour, or until silver knife inserted comes out clean. Serve cold. Serves 5.

SOFT CUSTARD
(or CUSTARD SAUCE)
81 calories per serving

2 eggs
2 cups skim milk
¼ teaspoon salt
1¼ teaspoon Sucaryl
    solution
1 teaspoon vanilla

Combine first 4 ingredients in top section of double boiler; beat slightly to blend. Cook over simmering water, stirring continuously, until mixture coats spoon. Remove from heat. Cool over cold water. Stir in vanilla; mix well. Chill. Serve cold as dessert, or as a sauce over pudding or fruit. Makes 4 servings.

Vary by using almond, rum, or sherry flavoring instead of vanilla.

BREAD CUSTARD
85 calories per serving

3 cups liquefied nonfat
    dry milk, or skim milk
3 slices bread
3 eggs
1 tablespoon Sucaryl
    solution
1 teaspoon vanilla
    cinnamon and nutmeg

Scald milk in 1-quart saucepan. Meanwhile, cube bread and place in 1-quart casserole. Combine eggs, Sucaryl, and vanilla, then blend into the scalded milk. Pour over the bread cubes. If desired, sprinkle top with cinnamom and nutmeg. Set in a pan of warm water and bake in a moderate (325°) oven 1 hour. Serves 8.

PUMPKIN CUSTARD
65 calories per serving

1½ cups canned pumpkin
1½ cups skim milk
2 eggs
2 teaspoons Sucaryl
    solution
½ teaspoon vanilla
1 teaspoon cinnamon
½ teaspoon ginger
¼ teaspoon salt

Place the pumpkin in a large mixing bowl. Combine skim milk, eggs, Sucaryl, vanilla, cinnamon, ginger, and salt. Add to pumpkin, blending well. Pour into 6 6-ounce custard cups. Bake in moderate (350°) oven 50 to 60 minutes, or until a silver knife inserted near the center of the custard comes out clean. (May also be baked in an 8-inch pastry shell. Add 109 calories per serving.) Serves 6.

PINEAPPLE-CHEESE CUSTARD
97 calories per serving

2 eggs, separated
1 cup skim-milk cottage
    cheese, sieved
1½ teaspoon Sucaryl
    solution
¼ teaspoon cinnamon
¼ teaspoon nutmeg
1 cup skim milk
1 8-ounce can unsweet-
    ened crushed or diced
    pineapple, drained

Beat egg yellows; add to cheese with Sucaryl and spices. Blend well. Add milk and drained pineapple. Beat egg whites stiff; fold in. Pour into 6 custard cups; sprinkle with additional nutmeg. Set cups in pan of warm water. Bake in moderate (350°) oven 45 minutes, or until silver knife inserted near rim comes out clean. Serves 6.

BASIC VANILLA RENNET DESSERT

27 calories per serving

- ⅔ cup nonfat dry milk powder
- 2 cups water
- ¾ teaspoons Sucaryl solution
- 1½ teaspoons vanilla
- 1 "Junket" rennet tablet nutmeg

Sprinkle dry milk on surface of water; beat with rotary eggbeater or in electric mixer until blended. Mix Sucaryl and vanilla with milk and heat to lukewarm (110°). Crush rennet tablet in 1 tablespoon water; when dissolved, add to lukewarm milk, stir a few seconds, and pour into serving dishes. Do not disturb for 10 minutes. Chill. Dust with nutmeg. Serves 4.

Other flavors can be made by following basic recipe and substituting for vanilla 1¼ teaspoons almond flavoring; 1 teaspoon lemon extract and several drops yellow food coloring; 1 teaspoon orange extract and several drops orange food coloring; 2 drops oil of peppermint and several drops red food coloring.

CHOCOLATE "JUNKET"

45 calories per serving

Follow basic recipe but substitute 1 tablespoon unsweetened powdered chocolate for vanilla.

PEACH "JUNKET"

50 calories per serving

Eliminate the vanilla in basic recipe and top 4 servings with 2 peaches fresh or canned without sugar, sliced.

PEAR "JUNKET"

57 calories per serving

Substitute 1 cup of quartered canned or fresh unsugared pears for peaches.

STRAWBERRY "JUNKET"

41 calories per serving

Substitute 1 cup of fresh strawberries.

APRICOT "JUNKET"

46 calories per serving

Use 1 cup of unsugared apricots.

APPLE "JUNKET"

48 calories per serving

Leave out vanilla in the basic recipe and top with 1 cup sliced apples divided among the 4 servings.

SWEET OMELET
45 calories per serving

2 eggs, separated
¼ teaspoon Sucaryl
   solution
   dash of salt
3 tablespoons diet
   preserves
2 tablespoons brandy

Beat egg yellows lightly with salt and Sucaryl. Beat egg whites with rotary or electric mixer. Fold whites into yellows and bake on grill or electric frying pan until done. Spread with your choice of unsugared preserves, jelly, or jam. Fold or roll, and transfer onto hot plate. Bring to table. Pour brandy over and light. Serve as soon as flame dies. Serves 4.

APPLE YOGURT MOUSSE
60 calories per serving

1 cup yogurt
2 cups unsweetened
   applesauce
¼ teaspoon powdered
   cinnamon
   fresh shredded coconut,
   for garnishing

Blend yogurt with applesauce and cinnamon, and put into glasses. Garnish with coconut before serving. Serves 6.

YOGURT COCONUT CREAM
130 calories per serving

1 jar Dannon or other
   yogurt (8 ounces)
2 ounces shredded fresh
   coconut
   Sucaryl (optional)
1 teaspoon powdered
   cinnamon

Blend yogurt with coconut and sweeten if desired. Put in 2 tall glasses and sprinkle with cinnamon. Serves 2.

COCONUT CREAMS
34 calories per piece

2 3-ounce packages
   cream cheese
2 teaspoons Sucaryl
   solution
1 teaspoon grated orange
   rind
½ cup shredded coconut,
   toasted

Mash cheese; whip until creamy. Add Sucaryl and orange rind and mix thoroughly. Form into balls about 1 inch in diameter, roll in coconut, and chill. Makes 24 pieces.

NECTAR RICE PUDDING
117 calories per serving

2½ cups Heart's Delight
   apricot, peach, or
   pear nectar
¼ cup rice
¼ teaspoon salt
2 teaspoons Sucaryl
   solution
¼ teaspoon nutmeg

Combine nectar, rice, salt, Sucaryl, and spice in lightly greased baking dish. Bake in moderately slow (325°) oven 2½ hours, stirring 3 times during first hour. Serve warm. Serves 4.

SWEET PILAU

111 calories per serving

1 1-pound can dietetic
    fruit cocktail
1 tablespoon Sucaryl
    solution
⅔ cup precooked rice
¼ teaspoon nutmeg
⅓ cup seedless raisins
⅓ cup chopped walnuts

*Drain and set aside fruit
cocktail. Measure liquid.
Add enough cold water to
make ¾ cup. Combine with
Sucaryl, rice, nutmeg, and*
raisins in saucepan; bring to
full boil. Remove from heat.
Cover. Let stand 10 min-
utes. Cool. Add fruit and
walnuts. Chill. Serves 8.

PREPARED PUDDINGS

There are several pud-
ding mixes (see Dietetic
and Low-Calorie Food Products) in addition to "Junket" tablets that are free of
sugar. These are either Sucaryl or saccharin sweetened and some of them also
contain substitutes for starch
and tapioca.

CAKES, PIES, COOKIES, AND BREADS

Here are some lower-cal-
orie cakes, cookies, pies, and
breads. It is not possible to
say "low calorie" because
to be baked successfully a
recipe must call for flour
and fat, two of the reducer's greatest enemies. Use
sparingly, as an occasional
change of taste from the
other desserts.

Store these baked goods
in the refrigerator or freezer
since they lack the sugar
that would otherwise act as
a preservative.

COCOA-FUDGE CAKE

133 calories per serving

½ cup hot water
1 teaspoon Sucaryl
    solution
3 tablespoons breakfast
    cocoa
2 tablespoons melted
    shortening
2 eggs, well beaten
1½ cups sifted flour
2 teaspoons baking
    powder
½ teaspoon baking soda
½ cup skim milk
1 teaspoon vanilla

*Add hot water and Sucaryl
slowly to cocoa, blending
thoroughly. Add shortening,
and cool. Add eggs gradu-
ally. Mix flour, baking powder, and soda and sift. Add
to cocoa mixture alternately
with mixed milk and vanilla.
Pour into lightly greased 8-
inch square cake pan. Bake
in moderate (350°) oven 30
to 35 minutes. Cool on rack.
Cut into 9 squares. Top
with Coconut Topping.
Serves 9.*

Coconut Topping
- ¼ cup dry skim milk
- ¼ cup cold water
- ½ teaspoon Sucaryl solution
- ½ teaspoon vanilla
- 2 tablespoons shredded coconut, toasted

Whip milk powder, water, and Sucaryl until stiff. Add vanilla. Fold in coconut. Spread on cake and serve immediately.

Harry Baker, a former bond salesman of Los Angeles, invented the Chiffon Cake. For almost twenty years he baked and sold them to the Brown Derby restaurants and never divulged the recipe. Then in 1947 he sold the secret to General Mills for $25,000 and soon the whole world was baking his cake. Sara Hervey Watts, home economic consultant for Abbott Laboratories, has revised the basic Chiffon Cake recipe by halving the amount of oil and leaving out sugar entirely. This cuts the calories per slice by a fat 82—from 178 to 96.

SUGARLESS CHIFFON CAKE

96 calories per serving
- 2¼ cups sifted cake flour
- 1 tablespoon baking powder
- 1 teaspoon salt
- ¼ cup salad oil
- ⅔ cup unbeaten egg yellows (8)
- ½ cup cold water
- 2 tablespoons lemon juice
- 2 teaspoons fine-grated lemon rind
- 2 teaspoons vanilla
- 1 cup egg whites (7 or 8)
- 1½ teaspoons cream of tartar
- 2 tablespoon Sucaryl solution
- ⅛ teaspoon yellow food coloring

Eggs should be at room temperature. Sift flour, baking powder, and salt into small mixing bowl; make a well in center. Add oil, egg yellows, water, lemon juice, rind, and vanilla. Beat with a wooden spoon until smooth. In large mixing bowl beat whites until foamy; add cream of tartar, Sucaryl, and coloring. Beat at high speed until very stiff peaks form (5 minutes). Do not underbeat. Gently fold in batter, smoothing out egg-white bumps. Do not stir. Pour at once into an ungreased 9- or 10-inch tube pan; smooth top. Bake in a slow (300°) oven 40 minutes, or until top springs back when lightly touched. Invert pan until cool, upside down, inserting small end of tube in neck of large funnel placed on tables. Serves 20.

For an 8- or 9-inch square cake, use half the recipe and bake 20 to 25 minutes. Cool by turning pan upside down and resting edges on 2 other pans.

ORANGE CHIFFON CAKE
98 calories per serving

Proceed as above, omitting vanilla and substituting orange juice for water and orange rind for lemon.

ORANGE DREAM CAKE
133 calories per serving

- ⅓ cup butter or margarine, melted
- 2 teaspoons Sucaryl solution
- ¼ teaspoon salt (optional)
- 2 eggs, slightly beaten
- 1¼ cups sifted cake flour
- 2 teaspoons baking powder
- ⅓ cup orange juice
- 2 tablespoons lemon juice

Add Sucaryl and salt to butter and blend. Add eggs and beat well. Sift flour and baking powder together and add alternately with the fruit juices to the egg mixture. Pour into a 9-inch greased pan and bake in moderate (375°) oven 25 to 30 minutes. Serves 8.

Topping
- juice and pulp of 1 ange
- poon Sucaryl tion

Boil Sucaryl and orange juice and pulp 2 or 3 minutes. Pour over cake about 10 minutes after it has been removed from the oven.

APRICOT UPSIDE-DOWN CAKE
157 calories per serving

- 3 8-ounce cans dietetic apricots
- 6 Maraschino cherries, cut in quarters
- 1 teaspoon cornstarch
- ¼ teaspoon Sucaryl solution
- ¼ cup shortening
- 2 egg yellows
- 1⅓ cups sifted cake flour
- 3 tablespoons sugar
- 1½ teaspoons baking powder
- ½ teaspoon salt
- ½ cup skim milk
- 1½ teaspoons Sucaryl solution
- ¾ teaspoon vanilla

Drain apricots and cherries on absorbent paper. Mix ¼ cup of apricot juice with cornstarch and ¼ teaspoon Sucaryl. Cook until thick. Brush 1 tablespoon of the mixture over bottom of an 8-inch layer-cake pan. Cream shortening until light and fluffy. Add egg yellows and beat well. Combine the sifted dry ingredients and add alternately with combined milk, additional Sucaryl, and vanilla to eggs and shortening. Place a piece of cherry in center of each apricot; place cut side down over bottom of pan. Pour batter over fruit. Bake in a moderate (350°) oven 35 minutes. Cool; invert on platter; brush with remaining thickened apricot juice. Serves 10.

Next you will find two recipes for cheese cake, the first made without baking. Either can be a delicious way to consume your daily allowance of egg, milk, and cheese.

NO-BAKE CHEESE CAKE
142 calories per serving

1 envelope Knox unflavored gelatine
⅛ teaspoon salt
1 egg, separated
½ cup skim milk
½ teaspoon grated lemon rind
1 tablespoon Sucaryl solution
1½ cups creamed cottage cheese
1 tablespoon lemon juice
1 teaspoon vanilla
6 tablespoons heavy cream, whipped

Mix together gelatine and salt in top of double boiler. Beat egg yellow and milk together; add to gelatine mixture. Cook over boiling water, stirring constantly, until gelatine is dissolved and mixture thickens—about 10 to 12 minutes. Remove from heat and add lemon rind and Sucaryl. Cool. Stir in cottage cheese, sieved, lemon juice, and vanilla. Chill, stirring occasionally, until mixture mounds slightly when dropped from a spoon. (While mixture is chilling, make Crumb Topping.) Fold stiffly beaten egg white and whipped cream into chilled gelatine mixture. Turn into 8-inch layer pan or 9-inch pie plate and sprinkle with Crumb Topping. Chill until firm. Serves 6.

Crumb Topping
Crush 2 graham crackers fine, mix with pinch of cinnamon and nutmeg, and sprinkle with Sucaryl sweetening powder.

If made with skim-milk cottage cheese, servings are 132 calories each.

CHEESE CAKE
182 calories per serving

4 eggs
1 tablespoon Sucaryl solution
½ cup flour
½ teaspoon salt
1 cup evaporated milk
1 teaspoon vanilla
2 tablespoons lemon juice
2 cups cottage cheese
nutmeg
1 slice bread, toasted and crumbed

Beat eggs; add Sucaryl. Beat in flour and salt. Add milk, vanilla, and lemo-

juice. Add slowly to cottage cheese, mixing well. Press through medium sieve; beat until smooth. Pour into shallow round (8-inch Pyrex) baking dish. Dust well with nutmeg; top with bread crumbs. Bake in very slow (250°) oven 1 hour. Turn off oven; leave cake in oven 1 hour longer. Cool slowly at room temperature. Chill. Serves 8.

ORANGE-CHEESE PIE
89 calories per serving

- 4 graham crackers, crushed
- 1 envelope unflavored gelatine
- 1 cup orange juice
- ¼ cup boiling water
- 1½ teaspoons Sucaryl solution
- 2 tablespoons lemon juice
- 1 tablespoon grated lemon rind
- 1 cup creamed cottage cheese
- nutmeg

Spread graham cracker crumbs evenly in 8-inch pie plate. Soften gelatine in a little of the orange juice; dissolve in boiling water. Combine dissolved gelatine, remaining orange juice, Sucaryl, and lemon juice. Chill until mixture is thickened, beginning to set. Whip until very light and fold in grated lem-

on rind and cottage cheese. Spoon gently into pie plate; sprinkle top with nutmeg. Chill. Serve with Whipped Topping. Serves 6.

Whipped Topping

- ¼ cup nonfat dry milk
- ¼ cup water
- 1 egg white
- ½ teaspoon Sucaryl solution
- 1 teaspoon grated lemon rind
- ½ teaspoon vanilla

Sprinkle milk powder over water. Whip rapidly until thick and foamy. Beat in egg white, Sucaryl, lemon rind, and vanilla. Continue heating until mixture is very thick and stands in peaks. Serve at once. Makes 2 cups.

The following is a fairly shallow deep-dish pie that saves 80 calories per serving by omitting the bottom crust.

CINNAMON APPLE PIE
176 calories per serving

- pastry for 1-crust pie
- 6 or 7 medium-sized tart apples, sliced
- 2 teaspoons Sucaryl solution
- 1 tablespoon lemon juice
- 2 tablespoons melted butter or margarine
- 2 tablespoons flour
- ½ teaspoon cinnamon
- ¼ teaspoon salt

Grease 9-inch pie pan lightly; spread apples in level
layer. Mix Sucaryl solution
in lemon juice. Blend to-
gether, until smooth, the
melted butter or margarine,
flour, cinnamon, salt, and
Sucaryl-lemon juice mixture.
Mix thoroughly. Spoon or
spread this entire mixture
over apples. Roll pastry into circle larger than filled
pie plate; fit pastry over
apples. Moisten rim of pie
plate; press pastry onto rim
with tines of fork. Cut several gashes in pastry. Bake
in hot (400°) oven 45 to 50
minutes. Cool. Serves 8.

In the search for a pie
shell that is least fattening,
the following was not only
first but also the easiest to
prepare.

GRAHAM-CRACKER CRUST
80 calories per ⅛th

6 saccharin or Sucaryl
   tablets
1 tablespoon water
¼ cup butter or
   margarine
18 2½-inch square
   graham crackers

Dissolve sweetener in water.
Cream butter until soft.
With rolling pin or potato
masher make fine crumbs of
graham crackers. (Should
make 1½ cups.) Mix butter
and crumbs thoroughly.
Work the dissolved sweet-
ener into crumb mixture.
Press over bottom and sides
of a deep 9-inch pie pan.
Bake for 10 minutes in oven
preheated to 325°. Cool.
Makes 8 sections.

LEMON ICEBOX PIE
176 calories per piece

Chill Graham-cracker Crust
and fill with Lemon Chiffon
Pudding (See Puddings,
Custards, Etc. section) that
is cool and soft but not firm.
Chill, and cut into 8 pieces.

SPANISH CREAM PIE
127 calories per piece

Chill Graham-cracker Crust.
Fill with Spanish Cream
(see Gelatine Desserts section) after it has been chilled and stirred once. Keep
chilled until serving time.
Cut into 8 pieces.

PEACH CREAM PIE
171 calories per serving

Proceed as for Spanish
Cream Pie, using Peach
Spanish Cream recipe and
topping with sliced peaches.

Make your own Icebox
Pie by using your choice of
pudding or prepared pud-
ding in that section or one
of the Gelatine Desserts
with Graham-cracker Crust
as shell and one of the
Whipped Toppings (also see
Sauces section) spread over
surface.

For Pumpkin Custard Pie,
see Page 249.

PEACH COBBLER
122 calories per serving

1 No. 2 can Diet Delight sliced peaches, drained
1 teaspoon lemon juice
⅛ teaspoon nutmeg
2 teaspoons melted butter
1 cup sifted cake flour
2 teaspoons baking powder
¼ cup shortening
1 egg, beaten
¼ cup skim milk
⅛ teaspoon Sucaryl solution
¼ teaspoon cinnamon

Heat oven to 350°. Combine first four ingredients and place in round 8 x 8 x 2 baking dish. Sift flour and baking powder. Work in shortening with pastry blender or two forks until consistency of corn meal. Stir in egg combined with milk and Sucaryl. Spread thinly over peaches. Sprinkle with cinnamon. Bake in moderate (375°) oven 40 minutes. Any Sucaryl-sweetened peaches may be used. Serves 8.

LEMON JELLY ROLL
76 calories per slice

5 eggs
3 tablespoons Sucaryl solution
2 tablespoons lemon juice
2 tablespoons grated lemon rind
2 teaspoons vanilla
¼ teaspoon yellow food coloring

¼ teaspoon salt
1 cup sifted cake flour

Have eggs at room temperature. Unshell them in large electric mixing bowl; beat at high speed until light— 5 minutes. Add Sucaryl, lemon juice, lemon rind, vanilla, coloring, and salt. continue beating at high speed until stiff peaks form—10 minutes. Sift flour into mixture while beating at low speed for 2 minutes. Line bottom of aluminum jelly-roll pan (15½ x 10½ x 1) with aluminum foil or well-oiled wax paper, then pour in batter. Smooth top. Bake in a slow (300°) oven 20 minutes, or until top springs back when lightly touched. Turn at once onto tea towel covered with wax paper. Peel off foil or paper from bottom of cake. Trim off ¼ inch on 4 sides. Roll up cake, towel and paper. Cool. Unroll and spread with Lemon Filling. Makes 12 slices.

Lemon Filling

1 cup water
2 tablespoons cornstarch
¼ teaspoon salt
¼ cup lemon juice
2 teaspoons Sucaryl solution
1 egg yolk
1 teaspoon butter
1 teaspoon grated lemon rind

Blend part of water with cornstarch and salt. Add remaining water, lemon juice, and Sucaryl. Cook, and stir over medium heat until thick—5 minutes. Stir small amount of hot mixture into egg yolk. Add to pan; cook and stir a few seconds longer. Add butter and lemon rind. Cool. Spread filling on cake. Roll cake up and chill again. Before serving, dust with Sucaryl sweetening powder or 1 tablespoon cornstarch mixed with 8 Sucaryl tablets crushed to fine powder.

If sugar had been used instead of Sucaryl, each slice would have been 173 calories.

CHOCOLATE SPONGE ROLL
74 calories per serving

5 eggs
5 teaspoons Sucaryl solution
1 tablespoon lemon juice
2 teaspoons vanilla
¼ teaspoon red food coloring
¾ cup sifted cake flour
¼ cup sifted cocoa
¼ teaspoon salt
¼ teaspoon soda

Have eggs at room temperature. Unshell eggs in large electric mixing bowl; beat at high speed until light—5 minutes. Add Sucaryl, lemon juice, vanilla, and food coloring. The red coloring gives a deep chocolate color when cake bakes. Continue beating at high speed until stiff peaks form—10 minutes. Sift dry ingredients together 3 times. Gradually blend cocoa-flour mixture into egg mixture at low speed for 2 minutes. Line bottom of jelly-roll pan (15½ x 10½ x 1) with well-oiled wax paper. Pour in batter; smooth top. Bake in a slow (300°) oven 20 minutes, or until top springs back when lightly touched.

While cake is baking, put tea towel on table; cover with wax paper. Sift with powder made of 1 tablespoon cornstarch and 8 finely crushed Sucaryl tablets. When roll is baked, turn onto prepared towel immediately. Peel paper from bottom of cake. Trim off crisp sides ¼ inch. Roll up cake, tea towel, and paper. Cool. Unwrap and spread with Cream Filling; then roll up again, rewrap, and place in refrigerator at least 2 hours before serving. Serves 12.

If made with sugar, each slice would contain 154 calories.

Cream Filling

2 tablespoons cornstarch
¼ teaspoon salt
1 cup water
1 tablespoon cream
1½ teaspoons Sucaryl solution
1 egg yolk, slightly beaten
¼ teaspoon vanilla

Put cornstarch and salt in saucepan; add water; stir until cornstarch dissolves. Add cream and Sucaryl. Cook over medium heat, stirring constantly, until mixture comes to a boil and is medium thick. Mix a small amount of the sauce with egg yolk and return to saucepan. Cook about 3 minutes longer, until well thickened. Stir in vanilla. Cool. Spread on Chocolate Sponge Roll.

If made with sugar, each rum baba would contain 158 calories. This recipe cuts the amount almost to half.

BABA AU RHUM
86 calories each

- 2 packages active dry yeast
- ⅓ cup warm water (90°)
- ½ teaspoon Sucaryl solution
- 2 cups sifted flour
- ½ teaspoon salt
- 3 eggs, beaten
- 1 tablespoon grated lemon peel
- 2 tablespoons melted butter or margarine

Sprinkle yeast on warm water; stir until dissolved. Add Sucaryl. Add ½ cup flour to yeast mixture. Cover; let rise in warm place until doubled in bulk. Add salt, eggs, melted butter, and remaining flour. Beat vigorously about 5 minutes.

Spoon into 12 cups of greased muffin pans 2 inches in diameter. Cover; let rise until double in bulk. Bake in moderate (350°) oven 20 to 25 minutes. Remove to cake rack. Cool. Prick bottoms with fork. Set in deep dish. Pour warm Rum Sauce over. Let cakes absorb sauce. Makes 12 babas.

Rum Sauce
Combine 1½ cups tea and 1½ teaspoons Sucaryl solution. Heat to boiling. Remove from heat; add 1 teaspoon rum flavoring.

Jimmy Hatlo, the "They'll Do It Every Time" cartoonist, always liked Banbury Tarts, so a lower-caloried version was created for him.

BANBURY TARTS
174 calories per tart

- 2 teaspoons Sucaryl solution
- 2 tablespoons cornstarch
- 1 egg, beaten
- 1 cup water
- juice 1 lemon
- 1 teaspoon grated lemon peel
- 1 cup seedless raisins
- 1 package pie pastry mix

Combine Sucaryl, cornstarch, egg, and water. Cook over low heat, stirring constantly, until thickened. Add lemon juice and grated lemon peel. Remove from heat; add raisins; cover; cool. Prepare pastry according to directions on package; roll out to ⅛-inch thickness. Cut into 10 4-inch squares. Spoon 1 tablespoon raisin mixture into center of each square; fold over to make a triangle. Press edges of triangles with tines of fork. Prick design in top of each tart to allow steam to escape. Bake in hot (425°) oven, 10 to 15 minutes, or until lightly browned. Makes 10 tarts.

STRAWBERRY TARTS

148 calories per tart

1 cup sifted flour
½ teaspoon salt
⅓ cup shortening
cold water
1 quart hulled strawberries
2 tablespoons Sucaryl solution

Mix and sift flour and salt; cut in shortening with two knives or pastry blender. Sprinkle with 1 tablespoon cold water. Mix in lightly with fork; continue adding water until pastry gathers around fork in soft ball. Roll out ⅛ inch thick on lightly floured board. Cut in 8 rounds large enough to fit over outside of fluted tart-shell pans. Turn pans upside down; press pastry circles on pans; trim edges. Prick pastry with fork. Bake upside down in hot (450°) oven 10 to 12 minutes. Cool

slightly; remove from pans. Cool thoroughly.
Measure 2 cups strawberries, crush slightly, add Sucaryl and 3 tablespoons water. Simmer 5 minutes. Cool. Remove berries to cool. Thicken liquid by cooking down. Place cooked strawberries in bottom of tart shells. Fill with remaining whole berries. Spoon liquid over berries. Makes 8 tarts.

CREAM PUFFS

82 calories per filled puff

¼ cup butter
½ cup water
½ teaspoon Sucaryl solution
½ cup flour
2 eggs

Heat butter and water over low heat in small saucepan until butter is melted. Add Sucaryl; stir. Add flour all at once; stir vigorously until mixture leaves sides of pan. Immediately remove from heat. Quickly beat in eggs, one at a time. Continue to beat until mixture forms dough. Drop with wet spoon, by heaping teaspoonfuls, on lightly greased cookie sheet, about 2 inches apart, shaping with wet spoon into 18 rounds. Bake in hot (425°) oven 25 to 30 minutes, or until puffed, dry, and golden brown. Cool. Makes 18 puffs.

Cream Filling

- 3 tablespoons cornstarch
- 1 egg
- 2 cups skim milk
- 2 teaspoons Sucaryl solution
- 1 teaspoon vanilla

Mix cornstarch and egg. Scald milk with Sucaryl; add to egg mixture. Cook in top of double boiler, stirring constantly, until thickened. Cover. Cook 10 minutes. Stir in vanilla. Cool. Cut baked puffs straight across close to bottom and fold top back. Fill with custard filling and close top.

SPICE STRIPS

47 calories per cookie

- ½ cup shortening, melted and cooled
- 1½ teaspoons Sucaryl solution
- 2 eggs
- 2 cups sifted flour
- 2 teaspoons double-acting baking powder
- ¾ teaspoon ground cloves
- 1 teaspoon cinnamon
- ½ teaspoon nutmeg
- ½ cup orange juice
- ¼ cup coarsely broken walnuts

Add Sucaryl to melted shortening. Beat eggs; add to shortening. Mix and sift flour, baking powder, and spices; add to egg mixture alternately with orange juice. Spread in shallow pan (15 x 10 x 1); sprinkle with walnuts. Bake in moderate (350°) oven 35 minutes. Cut 5 times across and 5 times down for 36 cookies.

CINNAMON SHORTIES

32 calories per cookie

- 5 tablespoons shortening
- 1 cup sifted all-purpose flour
- ¼ teaspoon baking powder
- 2 teaspoons Sucaryl solution
- 2 teaspoons vanilla
- 1 tablespoon milk, fruit juice, or coffee
- 1 teaspoon cinnamon

Cream shortening. Mix and sift flour and baking powder; blend in shortening. Mix Sucaryl in combined vanilla and milk or other liquid. Stir into flour mixture and mix thoroughly. Sprinkle cinnamon over dough; knead in so that dough presents a streaked appearance. Shape dough into small balls and arrange on lightly greased cookie sheet. Flatten balls with fork dipped in cold water. Bake in moderate (375°) oven 12 to 15 minutes, or until edges are brown. Makes 30 cookies.

CHOCOLATE-NUT BROWNIES
54 calories per square

1 square (1 ounce) un-sweetened chocolate
⅓ cup butter
2 tablespoons Sucaryl solution
2 teaspoons vanilla
2 eggs
1 cup sifted cake flour
½ teaspoon salt
½ teaspoon soda
¾ cup chopped walnuts

Melt chocolate and butter in saucepan over low heat. Remove from heat. Add Sucaryl, vanilla, and beaten eggs. Stir until well blended. Add flour, salt, and soda. Mix until blended. Stir in nuts. Pour into a greased 8-inch square pan. Level batter in pan. Bake in a slow (325°) oven 20 minutes. Cut into 32 squares. Without nuts the brownies are 37 calories each.

CITRUS SEED COOKIES
29 calories per cookie

¼ cup shortening
2 teaspoons Sucaryl solution
1 teaspoon vanilla
¼ cup orange juice
1 tablespoon coarsely grated orange rind
½ teaspoon aniseed
1 cup sifted flour
¼ teaspoon baking powder
¼ teaspoon salt

Cream shortening. Mix Sucaryl with vanilla and orange juice. Add rind and aniseed. Sift the dry ingredients together and add alternately with the liquid to the shortening. Shape dough into a roll and wrap in waxed paper. Chill until firm. Cut into 30 thin slices and place on an ungreased cookie sheet. Bake in a hot (400°) oven 12 to 15 minutes, or until edges become brown. Makes 30 cookies.

In Palm Springs, California, near the date groves, author Frank Scully persuaded his wife Alice to mix some of the local produce into her cookies.

DATE PINWHEEL COOKIES
36 calories per cookie

2 teaspoons Sucaryl solution
¾ cup butter or margarine, melted
1 teaspoon vanilla
2½ cups sifted flour
¼ teaspoon baking powder

Add Sucaryl to melted shortening and blend well. Add vanilla. Sift flour and baking powder together; add to shortening. Dough should be just moist enough to form a ball (if not, add water by teaspoonfuls until it does). Chill at least 1 hour. Roll out to a rectangle 10 by 20 inches.

Date Filling

1 cup chopped dates
¼ cup water
1 teaspoonful Sucaryl solution

Cook dates and water over low direct heat until just thickened. Add Sucaryl and cool.

Spread date filling over rectangle of cookie dough. Roll up, starting with 20-inch side nearest you. This will form a 20-inch roll. Chill overnight in refrigerator.

Cut into 60 cookies of ⅓-inch thickness. Bake on ungreased cookies sheet in moderate (375°) oven 12 to 15 minutes. Makes 60 cookies.

COCONUT KISSES
28 calories per kiss

2 saccharin or Sucaryl tablets
1 tablespoon evaporated milk
⅛ teaspoon vanilla
¾ cup shredded coconut (2 ounces)
few grains salt
1 tablespoon nonfat dry milk

Dissolve saccharin tablets in evaporated milk. Add vanilla and stir in coconut, salt, and dry milk. When blended, drop by teaspoonfuls an inch apart on a greased cookie sheet. Bake

on center shelf of moderate (375°) oven 10 minutes, or until light brown. Makes 12 pieces.

OATMEAL COOKIES
32 calories per cookie

1½ cups quick-cooking oatmeal (uncooked)
⅔ cups shortening, melted and cooled
2 eggs, beaten
1 tablespoon Sucaryl solution
1½ cups sifted flour
½ teaspoon salt (optional)
2 teaspoons baking powder
½ cup skim milk
1 teaspoon vanilla
¼ cup currants or raisins

Measure oatmeal into 1-quart mixing bowl. Stir in shortening, mixing well. Blend in combined eggs and Sucaryl. Sift dry ingredients together. Add alternately with combined milk and vanilla. Mix in currants or raisins. Drop by level teaspoonfuls on baking sheet. Bake in hot (400°) oven 10 to 15 minutes, or until golden brown. Makes 72 cookies.

If chocolate pieces are used instead of currants or raisins, add 1½ calories per cookie.

LEMON BRAN TEA WAFERS

18 calories each

2 eggs
1 teaspoon Sucaryl solution
½ cup melted butter
1 tablespoon lemon juice
1 tablespoon finely grated lemon rind
½ cup all-bran
2 cups sifted flour
1 teaspoon baking powder

Beat eggs, Sucaryl, butter, lemon juice, lemon rind, and all-bran in small mixing bowl until blended. Sift in flour and baking powder. Mix well. Shape into a 6-inch roll. Wrap in waxed paper and chill overnight. Cut into ¼-inch slices. Roll each slice into a thin 5-inch wheel on a floured board and cut into 4 quarters. Bake on ungreased cookie sheet in hot (400°) oven 6 minutes, until browned. Makes 100 cookies.

WALNUT BUTTER BALLS

43 calories per cookie

½ cup butter or margarine, melted and cooled
2 teaspoons Sucaryl solution
2 tablespoons sugar
1 cup sifted flour
1 teaspoon vanilla
¼ cup chopped walnuts

Add Sucaryl to shortening. Add sugar, flour, and va-nilla. Knead dough till well mixed. Add walnuts; knead again. Form into small balls about ¾ inch in diameter. Bake on ungreased cookie sheet in moderate (350°) oven 12 to 15 minutes, or until light brown. Makes 30 cookies.

ORANGE ANISE COOKIES

29 calories per cookie

1¾ teaspoons Sucaryl solution
¼ cup orange juice
1 teaspoon vanilla
4 tablespoons shortening
1 cup flour
¼ teaspoon salt
¼ teaspoon baking powder
1 scant teaspoon aniseed
1 tablespoon grated orange peel

Mix Sucaryl in combined orange juice and vanilla. Cream shortening. Sift dry ingredients together. Mix shortening, dry ingredients, and liquid together. Knead in aniseed and orange peel. Shape dough into roll and wrap in waxed paper. Chill until firm. Cut in slices ⅛-inch thick; place on un-greased cookie sheet and bake in hot (400°) oven 12 minutes, or until brown around edges. Makes 30 cookies.

NUT COOKIES

36 calories per cookie

Omit aniseed and add ¼ cup finely chopped walnut meats.

ORANGE NUT DROPS

34 calories per cookie

- ½ cup butter or margarine
- 2 teaspoons Sucaryl solution
- 1 egg
- 2 tablespoons orange juice
- 1 tablespoon grated orange rind
- ½ teaspoon vanilla
- 1¾ cups sifted flour
- ¼ teaspoon salt
- 1 teaspoon baking powder
- ½ teaspoon soda
- ½ cup skim milk soured with 1 teaspoon vinegar
- ½ cup chopped English walnuts

Cream butter in small electric mixing bowl at high speed until well softened. Mix Sucaryl with egg, orange juice, rind, and vanilla; add to butter. Sift dry ingredients together and add alternately with the soured milk. Blend in nuts. Drop by teaspoonfuls onto greased cookie sheet. Cut through batter with edge of spoon to flatten each cookie slightly. Bake in a moderate (375°) oven 18 to 20 minutes. Store cooled cookies in a container with a loose cover. Makes 56 cookies.

PEANUT-BUTTER COOKIES

34 calories per cookie

- 2 teaspoons Sucaryl solution
- 1 tablespoon butter or margarine, melted and cooled
- ½ cup peanut butter
- 2 eggs, slightly beaten
- 1 cup sifted flour
- ½ cup skim milk
- ¼ teaspoon baking soda

Add Sucaryl to shortening; add peanut butter; blend well. Add eggs; blend again. Add flour alternately with milk to which the baking soda has been added; blend well after each addition. Drop by heaping teaspoonfuls on ungreased cookie sheet. Bake in moderate (375°) oven 15 minutes. Makes 40 cookies.

BANANA-NUT MUFFINETTES

35 calories per piece

- 1 egg
- 1 banana, mashed
- 2 teaspoons Sucaryl solution
- 1¾ cups sifted cake flour
- 3 teaspoons baking powder
- ½ teaspoon salt
- ⅔ cup skim milk
- 1 teaspoon vanilla
- ¼ cup broken nut meats
- 2 tablespoons shortening, melted

Beat egg; add banana and Sucaryl. Mix and sift flour,

*baking powder, and salt;
add alternately with milk.
Add vanilla, nut meats, and
shortening, mixing well. Fill
very small muffin pans
(about 1½ inches bottom diameter) ¾ full. Bake in hot
(400°) oven about 20 min-
utes, or until golden brown.
Makes 30 muffinettes.*

CORN-MEAL-RAISIN MUFFINS
30 calories per small muffin, 63 per large

- 2 teaspoons Sucaryl solution
- 2 eggs, beaten
- ⅓ cup shortening, melted and cooled
- 1¼ cups corn meal
- ¾ cup sifted flour
- 2½ teaspoons baking powder
- ¾ teaspoon salt (optional)
- 1 cup skim milk
- ⅓ cup raisins

*Add Sucaryl and beaten
eggs to shortening; mix well;
stir in corn meal. Mix and
sift flour, baking powder,
and salt; add alternately
with milk to corn-meal batter. Add raisins. Place by
measured tablespoons in
muffin pans. If you use
small muffin pans, use 1 tablespoon of batter per cup.
If you use larger muffin
pans, use 2 tablespoons.
Bake in hot (400°) oven 25
minutes. Makes 44 small
muffins, 22 medium to large
muffins.*

If made with sugar, each
muffin would contain ⅓ more
calories.

BLUEBERRY CORN-MEAL MUFFINS
27 calories per small muffin, 57 per large

*Substitute blueberries for
raisins in above recipe and
increase amount of Sucaryl
solution slightly, according
to sweetness of berries.*

BLUEBERRY GLUTEN MUFFINS
58 calories per muffin

- 1 egg
- ½ cup skim milk
- ¼ cup Diamel or other self-rising gluten flour
- pinch of salt
- 2 teaspoons melted butter
- 3 ounces fresh or diet-canned blueberries

*Beat eggs and skim milk,
then stir into flour. Add
salt and butter; beat until
smooth. Add blueberries
and mix. Pour into greased
tins and bake in moderate
(350°) oven for about 25
minutes, or until muffins are
well browned. If sweeter
muffins are desired, add Sucaryl. Makes 6 muffins.*

HOME-MADE GLUTEN BREAD
57 calories per slice

- 1 cube compressed yeast or 1 package dry yeast
- 1 cup lukewarm water
- ½ pound Diamel or other gluten flour
- ⅛ teaspoon salt

*Dissolve yeast in water. Add
flour and salt. Combine all
ingredients and mix thor-
oughly. Knead dough until*

stiff. Place into bread pan and allow dough to rise in a warm place 1 hour. Bake in a moderate (350°) oven 45 minutes. Makes 1 loaf, or 16 slices.

This bread would have more than double the amount of calories if made with sugar.

PECAN BREAD
94 calories per slice

⅓ cup butter or margarine, melted and cooled
2¼ teaspoons Sucaryl solution
1 egg, slightly beaten
2 cups sifted flour
1 teaspoon salt (optional)
1 tablespoon baking powder
½ teaspoon cinnamon
¼ teaspoon ginger
⅛ teaspoon nutmeg
1 cup skim milk
½ cup chopped pecans

Add Sucaryl to butter or margarine and blend well. Add egg; mix well. Mix and sift dry ingredients; add to shortening alternately with milk. Stir in pecans well. Pour into greased loaf pan. Bake in moderate (350°) oven about 1 hour. Let stand 1 day, well wrapped in wax paper or foil, for easier slicing. Makes 20 slices.

Below is a simple recipe for pancakes that taste like blintzes but have the cheese right inside. Since they con-tain neither flour nor sugar, they are ideal for diabetics as well as other dieters. Using new electrical appliances, no butter or shortening is necessary.

CHEESECAKES
53 calories per cake

2 eggs
2 ounces pot or skim milk cottage cheese
1 tablespoon Escoffier Robert sauce
salt

Mix ingredients in Waring or other high-speed mixer for 1 minute. Pour into Sunbeam automatic frying pan or other controlled-heat frying pan heated to 320°. Cook until light brown. Cut into 4 sections, turn each, and cook until other side is done. Makes 4 pancakes.

SEASONINGS FOR BAKING

For all baking: Anise seed and powder, Caraway, Cardamon (especially for Danish pastry), Cinnamon, Cloves, Coriander, ground Ginger, Lemon rind, Licorice, Lime rind, ground Mace and Nutmeg, Saffron, Sesame seed, Vanilla.

Bread and Rolls: Cumin, Celery seed.

Cakes, Cookies: ground Allspice, Angelica, Fennel seed, Pistachio and Pine nuts, Poppy seed, Turmeric.

Pies: Cumin.

Let the dieter order eggs for breakfast at a restaurant and what does he get? 2 eggs, (154 calories), plus hash-brown or French-fried potatoes (470 to 640 calories), 2 pieces of toast (126 calories), buttered (80 to 100 calories), with jam or jelly (55 calories a level tablespoon) on the side.

This simple order will put on 885 to 1,185 calories where 154 are wanted. And two eggs, retail price around 15 cents, will cost you from 75 cents to a dollar, eating out.

This is the most horrible example of what the dieter faces away from home. Attempts to get waiters, waitresses, and kitchen help to cooperate with a dieter's needs will get results depending on the nature of the restaurant, the good nature of the serving people—and the dominant nature of the dieter.

Restaurants are run in ruts, and every effort is made to standardize orders, as anyone who has ever tried to get them to deviate from the standard can testify. However, they are beginning to encounter more and more dieters, who are breaking down resistance, getting green vegetables in place of the heavy starches, dry entrées instead of gravy-covered, and empty space on the plate in place of tempting, calorific potatoes, rice, noodles, dressing, sauces, and yams with marshmallows on top and a candied cherry on top of that.

But the battle is far from won. More expensive restaurants are more amenable to changing set orders, but they serve larger portions. Tearooms are your best bet for skimpy servings, but they counterbalance this with a tremendous variety of super-fattening desserts. In New York most waiters are too rushed or too surly to relay to the chef "no French fries with the steak," or "no gravy on the pot roast." On the other hand, they are so rushed that they snatch up your plate before you are finished, cutting down the size of your portion that way.

Until dieters win a permanent victory against grease, gravy, and starches in eating establishments, the most effective way to diet while dining out is to look your waiter straight in the eye, no mumbling or gazing down at the menu when you order, and say: "No bread or butter. A green vegetable instead of the potatoes. No gravy or sauce on the meat. Coffee black." Then smile, shrug, and let him have it: "Doctor's orders."

A waiter may dispute your need to reduce or argue that your diet ideas are all wrong, but there are very few of them who care to go up against a member of the medical profession.

WHAT TO DO ABOUT LUNCH

Eating wisely at lunchtime is difficult for dieters who work away from home. Luncheon is usually a rush job in a crowded place with only high-calorie foods available.

Frequently the choice is limited to sandwiches thick in bread, thin in protein ingredients, with fried potatoes or potato chips or potato salad on the side. If we discard the high-calorie, high-starch part of the sandwich, we are paying from 50 cents to a dollar for two ounces of meat or cheese. That means we are buying what we need at $4.00 to $8.00 a pound.

It isn't always feasible to pack and bring your lunch to work, but where it is, there are distinct advantages, nutritionally, budgetwise, and simply in solving the problem of where to eat and how fast you can begin.

The first step toward enjoying a balanced, healthful lunch is to have a good breakfast. This will mean that you have adequate blood sugar coursing through your veins so that you are not ravenous and your efficiency isn't impaired during the last hour before luncheon. It means you won't go off the rails and overeat, since it is the nature of the envelope, as Dr. Alexis Carrel called the body, to demand that we make up what we have denied it.

If you have a good foundation at breakfast, a lunch that is light in calories but adequate in bulk and taste satisfaction is sufficient to see you through the work-day. Today lunchboxes are attractive, compact and pro-tect the food, especially if hot-cold bottles with wide mouths are used. These al-low you to carry soups and even stews as well as hot and cold drinks. And paper and foil containers permit you to carry and eat in com-fort any non-perishable dish.

SANDWICH TIPS AND SUBSTITUTES

Of course sandwiches are the most convenient lunch dishes, and sandwiches mean bread at 130 calories for each 2 slices. Or do they? Why not slice your bread half as thick; use rolls and buns in which half the soft bread has been scooped out of the center (see 100- Cal-orie Sandwiches); try more low-calorie salad dressings as spreads in place of 100-calorie-per-tablespoon but-ter; cut down on the num-ber of sandwiches by re-placing one with a cup of salad, or a chicken leg or a piece of lean smoked fish?

VEGETABLE A DAY

Pack a different raw vege-table each day. Here are 28 varieties for 28 days: Wedges of green, white, and red cabbage; sauer-kraut; carrots, whole and in sticks; red and white rad-ishes; celery stalks, hearts, root; cucumber sticks and whole; egg, plum, and regu-lar tomatoes; cauliflowerets; scallions, sweet red and green bell peppers; endive or chicory; baby green peas; cress and water cress; Bibb, Romaine, and head lettuce; sour, dill, and diet sweet pickles; fresh pimentos; spin-ach leaves.

DESSERTS

Fresh fruit, in moderation, is your best bet. Vary this occasionally with a baked apple or pear. Also low-cal-orie custards and puddings or gelatine desserts that do not require refrigeration. Or take 2 or 3 low calorie cook-ies.

BEVERAGES

Almost any listed in the Beverage section. Also hot and cold soups to begin the meal. Skim milk and butter-milk, clear tea and coffee, and fruit or vegetable juices give you more choices.

100-CALORIE SANDWICHES

The ordinary sandwich (and it makes little differ-ence whether it is on white or dark bread) averages 300 calories, ranging from chicken-salad sandwich at 245 to club at 590.

To make sandwiches that frequently have less than 100 calories, start with a round bun or roll, such as are used for hamburgers. These average 1 ounce, and bread or rolls have about 78 calories per ounce. Split the roll and hollow out half of the soft bread in each half. This leaves you with around 40 calories of bread. Fill in each half with 2 tablespoons of a filling that does not exceed 15 calories per tablespoon, then press halves together, and you have a satisfying sandwich that is only ⅓ as fattening as the ordinary kind.

FILLINGS

In addition to any of the cottage-cheese combinations listed in Cheese, Pasta and Combination Dishes section and the spreads in the Anti-Appetizer section, try:

CARROT-PINEAPPLE SPREAD

1 cup skim-milk cottage cheese mixed with ¼ cup shredded carrot and ¼ cup drained crushed unsweetened pineapple, with a dash of salt. Makes 24 tablespoons, 10 calories each.

CARROT-OLIVE SPREAD

1 cup Sealtest or other skim-milk cottage cheese mixed with ¼ cup shredded carrot and 1 tablespoon fine-chopped olive, with dash of salt. Makes 20 tablespoons, 12 calories each.

EGG-PICKLE SPREAD

1 cup cottage cheese mixed with 1 hard-cooked egg, chopped, and ¼ cup chopped sweet dietetic pickles, seasoned with salt, pepper, and ¼ teaspoon Worcestershire. Makes 24 tablespoons, 13 calories each.

PICAPEPPER SPREAD

1 cup cottage cheese, ¼ cup each celery, diet sweet pickles, and green or sweet red pepper, all chopped fine. Makes 28 tablespoons, 9 calories each.

CHICKEN-SALAD SPREAD

½ cup chopped breast of fryer, ½ cup chopped celery, 2 tablespoons low-calorie mayonnaise-type dressing. Makes 10 tablespoons, 9 calories each. Lettuce or water cress can be substituted for celery.

Cod, crab meat, coleslaw, cucumbers, flounder, lobster, pimentos, radishes, and shrimps are other components for 100-Calorie Sandwich Spreads.

PRESERVING FRUITS—AND YOUR FIGURE

If the body is to remain trim and healthy, the good habits of sensible and nutritious eating you acquire while dieting should be kept up. For one thing, you can plan ahead to continue using less sugar by purchasing fruits when they are ripe and sweet (and least expensive), canning or freezing them with or without Sucaryl for use during the months when fresh fruit is not available.

With so many available brands of quick-frozen fruits (make sure by reading the label that they do not contain sugar or sugar syrup) and canned-without-sugar fruits, home preserving is no longer the essential activity it once was. Still, many people prefer the personally packed article, either because of family tradition, pride in their preserving ability, or just because it can be much less expensive.

Fruits such as apricots, nectarines, peaches, and strawberries will become discolored in freezing or canning unless a solution of ascorbic acid (Vitamin C) or citric acid (lemon juice) is added to the preserving liquid.

Some fruits (strawberries, cranberry sauce, plums) should be used within 3 months of canning because Sucaryl does not have the preserving qualities of sugar.

In pickling and preserving, where more than 2 or 3 tablespoons of Sucaryl are to be used, sweeten and taste gradually, since the sweetening power of Sucaryl tends to change when larger amounts are used.

273

HOME CANNING
WITH SUCARYL
(WATER-BATH METHOD)

To make 3-per-cent brine, dissolve 2 tablespoons salt in 1 quart water. Be sure fruit is completely covered with prepared liquid (Sucaryl or Sucaryl and ascorbic acid plus water or juice, according to the fruit) but leave ½-inch headroom above level of liquid. Remove air bubbles before processing by running a knife between fruit and jar.

Seal or partially seal jars before processing, depending on type of lid used. If partially sealed, complete seal as soon as jars are removed from water bath.

Obtain ascorbic acid powder at drugstore; make liquid solution by dissolving ½ teaspoon in 2 tablespoons of water.

SLICED APPLES
83 calories per medium apple

Select firm, tart cooking apples. Wash; pare; core; slice into 3-per-cent brine. Drain. Simmer in small amount of water 5 minutes. Drain, saving juice. Pack, hot, in sterilized containers. Fill containers with boiling hot liquid in the proportions of 1 teaspoon Sucaryl solution to 1 cup apple juice from cooking. Process 15 minutes; cool.

APPLESAUCE
100 calories per cup

Select firm, tart cooking apples. Wash; core; quarter; do not pare. Drop into 3-per-cent brine. Drain. Cook in small amount of water until soft. Put through food mill, grinder, or sieve. Measure. Add 1 teaspoon Sucaryl solution to every 1 cup applesauce. Bring to boil. Pour, boiling hot, into sterilized containers. Process 15 minutes. Cool. Label.

BLUEBERRIES
86 calories per cup

Pick over berries; wash; drain on absorbent paper. Pack in hot, sterilized containers. Cover berries with boiling hot liquid, using ½ teaspoon Sucaryl solution to each 1 cup water. Process 15 minutes. Cool. Seal.

BLACKBERRIES
82 calories per cup

Same as for blueberries, except use 2 teaspoons Sucaryl solution to 1 cup of water and process 20 minutes instead of 15.

STRAWBERRIES
54 calories per cup

Same as for blueberries, except use 1½ teaspoons Sucaryl solution plus ⅛ teaspoon ascorbic acid to 1 cup of water. Process 15 minutes.

Do not store canned strawberries longer than 3 months.

CRANBERRY SAUCE

54 calories per cup

Wash; pick out too soft or wrinkled berries. Cook 4 cups of berries with 1 cup water 5 minutes. Add 4 teaspoons Sucaryl solution and 1 cup water. Cook 3 minutes longer. Pack in hot sterilized jars. Process 5 minutes; cool; label. Use within 3 months.

PEACHES

77 calories per cup, sliced

Dip freestone peaches in boiling water; plunge into cold water; slip off skins. Cling peaches must be peeled by hand. Halve or slice; remove pits; drop into 3-per-cent brine. Drain. Pack in hot sterilized jars. Cover fruit with boiling hot liquid, using 1 tablespoon Sucaryl solution and ¼ teaspoon ascorbic acid for each cup of water. Process 20 minutes; cool; label.

PEARS

75 calories per cup

Peel; halve; core; drop into 3-per-cent brine. Drain. Pack in hot sterilized jars. Cover fruit with boiling hot liquid, using 2 teaspoons Sucaryl solution to each cup of water. Process 20 minutes; cool; label.

PLUMS

94 calories per cup of halves

Wash; halve; remove pits. Simmer 5 minutes in water ¼ inch deep in kettle. Drain, saving juice. Pack into hot sterilized containers. Cover fruit with boiling hot liquid, using 2 teaspoons Sucaryl solution to each cup of juice (add water to juice to make up cups). Process 15 minutes; cool; label.

Not recommended for storage longer than 3 months.

RHUBARB

20 calories per cup

Wash and trim stalks but do not peel. Cut in ¾-inch slices; measure. Add 1 cup water to 6 cups rhubarb. Cook 5 minutes. Drain, saving juice. Pack into hot sterilized containers. Cover fruit with boiling hot liquid, adding 1 tablespoon Sucaryl solution to each cup juice. Process 10 minutes; cool; label.

HOME CANNING WITHOUT SWEETENER

Fruits can be canned by eliminating the Sucaryl at the time of canning and adding it later when the fruit is used. Follow the directions above, except for the Sucaryl.

Lemon juice can be used instead of ascorbic acid to keep fruit from discoloring.

FRUIT JAMS
5 to 14 calories per tablespoon

By following directions on either packaged or bottled pectin (such as Certo or Sure-Jell) very low-calorie jams can be made, using any fruit and substituting Sucaryl for sugar.

The jam will not be as firm as when made with sugar and it must be kept in the refrigerator and used within 3 weeks, since Sucaryl provides only the sweetening and not the preserving qualities of sugar.

APRICOT JAM
4 calories per tablespoon

1 8-ounce can water-packed apricots
1 teaspoon Sucaryl solution
3 ounces liquid pectin

Mash apricots well with a fork, or purée in an electric blender, including all liquid. Add Sucaryl; bring to a fast boil. Add liquid pectin; continue to boil hard 1 minute. Pour into sterilized jars. After cooling, cover and store in refrigerator. (Keeps about 2 weeks.) Makes 16 tablespoons.

PEACH JAM
3 calories per tablespoon

1 8-ounce can water-packed peaches
1 teaspoon Sucaryl solution
3 ounces liquid pectin

Mash peaches well with fork, or purée in an electric blender, including all liquid. Add Sucaryl; bring to a fast boil. Add liquid pectin; continue to boil hard 1 minute. Pour into sterilized jars. After cooling, cover and store in refrigerator. (Keeps about 2 weeks.) Makes 18 tablespoons.

STRAWBERRY JAM
5 calories per tablespoon

2 cups large, firm berries
6 tablespoons Sucaryl solution

Wash and hull the strawberries. Then measure. Place a layer of berries in a kettle, then sweeten with Sucaryl and continue until all are used. Let stand overnight. Place on fire, bringing to a boil, and cook about 10 minutes. Pour into a bowl and let stand until the next day. Then fill jelly glasses and seal. Makes 1 to 1¼ cups.

Deaconess Maude Behrman, who was director of dietetics at Lankenau Hospital, Philadelphia, for twenty-five years and is now director of the Mercer House for Invalid Women of Atlantic City, supplies and edits the low-calorie and low-carbohydrate recipes in *Forecast,* the layman's magazine of the American Diabetes Association. Among diabetics she is considered Betty Crocker, Prudence Penny, and Clementine Paddleford all rolled into one, for she has given many years of valuable dietary instruction to readers whose lives depend on what they eat.

Here is a spread created by Deaconess Behrman which is practically calorieless.

RHUBARB SPREAD
No calories

12 Sucaryl tablets
½ cup water
2 cups rhubarb, cut fine
2 tablespoons pectin jelly powder

Dissolve Sucaryl in water pour over rhubarb, and cook together 4 to 5 minutes. Add pectin and cook 2 minutes more. Pour into a sterilized jar and seal. Makes 1 pint.

See Gelatine Dessert section for Grape Jelly.

HOME FREEZING WITH SUCARYL

By using Sucaryl instead of sugar in home preserving about 800 calories are eliminated for every cup of sugar called for in the recipe. Sucaryl provides only the sweetness, however, and not the bulk, the syrupy consistency, or the energy of sugar.

GENERAL DIRECTIONS

In packing, leave ½-inch headroom to provide for expansion during freezing.

Use 4 to 6 cups prepared liquid (Sucaryl or Sucaryl and ascorbic acid, and water or juice, according to the fruit) for 12 1-pint packages (about 10 pounds of fruit).

Ascorbic acid powder is on sale at any drugstore. Make liquid solution by dissolving ½ teaspoon in 2 tablespoons water.

To make 3-per-cent brine, dissolve 2 tablespoons salt in 1 quart water.

Calories indicated are for the raw fruits.

APPLE SLICES
83 calories per medium apple

Select firm, tart apples; core; pare; slice into 3-per-cent brine. Drain; simmer in small amount of water 3 minutes; drain, saving juice. Pack in pint or quart containers. Cover with liquid, using 1½ teaspoons Sucaryl solution plus ⅜ teaspoon ascorbic acid to each cup apple juice from cooking (add water to juice, if necessary, for desired amount). Cover containers; seal; label; cool; freeze.

APPLESAUCE
100 calories per cup

Select firm, tart apples (summer varieties preferred).

Wash; core; quarter; remove all blemishes. Cook in small amount of water until soft. Put through food mill or sieve. Measure. Heat to boiling. Add 1 teaspoon Sucaryl solution for each cup applesauce. Fill into pint or quart containers. Cover; seal; label; cool; freeze.

BERRIES
85 calories per cup

For blackberries, blueberries, boysenberries, dewberries, loganberries, red raspberries, youngberries.
Wash and pick over, discarding any soft or imperfect berries. Drain on absorbent paper. Add liquid, consisting of 1¼ teaspoons Sucaryl solution to ¼ cup water for each 6 cups berries. Mix thoroughly with berries, using a fork and being careful not to crush berries. Pack in pint or quart containers. Cover; seal; label; freeze.

STRAWBERRIES
54 calories per cup

Follow directions as for berries above, but add ⅛ teaspoon ascorbic acid for each ¼ cup of water.

CRANBERRY SAUCE
54 calories per cup

Wash and pick over cranberries, discarding any that are too soft or withered. For each 4 cups of cranberries add 4 tablespoons Sucaryl solution and 1 cup of water. Simmer 2 minutes. Fill into pint or quart containers; cover; seal; label; cool; freeze.

PEACHES
77 calories per cup, halves

Dip freestone peaches in boiling water; plunge into cold water; slip off skins. Cling peaches must be peeled by hand; slice directly into liquid consisting of 2½ teaspoons Sucaryl solution plus ¼ teaspoon ascorbic acid to 1 cup water for each 6 cups sliced peaches. Pack into pint or quart containers, making sure liquid covers fruit. Cover; seal; label; freeze.

PLUMS
94 calories per cup, halves

Wash; halve; remove pits. Pack in pint or quart containers. Completely cover with liquid in the proportions of 1¼ teaspoons Sucaryl solution plus ⅛ teaspoon ascorbic acid to each cup of water used. Cover containers; seal; label; freeze.

RHUBARB
20 calories per cup

Wash and trim stalks, but do not peel. Cut into ¾-inch slices; measure. To 5 quarts rhubarb add 2 cups water. Simmer 2 minutes; drain;

measure juice. Prepare liquid (1 tablespoon Sucaryl solution to each cup juice). Pack rhubarb in pint or quart containers; cover with sweetened liquid. Cover containers; seal; cool; label; freeze.

PICKLES AND
CONDIMENTS

The usual function of relishes, pickles, and catsups is to sharpen the appetite. Few dieters need such a stimulus. However, they are included here as an aid to dieting because they add zest and variety to otherwise restricted meals and because the pickled cucumbers and tomatoes listed are extremely low in calories.

DILL PICKLES

14 calories per cucumber

1 teaspoon garlic powder

1 teaspoon whole peppercorns

6 whole cloves

½ cup whole dill seed

2 quarts cider vinegar

1 quart water

1 cup salt
cucumbers (3 to 4 inches) for 4 quarts

Sterilize 4 quart jars. Combine all ingredients except cucumbers. Bring to a boil. Scrub cucumbers, but do not peel. Fill quart jars with the cucumbers. Cover with boiling vinegar. Seal. Makes 4 quarts.

CUCUMBER SLICES

40 calories per pint

10 pounds medium-sized cucumbers

1 cup salt

2¼ quarts vinegar

2 tablespoons Sucaryl solution

¼ cup mixed pickle spices
Wash and cut cucumbers into slices about ¼-inch thick. Mix cucumbers and salt. Let stand overnight. In the morning drain and press out all the juice possible. Rinse once in cold water. Combine vinegar, Sucaryl, and spices. Boil 1 minute. Add cucumbers, and simmer 5 minutes. Pack cucumbers into clean, hot, sterile jars to within 1 inch of top. Fill jars with hot liquid to top; seal tightly. Makes about 12 pints.

MIXED GARDEN PICKLES
53 calories per pint

- 3 cucumbers (6 or 7 inches)
- 2 medium green peppers
- 1 cup cauliflower flowerets
- ¼ pound fresh snap beans
- 8 small white onions
- salt
- 1 quart cider vinegar
- 2 tablespoons mixed pickling spice

Score cucumber rinds with a fork but do not peel. Cut into fourths lengthwise and then into ¾-inch chunks. Seed and cut peppers into ¾-inch pieces. Cut cauliflower into 1-inch pieces. Cut beans into 1-inch lengths. Peel onions. Combine all vegetables and cover with salt. Let stand 24 hours. Drain, and rinse. Heat vinegar and pickling spice. Add vegetables and simmer until just tender—about 15 minutes. Place in sterilized jars and seal. Makes 4 pints.

SPICED PICKLES
15 calories per pickle

- 100 small (3¾ inches) pickles
- 1 ounce whole cloves
- 1 ounce cinnamon
- 3 tablespoons Sucaryl solution
- ½ cup salt
- 1 ounce yellow mustard
- 1 pint cider vinegar

Scald pickles in boiling water. Drain. Mix cloves and cinnamon together. Place a layer of pickles in a 5-gallon crock and sprinkle with the spice mixture. Repeat until crock is full. Combine Sucaryl, salt, mustard, and vinegar, and bring to a boil; cook about 5 minutes. Pour brine over the pickles, filling the crock. More brine may be needed, depending on size of pickles. Cover crock and let stand in a cold place.

MUSTARD PICKLES
115 calories per pint

- 2 heads cauliflower
- 3 pounds small white onions
- ½ dozen green pepper shells (1 pound)
- 3 pounds green tomatoes
- 3 quarts white wine vinegar
- 2 to 3 tablespoons Sucaryl solution, or to taste
- ¼ pound dry mustard
- 2 tablespoons mustard seed
- 2 tablespoons celery seed
- 1 tablespoon turmeric
- 3 pints sweet spiced gherkins

Separate cauliflower into flowerets. Peel onions and slice pepper shells very fine. Slice tomatoes and combine all 4 ingredients. Cover with salt and let stand overnight. Drain. Cover with boiling water and cook until vegetables are soft. Drain. Heat vinegar, add Sucaryl, and pour over the thoroughly mixed mustard, celery seed, and turmeric. (A thicker mustard sauce can be made by adding flour.) Blend well. Add gherkins to the cooked vegetables. Pour all the liquid over them and cook about 10 minutes, or until mixture thickens. Pour into sterilized jars and seal. Makes about 12 pints

---

SWEET SPICED GHERKINS
40 calories per pint

- 5 pounds very small cucumbers
- ½ cup coarse salt
- 3 cups water
- 1 pint mild vinegar
- 1 pint water
- 5 tablespoons Sucaryl solution, or to taste
- 1 teaspoon cinnamon
- ¼ teaspoon ground allspice
- ¼ teaspoon ground cloves

Scrub cucumbers with a brush, then soak for 24 hours in brine made of salt and 3 cups water. Remove from brine and pour boiling water over. Drain quickly. Pack cucumbers closely, while hot, in sterilized jar. Cover at once with boiling mixture made from vinegar, 1 pint water, Sucaryl, and spices. Seal jars at once. Makes about 5 pints.

CHILI SAUCE
7 calories per tablespoon

- 18 tomatoes
- 2 green peppers
- 2 medium onions
- 3 tablespoons Sucaryl solution, or to taste
- 2 teaspoons salt
- 1 teaspoon ground cinnamon
- ½ teaspoon ground cloves
- 1 teaspoon allspice
- 2 cups vinegar

Peel, core, and chop tomatoes. Chop peppers and onions fine. Combine all ingredients. Boil slowly 4 hours, or until sauce reaches desired thickness. Fill, boiling hot, into hot sterilized ½-pint containers; seal. Makes about 6 ½-pint jars or 96 tablespoons.

PEPPER-ONION RELISH
4 calories per tablespoon

- 1 quart finely chopped onions
- 2 cups finely chopped sweet red peppers
- 2 cups finely chopped green peppers
- 2 tablespoons Sucaryl solution, or to taste
- 1 quart vinegar
- 4 teaspoons pure granulated salt

Combine all ingredients and bring slowly to boil. Cook until slightly thickened. Pour into clean, hot, sterile jars. Fill jars to top; seal tightly. Makes about 5 pints.

FRANKFURTER RELISH
19 calories per serving

3½ pounds sweet red peppers
3 pounds green peppers
3 pounds onions
1 quart vinegar
1 tablespoon Sucaryl solution
1 teaspoon mustard seed
1 tablespoon dry mustard
1 tablespoon celery seed
2 tablespoons salt

Wash peppers; remove cores and seeds. Peel onions. Put peppers and onions through food chopper, using medium knife. Cover with boiling water; let stand 5 minutes; drain. Add vinegar, Sucaryl, spices, and salt. Cook until vegetables are tender—about 15 minutes—stirring occasionally. Fill, boiling hot, into hot sterilized jars; seal. Makes about 8 pint jars or 64 servings, ¼ cup each.

PICKLED RED CABBAGE
10 calories per ounce

Shred red cabbage rather fine and sprinkle generously with salt. Set aside in a cool place 3 hours. Drain all moisture from cabbage; place it in the sun, allowing it to remain for several hours. In a saucepan place sufficient vinegar to cover the cabbage, adding 2 teaspoons Sucaryl solution for every quart of vinegar and a small amount of celery seed, pepper, mace, allspice, and cinnamon. Boil this together for 7 minutes; pour over cabbage. Put in stone jars, cover, and store in a cool place.

DINTY MOORE'S CABBAGE RELISH

While you wait for your order to be filled at Dinty Moore's fine old eating establishment off Broadway in New York you are given small portions of chopped cabbage, with just a bit of shredded carrot, marinated in white wine vinegar and sprinkled with dill and caraway seeds. Brings the digestive juices rushing out.

SEASONINGS FOR SAUERKRAUT
32 calories per cup

Sauerkraut, especially crisp and raw, gains much flavor when caraway or dill seeds or juniper berries are mixed with it. Also try a sliced or shredded raw carrot mixed with the kraut.

JIFFY CATSUP
12 calories per tablespoon

5 saccharin or Sucaryl tablets
3 tablespoons cider vinegar
¾ cup tomato paste
1 teaspoon salt
¼ teaspoon celery salt
½ teaspoon paprika
⅛ teaspoon ground cloves
¼ teaspoon dry mustard
⅛ teaspoon nutmeg
¼ teaspoon garlic powder

Dissolve sweetening in vinegar. Stir in the other ingredients. Stir well. Cover; store in refrigerator. Makes about 1 cup.

A regular 6-ounce can of tomato paste contains ¾ cup.

MUSHROOM CATSUP
3 calories per tablespoon

1 cup (8-ounce can) tomato purée
6 ounces chopped broiled mushrooms
2 tablespoons vinegar
⅛ teaspoon cinnamon
⅛ teaspoon allspice
¼ teaspoon dry mustard
¼ teaspoon celery salt
½ teaspoon Kitchen Bouquet
Sucaryl to taste

Blend all ingredients except Sucaryl until smooth—about 30 seconds—in electric blender or mixer. Pour into saucepan, sweeten to taste, and bring to boil. Simmer, covered, over low heat 15 minutes. Makes 2 cups.

HORSE-RADISH RELISH
8 calories per tablespoon

Grate sound horse-radish roots. Measure about ½ as much vinegar as horse-radish, add ¼ to ½ teaspoon salt for each cup of vinegar, and pour over grated horse-radish. Pack at once into clean, hot, sterile jars. Fill jars to top; seal tightly.

For Cranberry Relish see page 188; for Cranberry-Orange Relish, page 210.

SEASONINGS FOR PICKLING AND SPICING

Fruit Spices: Allspice, Cloves, Cinnamon bark, Lemon juice, grated Lemon rind, Cider Vinegar. For Mango: Fenugreek.

Meat Pickling Seasonings: Allspice, Bay leaves, Capers, Cloves, Mustard seed, Paprika, Tarragon.

Mustard Seasonings: fresh and dried minced Basil, Capers, Chervil, Chili powder, Curry powder, Dill, Garlic, Horse-radish, Lovage, Marjoram, Mushrooms, Mustard seed, minced or powdered Onion, Orégano, Paprika, Parsley, Rosemary, Sage, Tarragon, Thyme, Tomato paste, Turmeric and Cider, Garlic or Tarragon vinegars. Sweeten with Sucaryl solution.

Pickles, Sweet and Spiced: ground Allspice, Aniseed, Caraway seed, Cardamom seed, cassia buds, Celery seed, Cinnamon bark, Cloves, Coriander seed, Fennel, Ginger, Mace, Mint, Mustard seed, Nutmeg, Turmeric. Sweeten with Sucaryl solution.

Tomato Catsup Seasonings: Allspice, Cayenne, Celery seed, Cinnamon, Garlic, Ginger, Mace, chopped Onion or Onion salt, Paprika, Vinegar. Sweeten with Sucaryl solution.

MAKE YOUR OWN LOW-CALORIE RECIPES

Among the recipes in this book you will have observed a number of suggestions of how to substitute lower calorie ingredients for those that put the pounds where they are unwanted.

There is no reason why you cannot create new recipes of your own, as well as adapt your favorite dishes to less rich versions. Here are a few ways to switch.

Richard Tregaskis, the author and war correspondent, carries with him all over the world instant-beef broth powder (such as G. Washington) or bouillon cubes (about 2 calories each). Added to a cup of hot water, one of these makes a satisfying tea, an appetite-cutter, or a substitute for a can of bouillon or consommé (82 or 88 calories per can). And use them instead of canned soups in making dishes calling for beef stock. Vegetable bouillon cubes have only 8 calories each and Souplets 12.

Tomatoes in any form are tasty, filling, and very sparing of calories. Tomato juice, properly seasoned, makes a soup or a sauce by itself and replaces tomato soup, which has flour and salt, at a saving of 150 calories per can.

If you can stay away from the convenient canned tuna and salmon and use the lean fishes for salads and sandwiches you can save up to half the calories involved.

Veal is the leanest of the meats. Chickens vary in fat content according to age; use the youngest you can buy to get the fewest calories.

Butter is twice as fattening as cream cheese, which has four times the calories of skim-milk cottage cheese. The same amount of cottage cheese spread on your bread, instead of butter, saves ⅞ of the calories. Now, here is another way to use cottage cheese

SOUR CREAM SUBSTITUTE

Since sour cream is just as fattening as sweet cream, put cottage cheese or farmer's cheese or pot cheese into an electric blender with ⅓ as much water. Mix thoroughly and until it is the consistency desired (adding small amounts of water as necessary). This is a wonderful substitute that can almost be palmed off as the genuine article. Principal difference, only ⅙ as many calories.

For stews, pot roasts, etc., brown by searing on grill, soapstone griddle, or under flame, turning meat to seal juices in on all sides. This saves the high calories of flour and fat. If you must use fat or oil or butter or margarine, cut the amount to the barest minimum that will keep the food from sticking.

Green olives have ⅔ the calories of ripe; vinegar ½ the number of lemon juice; beef bacon, a new product, has half that of regular bacon; and green or sweet red peppers are ½ the caloric value of onions, while celery has even less calories than peppers. Egg noodles ready to eat, are half as fattening as spaghetti and macaroni.

Point up and intensify the flavor of foods (except sweet ones or plain egg dishes) with monosodium glutamate.

A quick, convenient form of mint extract is Mintit, which not only gives the full flavor in a concentrated liquid but is also useful to freshen fruits, canned fruit juices, and vegetables. It has no added alcohol, sweetening, or vinegar. Also, use it as a refreshing addition to dressings, soups, applesauce, or beverages.

Alice Richardson in her quick and practical cookbook, *Just a Minute*, suggests thickening cream sauces or soups with egg yellow instead of flour. Egg whites (16 calories each) or unflavored gelatine are also excellent thickeners instead of flour, tapioca, or butter.

SKIM MILK

Skim milk has all the food values of whole milk except the butterfat content. Powdered skim milk is inexpensive and convenient, since it keeps well on the kitchen shelf and mixes easily with water. It loses its slightly burnt taste when well chilled. In recipes using powdered skim milk, add less sweetener, since it is naturally sweet.

You can mix your own milk shakes with skim milk, or skim-milk powder and ice water, flavoring with fresh fruit or one of the uncaloried carbonated beverages or strawberry sauce.

To make an unsweetened, unflavored custardlike milk drink, dissolve ½ Junket rennet tablet in glass of cold skim milk and let stand undisturbed for 15 to 30 minutes.

Leading brands of skim milk are:

Borden's Instant Starlac
(The Borden Co., New York, N. Y. 10017; national distribution)
Nonfat milk solids

Carnation Instant
(Carnation Co., distributor, Los Angeles, Calif.; national)
Nonfat dry milk solids

Cellu Dried Skimmed Milk
(Chicago Dietetic Supply House, Inc., Chicago, Ill. 60612; national)

Loma Linda Soy Milk
(Soyalac)
(Loma Linda Food Co., Arlington, Calif.; national)
All-purpose, malt, powdered

Pet Instant
(Pet Milk Co., St. Louis, Mo.; national)
Nonfat dry milk

OTHER BOOKS ON DIETING, NUTRITION, AND COOKING

If you are interested in learning more about weight reduction by low-calorie eating, the part that proper nutrition plays in health or methods of preparing different foods, here is a list of suggested books and pamphlets.

MORE COMPLETE CALORIE TABLES

"Composition of Foods—Raw, Processed, Prepared." Handbook No. 8, United States Department of Agriculture (being revised).*

"Nutritive Value of Foods." United States Department of Agriculture, Home & Garden Bulletin No. 72, 20¢.*

"Food Values of Portions Commonly Used." Anna de Planter Bowes, 7th and Delancey Street, Philadelphia, Pa. 19106.

ON DIET AND NUTRITION

A Cookbook for Diabetics. Recipes from the A.D.A. *Forecast* by Deaconess Maude Behrman, Edited by Leonard Louis Levinson. American Diabetes Assn., 1 E. 45th St., New York, N. Y. 10017.

Eat, Think and Be Slender. Leonid Kotkin, M.D., with the assistance of Fred Kerner. Hawthorn Books, Inc., 70 Fifth Avenue, New York, N. Y. 10011.

Printing Office, Washington, D.C. 20402.
* Order from the Superintendent of Documents, Government

Everybody's Book of Modern Diet and Nutrition. Dr. Henrietta Fleck and Dr. Elizabeth Munves. Dell Distributing Company, Inc., 750 Third Ave., New York, N. Y. 10017.

How to Reduce Surely and Safely. Herbert Pollack, M. D., with Arthur D. Morse. McGraw-Hill Book Co., 330 West 42nd St., New York, N. Y. 10036.

Reduce and Stay Reduced. Norman Jolliffe, M.D. Simon and Schuster, Inc., 630 Fifth Avenue, New York, N. Y. 10020.

Weight Control. Iowa State College Press, Ames, Iowa.

FREE PAMPHLETS

"Calorie Saving Recipes with Improved Sucaryl." Abbott Laboratories, North Chicago, Ill.

"Diet Delight Low Calorie Menu Planner." Richmond-Chase Co., San Jose, California.

"Food Facts for Fun and Health." Kirsch Beverages, Inc., 921 Flushing Ave., Brooklyn, N. Y. 11206.

"Do You Really Want to Lose Weight?" Charles B. Knox Gelatine Co., Johnstown, N. Y.

"You Can Reduce With Safety and Comfort." National Live Stock and Meat Board, 36 S. Wabash St., Chicago, Ill.

"Overweight and Underweight"; "Hidden Calories That Tip the Scales"; "Food for the Family." Metropolitan Life Insurance Co., Health and Welfare Division, 1 Madison Ave., New York, N. Y. 10010.

Also write to the National Dairy Council, Chicago, Ill. 60606, for current information on weight control.

UNITED STATES GOVERNMENT PAMPHLETS*

"Apples in Appealing Ways." 10¢.

"Basic Fish Cookery." 25¢

"Conserving Nutritive Values in Foods." 10¢.

"Eat a Good Breakfast to Start a Good Day." 5¢.

"Family Fare . . . Food Management and Recipes." 35¢.

"Family Food Budgeting for Good Meals and Good Nutrition." 10¢.

"Food and Your Weight." 15¢.

"Green Vegetables for Good Eating." 10¢.

"Savory Herbs: Culture and Use." 15¢.

"Tomatoes on Your Table." 10¢.

* Order from the Superintendent of Documents, Government Printing Office, Washington, D.C. 20402.

NEW APPLIANCES
FOR LOW-CALORIE COOKING

In reading through the recipes you will have noticed that there are frequent instructions on the preparation of dishes using various electrical appliances and gadgets. That is because the search has been not only to find low-calorie foods but also the way to cook foods with the fewest possible calories.

Many of the new kitchen tools, and some we have known about for a long time, are very valuable in preparing appetizing meals for the weight loser.

These devices are of two kinds—to change the form of the food and thus make it more palatable, digestible, and convenient to eat, and to cook it with less or no fat at all.

In the first category comes the blenders, mixers, and juicers. Each of these has a different function. The blender cuts food at high speed until it is a powder, paste, or liquid. The mixer stirs, combines, and beats air into food. And the juicer squeezes the liquid out of fruits and vegetables. Many of the beverages in this book, as well as soups, salad dressings, desserts, and eggs can be made quickly and effortlessly with a blender. The mixers are useful in baking, for sauces, sherbets, puddings, and whipped vegetables. They frequently have juicer attachments and there are separate juicers that either squeeze or ream out citrus fruit. The squeezer type is used, too, for other fruits and vegetables.

Salad making and preparing vegetables can be so much less work if slicer-shredders and food grinders are used. The food is then in convenient-to-eat form, more "available" to the eater. The grinders are a big help when preparing leftovers or the tougher portions of meat.

ELECTRIC COOKING

The controlled, even heat that is possible when cooking with electricity helps cut the use of fats to a minimum or eliminate them altogether.

Using the new infra-red broilers and rotisseries, meats and fish can be cooked to a delicious turn, using barbecue bastings of spices and seasonings that are all but calorieless.

Another popular recent entry is the deep-fat kettle, which also doubles as a deep pot. It is the contention of nutritionists retained by manufacturers to test these deep-fat fryers that the quick immersing of the food in the high-temperature oil envelops the food in a thin, crisp coat that seals in the flavor and vitamins. They say that the heat quickly penetrates the food without soaking it in oil and suggest that further calorie savings can be made by removing the thin crust. At this writing there have not been enough disinterested opinions regarding this theory to judge it fairly.

Used as roasting, stewing, and simmering pots, these kettles do a fine, rapid job because of the even heat that comes from the round well as well as the bottom.

Automatic electrical skillets or frying pans, with their heavy aluminum or stainless-steel surfaces and controlled, dialed heat, make it possible to grill without grease rather than fry, saving calories at the rate of 100 per tablespoon of butter, 110 for shortening, and 126 for lard. If any grease is needed to prevent food from sticking, it can be a thin film wiped on with paper. In addition, they are used for making any dish where a shallow pot is indicated. And one company listed here makes a deep saucepan version. There is also an electric griddle on the market that will grill foods with little or no cooking oil.

Teflon, considered the world's most slippery solid, to which nothing will stick, is available as a cooking surface, either to be sprayed on existing utensils or new ones where it is bonded into the metal.

SOAPSTONE GRIDDLES

A much older device for greaseless cooking seems to be dying out—unless dieters are able to revive its use. This is the soapstone griddle, which gives a slow, even heat and is wonderful for cube steak, fish, hamburger, frozen meats, lamb chops, eggs, etc. without any added fat. It is cleaned with coarse salt.

Little of the soapstone quarried is used to make griddles any more and only two firms have been found that still deal in them. These are:

Vermont Maple Products Co., Barre, Vermont. Round griddles, 10 and 12 inches in diameter, with copper rim and 9 x 18 oval, with copper rim.

Vermont Country Store, Weston, Vermont. Round griddles range in size from 10 to 16 inches in diameter and oval ones from 8 x 16 to 12 x 24.

Pyrex glass dishes are also very useful for fatless frying.

PRESSURE COOKERS, ETC.

Preparing food with pressure cooker, pan, or canner is in another realm. It is a different way to cut calories, since cooking with little or no grease is one of its virtues. Another is the rapidity with which foods can be cooked, conserving vitamins, minerals, and flavor. There are both top-of-stove pressure cookers and the new electric pressure pans. In preparing recipes from this book in pressure equipment, consult the manufacturer's handbook for cooking time and amount of water.

Electric egg cookers and poachers and electric teapots are other quick-acting appliances which make reducing-diet cookery easier.

And an electric range is listed because this one had practically all the other new devices built in: griddle, rotary grill, deep-fat kettle, deep well cooker, adjustable broiler, and grill that turns over.

OTHER UTENSILS

The Aladdin Magic Cooker is a new idea in top-of-stove ware. It is a shallow aluminum pan with a cover that has a chimney or flue in the center. Because of its design it uses little oil or heat, cooks both sides at the same time, dry-frying most foods, and doing it in little time.

In addition, there has been much activity and development by makers of conventional-shaped pots and pans. The improvements have been in the kind and thickness of metals used, and now there are utensils of aluminum, stainless steel, and solid stainlees steel with aluminum bottoms that will cook foods without water or fat, much in the manner of pressure cookers. Heavy metal, even distribution of low heat, and tight-fitting, self-basting lids make this possible.

Aluminum metail foil is another great aid in the kitchen, especially for fatless food cooking. It is a must for un-messy broiling, and in roasting it retains the juices, permits high heat without burning and drying, and saves shrinkage. You will find several recipes here that are enhanced by the proper use of metal foil and you will undoubtedly discover new uses of your own.

MICROWAVE COOKING

Like the automobile makers, American kitchen-equipment manufacturers are quick to supply any new homemaking device where there is an indication of a demand. As low-calorie cooking increases, their research departments will be working, like the canners and food processors, to make the task of preparing low-calorie dishes easier. A glimpse into the future, showing us what it holds in store, is provided by the new radar ranges or electronic ovens.

RadaRange was the first to apply electronics to cooking. It uses electro-magnetic energy from a magnetron tube that sends short waves through the food, causing it to heat uniformly, silently, and swiftly.

The utensil (glass, china, plastic, or paper) and the stove, a stainless-steel wall cabinet, remain cold and clean, and the rate of cooking is amazing when compared with present-day oven times:

Fish, casseroles, steaks, bacon; 1 minute

Poultry, roast beef: 5 minutes a pound

An 8-inch layer cake: 4 to 5 minutes

Frozen turkey dinner, defrosted and heated: 5 minutes

Apple pie: 13 minutes

RadaRanges have been installed in commercial eating establishments and aboard the liner *United States*, where Executive Chef Otto Bismark has been using two large ones since the liner was commissioned in 1953. He finds them ideal for diet cookery, since the utensil remains cooler than the food and there is no need to use fat to prevent sticking. Shrinkage of meats is at a minimum and vegetables are cooked without water.

While test units are being used in homes, no domestic ranges have been available, and the two commercial models sell for $2,975 and $1,875.

General Electric, after ten years of experimenting, has also developed an electronic oven and has designed it primarily for home use. The performance of this appliance is also spectacular in time-cutting. An 8-pound frozen standing rib roast, which would ordinarily take 8 hours to thaw and another 4 to cook, was electronically roasted in 1½ hours.

APPLIANCES

Here are the appliances that help in preparing lower-caloried meals:

BLENDERS

Blend-Well; Dormeyer Corp., Chicago 10, Ill.

Eskimo Whiz-Mix; Bersted Mfg. Co., Div. of McGraw Electric Co., Boonville, Mo.

Hollywood Liquefier; Hollywood Liquefier Co., So. Pasadena, Calif.

Kenmore Blender; Sears, Roebuck & Co., Chicago 7, Ill.

Knapp-Monarch Liquidizer; Multi Speed Liquidizer; Knapp Monarch Co., St. Louis 16, Mo.

Liqui-Blender; Hamilton Beach Div., Scoville Mfg. Co., Racine, Wisc.

Manning-Bowman Automatic Food & Beverage Blender; Manning-Bowman Div., McGraw Electric Co., Elgin, Ill.

Osterizer; John Oster Mfg. Co., Milwaukee 17, Wisc.

Rival Aristocrat; Rival Mfg. Co., Kansas City 8, Mo.

Silex Blendette; Proctor-Silex Co., Chicago 38, Ill.

Sunbeam Automatic Blender; Mixmaster blender attachment; Sunbeam Corp., Chicago 50, Ill.

Universal Mixablend; Landers Frary & Clark, New Britain, Conn.

Waring Blendor; Waring Products Co., Winsted, Conn.

STANDARD MIXERS

Dormeyer Power Chef, Meal Maker, Silver-Chef, Mix-Maid; Dormeyer Corp., Chicago 10, Ill.

Hamilton Beach Food Mixer;

Hamilton Beach Co. Div., Scoville Mfg. Co., Racine, Wisc.

Kenmore Electric Mixer; Sears, Roebuck & Co., Chicago 7, Ill.

Kitchenaid; Hobart Manufacturing Co., Troy, Ohio.

Lady Casco Chef Mate Mixer-Blender-Juicer; Casco Prods. Corp., New York, N.Y.

Sunbeam Deluxe Automatic Mixmaster; Sunbeam Corp., Chicago 50, Ill.

Universal Food Mixer; Landers Frary & Clark, New Britain, Conn.

DETACHABLE MIXERS

(Lighter than standard mixers which may be removed from bases to serve as portable units.)

Dormeyer Mix-Well; Dormeyer Corp., Chicago 10, Ill.

PORTABLE MIXERS

Dorby Handi-Mixer; Dorby Co., Chicago 54, Ill.

Dormey Portable Mixer; Dormeyer Corp., Chicago 10, Ill.

Eskimo Hand Mixer; Bersted Mfg. Co., Div. of McGraw Electric Co., Boonville, Mo.

General Electric Portable Mixer; General Electric Co., Bridgeport 2, Conn.

Hamilton Beach Mixette; Hamilton Beach Co. Div., Scoville Mfg. Co., Racine, Wisc.

Kenmore Hand Mixer; Sears, Roebuck & Co., Chicago 7, Ill.

Oster Electric Portable Food Mixer, Oster Portable Electric Mixer; John Oster Mfg. Co., Milwaukee 17, Wisc.

Spee-dee Mixer Junior; Appli-ance Corp. of America, New York, N.Y.

Sunbeam Deluxe Automatic Mixmaster Hand Mixer; Sunbeam Mixmaster Hand Mixer; Cordless Mixmaster Hand Mixer; Sunbeam Corp., Chicago 50, Ill.

Universal Hand Mixer; Landers Frary & Clark, New Britain, Conn.

Westinghouse Portable Mixer; Westinghouse Electric Appliance Div., Mansfield, Ohio.

JUICE EXTRACTORS
Squeezer Type

Balanced Food Juicer; Balanced Foods, Inc., New York, N.Y. 10003.

Excell Juice Extractor; R.Y.P. Mfg. Co., White Plains, N.Y.

Juicex Electric Vegetable Juice Extractor (and Liquefier attachment); Drachenberg Products Mfg. Co., St. Clair Shores, Mich.

Super Juicer; Super Mfg. Co., Los Angeles, Calif.

Sweden Speed Juicer; Sweden Speed Juicer Corp., Seattle 99, Wash.

Waring Health Juice Extractor; Waring Products Co., Winsted, Conn.

Reamer Type

Dormeyer Meal-Maker; Dormeyer Mix-Well juicer attachments; Dormeyer Corp., Chicago 10, Ill.

Hamilton Beach Mixer, Juice Extractor attachment; Hamilton Beach Div., Scoville Mfg. Co., Racine, Wis.

Silex Juicit; Proctor-Silex Co., Chicago 38, Ill.

Sunbeam Mixmaster, Juice Extractor attachment; Sunbeam Corp., Chicago 50, Ill.

Westinghouse Food Crafter Mixer, Juicer attachment; Westinghouse Electric Corp., Electric Appliance Div., Mansfield, Ohio.

FOOD GRINDERS AND SLICER-SHREDDERS

Electric Grinders

Dormeyer Meal-Maker & Mix-Well Food Grinder attachments; Dormeyer Corp., Chicago 10, Ill.

Hamilton Beach Food Mixer, Food Grinder attachment; Hamilton Beach Div., Scoville Mfg. Co., Racine, Wisc.

Sunbeam Mixmaster, Food Grinder attachment; Sunbeam Corp., Chicago 50, Ill.

Hand Grinders

Enterprise Hand Food Grinder; Enterprise Mfg. Co., Philadelphia, Pa.

Grind-O-Mat, Hand Food Grinder; Rival Mfg. Co., Kansas City 8, Mo.

Electric Slicer-Shredders

Hamilton Beach Food Mixer, Slicer-Shredder attachment; Hamilton Beach Div., Scoville Mfg. Co., Racine, Wisc.

Sunbeam Mixmaster, Slicer-Shredder attachment; Sunbeam Corp., Chicago 50, Ill.

Hand Slicer-Shredders

Enterprise Hand Food Shredder; Enterprise Mfg. Co., Philadelphia, Pa.

Shred-O-Mat, Hand Food Shredder; Rival Mfg. Co., Kansas City 8, Mo.

Snitzler All-Purpose Hand Vegetable Shredder; Modern Products Co., Milwaukee, Wisc.

Combinations

Rival Kitcheneer, Hand Grinder-Chopper, Shredder, Slicer, Grater; Rival Mfg. Co., Kansas City 8, Mo.

BROILERS AND ROTISSERIES

Black Angus; Marlun Mfg. Co., Inc., Brooklyn, N. Y.

Broil King; International Appliance Corp., Brooklyn 8, N. Y.

Broil-Master; Sunburst Mfg. Co., Grosse Point Woods 36, Mich.

Farber "Open Hearth" Electric Broiler/Rotisserie; Farber "Open Hearth" Electric Broiler; S. W. Farber, Inc., New York 54, N. Y.

Fleck Infra-red Broiler; Fleck Inc., Asbury Park, N. J.

Knapp Monarch Redi-Baker table model; Knapp Monarch Redi-Oven; Knapp Monarch Co., St. Louis 16, Mo.

Magic-Quartz Rotisserie; Magic Quartz Corp., Jersey City, N. J.

Nesco Gourmet Rotiss-Oven; Nesco Roastryte; Nesco Industries, St. Louis 16, Mo.

Rotiss-O-Mat Broiler; Rotiss-O-Mat Corp., Long Island City, N. Y.

Roto-Broil; Jay Broiler Co., Long Island City, N. Y.

Sunbeam Carousel Rotisserie Broiler and Shish-Kabobber; Sunbeam Corp., Chicago 50, Ill.

KETTLES AND SKILLETS

Kettles

Broil-Quik Fryer-Cooker; Peerless Electric, Inc., New York 27, N. Y.

Dormeyer Fri-Well; Dormeyer

Deep-Fry Cooker; Dormeyer Corp., Chicago 10, Ill.

Cookryte Portable (round or oval); Nesco Industries, St. Louis 16, Mo.

Fry-o-mat Fryer Cooker; Rival Mfg. Co., Kansas City, Mo.

Fryryte Automatic Electric Deep Fryer (rectangular); Nesco Industries, St. Louis 16, Mo.

Kord Automatic Cooker-Fryer; Kord Mfg. Co., Inc., New York 70, N. Y.

Naxon Flavor Crock (all-purpose automatic cooker); Naxon Utilities Corp., Chicago 45, Ill.

Presto Electric Cooker-Fryer; National Presto Industries, Inc., Eau Claire, Wisc.

Roto Broil Automatic Electric Cooker-Deep Fryer; Jay Broiler Co., Long Island City, N. Y.

Sunbeam Automatic Cooker and Deep Fryer; Sunbeam Corp., Chicago 50, Ill.

Swifty Cooker-Deep Fry; Eastern Metal Products Co., Tuckahoe, N. Y.

Universal Deep Fryer; Universal Automatic Cooker-Fryer; Landers Frary & Clark, New Britain, Conn.

West Bend Electric Fryer-Roaster-Server; West Bend Aluminum Co., West Bend, Wisc.

Westinghouse Cook-N-Fryer; Westinghouse Electric Corp., Electric Appliance Div., Mansfield, Ohio.

Skillets

Dominion Fry Skillet; Dominion Electric Corp., Mansfield, Ohio.

Dormeyer Fry Skillet (square); Dormeyer French Fry Skillet (round); Dormeyer Corp., Chicago 10, Ill.

Farberware Stainless Steel Electric Automatic Skillet; Farberware Electric Buffet Server/Frypan; S. W. Farber, Inc., New York 54, N. Y.

G-E Electric Fry Pan; General Electric Corp., Bridgeport 2, Conn.

Presto Skillet; National Presto Industries, Inc., Eau Claire, Wisc.

Roto-Broil Automatic Electric Skillet; Jay Broiler Co., Long Island City, N. Y.

Sunbeam Multi-Cooker Frypans, Sunbeam Broiler Cover; Sunbeam Corp., Chicago 50, Ill.

Universal Broiler-Frying Pan; Landers Frary & Clark, New Britain, Conn.

Westinghouse "Long-Life" Broiler Fry Pan (no-stick cooking surface); Westinghouse Fryer; Westinghouse Electric Corp., Electric Appliance Div., Mansfield, Ohio.

SAUCEPAN

Sunbeam Automatic Electric Saucepan; Sunbeam Corp., Chicago 50, Ill.

GRIDDLES

Du-Wal Automatic Electric Griddle; Du-Wal, Inc., River Grove, Ill.

Sunbeam Automatic Electric Griddle; Sunbeam Corp., Chicago 50, Ill.

TOP OF STOVE PRESSURE COOKERS

Sunbeam Automatic Electric Griddle; Sunbeam Corp., Chicago 50, Ill.

Flex-Seal Stainless Pressure Cooker; Vischer Products Co., Chicago, Ill.

Mirro-Matic Pressure Pans; Pressure Canners; Aluminum Goods Mfg. Co., Manitowoc, Wisc.

Presto Meat-Master; Vege-Master; Cook-Master; Fry-Master; National Presto Industries, Inc., Eau Claire, Wisc.

Wear-Ever Pressure Cooker; Aluminum Cooking Utensils Co., New Kensington, Pa.

ELECTRIC PRESSURE COOKER

Mirro-Matic Electric Pressure Pan, for frying, boiling, braising, stewing, and food warming; Aluminum Goods Mfg. Co. Manitowoc, Wisc.

MISCELLANEOUS

Electric Egg Cooker and Poacher

Sunbeam Egg Cooker and Egg Poacher attachment; Sunbeam Corp., Chicago 50, Ill.

Electric Ranges

Hotpoint Electric 39-inch model, with golden griddle, rota-grill, automatic golden fryer (deep-fat kettle), handi-over grill, handi-raise broiler, deep well cooker; Hotpoint Co., Chicago 49, Ill.

Hotpoint Electric 30-inch model, with rota-grill, golden fryer (deep-fat kettle), deep well cooker; Hotpoint Co., Chicago 49, Ill.

Electric Teapot

Sunbeam Automatic 2-Quart Electric Kettle; Sunbeam Corp., Chicago 50, Ill.

Top-of-Stove Utensils

Aladdin Magic Cooker (aluminum), 8 in (1½ qt.), 11 in. (3 qt.) all-purpose; Gourmet Aluminum Co., Ltd., New York 36, N. Y.

Farberware (solid stainless steel with aluminum bottom); S. W. Farber, Inc., New York 54, N. Y.

Flint-Ware Radiant Core Waterless Cooker utensils (aluminum); Ekco Products Co., Chicago 39, Ill.

T-Fal Sauce Pan, Fry Pan, Bake Pan, Egg Pan, Chicken Fryer (no-stick utensils); T-Fal Housewares, Jersey City 5, N. J.

Wagner Fat-Free Fryer (cast iron); Wagner Mfg. Co., Sidney, Ohio.

Wagner Magnalite (stainless) utensils; Wagner Mfg. Co., Sidney, Ohio.

Wear-Ever New Method Cooking Utensils; Aluminum Cooking Utensil Co., Inc., New Kensington, Pa.

West Bend Flavo-Seal Waterless Cookware (aluminum); West Bend Aluminum Co., West Bend, Wisc.

Metal Foil

Alcoa Aluminum Foil; Aluminum Co. of America, New York, N. Y.

Crown Aluminum Foil; Crown Cork & Seal Co., Baltimore, Md.

Foil Wrap; Foil Wrap Inc., Seattle, Wash.

Minerva Wax Paper Co., Minerva, Ohio.

Quaker Wax Products Co., Philadelphia, Pa.

Reynolds Wrap Aluminum

Foil; Reynolds Metals Co., Louisville 1, Ky.

Wax Rite Products Co., Rochester, N. Y.

MICROWAVE STOVES

General Electric Electronic Oven; General Electric Co., Major Appliance Div., Louisville, Ky.

RadaRange; RadaRange Div., Raytheon Manufacturing Co., Waltham 54, Mass.

A bright new world is opening up for people who must reduce. New food products, prepared for low-calorie diets, are coming into our markets each day, and the markets themselves are setting up diet grocery sections for the convenience of low-calorie shoppers. Distribution of low-calorie beverages and canned fruits has reached out to blanket the nation, and other sugarless diet products are rapidly catching up.

Since there appears to be no law that restricts anyone from advertising his output as "Low Calorie" there are some misbranded products, so read the labels of new foods carefully and compare the fine-print with caloric count of similar foods that you know about, or with the tables in Composition of Foods.

For the guidance of dieters here is a list of more than 1200 different items that are being manufactured and sold for the reducing dieter. To our knowledge, nothing has been assembled and published before like this. So rapidly is this industry growing that this list may soon be considered incomplete. And undoubtedly the future will bring many more conveniences and improvements for those who want to eat less weight-forming foods.

If you cannot obtain listed products in your locality, a postcard to manufacturer (see Brands and their Distribution, page 314) will bring information on how to buy it. The vogue for 900 calorie liquid meals which occupied dieters for several years has waned, but several brands continue to do business, with the addition of various flavorings, ranging from banana to clam chowder. Among them are Borden (Borden Co., N. Y.) Metrecal (Edward Dalton Co., Div. of Mead Johnson, Evansville, Ind.) Nutrament (Dalton), and Sego (Pet Milk Co., St. Louis, Mo.).

DIETETIC AND LOW CALORIE FOOD PRODUCTS

("C.P.O." MEANS CALORIES PER OUNCE)

BAKED PRODUCTS

Baker Boy Diet Cakes
(Baker Boy Cakes, P.O. Box 15002, Los Angeles 15, Calif.)

Cellu Cookies
(Chicago Dietetic Supply House, Inc., Chicago 12, Ill; national distribution)
Almond, Chocolate Macaroons, 120 c.p.o.; Soy Oat Cookies, 76 c.p.o.

Century Low-Calorie Cookies
(Century Butter Cookies, 2020 White Plains Road, Bronx 62, N.Y.; Eastern distribution)
Av. 108 c.p.o.

Davidson's All-Butter Products (Sucaryl sweetened)
(Davidson's Bakeries, Chicago 40, Ill.; Midwest distribution)
Bread, 76.6 c.p.o.; Cinnamon Rolls, Coffeecake, 93 c.p.o.

Devonsheer Protein Whole-Grain Wafers
(Devonsheer Melba Corp., West New York, N.J.; national)
5 c.p. wafer

Devonsheer Rye Melba Toast
14 c.p. slice

Diamel Cookies
(Dietetic Food Co., Inc., Brooklyn 19, N.Y.; national)
Banana-flavored Tea, 18.7 c. each; Coconut Tea, 17 c. each; Fruit Tea, 16 c. each; Tayst-Tea, 29 c. each; Chocolate, Vanilla Kream Krax, 22 c. each; Chocolate, Vanilla-flavored Thins, 20 c. each;

Dietetic wafers, 12 c. each

Diamel Tasty Crackers
Dietetic, 18 c. each; Salted Bits, 14 c. each; Cheese Crax, 4½ c. each

Diamel Gluten Products
Bread, sliced and toasted, 35 c.p. slice; Breadsticks, 13 c.p. stick

Hol-Grain Protein Wafer-ets
(Hol-Grain Products Co., Seattle, Wash.; national)
5 c.p. wafer

Lite Diet Special Formula Bread
(Dugan Bros. Inc., Queens Village, N.Y.; N.Y. metropolitan area)
Without shortening, thin-sliced, 45 c.p. slice, 72 c.p.o.

Loeb's Aerated Gluten
(Loeb Dietetic Foods, New York 33, N.Y.; national)
Bread, 28 c.p. ¼-oz. serving; Rolls, 36 c. each (⅓ oz.)

Loeb's Gluten
Toast, 40 c.p. slice; Rusk, 33 c.p. slice

Loeb's Cookies (sugar-free)
Vanilla, Banana, Chocolate Chip, Frutee, 21 c. each; Coconutties, 64 c. each; Lemon, Vanilla, Chocolate Softeas, 42 c. each; Vanilla, Chocolate Cream Wafers, 38 c. each; Ginger, Chocolate, Lemon, Vanilla Snaps, 17.5 c. each; Vanilla, Chocolate Tea Cookies, 63 c. each; Almond Crisps, 25 c. each; Chocolate, Vanilla Biscuits, 22.5 c. each

Ry-Krisp
(Ralston Purina Co., St. Louis 2, Mo.; national)

21 c.p. double square wafer

Venus Wheat Wafers
(Venus Baking Co., Boston, Mass.; national)
17 c.p. wafer

BEVERAGES

Bubble Up
(Bubble Up Corp., Peoria, Ill.; national)
Citrus flavor, less than 2 c.p. 6 oz. serving

Canada Dry Low-Calorie Beverages
(Canada Dry Corp., New York, N. Y.; national)

Cantrell & Cochran Low Calorie Sodas
(Cantrell & Cochran, Inc., New York, N. Y.; national)

Cellu Cool-Sip Powder (artificially sweetened)
(Chicago Dietetic Supply House, Inc., Chicago 12, Ill.; national)
4 c.p. envelope (makes 1 qt.)

Cellu Cool Sip Syrup (saccharin sweetened)

Cellu Quench
Non-nutritive carbonated beverage

Clicquot Club Sugar Free (Sucaryl sweetened)
(Clicquot Club Co., Millis, Mass.; national by franchise)
Calories negligible

Coffee Time (Calcium Cyclamate, Sorbital sweetened)
(Nedick's New York Bottling Corp., New York, N.Y.˅
Coffee-flavored soda, sugar free

Colfax Sugar-fre' Home Mix (Sucaryl sweetened)
(Colfax Mineral Spring Co., Inc., Colfax, Iowa; national and bottled under franchise)
Calories negligible

Cott Sugar Free (Sucaryl sweetened)
(Cott Bottling Co., Inc., Manchester, N. H.; eastern seaboard)
7½ c.p. 6-oz. serving

Cott Syrups (Sucaryl sweetened)
For home use, 9 c.p. serving

Diamel Casein Cocoa
30 c.p. teaspoon

Diamel Choco-sip
Syrup, 19.4 c.p. tablespoon

Diamel Flavor-it
Syrups, no food value

Diet-50
(Sunrise Home Juices, Inc., Far Rockaway, N. Y.; East)
Low Calorie dietetic orange and grapefruit juice products, concentrated fruit juice, fresh fruit juice, Calcium Cyclamate, Citric Acid, Orange Oil, Ascorbic Acid (Vitamin C), Benzoate of Soda, 1 c.p.o.

Diet-Rite Cola
(Bottled under authority Royal Crown Cola Co. by N.Y. 7-Up Bottling Co., New Rochelle, N. Y.)
Less than 1 c.p. pint

Dietricious Dad's Root Beer (Sucaryl sweetened)
(Dad's Root Beer Co., Chicago 18, Ill; Pacific coast, Midwest bottlers)
5 c.p.o.

Di-ett (Sucaryl sweetened)
(Beverages by Hammer, Brooklyn 8, N. Y.; N. Y. metropolitan area)

Dr. Brown's Slim-Ray (Sucaryl sweetened)
(American Beverage Corp., Brooklyn 11, N. Y.; N.Y. and southeast)
Calories negligible

Dr. Pepper
Sucaryl-sweetened low calorie version

Glamor Sugar Free (Sucaryl sweetened)
(Canada Dry Ginger Ale Inc., New York, N. Y.; national)
Calories negligible

Hoffman Streamline (Sucaryl sweetened)
(Hoffman Beverage Co., Newark 6, N. J.; N. Y. metropolitan area)
Calories negligible

Kool-Aid
(Perkins Products Co., Chicago 29, Ill.; national)
Concentrated powder, calories negligible

Les-Cal (Sucaryl sweetened)
(Les-Cal Beverage Co., New York 67, N. Y.; franchised in 10 eastern states)
Calories negligible

Loeb's Beverage Concentrates (Hexitol sweetened)
6 c.p.o.

Loeb's Cocoa Beverage Mix (Sucaryl-saccharin sweetened)
16 c.p. tablespoon

Loma Linda Breakfast Cup
(Loma Linda Food Co., Arlington, Calif.; national)
Coffee substitute, no calories

Marvel Lemon Crystals
(California Fruit Juices Co., New York 72, N. Y.; national)
Unsweetened, 50 c.p. envelope makes 1 qt.

Metri-Cola
Sugar-free beverage bottled by Cott under license from Mead Johnson

Nestlé Instant Beverages
(Nestlé Co., White Plains, N. Y.; national)
Instant Coffee, Decaf, Nes-

café, no calories; Nestea, 2 c.p. cup

No-Cal (Sucaryl sweetened)
(Kirsch Beverages, Inc., Brooklyn 6, N. Y.; franchised, national)
Calories negligible

Patio Cola
(Pepsi Cola Co., New York, N. Y.; national)
Sugarless

Rock Creek Trim (Sucaryl sweetened)
(Rock Creek Ginger Ale Co., Inc., Washington 24, D. C.; Washington metropolitan area)
Calories negligible

Shasta "Sweetness Without Sugar" (Sucaryl sweetened)
(Consolidated Foods, San Francisco 4, Calif; national)
Calories negligible

Slender (Sucaryl sweetened)
(E. L. Kerns Co., Trenton, N. J.; Southern N. J.; Northeastern Penna.)
Calories negligible

Smithers Low Calorie Chocolate Milk Shake
(Smithers Sons, Ltd., Los Angeles, Calif.; national)
Mix, non-fat milk powder, defatted cocoa, Sodium Cyclamate sweetened

Tab
Coca-Cola's low calorie cola drink

Tastee Cola
(Mother's Pride, Div. of National Drinks, Gardena, Calif.; West)

Tillie Lewis Tasti-Diet Topping
(Tillie Lewis Foods, Inc., Stockton, Calif.; national)
Chocolate-flavored, mixed with milk makes hot or cold

drink, 2 c.p. teaspoon of syrup

Trim (Sucaryl sweetened)
(B-1 Beverage Co., St. Louis 10, Mo.; Middle West and franchises)
Calories negligible

U-Bet Beverage Mixer (Sucaryl sweetened)
(H. Fox & Co., Inc., Brooklyn 12, N.Y.; eastern seaboard, California)
Pure fruit flavors: 18 c.p. 8-oz. serving; Ginger Ale, 13 c.p. 8-oz. serving

Vernor's Ginger Ale
(Vernor's Ginger Ale Co., Los Angeles, Calif.; West)
1 c.p. 6 oz. serving

White Rock Dietonic (Sucaryl sweetened)
(White Rock Bottlers Co., Los Angeles 58, Calif; Southern Calif., Nevada, New York, franchise bottlers nationally)
Calories negligible

CANDIES AND GUM

Dietetic candies and gums, with but few exceptions, not only taste much less appetizing than regular sugar confections, but frequently have almost as many calories. They are manufactured mainly for diabetics who are unable to handle sugar and for whom the calorie problem is not so serious.

Amurol Sugarless Mints
(Amurol Products Co., Chicago 2, Ill.; national)
calories negligible

Amurol Sugarless Chewing Gum
Cinnamon, Spearmint, Peppermint, Fruit, Chlorophyll Mint, Clove, Licorice, no calories

Balanced Sugarless Mints
(Balanced Foods, Inc., New York 3, N.Y.; national)
12 flavors

Balanced Sugarless Chewing Gum
8 flavors

Be*Lean
(Be Lean Candy Co., Inc., New York 34, N.Y.; national)
Orange, Rum, Mocha Chocolates, 15 c. each; Cherry, Orange, Lemon Wonderjels, 3 c. each

Cellu Sugar-Free Chewing Gum
Peppermint, Cinnamon, Licorice, no food value

Cellu Sugar-Free Sweets
Hard Gum Drops, Cough Drops, Lickalots, Lister's Sweets, calories negligible

Dental Gum
(Fan Tan Gum Corp., Pittsburgh, Pa.; national)
Hexitol-sweetened, calories negligible

Diamel Dietetic Sweets
Butterscotch, Coffee, Wild Cherry Drops, Crystal-Mints, 4 c.p. piece; Root Beer Drops, 1 c.p. piece; Bon-Bons, 28½ c.p. piece; Candi-Treats, 13 c.p. piece; Chocolate Miniatures, 21 c.p. piece; Choco-Almonds, 34.5 c.p. piece; Orange, Lemon, Raspberry, Licorice, Peppermint Soft Drops, 1 c.p. piece; Candy Jellies, 5 c.p. piece; Chocolate Nut, Orange, and Plain bars, Chocolate-flavored bar with milk solids, 200 c.p. bar; Chocolate-covered Mint pattie, 124 c.p. pattie; Chocolate-covered Coconut bar,

140 c.p. bar; Chocolate-covered Fudge bar, 154 c.p. bar; Chocolate-covered Marshmallow bar, 130 c.p. bar; Chocolate-covered Hazel Nut Delights, 122 c.p. bar; Chocolate-covered Nut Chew bar, 130 c.p. bar.

Diamel Twin Pops
   Orange, Lemon, Lime, Raspberry, 3½ c. each

Dietician Chewing Gum
   Peppermint, Spearmint, Cinnamon, Fruity, 3 c.p. piece

Drake's Sugarless Chocolates (Amurol Products Co.)
   Plain, Mint, Orange, Coconut, Roasted Almond, Mocha, Milk-type Chocolate bars, Bittersweet with Roasted Almonds Chocolate bars, 148 c.p.o.; Mocha, Mint, Orange, Milk-type Chocolate Perfections; Mint, Filbert, Almond, Orange Bittersweet Chocolate Perfections, 57 c.p.o.

Droste Chocolate for diabetics (Droste, Haarlem, Holland; national)
   Sugar-free chocolate-sweetened with Sorbitol, Plain, Milk, Coffee Milk, Hazelnut Milk, Hazelnut Plain, 154 calories for ⅞ ounce

Estee Low Calorie candies (Estee Cando Co., New York 32, N. Y.; national)
   Complete line of sugarless candies and cookies

Featherweight Sweets (Chicago Dietetic Supply House, Inc., Chicago 12, Ill.; national)
   Sugarless candies

Gregg's
   (Dalt International, Inc., New York 62, N. Y.; national)

Finnish pure fruit base marmalaad Apricot, Black-currant, Duchess-pear, Lemon and Strawberry candies, 18.3 c. each

Harvey's Sugarless Gum (National Chicle Products Co., Redwood City, Calif.; national)
   Pop. flavors, 1½ c.p. stick

Loeb Candy Bars (Hexitol sweetened)
   Vanilla, Swiss, Milk, Mocha solid chocolate, 162 c.p.o.; Dee Bar (milk chocolate with aerated wheat meal) 147 c.p.o.; Peppermint Creme pattie, chocolate-covered, 105 c.p.o.; plain Cherry Marshmallow, chocolate-covered, 85 c.p.o.; Fudge, chocolate-covered, 110 c.p.o.; Coconut Creme, 123 c.p.o.; Orange Coconut, 106 c.p.o.; Nougat, 116 c.p.o.

Loeb Hard Candies (Hexitol sweetened)
   Coffee Gems, Cool Mints, Fruitdrops, 1¼ c. each

Loeb Chocolates (Hexitol sweetened)
   Fruit, Nut, Cream centers, 33.5 c. each

Loeb Chewing Gum (Hexitol sweetened)
   Peppermint, Spearmint, Frutee, 8 c.p. stick

Loft's Dietetic Chocolate Bars (Loft Candy Corp., Long Island City 1, N. Y.; national)
   Light and dark chocolate, with and without nuts, with Mannitol

Mrs. Sittler's Dietetic Milk Chocolates
   (Mrs. Sittler's Candies, Inc., Cicero 50, Ill.; national)

With Mannitol, 196 c.p. 1¼ oz. bar

Nutra*Slim Dietetic Candies
(Nutra Foods Corp., Valley Stream, N. Y.; national)
Chocolate Stars, Coconut Royals, Fruit and Nut Cubes, Nutraslimz, Ten-Cal bars, sweetened with Mannitol, Saccharin, Sucaryl Calcium

Park's Sugarless Gum
(Chiclecraft, Inc., Knoxville, Tenn.; national)
Mountain Berry, Grape, Clove, Spearmint, Peppermint, Fruit, Cinnamon, Licorice, with Mannitol, Sorbitol

Wander Diabetic Nut Chocolate
(A. Wander, London W.1., England; international)
Sugar-free, vitamin-enriched

CEREALS, FLOUR, AND PASTAS

Battle Creek Gluten Flour
(Battle Creek Food Co., Battle Creek, Mich.; national)

Battle Creek Vegetable Entrées
Vegetable "Steaks," 30 c.p.o.; Vegetable Skallops, 40 c.p.o.; Protose, 57 c.p.o.; Nuttose, 75 c.p.o.

Battle Creek Waffle Mix, 56 c.p.o.

Buitoni Pastas
(Buitoni Foods Corp., So. Hackensack, N. J.; national)
20 per cent protein Macaroni products, dry, 100 c.p.o.; cooked, 35 c.p.o.
40 per cent protein Special Dietetic Macaroni, dry, 134 c.p.o.; cooked, 38.6 c.p.o.

Cellu Breakfast Crisp
46 c.p.o.

Cellu Muffin Flour
1 envelope makes 6 muffins, 43 c.p. muffin

Diamel Cereals
Breakfast Crunchies, 37 c.p.o.; Soyrina Breakfast Food, 75 c.p.o.

Diamel Dietetic Flours
Genuine Gluten, 110 c.p.o.; Self-Rising Gluten, 105 c.p.o.; Soy Bean, 130 c.p.o.

Diamel Gluten Products
Noodles, 90 c.p.o.; Spaghetti, 90 c.p.o.; Elbow Macaroni, 90 c.p.o.

Loeb's Gluten Flour
102 c.p.o.

Loeb's Gluten Spaghetti and Noodles
108 c.p.o., dry

Loeb's Prepared Mix
For waffles, griddle cakes, cookies, etc., 94 c.p.o.

Loeb's Soya Farinette
Hot breakfast cereal, very low starch content, 115 c.p.o.

Loma Linda Vegetable Proteins
Vegemeat Burger, 26 c.p.o.; Vegemeat Steaks, 25 c.p.o.; Linkettes (vegetable wieners), 55 c.p. wiener

Worthington Vegetable Protein Foods
(Worthington Foods, Inc., Worthington, Ohio; national)

FRUITS AND JUICES
Calorie Count

Caloric values of most brands of dietetic fruits and unsweetened juices are sufficiently alike so that, instead of listing them for each brand each time, they are given here on an approximate calories-per-ounce basis:

Applesauce, 11—13
Apricots, 10—11
Blackberries, 11.5—14.5
Blueberries, 13
Boysenberries, 11
Cherries, Bing, 14—17
Cherries, Red Tart Pitted, 14
Cherries, Royal Anne, 14—17
Cranberries, 13.5
Figs, Kadota, 14—16
Fruit cocktail, 11—13
Fruits for salad, 11—13
Grapefruit sections, 10
Grapes, Seedless, 15—16
Orange and Grapefruit sections, 11
Peaches, Cling, 8—11
Peaches Freestone, 8—10
Pears, Bartlett, 8—11.3
Pineapple, 15.4—17
Plums, Green Gage, 10
Plums, Prune, 15
Raspberries, Red, 12
Raspberries, Black, 12—14
Rhubarb, 4.5
Strawberries, 10

Water-packed fruits are usually 1 or 2 c.p.o. less than juice-packed or artificially sweetened fruits.

Apple juice, 13.5
Apricot nectar, 11—13
Grape juice, 19
Grapefruit juice, 11
Orange, 13—16
Pineapple, 14—16
Prune, 19

Products

Arcadia (water pack)
(Sherman Foods, Inc., New York 16, N. Y.; national)
Applesauce, Apricot halves, Blackberries, Blueberries, dark sweet Cherries, Royal Anne Cherries, Fruit cocktail, Fruits for salads, Grapefruit sections, Kadota Figs,

Peaches, halves and sliced, Bartlett Pears, crushed Pineapple, sliced Pineapple, Pineapple tidbits, Purple Plums, Red Raspberries, Strawberries

Arcadia Juices (unsweetened)
Apple, Apricot, Blackberry, Black Cherry, Blueberry, Grape, Grapefruit, Orange, Pineapple, Prune

Balanced Pack (water pack)
(Balanced Foods, Inc., New York 3, N. Y.; national)
Applesauce, Apricots, Blackberries, Blueberries, Bing Cherries, Royal Anne Cherries, Cranberries, Fruit cocktail, Grapefruit sections, Kadota Figs, Peach halves, sliced Peaches, Bartlett Pear halves, sliced Pineapple, Purple Plums, Strawberries

Balanced Juices (unsweetened)
Apple, Grape, Grapefruit, Orange, Pineapple, Prune, Fig, Apricot, Blackberry, Black Cherry, Blueberry, Cranberry, Pomegranate

Blue Boy (water pack)
(Haxton Foods, Inc., Oakfield, N. Y.; national)
Applesauce, dark sweet Cherries, sliced Peaches, Red Raspberries, Strawberries

Bordo Grapefruit
(Bordo Products Co., Chicago, Ill.; national)
No sugar added

Cellu Juice-Pak
Apricot halves, Black Cherries, Fruit cocktail, Grapefruit, Cling Peach halves, sliced Cling Peaches, Freestone Peach halves, Bartlett Pear halves, crushed Pineapple, sliced Pineapple,

Pineapple tidbits

Cellu Strained Fruits (unsweetened)

Apricot, Freestone Peach, Bartlett Pear, Pineapple

Cellu Water-packed Fruits

Applesauce, Apricot halves, Blackberries, Blueberries, Boysenberries, Black Cherries, Red Pitted Cherries, Royal Anne Cherries, Kadota Figs, Fruit Cocktail, Fruits for salad, Seedless Grapes, Cling Peach halves, sliced Cling peaches, Freestone Peach halves, Bartlett Pear halves, sliced Pineapple, Pineapple chunks, Prune-Plum halves, whole Prune-Plums, Black Raspberries, Red Raspberries, Rhubarb, Strawberries

Cellu Cranberries, (Sucaryl sweetened)

Cellu Fruit Juices

Apple, Apricot, Red Tart Cherry, Grape, Grapefruit, Orange, Peach, Pear, Pineapple

Diet Delight (Cyclamate Calcium and Sodium sweetened)

(Richmond-Chase Company, San Jose, Calif.; national)

Fruit cocktail, Bartlett Pears, sliced Peaches, Peach halves, Apricots, Cherries, Pineapple chunks, Pineapple tidbits, Kadota Figs, Mandarin Oranges, Grapefruit, Apple Sauce, fruits for salad

Diet Delight Apricot Nectar

Diet-Sweet (Sucaryl-saccharin sweetened)

(Pratt-Low Preserving Co., Santa Clara, Cal., national)

Apricot halves, Royal Anne

Cherries, Kadota Figs, Fruit cocktail, Thompson Seedless Grapes, sliced Cling Peaches, Cling Peach halves, dessert-cut Elberta Peaches, Bartlett Pear halves, Green Gage Plums

Ditex Dietetic Foods (Saccharin-Sorbitol sweetened)

(Ditex Foods, Inc., Chicago 14, Ill.; national)

Apricot halves, Cling Peaches, Light Sweet Cherries

Dole Dietetic Pack Pineapple (in unsweetened juice)

(Dole Corp., Honolulu, Hawaii; national)

Tidbits, sliced

Dole Unsweetened Pineapple Juice

Iris Diet Fruits

(Smart & Final Co., Los Angeles, Calif.; national)

Full line of sugarless fruits and juices

Loma Linda Fig Juice (unsweetened)

Lucky Leaf Apple Sauce (artificially sweetened)

(Knouse Foods, Corp., Inc., Peach Glen, Penna.; national)

Lyndonville Dietetic Apple Sauce

(Lyndonville Canning Co., Lyndonville, N.Y.; national)

Unsweetened apple sauce

Monarch Diet Dessert (Sucaryl sweetened)

(Consolidated Grocers Corp., Chicago, Ill.; national)

Applesauce, Apricot halves, Blackberries, Boysenberries, Black Bing Cherries, Red Tart pitted Cherries, Royal Anne Cherries, Kadota Figs, Fruit cocktail, Fruits for salad, Grapefruit sections,

Seedless Grapes, sliced Elberta Freestone Peaches, Elberta Freestone Peach halves, sliced Cling Peaches, Cling Peach halves, sliced Bartlett Pears, Bartlett Pear halves, Prune Plums, Black Raspberries, Red Raspberries, Strawberries, Grapefruit and Orange sections

Monarch Unsweetened Fruits (water pack)
Apple Sauce, Apricot Halves, Black Bing Cherries, Royal Anne Cherries, Kadota Figs, Fruit Cocktail, Fruits for Salad, Grapefruit sections, Sliced Elberta Peaches, Elberta Peach Halves, Sliced Cling Peaches, Cling Peach Halves, Prune Plums

Monarch Unsweetened Fruits (juice pack)
Crushed Pineapple, Sliced Pineapple, Pineapple Tidbits

Monarch Unsweetened Fruit Juices
Apple, Grape, Orange, Grapefruit, Pineapple

Mott's Figure Control Fruits (Cyclamate - Saccharin sweetened)
(Duffy-Mott Co., Inc., New York, N.Y.; national)
Applesauce, Apricots, Fruit Cocktail, Grapefruit Sections, Kadota Figs, Sliced Peaches, Peach Halves, Pear Halves, Sliced Pineapple, Pineapple Tidbits, Cooked Prunes, Royal Anne Cherries, Spiced Apple Rings, Chunky Apples and Fruit

Mott's Figure Control Fruit Drinks
Apple-Grape drink, Apricot Nectar, Five Fruit Breakfast drink, Pineapple-Grapefruit drink

Nutradiet (water pack)
(S & W Fine Foods, Inc., San Francisco, Calif.; national)
Applesauce, Apricots, Royal Anne Cherries, Figs, Fruit cocktail, Grapefruit, yellow Cling Peaches, Pears, Pineapple, Prunes

Nutradiet (artificially sweetened)
Applesauce, Apricots, Royal Anne Cherries, Figs, Fruit cocktail, Grapefruit, Cling Peaches, Pears, Strawberries, Salad Fruits

Nutradiet Unsweetened Fruit Juices
Apple, Grapefruit, Orange, Grape, Orange and Grapefruit, Pineapple, Prune

Nutradiet Low Calorie Nectars
Apricot, Apricot and Pineapple

Ocean Spray Cranberry Sauce (Sucaryl sweetened)
(National Cranberry Assn., Hanson, Mass., national)
Whole berries

Ocean Spray Cranberry Juice (sugar-free)

Pratt-Low Diet Sweet Fruits

Pratt-Low Diet Pack Hawaiian Pineapple (in unsweetened juice)

Pratt-Low Diet Pack Applesauce (water pack)

Premier (Sucaryl sweetened)
(Francis H. Leggett & Co., New York; national)
Apricot halves, Royal Anne Cherries, Fruit cocktail, Fruits for salad, sliced yellow Cling Peaches, Bartlett Pear halves

Premier (water pack)
Applesauce, Apricot halves, Royal Anne Cherries, dark sweet Bing Cherries, Fruit cocktail, Fruits for salad, Kadota Figs, Grapefruit sections, yellow Cling Peach halves, sliced yellow Cling Peaches, Bartlett Pear halves, Pineapple tidbits, sliced Pineapple, Purple Plums

Premier Juices (unsweetened)
Grapefruit, Grapefruit and Orange, Concord Grape, Orange

S. S. Pierce Epicure Dietetic Fruits
(S. S. Pierce Co., Boston, Mass.; national)
Pitted Cherries, Fruit Cocktail, Grapes, Peaches, Pineapple, Pears, etc.

Starlet Low Calorie Fruits
(Paramount Citrus Assn., San Fernando, Calif., national)

Tillie Lewis Tasti-Diet (Saccharin-Sucaryl sweetened)
Apricots, whole and halved, light sweet Cherries, Fruit cocktail, Kadota Figs, sliced Cling Peaches, Bartlett Pears

Tillie Lewis Tasti-Diet Prune Plums (Sorbitol - saccharin-sweetened)

Tillie Lewis Tasti-Diet Applesauce (unsweeetened)

Tillie Lewis Tasti-Diet Apricot Nectar (saccharin sweetened)

White Rose (water pack)
(Francis H. Leggett & Co., Subsid. of Seeman Bros., Inc., New York; N.Y. metropolitan area and partial national)
Applesauce, Apricots, Royal Anne Cherries, Kadota Figs, Fruits for salad, Fruit cock-tail, Peaches, Bartlett Pears, sliced Pineapple

PUDDINGS, GELATINES AND ICE CREAM

Ardsley Artificially Sweetened Ice Cream
(Whitelawn Dairies, Inc., Brooklyn, N. Y.; 50 mile area around metropolitan New York)

Borden's Artificially Sweetened Ice Cream
(Borden Co., Pioneer Ice Cream division, Brooklyn 38, N. Y.; metropolitan New York)
51 c.p.o.

Cellu Gelatin Dessert (Sucaryl-saccharin sweetened)
13 c.p. serving

Cellu Granulated Gelatin
Unflavored

Cellu Freezette
Vanilla, Chocolate ice-cream mix, has no food value

Cellu Pudding Powder
Cellu Rennet Powder
Has no food value

Diamel Puddings
19 c.p. serving

Diamel Gelatin Desserts
9 c.p. serving

Diamel Freez-it
30 c.p. serving

Diet-Freeze (Sucaryl sweetened)
(Maple Island, Inc., Stillwater, Minn.; national)
Ice-cream-type mix, 121 c.p.o., 126 c.p. serving

Dietician Ice Cream
Vanilla, no calories; Chocolate 15 c.p.o., add 60 c. each per 1-oz. serving for cream

D-Zerta Gelatins (Saccharin sweetened)

(General Foods Corporation, White Plains, N.Y.; national)

12 cal. per ½-cup serving

D-Zerta Puddings (Sucaryl-saccharin sweetened)

54 c. per portion made with skim milk

Fortissimo Starchless Mocha Pudding

1 tablespoon makes 3½ ozs., or 2 servings, 6 c.p. serving

Fro-sun (Sucaryl-Sorbo sweetened)

(Land O' Sun Dairies, Inc., Miami Beach 39, Fla.; Southern Florida)

Dietetic ice milk 24.4 c.p.o.

Jellathin Dietetic Gelatin Dessert

(Perkins-Kellog Food Co., Los Angeles 57, Calif.; West Coast)

Calcium - Cyclohexl - Sulfamate - sweetened; various flavors

Jelex (Sucaryl sweetened)

(Enzo Jel Co., Sheboygan, Wisc.; partial national)

9 c.p. ⅕-pt. serving

"Junket" Rennet tablets

(Chr. Hansen's Laboratory, Inc., Little Falls, N.Y.; national)

No calories

Knox Gelatine

(Chas. B. Knox Gelatine Co., Inc., Johnstown, N.Y.; national)

Unsweetened, unflavored, 112 c.p.o. but 4 c.p. serving

Loeb's Gelatin (Saccharin-Sucaryl sweetened)

15 c.p. portion

Loeb's Pudding Desserts

Chocolate, 17 c.p. serving; others, 20 c.p. serving

Monarch

Low calorie gelatin, 2 c.p.o.,

and pudding desserts, 20 c.p.o. made with whole milk

Mott Figure Control Desserts

Gelatin Custards, 19 c.p.o.; Gelatins, 3 c.p.o.

Puddex (Sucaryl sweetened) (Enzo Jel Co.)

4 c.p. ⅕-pt. serving, plus milk

Smithers Gelatin Custard Dessert, 10 c.p.o.

Tillie Lewis Tasti-Diet Gelatin

7 cp. 4-oz. serving

Tillie Lewis Tasti-Diet Pudding

34 c.p. serving when made with skim milk; Chocolate, 41 c.p. serving

SALAD DRESSINGS

Cellu Salad Topping (Sucaryl sweetened)

8 c.p.o.

Chef Milani's Diafoods Dressing

(Louis Milani Foods, Inc., Chicago, Ill.; national)

1.8 c.p. teaspoon

Diamel

Diet Whip (mayonnaise type) 10 c.p. tablespoon; Tangy, 1 c.p. tablespoon; Superb, 11 c.p. teaspoon

Diet Delight

Chef's Herb, 2 c.p. tablespoon; Bleu Cheese, 8 c.p. tablespoon; Dietetic Whipped, 24 c.p. tablespoon

Diet-Sweet Normandy Diet Dressing

(Pratt-Low)

Kraft

(Kraft Cheese Co., Chicago, Ill.; national)

Kraft Low Calorie Dressings, about 8 c.p. teaspoon

Monarch

Low-calorie Dressing, 4 c.p.

tablespoon; Whipped Dressing, 21 c.p. tablespoon

Mott
French Style Dressing, 11 c.p. tablespoon; Italian Style, 8 c.p. tablespoon; Whipped 24 c.p. tablespoon

Pratt-Low Diet-Sweet Whipped Diet Dressing

Smithers
Low Calorie Tawny Dressing, 39 c. p. tablespoon; Low Calorie Fine Herb Dressing, 3 c.p. tablespoon

Sylph Dressing
(House of Herbs, Salisbury, Conn.; national)
4 c.p. teaspoon

Tillie Lewis Tasti-Diet
Imitation French, 0.3 c.p. level teaspoon; One Calorie, 1 c.p. 2 rounded teaspoons; Chef's, 0.7 c.p. level teaspoon; Blue Cheese, 1 c.p. level teaspoon; Whipped, 6 c.p. teaspoon

SPREADS

Balanced Dietetic Preserves
Various flavors.

Cellu Fruit Spreads (saccharin sweetened)
Apricot, 12 c.p.o., Grape, 18 c.p.o., Pineapple, 14 c.p.o.

Cellu Jellies (saccharin sweetened)
5 c.p.o.

Davidson's Dietetic Spreads and Jels
(Davidson's Pure Food Products, Ltd., Montreal 28, Canada; distributed in U.S. by Andre Prost, Inc., East Elmhurst, N.Y., and MacDowell Bros., Ogdensburg, N.Y.)
Spreads: 2½ c.p.o.; Jels: 1⅘ to 3 c.p.o.

Diamel Diet Jelly
1 c.p. teaspoon

Diet-Sweet Jellies

Diet-Sweet Preserves
Honeydew (Sucaryl sweetened)
(General Preserve Co., Inc., Brooklyn 31, N.Y.; eastern seaboard)
Raspberry jelly, 3.5 c.p.o.; Concord Grape jelly, 12.5 c.p.o.; Blueberry preserves, 6.2 c.p.o.; Strawberry preserves, 3.5 c.p.o.

Loeb's Fruit Spreads (Saccharin-Sucaryl sweetened)
Cherry, Apricot, Raspberry, 8 c.p.o.; Strawberry, Plum, 6 c.p.o.; Pineapple, 10 c.p.o.; Grape 9½ c.p.o.

Louis Sherry Fruit Jellies and Preserves
(Louis Sherry Preserves, Inc., Long Island City, N. Y.; national)
About 7 c.p.o.

Monarch Dietetic Jelly and Preserves

MacTavish Fruit Spreads (Sucaryl sweetened)
(MacTavish Preserves Co., Inc., Brooklyn 15, N.Y.; national)

Mott Figure Control Jellies and Preserves
18 c.p.o.

M.C.P. Low Sugar Pectin
(Mutual Citrus Products Co., Anaheim, Calif.; West Coast and mail order)
For making low sugar jams, desserts, custards, toppings

Orchard Maid Diet Preserves (Sucaryl sweetened)
(Orchard Products Co., Chicago 7, Ill., distributed in Illinois)
Seedless Red Raspberry, Strawberry, 10 c.p.o.; Seed-

less Concord Grape, 8.5 c.p.o.; Elberta Peach, 10.5 c.p.o.

S. S. Pierce Fruit Jams
Artificially sweetened

Polaner
(M. Polaner & Son, Inc., Newark, N.J.; eastern seaboard from Maine to Virginia, Ohio, Illinois)
Cyclamate and Saccharin sweetened, Preserves: Apricot, 16 c.p.o.; Blackberry, 14 c.p.o.; Wild Blueberry, 14 c.p.o.; Peach, 16 c.p.o.; Damson Plum, 14 c.p.o.; Red Raspberry 14 c.p.o.; Strawberry, 10 c.p.o.; Concord Grape Jelly, 14 c.p.o.; Orange Marmalade, 14 c.p.o.

Slenderella Jellies
(J. M. Smucker Co., Orrville, Ohio; national)
Low Calorie Grape Jelly, 13 c.p.o.

Tillie Lewis Tasti-Diet (Sucaryl sweetened)
9 c.p. tablespoon

SYRUPS, SEASONING, SAUCES, BROTH, CHEESE AND PICKLES

Ac'cent
(International Minerals & Chemical Corp., Chicago 6, Ill.; national)
Monosodium Glutamate, seasoning, 8 c.p. teaspoon

Borden's Eagle Brand Neufchatel Cheese
30% lower in fat than cream cheese, 72 c.p.o. *vs.* 106 c.p.o.

Buitoni Sauces
Meat, 33 c.p.o.; Mushroom, 24 c.p.o.; Marinara, 19 c.p.o.; Pizza, 16 c.p.o.

Cellu Bouillon Cubes
Chicken, vegetable, beef

Cellu Chili Sauce (sugar free)

Cellu Maple Topette
Sugar free, without food value

Diamel Choco-Sip
Syrup, 19.4 c.p. tablespoon

Diamel Pancake Sweetener
Maple flavor

Diamel Vegetable Broth-Mix
11 c.p. teaspoon

Dairy Diet Cheese Spread
(Calumet Cheese Co., Inc., Hilbert, Wisc., national)
Cheddar, 84 c.p.o.

Diet Delight Imitation Maple Table Syrup
Artificially sweetened, 5 c.p.o.

Dietician Souplets
For vegetable broth, 12 c. each

Dietician Syrup
Choc-Low, 5 c.p. teaspoon

Escoffier sauces
(Julius Wile Sons & Co., Inc., New York, N.Y.; national)
Sauce Robert, 21 c.p. tablespoon; Sauce Diable à la Provençale, 22 c.p. tablespoon; Sauce Melba, 38 c.p. tablespoon

Fortissimo Garden Vegetable Broth
3 c.p. teaspoon concentrate

Fortissimo Mock Honey (Cyclamate and Sorbitol sweetened)
Sugar free, 34 c.p.o.

Fortissimo Red Raspberry Syrup
(Cyclamate and Sorbitol sweetened)

Fortissimo Dietetic Simulated Maple Syrup
(Sweetened with Sorbitol, Cyclamate and Levulose, 46 c.p.o.)

Fortissimo Dietetic Romano Cheese Flavor
68 c.p.o.

Grape-serv
(Grape-serv Food Products, Co., Brooklyn, N.Y.)
Sauce for meats, poultry, fish, salads, 6 c.p. tablespoon

L'art Sweet Pickles (Sucaryl sweetened)
(Green Bay Food Co., Green Bay, Wisconsin; Midwest)
calories negligible

Loma Linda Gravy Quik
11 c.p.o. when made according to label recipe

Loma Linda Soy Cheese
27 c.p.o.

Mintit
(Rye Oldfarms Co., Rye, N.Y.; national)
Liquid natural mint concentrate, bottled, calories negligible

Monarch Low Calorie Maple Syrup
1 c.p.o.

Monarch Low Calorie Sweet Pickles
4 c.p.o.

Mott Figure Control Sauces
White, 16 c.p.o.; Newburg, 14 c.p.o.; Welsh Rarebit (Cheese Sauce), 18 c.p.o.

Mott Figure Control Pie Fillings
Apple, 20 c.p.o.; Cherry, 20 c.p.o.

Mott Figure Control Toppings

Chocolate, 16 c.p.o.; Pineapple, 18 c.p.o.

Mott Figure Control "Maplette" Syrup
18 c.p.o.

Nestlé Bouillon
Chicken, 8 c.p. cube; Beef, 8 c.p. cube

Nu-diet Sugar Free Waffle Syrup (Sucaryl sweetened)
(Colfax Mineral Springs Co., Inc., Colfax, Iowa; national)
Maple flavor

Smithers Low Calorie Foods
English Beef Tea, 2 c.p.o.; Newburg Sauce, 15 c.p.o.; White Sauce, 18 c.p.o.; French Dip Gravy, 8 c.p.o.; Thick Brown Gravy, 15 c.p.o.

Spice Club Mushroom Seasoning Powder
(Spice Club Foods, Inc., 2-15 26th Ave., Long Island City, N.Y.)

Spice Club Fiber-free Dietetic Chocolate Syrup
Sugarless, 24 c.p.o.

Tillie Lewis Tasti-Diet Topping (Sucaryl-saccharin sweetened)
Chocolate-flavored, 2 c.p. teaspoon; Maple - flavored, syrup-style, 1 c.p. tablespoon

G. Washington's Instant Broth
(American Home Products Corp., New York, N.Y.; national)
Light, dark powder, calories negligible

BRANDS AND THEIR DISTRIBUTION

AMUROL (Amurol Products Co., Chicago 2, Ill.; national distribution)

ARCADIA (Sherman Foods, Inc., New York 16, N.Y.; national)

BALANCED (Balanced Foods, Inc., New York 3, N.Y.; naational)

BATTLE CREEK (Worthington Food Co., Worthington, Ohio; national)

BE LEAN (Be Lean Candy Co., Inc., New York 34, N.Y.; national)

BLUE BOY (Haxton Foods, Inc., Oakfield, N.Y.; national)

BORDO (Bordo Products Co., Chicago, Ill.; national)

BORDEN'S (The Borden Co., New York, N.Y.; national)

BUITONI (Buitoni Foods Corp., So. Hackensack, N.J.; national)

CANADA DRY (Canada Dry Corp., New York, N.Y.; national)

C & C (Cantrell & Cochran Co., New York, N.Y.; national)

CELLU (Chicago Dietetic Supply House, Inc., Chicago 12, Ill., national)

CLICQUOT CLUB (Clicquot Club Co., Millis, Mass.; national by franchise)

COLFAX (Colfax Mineral Springs, Co., Inc., Colfax, Iowa; national and bottled under franchise)

COTT (Cott Bottling Co., Inc., Manchester, N.H.; eastern seaboard)

COUNTDOWN (Slenderella, Inc., Long Island City, N.Y.; national)

DAIRY DIET (Calumet Cheese Co., Inc., Hilbert, Wisc.; national)

DAVIDSON'S SPREADS (Davidson's Pure Food Products Ltd., Montreal 28, Canada; distributed in United States by MacDowell Bros., Ogden, N.Y.)

DAVIDSON'S ALL-BUTTER PRODUCTS (Davidson's Bakeries, Chicago 40, Ill.; Midwest distribution)

DENTAL GUM (Fan Tan Gum

Corp., Pittsburgh, Pa.; national)

DEVONSHEER (Devonsheer Melba Corp., West New York, N.J.; national)

DIAMEL (Dietetic Food Co., Inc., Brooklyn 19, N.Y.; national)

DIET DELIGHT (Richmond-Chase Company, San Jose, Calif.; national)

DIET-FREEZE (Maple Island, Inc., Stillwater, Minn.; national)

DIETICIAN (American Dietaids Co., Inc., Yonkers, N.Y.; national)

DIETRICIOUS DAD'S ROOT BEER (Dad's Root Beer Co., Chicago 18, Ill.; Pacific coast, Midwest bottlers)

DIET SWEET (Pratt-Low Preserving Co., Santa Clara, Calif.; national)

DI-ETT (Beverages by Hammer, Brooklyn 8, N.Y.; N.Y. metropolitan area)

DITEX (Ditex Foods, Inc., Chicago 14, Ill.; national)

DOLE (Hawaiian Pineapple Company, San Jose 8, California; national)

DRAKE'S (Amurol Products Co., Chicago 2, Ill., national)

DR. BROWN'S SLIM RAY (American Beverage Corp., Brooklyn 11, N.Y., N.Y. and southeast)

D-ZERTA (General Foods Corporation, White Plains, N.Y.; national)

ESCOFFIER SAUCES (Julius Wile Sons & Co., Inc., New York, N.Y., national)

FORTISSIMO (Spice Club Foods, Inc., Long Island City N.Y.; national)

FRO-SUN (Land O' Sun

Dairies, Inc., Miami Beach, 39, Fla.; Southern Florida)

GLAMOR SUGAR FREE (Canada Dry Ginger Ale Inc., New York, N.Y.; national)

GRAPE-SERV (Grape-serv Food Products Co., Brooklyn, N.Y.)

GREGG's (Dalt International, Inc., New York 62, N.Y.; national)

HARVEY'S SUGARLESS GUM (National Chicle Products Co., Redwood City, Calif.; national)

HOFFMAN STREAMLINE (Hoffman Beverage Co., Newark 6, N.J.; N.Y. metropolitan area)

HOL-GRAIN (Hol-Grain Products Co., Seattle, Wash.; national)

HONEYDEW (General Preserve Co., Inc., Brooklyn 31, N.Y.; eastern seaboard)

JELEX (Enzo Jel Co., Sheboygan, Wisc.; partial national)

JELLATHIN (Perkins - Kellog Food Co., Los Angeles 57, Calif., West Coast)

"JUNKET" (Chr. Hansen's Laboratory, Inc., Little Falls, N.Y.; national)

KNOX (Chas. B. Knox Gelatine Co., Inc., Johnstown, N.Y.; national)

KOOL-AID (Perkins Products Co., Chicago 29, Ill. national)

KRAFT (Kraft Cheese Co., Chicago, Ill.; national)

L'ART (Green Bay Food Co., Green Bay, Wis., Midwest)

LES-CAL (Les-Cal Beverage Co., New York 67, N.Y.; franchised in 10 eastern states)

LOEB's (Loeb Dietetic Foods,

New York 33, N.Y.; national)

LOMA LINDA (Loma Linda Food Co., Arlington, Calif.; national)

LOUIS SHERRY (Louis Sherry Preserves, Inc., Long Island City, N.Y.; N.Y.-Philadelphia)

LUCKY LEAF (Knouse Foods Corp., Inc., Peach Glen, Pa., national)

LYNDONVILLE (Lyndonville Canning Co., Lyndonville, N.Y.; national)

MAC TAVISH (MacTavish Preserves Co., Inc., Brooklyn 15, N.Y.; national)

MARVEL (California Fruit Juices Co., New York 72, N.Y.; national)

MINTIT (Rye Oldfarms Co., Rye, N.Y.; national)

MONARCH (Monarch Foods Div. of Consolidated Foods Corp., Somerville, Mass.; national)

MOTT's (Duffy-Mott Co., New York, N.Y.; national)

NESTLE (Nestlé Co., White Plains, N.Y.; national)

NO-CAL (Kirsch Beverages Inc., Brooklyn, N.Y.; national)

NU-DIET (Colfax Mineral Springs Co., Inc., Colfax, Iowa; national and bottled under franchise)

NUTRADIET (S. & W. Fine Foods, Inc., San Francisco, Calif.; national)

NUTRA*SLIM (Nutra Foods Corp., Valley Stream, N.Y.; national)

OCEAN SPRAY (National Cranberry Assn., Hanson, Mass.; national)

ORCHARD MAID (Orchard

Products Co., Chicago 7, Ill.; distributed in Illinois)

POLANER (M. Polaner & Son Inc., Newark, N.J.; East)

PRATT-LOW (Pratt-Low Preserving Co., Santa Clara, Calif.; national)

PREMIER (Francis H. Leggett & Co., New York; national)

PUDDEX (Enzo Jel Co., Sheboygan, Wisc., partial national)

ROCK CREEK TRIM (Rock Creek Ginger Ale Co., Inc., Washington 24, D.C.; Washington metropolitan area)

S. S. PIERCE EPICURE DIETETIC (S. S. Pierce Co., Boston, Mass.; national)

SHASTA (Shasta Water Co., San Francisco 4, Calif.; western)

SLENDER (E. L. Kerns Co., Trenton, N.J.; southern N.J., northeastern Penna.)

SLENDERELLA (Slenderella, Inc., Long Island City, N.Y., national)

SLENDERELLA (J. M. Smucker Co., Orrville, Ohio; national)

STARLET (Paramount Citrus Assn., San Fernando, Calif.; national)

SYLPH DRESSING (House of Herbs, Salisbury, Conn.; national)

TILLIE LEWIS (Tillie Lewis Foods, Inc., Stockton, Calif.; national)

U-BET (H. Fox Co., Inc., Brooklyn 12, N.Y.; eastern seaboard, California)

TRIM (B-1 Beverage Co., St. Louis 10, Mo.; Middle West and franchises)

VENUS (Venus Baking Co., Boston, Mass.; national)

VERNOR'S (Vernor's Ginger Ale Co., Los Angeles, Calif., West Coast)

WHITE ROCK (White Rock Bottlers Co., Los Angeles 38, Calif.; national)

WHITE ROSE (Francis H. Leggett & Co., Subsid. of Seeman Bros., Inc., New York; N.Y. metropolitan area and partial national)

WORTHINGTON (Worthington Foods, Inc., Worthington, Ohio; national)

Common Household Units	Calories	Protein, Grams	Fat, Grams	Carbohydrate, Grams	Calories in One Pound*
Apple, raw, 1 large	117	.6	.8	30.1	263
Apple juice, 1 cup	124	.2	0.¶	34.4	227
Applesauce, unsweetened, 1 cup	100	.5	.5	26.1	189
Apricots, raw, 3 canned, water pack, 1 cup	54 77	1.1 1.2	.1 .2	13.8 19.8	225 144
Asparagus, cooked, 1 cup	36	4.2	.4	6.3	92
Bacon, medium, cooked, drained, 2 slices	97	4.	8.8	.2	2,761
Banana, raw, 1 large	119	1.6	.3	31.	401
Beans, snap (green, yellow, or wax) cooked or canned, 1 cup	27	1.8	.2	5.9	99
Beef cuts, cooked chuck, 3 ounces without bone	265	22.	19.	0.	1,406
flank, 3 ounces without bone	270	21.	20.	0.	1,425
hamburger, 3 ounces	316	19.	26.	0.	1,654
porterhouse, 3 ounces without bone	293	20.	23.	0.	1,554
rib roast, 3 ounces without bone	266	20.	20.	0.	1,449
round, 3 ounces without bone	197	23.	11.	0.	1,057
rump, 3 ounces without bone	320	18.	27.	0.	1,714
sirloin, 3 ounces without bone	257	20.	19.	0.	1,346
Beef, canned, corned beef, lean, 3 ounces	159	22.5	7.	0.	837

Common Household Units	Calories	Protein, Grams	Fat, Grams	Carbo- hydrate, Grams	Cal- ories in One Pound*
roast beef, 3 ounces	189	21.	11.	0.	1,019
Beef, dried or chipped, 2 ounces	115	19.4	3.6	0.	923
Beets, cooked or canned, 1 cup diced	68	1.6	.2	16.2	187
Blackberries, raw, 1 cup	82	1.7	1.4	18.0	260
canned, waterpack, 1 cup	104	2.2	1.7	22.9	194
Blueberries, raw, 1 cup	85	.8	.8	21.1	279
canned, water pack, 1 cup	90	1.0	1.0	21.8	168
frozen, without sugar, 3 ounces	52	.5	.5	12.8	279
Bluefish, cooked, baked, 1 pound	704	124.4	19.1	0.	704
Bouillon, 1 cube	2	.2	.1	0.	219
Bread, white, 1 slice	63	20.	.7	12.	1,254
Broccoli, cooked, 1 cup	44	5.0	.3	8.2	133
Brussels sprouts, cooked, 1 cup	60	5.7	.6	11.6	212
Butter, 1 tablespoon	100	.1	11.3	.1	3,251
1 square	50	.0	5.7	.0	3,251
Buttermilk, from skim milk, 1 cup	86	8.5	.2	12.4	162
Cabbage, raw, 1 cup shredded finely	24	1.4	.2	5.3	109
cooked, 1 cup	40	2.4	.3	9.0	109
Cantaloupe, raw, 1 cup diced	30	.9	.3	6.7	93
Carrots, raw, 1 medium or ½ cup grated	21	.6	.2	4.6	188
cooked, 1 cup diced	44	.9	.7	9.3	138
Cauliflower, raw, 1 cup buds	30	2.9	.2	5.9	113
Celery, raw, 3 small inner stalks	9	.6	.1	1.8	82
cooked, 1 cup diced	24	1.7	.3	4.8	82
Cheese					
Camembert, 1 ounce	85	5.0	7.0	.5	1,356
Cheddar, 1 ounce	113	7.1	9.1	.6	1,806
cottage, 1 cup	215	43.9	1.1	4.5	433
cream, 1 tablespoon	56	1.4	5.6	.3	1,686
Parmesan, 1 ounce	112	10.2	7.4	.8	1,786
Swiss, 1 ounce	105	7.8	7.9	.5	1,680

Common Household Units	Calories	Protein, Grams	Fat, Grams	Carbo- hydrate, Grams	Cal- ories in One Pound*
Cherries, raw, 1 cup	65	1.2	.5	15.8	277
Chicken, raw, bone out,					
broilers, ½ bird	332	44.4	15.8	0.	685
roasters, 4 ounces	227	22.9	14.3	0.	909
stewing hens, 4 ounces	342	20.4	28.3	0.	1,372
fryers, 1 breast, 8 ounces	210	47.0	1.0	0.	472
fryers, 1 leg, 5 ounces	159	29.1	3.8	0.	507
canned, 3 ounces	169	25.3	6.8	0.	905
Chili sauce, 1 tablespoon	17	.5	.1	4.0	445
Clams, meat, raw, 4 ounces	92	14.5	1.6	3.9	369
Cod, raw, 4 ounces	84	18.7	.5	0.	336
Coleslaw, 1 cup	102	1.6	7.3	9.2	388
Corn, cooked, 1 ear	84	2.7	.7	20.0	383
canned, drained, 1 cup	140	4.5	1.2	33.3	384
Crab meat, canned or					
cooked, 3 ounces	89	14.4	2.5	1.1	389
Cranberries, raw, 1 cup	54	.5	.8	12.8	218
Cream, light, 1 tablespoon	30	.4	3.0	.6	925
Cress, water, raw, 1 ounce	5	.5	.0	1.0	84
Croaker, raw, 4 ounces	109	20.2	2.5	0.	435
Cucumber, raw, 6 slices	6	.4	.0	1.4	55
Currants, raw, 1 cup	60	1.3	.2	15.0	248
Dandelion greens, cooked,					
1 cup	79	4.9	1.3	15.8	200
Egg, 1 medium whole	77	6.1	5.5	.3	736
1 medium white only	15	3.3	0.	.2	227
1 medium yellow only	61	2.8	5.4	.1	1,640
Endive or escarole, 1 ounce	6	.5	0.	1.1	173
Figs, raw, 3 small	90	1.6	.5	22.3	357
Flounder, raw, 4 ounces	78	16.9	.6	0.	310
Gelatin, dry, plain,					
1 tablespoon	34	7.6	.0	0.	1,520
Gooseberries raw, 1 cup	59	1.2	.3	14.6	178
Grapefruit, raw,					
½ medium or 1 cup	75	.9	.4	19.0	180
Grapefruit juice,					
unsweetened, 1 cup	87	1.2	.2	22.6	162
concentrate, 1 can	297	3.8	.8	77.0	667
Grapes, slip skin, 1 cup	84	1.7	1.7	17.7	318
adherent skin, 1 cup	102	1.2	.6	25.9	301
Grape juice, 1 cup	170	1.0	.0	46.2	303
Haddock, raw, 4 ounces	87	20.2	.1	0.	356
fried, 1 fillet	158	18.7	5.5	7.0	676
Halibut, raw, 4 ounces	139	20.6	5.8	0.	573

Common Household Units	Calories	Protein, Grams	Fat, Grams	Carbo- hydrate, Grams	Cal- ories in One Pound*
broiled, 1 steak	228	32.8	9.8	0.	827
Honeydew melon, raw,					
1 wedge trimmed	49	.8	0.	12.8	146
†Ice Cream, plain,					
1 8-ounce container	294	5.7	17.8	29.3	938
Kale, cooked, 1 cup	45	4.3	.7	7.9	182
Lamb, cooked without bone					
rib chop, 3 ounces	356	20.	30.	0.	1,900
shoulder roast, 3 ounces	293	18.	24.	0.	1,551
leg roast, 3 ounces	230	20.	16.	0.	1,241
Lard, 1 tablespoon	126	0.	14.	0.	4,095
Lemon juice, unsweetened,					
1 tablespoon	4	.1	.0	1.2	108
Lemon, 1 medium	20	.6	.4	5.4	88
Lettuce, raw, 2 large leaves	7	.6	.1	1.4	47
Lime juice, fresh, 1 cup	58	1.0	.0	20.4	104
Lime, 1 medium	19	.4	.1	6.4	126
Lobster, canned, 3 ounces	78	15.6	1.1	.3	417
Loganberries, raw, 1 cup	90	1.4	.9	21.6	283
Macaroni, dry, 1 cup, elbow	463	15.7	1.7	94.1	1,712
Mackerel, canned, 3 ounces	153	17.9	8.5	0.	819
Mango, raw, 1 medium	87	.9	.3	22.7	300
Margarine, 1 pat	50	.0	5.7	.0	3,269
Milk, cow, whole, 1 cup	166	8.5	9.5	12.0	309
nonfat (skim), 1 cup	87	8.6	.2	12.5	162
nonfat powder,					
1 tablespoon	28	2.7	.1	3.9	1,643
evaporated, 1 cup	346	17.6	19.9	24.9	625
half and half, 1 cup	330	7.7	29.0	10.9	620
Mushrooms, canned,					
with liquid, 1 cup	28	3.4	.5	9.0	51
Mustard greens, cooked,					
1 cup	31	3.2	.4	5.6	102
Noodles, egg, dry, 1 cup	278	9.2	2.5	53.4	1,729
Oils, 1 tablespoon	124	0.	14.	0.	4,013
Okra, cooked, 8 pods	28	1.5	.2	6.3	148
Olives, 10 green	72	.8	7.4	2.2	600
10 ripe	106	1.0	11.6	1.4	866
Onions, raw, mature,					
1 tablespoon chopped	4	.1	.0	1.0	205
cooked whole, 1 cup	79	2.1	.4	18.3	172
young green, 6 small	23	.5	.1	5.3	205
Orange juice, unsweetened,					
1 cup	109	2.0	.5	27.3	201

Common Household Units	Calories	Protein, Grams	Fat, Grams	Carbo- hydrate, Grams	Cal- ories in One Pound*
concentrate, frozen, 1 can	300	5.5	1.4	74.9	1,039
Orange, 1 medium	70	1.4	.3	17.4	204
Oysters, meat only, raw, 1 cup	200	23.5	5.0	13.4	380
Papayas, raw, 1 cup	71	1.1	.2	18.2	178
Parsnips, cooked, 1 cup	94	1.6	.8	21.5	274
Peaches, raw, 1 medium	46	.5	.1	12.0	208
canned, solids and liquid water pack, 1 cup	66	1.2	.2	16.6	123
Peanut butter, 1 tablespoon	92	4.2	7.6	3.4	2,615
Peanuts, 1 tablespoon, chopped	50	2.4	4.0	2.1	2,540
Pears, raw, 1 pear	95	1.1	.6	23.9	285
water pack, 1 cup	75	.7	.2	19.8	143
Peas, young, green, cooked, 1 cup	111	7.8	.6	19.4	316
canned, drained, 1 cup	145	7.2	1.0	27.5	411
Pepper, green, raw, 1 medium	16	.8	.1	3.6	113
cooked, 1 medium	17	.8	.1	3.9	119
Persimmon, 1 raw with seeds	74	.8	.4	19.0	355
Pickle, dill, 1 large	15	.9	.3	2.8	49
bread and butter, 6 slices	29	.4	.1	7.1	316
sour, 1 large	15	.7	.3	3.0	49
sweet, 1 tablespoon	14	.1	.1	3.4	488
Pimento, canned, 1 medium	10	.3	.2	2.2	123
Pineapple, raw, 1 cup diced	74	.6	.3	19.2	240
Pineapple juice, canned, 1 cup	121	.7	.2	32.4	221
Plum, 1 raw	29	.4	.1	7.4	205
Pork without bone fresh ham, 3 ounces	338	20.	28.	0.	1,818
loin or chops, 3 ounces	284	20.	22.	0.	1,508
cured ham, 3 ounces	339	20.	28.	.3	1,804
Prune juice, canned, 1 cup	170	1.0	0.	46.3	321
Pumpkin, canned, 1 cup	76	2.3	.7	18.0	151
Radishes, raw, 4 small	4	.2	.0	.8	92
Raspberries, red, raw, 1 cup	70	1.5	.5	17.0	259
Rhubarb, raw, 1 cup, diced	19	.6	.1	4.6	73
Salmon, Pacific, broiled or baked, 1 steak	204	33.6	6.7	.2	761

Common Household Units	Calories	Protein, Grams	Fat, Grams	Carbo-hydrate, Grams	Cal-ories in One Pound*
canned, Chinook, with liquid, 3 ounces	173	16.8	11.2	0.	922
canned, Chum, with liquid, 3 ounces	118	18.3	4.4	0.	630
canned, Coho with liquid, 3 ounces	140	17.9	7.1	0.	753
canned, pink with liquid, 3 ounces	122	17.4	5.3	0.	651
canned, red with liquid, 3 ounces	147	17.2	8.2	0.	785
Sardines, canned in oil, Atlantic, drained, 3 oz.	182	21.9	9.4	1.0	976
pilchards, Pacific with liquid, 3 oz.	171	15.1	11.5	.6	909
in tomato sauce, 3 oz.	184	15.1	12.6	1.4	983
Sauerkraut, canned, drained, 1 cup	32	2.1	.4	6.6	99
Sausage, bologna, 1-in. slice	467	31.2	33.5	7.6	1,005
1 frankfurter, cooked	124	7.	10.	1.	1,131
liverwurst, 2 ounces	150	9.5	11.7	.9	1,193
pork, links or bulk, raw, 4 oz.	510	12.2	50.8	0.	2,044
Vienna, canned, 4 oz.	244	17.9	18.6	0.	978
Scallops, raw, 4 oz.	89	16.8	.1	3.9	355
Shad, raw, 4 oz.	191	21.2	11.1	0.	764
‡Sherbet, ½ cup	118	1.4	.0	28.8	558
Shrimp, canned, drained, 3 oz.	108	22.8	1.2	—§	577
Soup, canned, ready to serve:					
bouillon, broth, or consommé, 1 cup	9	2.	—	0.	21
chicken, 1 cup	75	3.5	2.5	9.5	137
tomato, 1 cup	90	2.2	2.2	17.9	167
vegetable, 1 cup	82	4.2	1.8	14.5	149
Soybean sprouts, raw, 1 cup	49	6.6	1.5	5.7	208
Spinach, raw, 4 ounces	22	2.6	.3	3.6	89
cooked or canned, 1 cup	46	5.6	1.1	6.5	115
Squash, summer, cooked, diced, 1 cup	34	1.3	.2	8.2	74
Squash, winter, baked, mashed, 1 cup	97	3.9	.8	22.6	215
boiled, mashed, 1 cup	86	3.4	.7	20.1	171

Common Household Units	Calories	Protein, Grams	Fat, Grams	Carbo- hydrate, Grams	Cal- ories in One Pound*
Starch, corn, etc., 1 tablespoon	29	.0	.0	7.0	1,644
Strawberries, raw, capped, 1 cup	54	1.2	0.7	12.4	160
Sugar, granulated, 1 cup	770	0.	0.	199.0	1,748
Swordfish, broiled, 1 steak	223	34.2	8.5	0.	793
Tangerine, juice, fresh or canned, 1 cup	95	2.2	.7	22.6	176
Tangerine, 1 medium	35	.6	.2	8.8	203
Tomato juice canned, 1 cup	50	2.4	.5	10.4	93
Tomato purée, canned, 1 cup	90	4.5	1.2	17.9	165
Tomato catsup, 1 tablespoon	17	.3	.1	4.2	446
Tomatoes, raw, 1 medium	30	1.5	.4	6.0	81
canned or cooked, 1 cup	46	2.4	.5	9.4	93
Tuna fish, canned, drained, 3 ounces	169	24.7	7.0	0.	1,318
Turkey, medium fat, raw, 4 ounces	304	22.8	22.9	0.	1,216
Turnips, cooked, 1 cup diced	42	1.2	.3	9.3	122
Turnip greens, boiled, 1 cup	43	4.2	.6	7.8	135
Veal, cooked, without bone cutlet, 3 ounces	184	24.	9.	0.	993
shoulder roast, 3 ounces	193	24.	10.	0.	1,029
stew meat, 3 ounces	252	21.	18.	0.	1,344
Vinegar, 1 tablespoon	2	0.	—	.8	56
Watermelon ½ slice (¾ by 10 in.)	45	.8	.3	11.0	126
Wheat flour (bread), 1 cup	408	13.2	1.2	83.7	1,656
Yogurt, plain, 1 cup	160	6.53	6.76	11.0	320

* Indicates number of calories in one edible pound.

† Based on 5 pounds of ice cream to the gallon, factory packed.

‡ Based on 6.8 pounds to the gallon, factory packed.

§ A dash shows that no basis could be found for imputing a value although there is some reason to believe that a measure-able amount of the constituent may be present.

¶ A zero followed by a decimal point (0.) indicates that there may be up to 0.5 of a gram present but bases for showing the amount were inadequate. Where no values exist, the figure .0 is used.